Man in the Music

The Creative Life and Work of
Michael Jackson

JOSEPH VOGEL
Foreword by Anthony DeCurtis

STERLING
New York

An Imprint of Sterling Publishing
387 Park Avenue South
New York, NY 10016

STERLING and the distinctive Sterling logo are registered trademarks of Sterling Publishing Co., Inc.

ISBN 978-1-4027-7938-1 (hardcover)

ISBN 978-1-4027-8934-2 (ebook)

Library of Congress Cataloging-in-Publication Data

Vogel, Joseph, 1981-

Man in the music : the creative life and work of Michael Jackson / Joseph Vogel ; with a foreword by contributing editor Anthony Decurtis.

p. cm.

Includes bibliographical references and index.

ISBN 978-1-4027-7938-1

1. Jackson, Michael, 1958-2009—Criticism and interpretation. 2. Popular music—United States—History and criticism. I. Title.

ML420.J175V65 2011

782.42166092—dc22

[B]

2010051263

Distributed in Canada by Sterling Publishing

c/o Canadian Manda Group, 165 Dufferin Street

Toronto, Ontario, Canada M6K 3H6

Distributed in the United Kingdom by GMC Distribution Services

Castle Place, 166 High Street, Lewes, East Sussex, England BN7 1XU

Distributed in Australia by Capricorn Link (Australia) Pty. Ltd.

P.O. Box 704, Windsor, NSW 2756, Australia

For information about custom editions, special sales, and premium and corporate purchases, please contact Sterling Special Sales at 800-805-5489 or specialsales@sterlingpublishing.com.

Manufactured in China

2 4 6 8 10 9 7 5 3 1

www.sterlingpublishing.com

CONTENTS

Dedicated to Prince Michael, Paris, and Blanket

"In many ways, an artist is his work."

—Michael Jackson

"Deep inside, I feel that this world we live in is really a big, huge, monumental, symphonic orchestra. I believe that in its primordial form all of creation is sound and that it's not just random sound, that it's music. . . . Music governs the rhythm of the seasons, the pulse of our heartbeats, the migration of birds, the ebb and flow of ocean tides, the cycles of growth, evolution, and dissolution. It's music, it's rhythm. And my goal in life is to give to the world what I was lucky to receive: the ecstasy of divine union through my music and my dance."

—Michael Jackson

PREFACE

This book began in 2005 at a time that was undoubtedly Michael Jackson's darkest hour. For almost two years—following Martin Bashir's infamous documentary, *Living with Michael Jackson*—he had been the subject of an insatiable global media feeding frenzy. His trial drew more than 2,000 reporters from at least 35 countries. It garnered more coverage than the war in Iraq or the genocide in Sudan. The tabloid punditry—led by infotainment hosts such as Nancy Grace and Diane Dimond—merged seamlessly into mainstream cable news, in which speculation about Jackson was the lead topic on nearly every news and entertainment channel, nearly every night, for more than six months. Most assumed Jackson's guilt and used the occasion to ridicule everything from his physical appearance to his children to his various eccentricities. "America is done with this guy," proclaimed conservative *Fox News* host, Bill O'Reilly. "He's a weirdo."

When I arrived in Santa Maria, California, that summer, I witnessed a circus-like atmosphere. The media had set up a small city. Trailers, tents, and satellites surrounded the courthouse; reporters were everywhere—standing in front of cameras, conducting interviews, and talking into cell phones. Hundreds of fans were there too, of course—and others who simply wanted to sell something, gawk or get on TV.

What quickly became apparent, however, was how little interest there was in evidence or decency, nuance or objectivity. Ratings and headlines depended on an incessant stream of sensationalism, innuendo, hearsay and speculation, and this is exactly what audiences received. Jackson himself was reduced to a circus freak. He was the modern-day Elephant Man, begging to be treated like a human being amidst a crowd of finger-pointing spectators. British journalist Charles Thomson called it "one of the most shameful episodes in journalistic history." Political observer Jeff Koopersmith characterized it as a "high-tech lynching."

Jackson, of course, was ultimately acquitted of all charges. Yet the damage was done. The groundbreaking music had been smothered in a cacophony of noise, the videos and dances erased and replaced with footage of a broken man, walking gingerly out of a courtroom.

When I began the book, then, my objective was to recover Michael Jackson, the artist. The scandals and eccentricities had been covered ad nauseam (and most often in very speculative, superficial ways). His actual creative work, it seemed to me then and now, was infinitely richer, more interesting, and compelling. That's what I hoped to bring back into focus.

Over the next five years, I read nearly every book written about the pop star. Given his cultural impact, it was remarkable how little of substance was available. While one could find a range of serious, in-depth books on Elvis Presley or the Beatles, most titles on Jackson fell into two categories: self-published fan adulation or sensationalized tabloid "tell-alls." There were some exceptions, most notably, Jackson's 1988 autobiography *Moonwalk* and J. Randy Taraborrelli's voluminous *Michael Jackson: The Magic and the Madness*. Over the period of my research (and particularly following his death), other substantive books appeared, including Chris Cadman and Craig Halstead's reference catalog, *Michael Jackson: For the Record*; Armond White's eloquent collection of essays, *Keep Moving: The Michael Jackson Chronicles*; Mark Fisher's edited volume, *The Resistible Demise of Michael Jackson*; and recording engineer Bruce Swedien's technical, but illuminating *In the Studio with Michael Jackson*.

While each of these books offered important contributions, however, I still felt a book assessing Jackson's entire body of work—album-by-album, song-by-song—was missing. My early model was Ian MacDonald's classic, *A Revolution in the Head: The Beatles' Records and the Sixties*. Though in many ways my book ended up being structured quite differently—I chose to organize by album, and emphasize context and interpretation over more technical breakdowns—I still hope it will serve a similar role in terms of depth, breadth and comprehensiveness.

Yet it wasn't just coverage I was aiming for. So much music criticism (particularly about Jackson) has been reductive and condescending. I wanted to write something historically and critically rigorous, but approach the subject with less cynicism and more curiosity. What was Jackson trying to convey? What did his work illuminate, challenge, provoke, express? How was it made? And what type of response(s) did he hope to elicit? I agreed with literary critic, Mark Edmundson, that the art of interpretation should at least begin with an attempt to see the world from the perspective of the artist—to "arriv[e] at a version of the work that the [artist]—as we imagine him, as we imagine her—would approve and be gratified by."

The book that developed from this philosophy was inevitably daunting to write. Doing justice to any great artist is a challenge, but Michael Jackson poses especially unique ones. Perhaps most difficult was a) accumulating enough reliable information to develop a clear sense of when, where, why, how, and with whom his work was made, and b) developing some degree of fluency in all the media his work utilized: music, singing, dance, film, studio technology, etc. What I quickly realized is that my role would necessarily be as much researcher and interviewer as author, and that I would allow people who knew far more than I did to speak for themselves. To this end, I read a wide range of inside accounts, reviews, and analyses of Jackson's work; I read every interview Michael Jackson gave from 1977 forward; and I read as many interviews as I could find from those who worked with him, including Quincy Jones, Bruce Swedien, Rod Temperton, Teddy Riley, Rodney Jerkins, Matt Forger, Brad Buxer, and Bill Bottrell. Perhaps most enlightening, however, were the personal interviews I conducted with many of these people and others who worked closely with Jackson. Speaking with Jackson's creative partners—producers, engineers, music directors, musicians, and technicians—provided fascinating insights into how Jackson operated as an artist and how specific songs and albums came into being. Many of the people I conversed with had rarely spoken about Jackson publicly before. Yet, all were generous with their time and pleased that the Jackson they knew was finally being represented in print.

Also extremely helpful in my research was *Rolling Stone*, whose archives provided rich and relevant material from nearly every stage of Jackson's career. In addition, the online archives of *Time* magazine, *The New York Times*, *Ebony*, and The Michael Jackson Archives website were invaluable. The Estate of Michael Jackson was also very generous with their feedback and support.

Unfortunately, I was never able to interview Michael Jackson himself. The night before he died I was working on the book. I had hoped to interview him in London during his *This Is It* concert series. I knew from a rare 2007 interview he gave to *Ebony* that he was eager to get the focus back on his work, to be perceived as an artist, not a tabloid oddity. But then came the tragic news.

I was stunned. Like many people, I had grown up with Michael Jackson. He meant to me what transformative artists like Elvis Presley, John Lennon, and Bob Dylan had meant to previous generations of young people. The first time I saw the Motown 25 performance, at the age of nine, I was absolutely captivated. I wore out my VHS of *Michael Jackson: The Legend Continues* having played it so many times, and used to ride my bike to school listening to songs like "Beat It," "Man in the Mirror," and "Black or White" on my Walkman. Over the years, my musical interests changed and evolved, but my fascination with Jackson persisted—I could always appreciate his work in new ways and on new levels.

With his death, then, came a profound sense of loss and sadness about what might have been. Yet as Jackson presciently put it just two years earlier (quoting one of his own artistic heroes, Michelangelo): "I know the creator will go, but his work survives. That is why to escape death, I attempt to bind my soul to my work." It was perhaps the most revealing comment he ever made about what he hoped for his legacy.

In creating this book, I traveled deep inside that soul-filled work. With each return visit, new and exciting discoveries unfolded.

It is my hope that *Man in the Music* will inspire a similar experience for others, serving as a gateway into the creative world of one of the most unique artists of the past century.

JOSEPH VOGEL
April 2011

FOREWORD

ANTHONY DECURTIS

Over the summer of 2001, I worked as the lead writer for what was billed as the Michael Jackson 30th Anniversary Celebration, two concerts that were to be held at Madison Square Garden in New York on September 8 and 10. The shows would be filmed and later shown on television in edited form and made available on DVD. The anniversary celebrated was the 1971 release of "Got to Be There," Jackson's first solo single and a Top 5 hit. The occasion was part of the buildup for the release of *Invincible*, his first album of new material in six years. It would come out the next month, and though no one knew it at the time, it would be Jackson's last studio album.

The preparations for the show were chaotic, to say the least. David Gest was the producer—need I say more?—and special guests included the likes of Liza Minelli (whom Gest would later marry and divorce), Marlon Brando, Elizabeth Taylor, and other stars who would seem wildly out of place at an arena pop concert, especially at a time when Jackson needed more than anything else to redefine himself in contemporary terms. For me the stress of those weeks of working on the script was compounded by the fact that I was getting married on September 8 in upstate New York. Consequently I wasn't going to be able to attend the concerts myself, so the whole effort, bizarre and exciting as it was, felt a bit abstract.

The event that grounded that period for me was the evening of rehearsals I attended a couple of days before the first show. The Garden's twenty thousand or so seats were empty, save for other members of the film crew, workers setting up the venue for the concerts, and representatives of the various artists scheduled to rehearse that night. Whitney Houston was on the scene looking hollowed out and vacant. On stage, Michael Jackson, his brothers, and a backing band were rehearsing.

Michael Jackson wasn't in stage clothes; I recall him wearing slacks and a loose-fitting shirt, and having reading glasses available to look at papers he was consulting. If he didn't speak into his microphone, I wasn't close enough to hear what he was saying. However, Jackson would often talk into the mike to make sure everyone on stage could hear him, and it was in his hand at all times, occasionally picking up his voice even when he wasn't holding it to his face. His primary concern was with blocking his choreography for the show—and it was evident that he was relaxed and completely in control. He spoke primarily with his musical director, Greg Phillinganes;

his tone was always friendly, respectful, and professional. Jackson was very focused about how he wanted his movements and those of his brothers to work with the music—where he would be when the beats landed, the fillips he needed in the music to make his moves hit with the most compelling impact.

When they spoke off-mike, one could see Jackson and Phillinganes alternately concentrating and laughing. They wanted to get things right, but they were also having fun, excited about the upcoming shows. Jackson seemed a bit distant from his brothers, though not cold or peremptory, just removed. Mostly, he seemed very much a musician and performer who knew exactly what he wanted but who also appreciated the necessary efforts being made by others. He knew that his name was on the marquee and whatever happened would ultimately be a reflection of him, not of anyone else.

Over the years, I had written about Michael Jackson a great deal, watched him perform many times, and discussed and debated about him on news and entertainment television shows. The next month I would conduct a lengthy telephone interview with him, drawing on questions submitted by his fans (and screened by his innumerable handlers) that would be broadcast live on the Internet. However, I had never witnessed him in a situation like this, and it was impressive to see.

It reminded me, first of all, of why anybody cared about Michael Jackson from the very start. He was among the greatest performers I had ever seen, and his music could light up a dance floor instantaneously. Every time I listen to his songs, I discover new things to love about them, inventive touches that I had never noticed before. In this one specific sense his death was a blessing: It forced people to re-encounter his artistry and to realize once again how important he had been to them, how much his music had meant to their lives. For younger people who had not grown up with Michael Jackson, it provided perhaps their first opportunity to hear his music free of clichéd preconceptions about him.

However, there's no point making excuses. No question: Jackson must bear some of the responsibility for why he eventually became little more than a punch line in the years before his death. His behavior and eccentricities frequently drew attention away from his work. What was once a bracing ambition evolved into megalomania. One time in an interview for a *Rolling Stone* cover story, I asked Janet Jackson if she could accept the idea that she might possibly make a great record that didn't sell. She gave me a benign, quizzical look as if I had suddenly begun speaking a foreign language that she couldn't conceivably be expected to understand. What could it possibly mean to make a "great" record that people didn't buy?

That was the commercial ethic the Jacksons subscribed to, and Michael was a far more fervent believer in it even than Janet was. There are understandable cultural reasons for that as well as personal ones, but there is no way around the fact that Michael's efforts to recreate the success and impact of *Thriller*—to relive the moment that made the world make the most sense to him—damaged him. Still, there can also be no doubt that the media fell into the psychological trap that Jackson unconsciously set, and measured all of his post-*Thriller* work by an unattainable commercial standard, to everyone's inevitable disappointment—his, most of all.

But, as Joe Vogel convincingly demonstrates in this fine, comprehensive book, Jackson created great and important work throughout his career. By the time of Jackson's death, the man and his problems had utterly eclipsed the music. Like everyone who paid close attention to Jackson, I, of course, understood how he experienced the stage as the place of his most profound happiness. Until that night at Madison Square Garden, I thought that was simply about the white heat of performance burning away all other issues with its hard, gemlike flame.

When I saw Michael prepare for his thirtieth anniversary performances with undeniable ease and calmness, however, it became clear that he was happy on stage because he was, first and foremost, an artist; and his music meant more to him than anything else. I find that same steady focus and command I witnessed that night in the pages of *Man in the Music*, a tribute that Michael Jackson's spellbinding work more than lives up to and more than deserves.

Anthony DeCurtis *is a contributing editor at* Rolling Stone, *where his work has appeared for more than twenty-five years, and he occasionally writes for the* New York Times *and many other publications. He is the author of* In Other Words: Artists Talk About Life and Work, *as well as* Rocking My Life Away. *He is also the editor of* Present Tense: Rock & Roll and Culture, *and co-editor of* The Rolling Stone Illustrated History of Rock & Roll *and* The Rolling Stone Album Guide *(3rd edition). His essay accompanying the Eric Clapton box set* Crossroads *won a Grammy Award in the Best Album Notes category. He holds a PhD in American literature and teaches in the writing program at the University of Pennsylvania.*

INTRODUCTION

A GREAT ADVENTURE

Michael Jackson often explained his creative process as an act of recovering something that already existed. He was just a "courier" bringing it into the world, a medium through which the music flowed. He cited Michelangelo's philosophy that inside every piece of stone or marble was a "sleeping form." "He's just freeing it," Jackson insisted. "It's already in there. It's already there."

As an artist, then, Jackson's work was about liberation. He wanted to free what was bound, transform what was petrified, and awaken what was dormant. He wanted to break through any obstacle that constrained the imagination, any chains—psychological, social, or political—that imprisoned the body or mind. This is what art meant to him personally, and it was his intended effect on his audience as well.

For millions around the world, of course, this is exactly what he accomplished. To admirers, he was always far more than a mere celebrity or pop star. He was music incarnate. Listening to his songs or watching him perform was an injection of life, a torrent of powerful emotions. Some likened it to a sort of spiritual ecstasy. Others compared it to an exorcism. Fans spoke of feeling transported, empowered, connected, inspired. After witnessing a concert on his *Bad* World Tour in 1988, *Newsweek* journalist Jim Miller described him as possessing "the breathtaking verve of his predecessor James Brown, the beguiling wispiness of Diana Ross, the ungainly pathos of Charlie Chaplin, the edgy joy of a man startled to be alive. The crowd gasps and screams …"

Jackson sometimes compared the reciprocal energy of a performance to a Frisbee—"you hold it, you touch it, and you whip it back." Audiences, he believed, were more than passive spectators; they were a vibrant community, composed of all ages, races, religions, and cultures, standing shoulder to shoulder, temporarily bound up in the collective spell of his music, imagining the world anew. "You can take them anywhere," he effused. This was his gift as an artist: the ability to dissolve into the stories, the emotions, the *magic* of his music—and to take masses of people from all walks of life with him. He called this creative bond many things over the years: escapism, entertainment, showmanship, art. But ultimately, for Jackson, it was about sharing and receiving love.

Jackson in a moment of discovery on his *Bad* World Tour in 1987.

Jackson performing his iconic "Billie Jean" routine on his Victory Tour in 1984.

THE EMBODIMENT OF MUSIC

Jackson's body was his most instinctual canvas. He was a dancer to the core. He danced in private as a form of exercise and release. He danced while recording in the studio. On stage, his body seemed to become possessed by the music. "I am a slave to the rhythm," he explained. "I am a palette. I just go with the moment. You've got to do it that way because if you're thinking, you're dead. Performing is not about thinking; it's about feeling." Choreography, to Jackson, was like lines in painting: it gave borders within which to operate. It wasn't about counting or steps; it was about exploring and expressing within those confines.

In this creative space, he would become the "embodiment" of each piece. "When you're dancing," he revealed, "you are just interpreting the music and the sounds and the accompaniment. If there's a driving bass, if there's a cello, if there's a string, you become the emotion of what the sound is." This ability to fully occupy the music is what set him apart as a dancer. Many of his moves had been done before, including the moonwalk; but he got deep inside them, understood what they could convey, and made them his own.

AN UNUSUAL EDUCATION

Understanding Jackson as a dancer and performer is crucial to understanding him as a singer and songwriter since, if ever there was someone who exemplified the title "song and dance man," it was Michael Jackson. He learned from the best: showmen like Sammy Davis Jr., James Brown, Jackie Wilson, Fred Astaire, and Gene Kelly. When he was just eight years old, he watched from the sides of stages in legendary theaters such as the Regal and the Apollo, absorbing and learning.

The biggest revelation to young Michael Jackson was "the Godfather of Soul," James Brown. As Elvis Presley was to a young John Lennon, so James Brown was to Michael. Jackson, however, had the advantage of seeing his idol up close and in person. "After studying James Brown from the wings," he recalls, "I knew every step, every grunt, every spin and turn. I have to say he would give a performance that would exhaust you, just wear you out emotionally. His whole physical presence, the fire coming out of his pores, would be phenomenal. You'd feel every bead of sweat on his face and you'd know what he was going through. I've never seen anyone perform like him."

It wasn't just Brown's performing and dancing that Jackson incorporated. Brown's trademark rhythmic singing, his staccato vocals (featuring short syllables, grunts, screams, and exclamations), and his pure elemental funk are all over Jackson's music. Jackson, of course, adapted and fused Brown's style with others, but Brown was unquestionably Jackson's most profound early influence.

Jackson's musical education continued at Motown, where he was surrounded by some of the most renowned musicians of an era, including Marvin Gaye, Gladys Knight, and Smokey Robinson. As a young boy, he was especially enthralled with Diana Ross, whom he lived with for several months upon arriving in Los Angeles in 1970. "She was art in motion," he later wrote. "I watched her rehearse one day in the mirror. She didn't know I was watching. I studied her, the way she moved, the way she sang, the way she was." As a young teenager, he would also sit in the studio with Stevie Wonder, watching him record some of his classic albums, including *Songs in the Key of Life*. "He would always come into the studio curious about how I worked and what I did," recalls Wonder. "'How do you do that? Why do you do that?' I think he understood

James Brown, the "hardest working man in show business," in a signature pose. Brown was Jackson's biggest early influence.

clearly from seeing various people do the music scene that it definitely took work." Jackson later referred to Stevie Wonder as a "musical prophet."

There were many other important influences during his years at Motown who helped polish and season Jackson's natural ability: Suzanne de Passe, the Jackson 5's early manager, choreographer, stylist, P. R. instructor, and stand-in mom; a group of talented songwriters and producers called "the Corporation," which included Deke Richards, Freddie Perren, and Alphonzo Mizell; and Hal Davis, who wrote many of the Jackson 5's and Michael's Motown songs, from "I'll Be There" to "Dancing Machine." Yet, arguably no one had as profound an impact on young Michael's development as the creator of Motown Records himself, Berry Gordy. Gordy taught Jackson perfectionism and meticulous attention to detail in the studio. If a song took more than a hundred times to get right, they would record it more than one hundred times. It was exhausting training, especially for a young boy; but Jackson learned. "I'll never forget his persistence," he later wrote." I observed every moment of the sessions where Berry was present and never forgot what I learned. To this day I use the same principles."

Yet perhaps Gordy's biggest impact on Michael was engraining in him the ambition for crossover, chart-topping, world-conquering music and entertainment. Gordy was a savvy, shrewd executive who felt black music could (and should) reach a mass, multiracial, even international audience. Though some felt this was primarily a commercially motivated ambition that sanitized or mainstreamed black music, there is no question it made significant inroads in an industry that was, at the time, still almost completely racially segregated.

Gordy's blueprint was important, then, not only because it created a climate for artists like Jackson to be accepted by white and international audiences, but also because it was an ideology of inclusion that Jackson later adopted wholeheartedly. For the rest of his career, he refused to be pigeonholed by race, genre, nationality, or anything else. Music, he felt, was universal. And a black boy from Gary, Indiana, could be its "king."

This philosophy, indeed, was a big part of why Jackson was later drawn to Quincy Jones. Jones, he explained in a 1980 interview, was "unlimited musically": he did everything from jazz to pop to classical scores. He was also "all colors," which meant to Jackson that his work wouldn't be boxed in as "black music."

Indeed, while Jackson was clearly rooted, musically and otherwise, in the African American tradition, his range of influences grew far beyond any one race or ethnicity. "I love great music," he explained. "It has no color, it has no boundaries." Jackson's own early musical interests spanned from funk pioneers like P-Funk and Sly and the Family Stone to folk groups like the Carpenters and the Mamas & the Papas; from Broadway balladeers like Julie Andrews and Barbra Streisand to disco sensations like the Bee Gees.

Jackson loved experiencing art for its own sake (what he often called "the magic"), but he also wanted to understand its "anatomy." He wanted to understand everything about the way it worked, its history, what had withstood the test of time, what its possibilities were. By the time he met Quincy Jones in the late seventies, though still a teenager, he already had nearly a decade of experience learning firsthand from some of the most renowned musicians and songwriters in the industry. Jones described him as a "sponge." "He wanted to be the best of everything—to take it all in," Jones said. "He went to the top model in each category to create an act and persona that would be unequaled."

A WORLD OF IMAGINATION

Throughout his life, Jackson always had his finger to the pulse of the music industry—both as a fan and as an artist searching for new sounds and ideas. He was fascinated by both the "mystique" and artistry of the two major pop phenomena before him: Elvis Presley and the Beatles (it was no coincidence that he married the daughter of the former and purchased the song catalog of the latter). Whenever he thought of his own artistic and cultural legacy, Presley and the Beatles lingered in the back of his mind. His musical interests, however, also included less obvious influences such as Led Zeppelin, Yes, Grace Jones, and Radiohead. "I have all kinds of tapes and albums people would probably never think were mine," he once said. This vast reservoir of musical knowledge comes through in his songs. For "Wanna Be Startin' Somethin'" he included an African chant inspired by Cameroonian saxophonist Manu Dibango's "Soul Makossa"; on "Little Susie" he used a section from French composer Maurice Duruflé's choral work, Requiem Op. 9; on "2Bad" he sampled hip-hop pioneers Run-D.M.C. As Greg Tate observes, Jackson was willing to pull from "anybody he thought would make his own expression more visceral, modern, and exciting."

Charlie Chaplin (as the Little Tramp) and Jackie Coogan in the film, *The Kid*. Jackson idolized Chaplin and recreated this picture for his cover of "Smile."

One of the things that made Jackson unique as an artist, however, is that many of his influences were anything but hip and contemporary. When asked what his biggest inspiration was for *Thriller*, he didn't answer Prince or the Police; he said it was nineteenth-century Russian composer Tchaikovsky. "If you take an album like *Nutcracker Suite*," he explained, "every song is a killer, every one. So I said to myself, 'Why can't there be a pop album [like that?]'" It wasn't just a vision for consistent quality that classical music inspired. Since his youth, Jackson had listened to composers such as Tchaikovsky, Debussy, Prokofiev, Beethoven, Bernstein, and Copland. Jackson was particularly drawn to Romantic and Impressionistic pieces that contained strong melodies and vivid, emotional color. To Jackson, music was always very visual; he was drawn, therefore, to pieces that were attached to or evoked some kind of visual presentation, such as Debussy's *Arabesque No. 1* or Prokofiev's *Peter and the Wolf*. Classical influence permeates Jackson's work, at times even literally attached as preludes to his own compositions.

Jackson was also a devoted fan of musicals—including *The Sound of Music*, *Singin' in the Rain*, *My Fair Lady*, and *West Side Story*—and incorporated their styles into both his videos and albums. It was an influence that sometimes put him at odds with traditional rock critics who felt he was too "theatrical." Yet Jackson never deviated from his love of show tunes. He was also obsessed with film: all the old MGM movies, everything Disney, Spielberg, Lucas, Hitchcock, and Francis Ford Coppola. He would watch films such as *E.T.*, *The Elephant Man*, and *To Kill a Mockingbird* repeatedly and cry every time. "In film, you live the moment," he explained. "You have the audience for two hours. You have their brain, their mind—you can take them any place you want to take them. You know, and that idea is mesmerizing to me—that you can have the power to move people, to change their lives."

Jackson's intense love of the silver screen generated many passions. He was enamored of all things Shirley Temple and Elizabeth Taylor (the rumors of "shrines" to both were true). He boasted a bigger cartoon collection than Paul McCartney. He could watch the Three Stooges for hours on end. He famously claimed he "was Peter Pan," so great was his kinship for J. M. Barrie's iconic boy-hero. Jackson studied the work of every major dancer of the century, including Fred Astaire, Gene Kelly, Bob Fosse, Martha Graham, Alvin Ailey, and Jeffrey Daniel (all of whom likewise admired him). His deepest kinship, however, might have been with cinema legend Charlie Chaplin, a similarly paradoxical figure who rose from poverty to become the biggest entertainer of his age. One can find Chaplin's movements, stylizations, and combination of exuberance and pathos throughout Jackson's work.

Not only did he watch or listen to these people, he read about them. Jackson was a voracious reader. From his childhood until his final years, he would visit bookstores and come home with stacks of books. His personal library contained more than 20,000 titles, including biographies, poetry, philosophy, psychology, and history. Jackson read about African American slavery and the civil rights movement, about Edison and Galileo, about religion and spirituality. He read novels

Jackson acting as director on the set of his music video, *Liberian Girl*, in 1988. By this time he had already revolutionized the medium and preferred calling his videos "short films."

In 1983, however, Jackson completely reinvented the possibilities. *Billie Jean* and *Beat It* initiated this transformation, replacing cheap, montage-like promos with elaborate, fully conceived productions that contained stronger narratives, spectacular visuals and effects, and, of course, Jackson's signature choreography and dance moves. Then came the groundbreaking fourteen-minute video for "Thriller," which cost more than a half-million dollars to make and became the best-selling VHS home movie of all time. *Thriller* is now almost universally considered the most influential music video in history.

Such innovation in the medium continued throughout Jackson's entire career, making him the defining visual artist of the MTV generation. From the pioneering 4-D attraction, *Captain EO*, to the forty-minute Gothic spectacle, *Ghosts*, Jackson was always ahead of the curve, expanding the possibilities of the medium, while igniting viewers' imaginations. Indeed, in retrospect, as cultural critic Hampton Stevens notes, "The oft-repeated conventional wisdom—that Jackson's videos made MTV and so 'changed the music industry' is only half true. It's more like the music industry ballooned to encompass Jackson's talent and shrunk down again without him. Videos didn't matter before Michael, and they ceased to matter at almost the precise cultural moment he stopped producing great work."

SINGING BEYOND LANGUAGE

While this book acknowledges Jackson's contributions to dance and film, however, its emphasis is on his work as a singer and songwriter. Perhaps, in part, because of Jackson's abilities in these other areas, his remarkable skills as a vocalist and composer are often overlooked. There are, no doubt, a variety of reasons for this neglect—one being that assessing Jackson's work is much different from that of a traditional singer–songwriter like Bruce Springsteen or Bob Dylan. With Dylan, the lyrics are often out front and focused upon heavily in critical assessments; however, for Jackson, they can often be ancillary, or at least one of several media to consider. Indeed, even in his vocalizing, part of Jackson's distinctive style is his ability to convey emotion without the use of language: there are his trademark gulps, grunts, gasps, cries, and exclamations; he also frequently scats or twists and contorts words until they are barely decipherable. The idea is to make the audience "feel" the song as a sense impression, rather than focusing entirely on the words. Such "impressions," of course, can be more difficult to analyze.

Jackson's more instinctual method was something he had learned watching the masters of funk, soul, and rhythm and blues. Yet he developed a style that was unmistakably his own. It was a voice that could brilliantly conjure emotional extremes, injecting the most ordinary lyric with depth and pathos. "[Michael]," observed Quincy Jones, "has some of the same qualities as the great jazz singers I'd worked with: Ella, Sinatra, Sassy, Aretha, Ray Charles, Dinah. Each of them had that purity, that strong signature sound and that open wound that pushed them to greatness. Singing crushed their pain, healed their hurts, and dissolved their issues. Music was their release from emotional prisons."

From a technical standpoint, Jackson's broad range allowed him to move fluidly through nearly four octaves (this was something he worked very hard to achieve as an adult, though he rarely pushed his range to the limits). A natural tenor, his singing in the upper register was smooth and sublime, yet he could also be effective in his lower register, occasionally even dropping down to a baritone. Everyone who worked with him commented on his perfect pitch. His longtime voice coach, Seth Riggs, marveled at both his ability and dedication. Jackson, after all, was one of the most gifted child singers of all time. People often take for granted his transition into an adult singer, but it took an enormous amount of effort and development. He had to find new ways of approaching songs and new ways of employing his skill set.

What Jackson may have lost in youthful elasticity, he made up for in creativity and versatility. Moving through *Off the Wall* alone, one travels from the falsetto ecstasy of "Don't Stop 'Til You Get Enough," to the subtle warmth of "Rock With You," to the primal percussiveness of "Workin' Day and Night," to the jazz improvisation of "I Can't Help It," to the vulnerable crooning of "She's Out of My Life." On subsequent albums, he soared on majestic anthems alongside gospel choirs, delivered gritty scratch vocals on rock songs like "Dirty Diana" and "Give In To Me," and implemented spoken raps and beatboxing on many of the rhythm tracks. "Jackson was a dancer at heart," writes music critic Neil McCormick, "and his vocal prowess expressed itself playfully within and around the rhythm. He liked to multitrack himself so that he was spinning off his own vocal, providing his own calls and response. I often think that it is one of those voices that would stand out in any context, which you cannot say of many pop singers, hitting a space that is emotionally right on the button but is almost more than human, transcending all divides in the way that, sometimes, a great world singer can, moving beyond language into pure

Singing, as Quincy Jones put it, was Jackson's "release from emotional prisons."

music." This, indeed, was what he aimed to achieve with his singing. Listen to Jackson's wordless cries in the chorus of "Earth Song," or his scatting in the unfinished, "In the Back." Words aren't necessary—the deep emotion is communicated perfectly in his delivery. His voice *is* the music.

MUSIC AS TAPESTRY

Jackson used his intuitive musicality as a songwriter as well. While he didn't read music or play instruments proficiently, he could vocally convey the arrangement, rhythm, tempo, and melody of a track, including nearly every instrument. "He starts with an entire sound and song," explains producer Bill Bottrell. "Usually he doesn't start with lyrics, but he hears the whole arrangement of the song in his head.... He hums things. He can convey it with his voice like nobody. Not just singing the song's lyrics, but he can convey a feeling in a drum part or a synthesizer part. He's really good at conveying those things." Often Jackson would vocalize a new song into a tape recorder until he could get to a studio; other times he would call a musician or producer and dictate to him or her directly. "One morning [Michael] came in with a new song he had written overnight," recalls assistant engineer Rob Hoffman. "We called in a guitar player, and Michael sang every note of every chord to him. 'Here's the first chord, first note, second note, third note. Here's the second chord, first note, second note, third note,' etc. We then witnessed him giving the most heartfelt and profound vocal performance, live in the control room through an SM57. He would sing us an entire string arrangement, every part. Steve Porcaro once told me he witnessed [Jackson] doing that with the string section in the room. Had it all in his head, harmony and everything. Not just little eight bar loop ideas. He would actually sing the entire arrangement into a microcassette recorder complete with stops and fills."

Once Jackson got down the foundation of the song, he would begin fleshing it out, layer by layer, a process that would sometimes take a few weeks and sometimes take years. "Music is tapestry," he explained. "It's different layers, it's weaving in and out, and if you look at it in layers, you understand it better." He liked to allow time for the song to reveal itself. If it wasn't quite there, he would move on to something else and come back to it later. Those who worked with him speak of his patience, focus, and genuine commitment to his craft. "He was a consummate professional," recalls technical director Brad Sundberg. "If his vocals were scheduled for a noon downbeat, he was there at 10 a.m., with his vocal coach Seth [Riggs], singing scales. Yes, scales. I would set up the mic, check the equipment, make coffee, and all the while he would sing scales for two hours."

In the studio, Jackson had very specific preferences. Before singing, he would often request a scalding hot drink with cough drops to relax his vocal chords. He liked the music so loud his collaborators often had to wear earplugs or leave the room. He usually sang with the lights off, as the darkness allowed him to totally immerse himself in the song without feeling self-conscious.

As he sang, he also danced, stomped, or snapped his fingers. If he didn't have the lyrics written yet, he would simply scat through the song or make up words as he went along. In between sessions he liked to doodle on stray pieces of paper or play with animals he brought in, including his chimpanzee, Bubbles, and his python, Muscles (who enjoyed the warmth of the control board).

Jackson enjoys a lighter moment on stage. His collaborators describe him as having a wonderful sense of humor.

In spite of his quirks, it is nearly impossible to find someone Jackson worked with who didn't walk away with a profound level of respect and appreciation. Even when his personal life was in disarray, his creative colleagues witnessed an individual far different than the man depicted in the tabloids. From producers to assistant engineers to fellow musicians, they describe him as possessing a certain "aura," but being down-to-earth, humble, and polite. They describe his sense of humor and "boisterous" laugh; they describe his curiosity; they describe his passion and excitement for each new project. "All of Michael's recordings were done with a sense of *joy* that I have never experienced with another artist," recalls longtime recording engineer Bruce Swedien. "Not just fun and laughing and stuff, I mean real musical *joy*.... His passion for what we were doing was boundless."

Producer Bill Bottrell, who worked closely with Jackson during the *Bad* and *Dangerous* sessions, praises him for challenging and stretching Bottrell as a fellow artist. "[He] just started asking me to take more responsibility, play more music, write music, play more instruments.... He changed my life. And it never stopped feeling that way." Bottrell and others not only speak of being treated as equals, but also of Jackson's sincere appreciation for their talent and contributions. Songwriter/musician Brad Buxer, who worked intimately with Jackson for twenty-five years, recalls the thrill of finding just the right chord or beat. "When you did something [Michael] liked," Buxer says, "He would say, 'That's it. That's perfect. Lock this in cement.' We called the versions that were special 'Bible versions.' We'd go through thousands of versions, but we'd put 'Bible' by the best one.... It was just an extremely pleasant, fun time because of the musical freedom. You knew at the end of the day, you would have something.... It never got old; it never got stale."

Making music, for Jackson, then, was rarely an isolated act. The idea might come in a moment of solitude, but it was realized in much the same way a director realizes a film: through a dynamic, decentralized interplay of creativity. Jackson loved assembling talent and being part of a creative team. Once he found the right people, from the earliest *Off the Wall* sessions with Quincy Jones and Bruce Swedien to his latest projects, the motto remained the same: music first.

The music that resulted was high quality indeed. It is also far more diverse than the average music listener realizes. In addition to funk, R&B, rock, soul, jazz, and disco, he also experimented with classical, Broadway, gospel, Latin, hip-hop, electronic, and industrial, among numerous other styles. Jackson was often criticized for this eclecticism, with people claiming he was simply targeting demographics; but he defended himself by arguing for a borderless music. "I don't categorize music," he said in a 2002 interview, "Music is music.... How can we discriminate?"

This was his philosophy, and it is the hallmark of his music and artistry. Just as the Beatles made rock inclusive enough to contain elements of folk, blues, psychedelic, Eastern music, and classical, Jackson made "pop" a multigenre, multimedia affair that was limitless in its range of sounds, styles, and possibilities.

ARTISTIC EVOLUTION

In spite of his experimentation and evolution, however, the conventional wisdom from most media and music critics for decades was that Michael Jackson reached his artistic peak with *Off the Wall* and *Thriller*, and everything that followed revealed a slow and steady decline. In its 2009 obituary, the *New York Times* referred to his post-*Thriller* career as a "bizarre disintegration." What made his work so "bizarre" in these years? Nothing specific is mentioned, other than that his "bizarre private life" somehow equated with bad music. Similarly, in *Time's* retrospective, Josh Tyrangiel writes, "Given the tumult in his personal life, it's no surprise that the 1990s were a barren period for Jackson creatively." Tyrangiel doesn't explain why personal tumult has proven so creatively fertile for other artists—Ray Charles, John Lennon, and Kurt Cobain (among thousands of others)—but not for Jackson. He also doesn't explain how Jackson's prolific creative output during this time—Jackson wrote and recorded more songs and released more albums and music videos in the nineties than he did in the eighties—equates to a "barren period." Music critic Jon Pareles at least offers a slightly more specific criticism, claiming it was Jackson's loss of innocence that led to his artistic decline. "The underlying sweetness that had made Mr. Jackson endearing, even at his strangest, had curdled," he wrote. The criteria that made Jackson's work resonant, then, for Pareles is its "sweetness," though he doesn't attempt to reconcile this with early, lyrically disturbing songs such as "Billie Jean" and "Wanna Be Startin' Somethin'." The expectation of perpetual "sweetness" is also rather strange, given that conflict, anger, unrest, social protest, and disillusionment have been stimuli for some of the most powerful music.

A serious assessment of Michael Jackson's entire body of work has been missing with critics, who have frequently resorted to vague generalizations, patronizing dismissals, and petty moralizing. The range of his work, as a result, is frequently both fundamentally mischaracterized and misunderstood. Indeed, contrary to most media narratives, a closer analysis of Jackson's solo career reveals a remarkable artistic evolution. An apt parallel, in fact, is the Beatles, who likewise began by singing exuberant love songs but continued to challenge themselves and their audiences with new sounds and arrangements, more complex and socially conscious lyrics, and *delectus personae* that challenged the normative values and assumptions of their time. Similarly, observes cultural critic Armond White, "Jackson's career arc from beloved child star to dazzling young adult to ever-perplexing world conqueror shows a restless imagination. He pushed the culture forward—challenging it—as he also challenged himself. His idiosyncratic nature proved puzzling and alluring, yet it also torments the status quo—which is highly ironic for pleasurable pop art to do." White's recognition, however, has proven to be the exception, not the rule. While many critics, then and now, have lavished praise on the Beatles for their growth and transformations, Jackson has more often been characterized as a shallow record-chaser, whose failure to surpass the commercial success of *Thriller* somehow validated the perception that the music had lost its value.

More recently, such conventional thinking is being reconsidered as the public and critics alike go back to the albums and videos—often, in the case of his later work, hearing it for the first time—and reassess their aesthetic and cultural value. What this reassessment has revealed, and will undoubtedly continue to reveal, is that while the sales numbers and cultural impact in the United States might have declined, the richness, depth, and artistry did not. One need look no further than the haunting, poetical "Stranger in Moscow," one of the most powerful expressions of alienation since the Beatles' "A Day in the Life"; or the Gothic pop masterwork, "Is It Scary," which turns a mirror on an accusing society, forcing it to look at its own grotesque reflection; or the music video for "Black or White," which mixes satire and idealism, before unleashing an utterly fearless (and artistically sophisticated) coda.

Such work may have showcased a different, less cheerful version of Jackson, but it certainly wasn't barren or boring. "What is interesting," observes *Rolling Stone's* Mikal Gilmore of this oft-overlooked creative period, "is that this was…the time in which Jackson made some of his most interesting art: some of his wittiest, his most pain-filled, his angriest, and by far his most politically explicit or troubling."

Yet it is a mistake to think that these more challenging themes only emerged later in his career. Certainly some of his social commentaries became sharper and more direct as

Jackson on the set of his *Black or White* video; Jackson's artistry continued to evolve in interesting and challenging ways in the 1990s.

"Who Is It," "Stranger in Moscow"); and, of course, there are the anthems ("We Are the World," "Man in the Mirror," "Heal the World," "Earth Song").

If there is an overarching thread to Jackson's work, however, it is its persistent dissatisfaction with the world as it is, and its attempt to provide some kind of escape, liberation, or transformation as antidote. It is a fundamentally Romantic paradigm. Art, as the poet Percy Shelley put it, is "the mirror which makes beautiful that which is distorted." It is a journey, in other words, toward wholeness or integration. Yet, it doesn't do this by ignoring the distorted; the goal of the artist is to reveal the struggle, the contrast. "Many of his most affecting performances," observes Jeff Chang, "were about distance and displacement, the desire to be somewhere else, the inability to return to a lost past." Indeed, this struggle permeates Jackson's work. He's "searching for the world that he comes from" in "Childhood"; he doesn't know "whether to live or die" in "She's Out of My Life"; he's trapped in "Leave Me Alone"; he's "confused" in "Will You Be There"; he's "abandoned" in "Stranger in Moscow." These are the repercussions of what Jackson calls the "wounded world." It is "the result of the alienation people feel from each other and their environment." They are narratives of estrangement and sadness.

"I used to dream," he sings in "Earth Song," "I used to glance beyond the stars/Now I don't know where we are/Although I know we've drifted far." In "Man in the Mirror," he implicates himself, confessing he's "been a victim of a selfish kind of love." In "Jam" he is "conditioned by the system." And in "Wanna Be Startin' Somethin'" he is "stuck in the middle/And the pain is thunder."

Jackson on the set of his *You Are Not Alone* video.

Yet Jackson always believed the music could get him out and that he could take his audience with him. Thus, in "Startin' Somethin,'" there is a remarkable finale in which Jackson screams out, "I know I am someone!" before symbolically linking himself to a community with the collective African chant: "ma ma se ma ma sa ma ma coo sa." Likewise, in "Man in the Mirror," selfish love is replaced by compassion, creating an identity that is integrated with others. Of course, not every song provides this type of connection and transformation. However, it was what Jackson believed, in principle, music could accomplish.

An iconic photo of Michael Jackson during the *Thriller* era, when his image and music were ubiquitous.

BREAKING BARRIERS

Given the nature of his artistry, it should come as no surprise that Michael Jackson's primary cultural achievement—more than his sales numbers, awards, countless protégés, or even philanthropy—is in breaking barriers that typically divide humanity. This trailblazing began most prominently with race, in which Jackson's mass-popularity forced radio, magazines, and television stations like MTV to finally drop the excuse of rock/R&B divisions or lack of commercial viability and open the gates of opportunity for black artists. There were, of course, many successful black artists before Jackson. However, none had reached the stratospheric level of Elvis Presley or the Beatles. To many, it simply seemed natural and inevitable that a white artist would be bigger and better than a black artist. Yet in the eighties, Michael Jackson finally put that myth to rest. *Thriller* wasn't merely the best-selling album by a black artist, or the best-selling album of the decade; it was the best-selling album, period. Bigger than Elvis. Bigger than the Beatles. Bigger than the Stones. For African Americans, then, it was an enormous source of affirmation and achievement. The music they invented was finally being recognized at the highest level. As Greg Tate put it: "Black people cherished *Thriller's* breakthrough as if it were their own battering ram [against] apartheid."

His success, of course, wasn't only meaningful to African Americans. "Even though rooted in Black experience," writes cultural critic Michael Eric Dyson, "he felt it would be a crime to limit his music to one race, sex, gender, ethnicity, sexual orientation or nationality. Michael's art transcended every way that human beings have thought of to separate themselves, and then healed those divisions, at least at the instant that we all shared his music." It was a boundary-less universality Jackson always aimed for: "From a child to older people," he explained, "from the farmers of Ireland to the lady who scrubs toilets in Harlem ... I want to reach every demographic I can through the love and joy and simplicity of music."

This, indeed, is largely what he accomplished. Especially after *Thriller*, he and his music were embraced around the world. "Michael is now, quite simply, the biggest star in the pop-cultural universe," wrote *Rolling Stone* in 1984, "if not bigger than Jesus, as John Lennon once boasted of the Beatles, then certainly bigger than that group, or any other past pop icons." By the early 1990s, his concerts sold out from Germany to Japan, South Africa to Australia, Moscow to Prague. His songs played in every corner of the world. His lyrics were better known than national anthems.

After *Thriller*, of course, things changed. Jackson remained the biggest entertainer in the world, but he became increasingly polarizing. Michael Jackson had always been "different"; in fact, people often forget how strange it was that mainstream America ever embraced a man who wore makeup, spoke in a high voice, dressed in sequins, and lived in a miniature Disneyland. As the eighties wore on, however, Jackson's eccentricities became more apparent and pronounced, including his ever-changing physical appearance. Michael Jackson represented something different and unusual—and Americans in particular had a difficult time processing it. He was stigmatized as "weird" and "bizarre." By the mid-eighties, the "Wacko Jacko" label had already taken hold.

In the ensuing years, Jackson's cultural dominance began to wane as the media and the public increasingly marginalized him. Each tabloid story, each scandal, each public appearance, made him seem more strange and threatening. He was an outsider who nonetheless continued to fascinate people. Yet, these years also allowed him a new cultural role: already different, he become doubly marked as the "other"—and thus, millions of people around the world who didn't fit in, for whatever reasons, could identify with him. While the media ruthlessly mocked and objectified him, fans saw him as a victim of a cruel and callous culture of exploitation. Michael Jackson, they felt, was a pure, fragile soul, a Keats-like hero "whose achievement could not be separated from agony, who was 'spiritualized' by his decline, and... simply too fine-tuned to endure the buffetings of the world." Steven Spielberg once described him as a "fawn in a burning forest." Jackson himself often reinforced this delicate persona. He was the innocent man-child, forever compensating for his lost childhood, the seraphic singer who received inspiration from the branches of his "giving tree."

Jackson performs at Super Bowl XXVII in 1993, earning the broadcast its highest ratings ever. At this time, Jackson's global popularity was as high as ever.

Yet as the nineties wore on, he also became increasingly adept at striking back at the society that scorned him. He was the archetypal misunderstood artist: an eccentric genius perpetually at odds with the world around him, committed to his creative vision regardless of cultural expectations. He was also willing to embrace the darker side of Romanticism—the Gothic—to express the horror, isolation, and anxieties of being a "monster" in a monstrous world. In his 1997 film, *Ghosts*, he plays the role of the strange, misunderstood outsider as the citizens of "Normal Valley" seek to drive him out of town. Yet he doesn't act as mere innocent victim. "If you wanna see/Eccentric oddities," he sings, "I'll be grotesque before your eyes." In the final track on *Invincible*, he likewise flaunts his "monstrous" persona, provocatively saying "you should feel threatened by me."

In the final two decades of his life, then, Jackson played a less mainstream, but still valuable, cultural function. He was no longer the beloved superstar; he was the superstar who now spoke

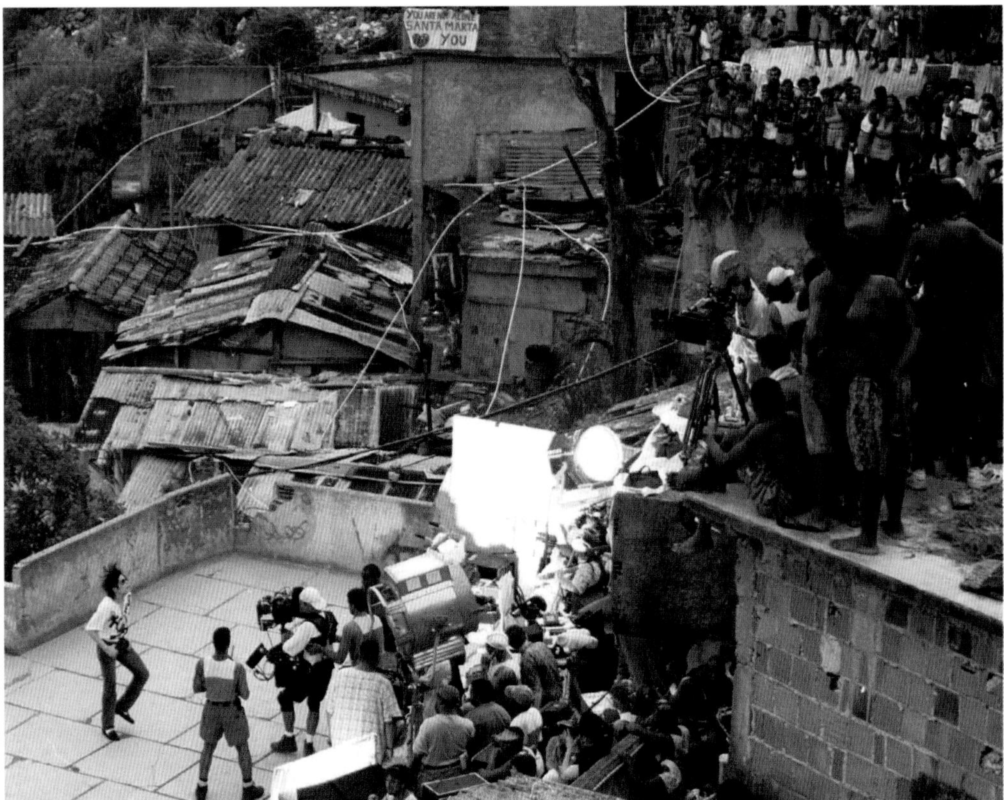

Hundreds of locals look on as Jackson performs in an impoverished *favela* in Rio de Janeiro, Brazil, the location of his controversial video, *They Don't Care About Us*, directed by Spike Lee.

Jackson on the set of his 1992 music video, *Remember the Time*. Many fans and admirers saw Jackson as a pure soul in a corrupt world. Steven Spielberg described him as a "fawn in a burning forest."

from the margins, from the perspective of the wounded or forgotten. Songs like "We've Had Enough" and "They Don't Care About Us" express an identification and solidarity with the oppressed. The former is an antiwar plea, the latter a chant of empowerment for all who have suffered injustice. It is a voice at odds with the status quo, indicting the media in "Tabloid Junkie," shouting apocalyptic anthems like "Earth Song," or narratives of quiet desperation like "Little Susie."

For most media and critics, however, this cultural import was overlooked in favor of a reductive dismissal. "Unlike the Beatles," observed *Time's* Jay Cocks, "[Jackson] has a vast audience, but a small constituency." In 1990, renowned music critic Greil Marcus famously claimed Jackson was the "first pop explosion not to be judged by the subjective quality of the response it provoked, but to be measured by the number of objective commercial exchanges it elicited." He was, in other words, a diversion, a phenomenon, a spectacle with surface-level resonance. His artistry and influence, in this way, were easily reduced and rationalized. Elvis and the Beatles changed the world; Jackson was just a commercial entertainer.

DEATH AND REBIRTH

It took something completely unexpected—and tragic—to finally begin to put Michael Jackson's artistic and cultural achievement into some perspective. Exactly thirty years after his solo career began, on a Thursday morning in June, Michael Jackson died in his home at the age of fifty.

The news sent shock waves around the world. From America to Africa, Europe to Asia, people learned of the tragedy via cell phone, text message, Twitter, TV, radio, Internet news sites, and social networks. Interest was so overwhelming that many prominent websites temporarily froze or crashed, including Wikipedia, Google, TMZ, and the *Los Angeles Times*. "Today was a seminal moment in Internet history," said a spokesperson for America Online. "We've never seen anything like it in terms of scope or depth."

Indeed, due in part to new media, the global response to Jackson's death was simply without historical parallel. It was bigger than Elvis Presley's, bigger than John Lennon's, bigger than Pope John Paul II's, John F. Kennedy's, and even Princess Diana's. Media experts estimated that Jackson's memorial was watched on TV or online by an astounding one billion people.

Meanwhile, within hours of the tragic news, Jackson's music and videos began flying off the shelves. In the week following his death, nine of the top ten positions on the *Billboard* Catalog Albums Chart in the United States belonged to Jackson, a feat never before accomplished. By the next week, he occupied the top twelve positions. He also became the first artist to top the *Billboard* 200 with a catalog album (*Number Ones* appropriately stayed at #1 for six non-consecutive weeks).

On iTunes and other online retailers, the King of Pop similarly reigned supreme, shattering record after record for digital sales. In the United States, no artist had ever sold one million downloads in a week; in the week following his death, with stock wiped clean in brick-and-mortar stores, Jackson sold 2.6 million. Across the world, Jackson's songs and albums reached #1 in every country with digital charts, including Australia, Japan, New Zealand, Argentina, and Germany. "In life," wrote *USA Today's* Jerry Shriver, "Michael Jackson was the king of pop. In death, he also reigns as the king of on-line retailing."

The benchmarks went on and on. By the end of 2009, Jackson had sold more than eight million albums in the United States, and an estimated thirty million worldwide, not only becoming the best-selling artist of the year by a landslide, but also surpassing even his own stratospheric sales records from the glory years of *Thriller*.

These staggering numbers, of course, didn't even account for various tributes and Jackson marathons on TV and radio, in magazine commemorations, or on the estimated fifteen billion Jackson-related views on sites like YouTube. They also didn't account for the millions of people who would go to theaters that fall to watch Michael Jackson's *This Is It*, a documentary of the singer's final concert rehearsals that became the best-selling music film of all time.

It was a remarkable reascent for the King of Pop, made even more so considering the context. Jackson hadn't released a new album in eight years; he had only performed two concerts (at Madison Square Garden in 2001) in the past decade; and his last major public appearance was his 2005 acquittal, following months of lurid headlines and assumed guilt. Now, even for detractors, the truth was undeniable: Regardless of the controversy, scandal, and perceptions of "strangeness," Michael Jackson's artistic and cultural legacy was enormous.

There were those, of course, who claimed the response to Jackson's death was simply a sad cable marathon of media hype and celebrity worship. It was partially true. Certainly, as is the case in all high-profile deaths, the media were quick to exploit Jackson's passing for ratings, sometimes at the expense of other important news. Yet regardless of the excess and mythologizing, his cultural import was unquestionable. In the United States, Jackson now stood with Elvis Presley and the Beatles as the most culturally momentous popular acts in music history. Globally, his reach was even greater. Some have argued rather persuasively that

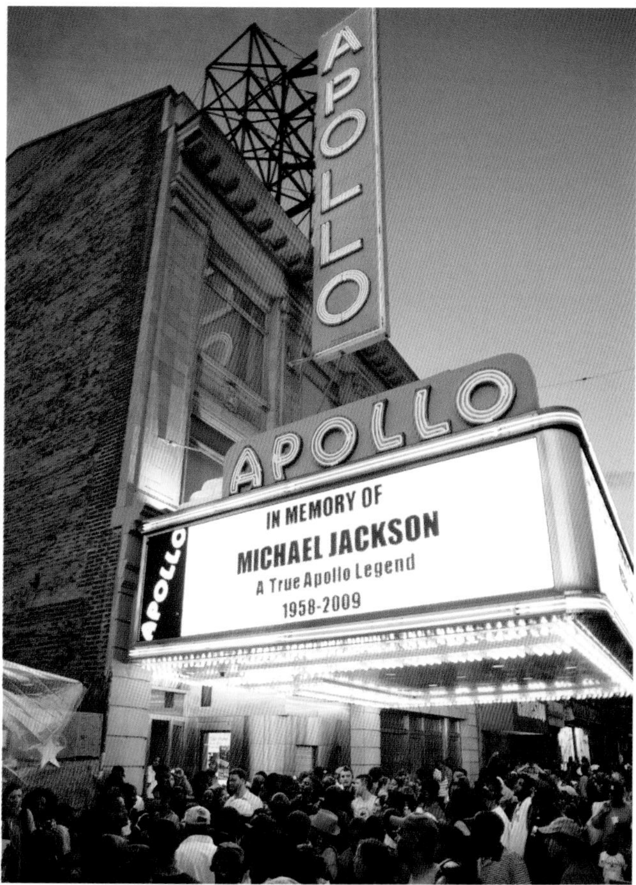

Hundreds of fans gather at the legendary Apollo Theater in Harlem upon hearing of Michael Jackson's death. Similar impromptu gatherings took place around the world.

he was "the most influential artist of the twentieth century."

In the wake of his death, this enormous international influence was on full display. Spontaneous gatherings from Los Angeles to London, Rio de Janeiro to Russia, Kenya to Korea, played his music and conducted vigils. Many people cried; others sang and danced. In the Philippines, hundreds of prisoners reunited for a routine of "Thriller" that had become a YouTube sensation. In Iran, protestors of a repressive regime blasted "Beat It." In Gary, Indiana, the industrial city of Jackson's birth, thousands converged to pay their respects at the humble home on 2300 Jackson Street. People brought flowers and pictures, letters and candles. In Harlem, outside the legendary Apollo Theater, grandparents, parents, and children came together to grieve and remember; each generation knew and sang the words to his songs. Michael Jackson's music, as it had for decades, crossed barriers, connected people. "It was a moment," writes Rob Sheffield, "that summed up everything we loved about Michael Jackson, as every car, every bar, every open window seemed to throb with the same beat, as if Jackson had successfully syncopated the whole world to his own breathy, intimate, insistent rhythmic tics."

Indeed, what was perhaps most surprising to many media commentators was the emotional outpouring Jackson's death inspired. His death didn't just take people by surprise; it reminded them of what he meant to them. The response was particularly deep in the African American community. "From Compton to Harlem," wrote Greg Tate, "we've witnessed grown men broke-down crying in the 'hood over Michael; some of my most hard-bitten, 24/7 militant Black friends, male and female alike, copped to bawling their eyes out for days after they got the news. It's not hard to understand why: For just about anybody born in Black America after

Jackson, on his *Dangerous* World Tour, in a moment of transcendence.

1958—and this includes kids I'm hearing about who are as young as nine years old right now—Michael came to own a good chunk of our best childhood and adolescent memories."

Over the subsequent weeks, in interviews and comments, person after person spoke of feeling connected to Michael Jackson, of "growing up" with him, of feeling his music was part of the "soundtrack" to their lives.

"Michael Jackson and the Jackson Five were a big part of my childhood," wrote one fan. "He was my first crush, my first lip sync, the first poster put on my wall, my first concert. I am 44, the Jacksons were the first time I as a child had my own music. I will always love him for his talent and also all of the special childhood memories that I hold dear. Rest in peace. Michael. I will always love you."

"As a single child," recalled another commenter, "I remember coming back home every summer from boarding school and blasting MJ's songs on my stereo as soon as my parents left for work and dancing silly around the house. I never felt alone. Thank you, Michael for unforgettable music and your amazing spirit."

"I remember when I would drive 200 miles every day in order to attend a university," shared another admirer, "I would always rely on his up-beat album *Thriller* to keep me awake on the long drive home over the Cajon pass. In many ways, he saved my life on those long late night drives. I must tell you, very little ever shakes me up.... But the death of Michael Jackson shook my world to the core even though it was expected.... When I think of Michael, I always think of the love he could never give to himself but brought to the world through his music."

Many spoke of Jackson's impact on race. "I was 11 years old and the daughter of a policeman when the Jackson 5 came on the TV," recalled one woman. "I watched for a minute, then I said, 'He's cute.' The rage in our house from that innocent comment will never be forgotten. I had never seen a black person; my dad's racism and anger was unstoppable. I defended Michael Jackson that night and [my dad] took me in my room and beat me till I promised never to talk about him again. Until today I really haven't been able to talk about what happened. I just saw for the first time the video 'Black or White' and I wished I had seen it years ago! I was right and Michael Jackson was right. Thank you Michael from a little white girl who didn't see black or white."

"I can still remember being 3 years old in the living room with my older brothers and they were watching the 'Rock With You' video," recalled one commenter. "All the green lasers and sequins, I thought MJ was [a] black super hero.... He gave me the inspiration to know that you can be born a poor little black boy in America, and become a King to the world, just by using the talents and gifts that God blesses you with."

Numerous comments, meanwhile, revealed Michael Jackson's international following. "We've been deprived of so many things for so many years that his music opened a whole new world for us," said Russian fan, Valentina Gromova. "There was so much energy in him."

"When I was a kid," wrote another commenter, "he was very popular in our remote village in India. At that time, we didn't even know who the American president was but we knew Michael Jackson. We enjoyed his music so much even without understanding the meaning of a single word. That was the power of his music."

"Michael Jackson was very much loved in Africa," recalls Nana Koram. "I grew up in Ghana adoring this King of Pop. He was one of the most gifted and iconic figures of the music industry, who transgressed all cultural barriers, despite the fact that he only sang in English."

In the weeks following Jackson's death, comments and memories like these came pouring in from every corner of the world. Besides the millions of comments on news, music, and fan sites, Jackson's official website received more than five hundred thousand entries from people wanting to pay their respects. Statements of condolence and respect also came pouring in from world leaders.

"He will go down in history as one of our greatest entertainers," said U.S. president Barack Obama (though his failure to more forthrightly recognize Jackson's artistry justifiably irked some fans). Former South Korean president and Nobel Peace Prize winner Kim Dae-jung called Jackson "a hero of the world." In Rio de Janeiro (where Jackson once shot a music video with Spike Lee for "They Don't Care About Us"), Mayor Eduardo Paes announced that the city would erect a statue in Jackson's honor. Former South African president and civil-rights icon Nelson Mandela, who collaborated with Jackson on several human-rights projects and charities, called his friend "a close member of our family.... We had great admiration for his talent and that he was able to triumph over tragedy on so many occasions in his life."

The admiration extended to Jackson's peers. "It's so sad and shocking," said Paul McCartney. "I feel privileged to have hung out and worked with Michael. He was a massively talented boy-man with a gentle soul. His music will be remembered forever and my memories of our time together will be happy ones." Fellow pop icon Madonna likewise spoke of her deep admiration for Jackson as both an artist and a person. "In a desperate attempt to hold onto his memory, I went on the Internet to watch old clips of him dancing and singing on TV and onstage and I thought, 'My God, he was so unique, so original, so rare. And there will never be anyone like him again.' He was a king. But he was also a human being and alas, we are all human beings and sometimes we have to lose things before we can truly appreciate them."

In Barcelona, U2 paid tribute while on tour, dedicating "Angel of Harlem" to the singer, before segueing into "Man in the Mirror" and "Don't Stop 'Til You Get Enough" as ninety thousand fans sang along. In Glastonbury, Lady Gaga, also on tour, sobbed over the news, later praising Jackson as revolutionary and one of her biggest influences. In the subsequent weeks, recognition came from nearly every individual in the music and entertainment industry, from rock artists such as Slash and Eddie Van Halen to rappers such as Kanye West and Jay-Z to filmmakers such as Steven Spielberg and Martin Scorsese.

MAN IN THE MUSIC

Yet of all the heartfelt statements and tributes, one of the most intimate and powerful eulogies came from Jackson's longtime friend and peer from Motown, Stevie Wonder. Wonder, of course, never saw Jackson perform; he never witnessed the changes in his appearance; he never saw the music videos or costumes or masks. However, he knew Jackson on a much deeper level than most. And he heard his music. Michael, he often said, was a gift.

In the midst of the media frenzy following Jackson's death, Stevie Wonder made no public statement or appearance. "He is emotionally distraught and chooses to be quiet right now," said a representative. Weeks later, when he took the stage at Michael's memorial, it was clear he was still devastated. "This is a moment that I *wished* I didn't live to see come," he says. As he begins playing the opening chords to "I Can't Help It," however—a song he had written for Michael's *Off the Wall* album in 1979—he seems to be channeling Jackson's energy: that familiar, but strange mixture of yearning tinged with sadness.

In the medley that followed—an impassioned combination of "Never Dreamed You'd Leave in Summer" and "They Won't Go When I Go"—Wonder allows the music to simultaneously recover, lament, and testify. "No more lying friends/Wanting tragic ends," he sang in the latter

Stevie Wonder performs a moving medley of songs at Jackson's 2009 memorial in Los Angeles.

song, as a hushed audience listened. It was a deep, gospel soul that conjured a very heavy, personal, visceral pain. It was a song about losing a friend, not an icon.

Yet it wasn't just loss Wonder conveyed; it was righteous indignation. "Unclean minds mislead the pure," he exclaimed, "The innocent will leave for sure/For them there is a resting place." As the song built to its emotional climax, an anguished Wonder poured every last ounce of his soul into it, as if singing its words would finally push through the surrounding circus, the trivial noise, and reveal the essence, the humanity, and the tragedy of Michael Jackson.

"Michael, they won't go," he cried, "they won't go, where you go."As Wonder finished, the crowd applauded, but, like Michael, he seemed to be in another place.

For Wonder (and many others), Jackson's death at least meant his prolonged suffering was over, and he could finally escape completely into the vibrant creative world he "conceived." For those left behind, however—including his children, his friends, and his fans—there remains a profound sense of loss. As Jackson ironically wrote in his 1988 autobiography: "Often in the past, performers have been tragic figures. A lot of the truly great have suffered or died because of pressure and drugs.... It's so sad. You feel cheated as a fan that you didn't get to watch them evolve as they grew older."

In the mid-nineties, Jackson's former wife, Lisa Marie Presley, remembered him, in the midst of a conversation about her father, staring at her very intensely and saying with "an almost calm certainty, 'I am afraid I am going to end up like him, the way he did.'" It was not something he wanted; in fact, he often expressed fears about dying. Yet he had read and seen enough to know it wasn't easy to survive a lifetime of fame. For more than forty years he wrestled with it, played with it, exploited it, ran from it, hid from it, denounced it, and described its effects in his work. In the end, the world lost him, but gained "Billie Jean" and "Stranger in Moscow" and "Man in the Mirror."

"Whatever his life felt like from inside," writes journalist David Gates, "from outside it was manifestly a work of genius, whether you want to call it a triumph or a freak show—those are just words. We'd never seen anyone like this before, either in his artistic inventiveness or his equally artistic self-invention, and we won't forget him—until the big Neverland swallows us all."

Michael Jackson continued to create and perform until his final night. He told his fellow collaborators he couldn't sleep because he "couldn't turn it off"; the ideas kept coming; his imagination was restless. He had big plans for the future. "It's an adventure," he told his final creative team, "a great adventure."

I'm interested in making a path instead of following a trail and that's what I want to do in life—in everything I do."

MICHAEL JACKSON, *EBONY*, 1979

inclined psychedelia of the late-seventies, and the clubs were the new hippy communes: the space in which music, drugs, and sex converged. Jackson, who celebrated his twenty-first birthday at Studio 54, in many ways "seemed entirely in tune with the times, coming of age at the epicenter of the urban nightlife scene sweeping the culture, and creating a smart, sexy sound for it." Yet he was also somehow detached from it all, "a strangely innocent boy-child in the era of *Boogie Nights'* fleshpots, untouched by sex or drugs despite the manic indulgence all around him, a Jehovah's Witness lost in the pleasure dome."

"People came to [Studio 54] like characters," he observed, "and it's like going to a play."

Indeed, while Jackson refrained from the hedonistic pleasures of the club life, he was also fascinated by its theatricality. "People came to [Studio 54] like characters," he observed, "and it's like going to a play. I think that's the psychological reason for the disco craze: you get to be that dream you want to be. You just go crazy with the lights and the music and you're in another world."

This "escapism," as Jackson often referred to it, became a lifelong fascination, as did the idea of transformation, of becoming something different and new. Not everyone, however, was as intrigued by disco's transformative effect. The year 1979 saw a serious backlash against the dance-driven aesthetic, as demonstrated in the "Disco Sucks" movement and the infamous "Disco Demolition Night" at Comiskey Park in Chicago, where a huge pile of disco records were burned at centerfield, causing a near riot from a raucous crowd of ninety thousand. *Off the Wall*, interestingly, was released less than a month after this event.

In addition to public demonstrations, music critics at the time were almost universally skeptical of disco, favoring instead the "authenticity" and "seriousness" of rock. While rock pushed boundaries and opposed mainstream culture, critics argued, disco was a slick, shallow product aimed at a mass consumer audience. While this assessment contained some truth—disco, like all genres of popular music, could be, and was sometimes vapid and commercially calculated—it also disclosed some obvious biases. By 1979, after all, formulaic, commercial rock was just as prevalent as disco. At least part of the distaste seemed to stem from a long-held, sometimes subconscious stigmatization of "black" music that had previously manifested itself in the segregation of R&B, soul, and funk from rock.

Disco evolved out of predominantly black musical styles, transforming funk with a more lavish accompaniment of strings, horns, keyboards, electric guitars, and synthesized, four-on-the-floor beats. Inclusive in its sound, message, and audience, disco, at its best, encouraged diversity, acceptance, and experimentation, making it the musical aesthetic of choice for many minorities, including not only blacks, but also gays, Hispanics, and women in the mid- to late-seventies. "Disco was diametrically opposite to the macho posturing of white rock," observes cultural critic Daryl Easlea, "and since there were no bands in disco, no tours,

An eighteen-year-old Jackson looks out at New York City in wonder.

or souvenir T-shirts, it was difficult to quantify. A few journalists wrote passionately about it, but in the main it was ignored or treated with disdain." Indeed, derisive descriptions of its effeminacy, its theatricality, its emotional extravagance, and even its ability to make people want to dance were not merely neutral observations. As Craig Werner writes, "The attacks on disco gave respectable voice to the ugliest kinds of unacknowledged racism, sexism and homophobia." (Interestingly, from early in Jackson's adult career, these same attacks—particularly of perceived effeminacy, androgyny, and homosexuality—were consistently hurled at him as well.)

Disco, of course, wasn't the only presence in music. The late seventies also gave birth to Stevie Wonder's *Songs in the Key of Life*, Pink Floyd's *The Wall*, The Eagles' *Hotel California*, Fleetwood Mac's *Rumours*, and Queen's *News of the World*. Disco, prog rock, glam rock, soft rock, punk, and pop all competed in an evolving, eclectic music scene. The world was still feeling the reverberations of 1977's blockbuster album, *Saturday Night Fever*, and artists such as the Bee Gees, Donna Summer, Chic, and the Sledgehammer Sisters dominated the charts.

In this context, *Off the Wall*'s visceral disco-pop sound seems very much a reflection of the tastes of the time. Yet part of what sets the album apart, then and now, stems from its dynamism, the sustained tension it strikes between opposites. Unlike much late-seventies disco, *Off the Wall* is not merely a celebration of excess. It is an album of innocence as much as experience, of timidity and wonder as much as indulgence. It is highly sensual, but subtly, often euphemistically. It never speaks of politics, yet it is implicitly political. It never speaks of race, yet it broke numerous racial barriers. It references nothing specific about its historical context, yet it clearly signifies for many listeners a specific moment in time. It is disco, but it is also jazz, pop, funk, soul, R&B, and Broadway. *Off the Wall*, then, is a difficult album to pin down. This elusiveness, however, is part of what makes it so compelling.

Work on *Off the Wall* officially began in December 1978 at Allen Zentz recording studios in Hollywood. The past year had been a time of dramatic change and evolution for Michael Jackson. After years of feeling beholden to family expectations, he finally began to cut ties with his domineering father. *Off the Wall* would also be his first album without the involvement of his brothers, Motown, or the Philly duo of Kenny Gamble and Leon Huff. In addition, he had also just landed the role of the Scarecrow in *The Wiz*, an urban adaptation of the Broadway hit, alongside his idol, Diana Ross. Other than touring, it was his first time living away from home. In this new setting, producer Rob Cohen observed, he was "like a little kid in the Manhattan playground." While *The Wiz* ultimately disappointed at the box office, Jackson was generally seen as one of the few bright spots, garnering praise for his "genuine acting talent" and professionalism.

More importantly, *The Wiz* connected Jackson and legendary producer Quincy Jones, who was writing the score for the film. Jones carried with him a wealth of experience, knowledge, and skills. Born on the south side of Chicago, he was a talented and ambitious child, already arranging and writing songs in his teens. By the time he met Jackson in 1977, his résumé included traveling the world many times over with fellow

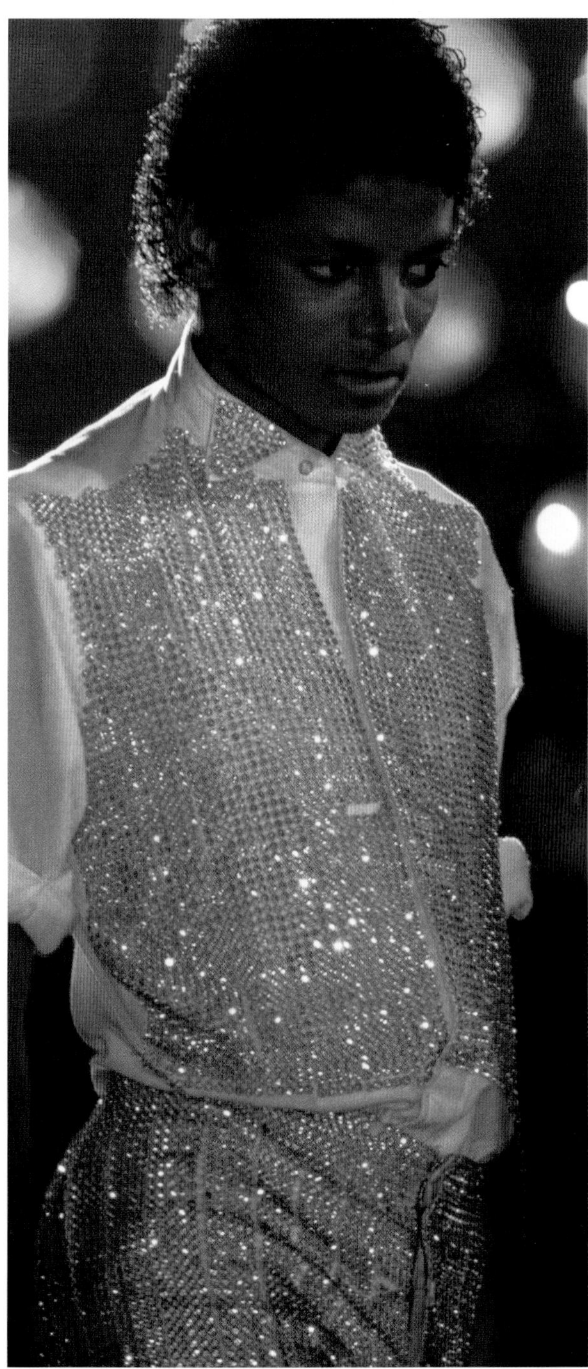

jazz musicians, receiving a classical education in Paris, composing award-winning film scores, and working with legends such as Frank Sinatra, Sammy Davis Jr., Dinah Washington, Nat King Cole, Ray Charles, and Count Basie. Like Berry Gordy, Jones was a pioneer for African Americans in the music industry, and like Jackson, he was also a compulsive perfectionist.

Given this pedigree, it is remarkable how quickly Quincy Jones was sold on the then eighteen-year-old Michael Jackson. Jackson's role in *The Wiz* was his first as an actor. When filming began, he didn't even have a feature song. "Most of the people involved with the film had no idea what Michael Jackson was about," Jones recalls. However, as Jones watched Jackson in action—his preparation, his instincts, his ambition—he became convinced that the young performer was a once-in-a-generation talent, comparing him to Sammy Davis Jr. and Frank Sinatra. "Michael was the best thing that came out of *The Wiz* for me," he later wrote. "As we rehearsed the musical scenes . . . I became more and more impressed. He was always super-prepared. He showed up at 5 a.m. for his scarecrow makeup call and had every detail of what he needed to do memorized for every shooting. He also knew every dance step, every word of dialogue, and all the lyrics to every song by everyone in the entire production." Beyond preparation, Jones saw in Jackson that rare "it" factor. "[Michael Jackson] had the wisdom of a sixty-year-old and the enthusiasm of a child," Jones observed. "He was a genuinely shy, handsome kid who hid his amazing intelligence with small smiles and giggles. But beneath that

Jackson's music and personality paradoxically embodied and defied the qualities of disco.

Jackson at the 1978 premiere of *The Wiz*, where he first met Quincy Jones. They would begin work on his first solo album, *Off the Wall*, that same year.

shy exterior was an artist with a burning desire for perfection and an unlimited ambition to be the biggest entertainer in the world."

While filming *The Wiz*, Michael Jackson likewise developed an admiration for Jones and became convinced he would be the perfect producer for his first solo album. "Quincy does jazz, he does movie scores, rock 'n' roll, funk, pop—he's all colors, and that's the kind of people I like to work with," Jackson explained in a 1980 interview. "[*Off the Wall*] was the first time that I fully wrote and produced my songs, and I was looking for someone who would give me that freedom, plus someone who's unlimited musically."

That Jones could not only see Jackson's enormous potential but also encouraged him to reach it sealed the deal for the singer. When Epic Records balked at the idea of a Jackson–Jones collaboration because Jones was "too jazzy" and couldn't produce solid dance hits, Jackson didn't back down. "He marched back into Epic with [his managers]," Quincy recalled, "and said, 'I don't care what you think, Quincy is doing my record.'" Jackson won—and eventually so did Epic Records.

Beyond acting as producer, Quincy Jones helped Jackson assemble an all-star supporting cast, including highly regarded recording engineer, Bruce Swedien, who Jones had been close friends with since the fifties. Swedien would remain with Michael Jackson for his entire solo career, providing both friendship and "one of the best pairs of ears" in the business. Completing what was often referred to as the "Big Three" was British songwriter Rod Temperton, a member of the international funk-disco band, Heatwave. Temperton was a talented musician who Jones described as "one of the best songwriters who ever lived, with the melodic and contrapuntal gifts and instincts of a classical composer." Given his reputation as a hip, funky member of the disco group Heatwave, many of the musicians working on *Off the Wall* were surprised to learn he was a "little white guy" from North Lincolnshire, England. Yet musically, Temperton was a natural fit with Jones, Swedien, Jackson, and the rest of the team. "Rod was a kindred spirit in many ways," said Jackson. "Like me, he felt more at home singing and writing about the nightlife than actually going out and living it."

In addition to the Big Three, Jones and Jackson tapped the songwriting talent of some of the biggest names in the music industry, including Paul McCartney, Stevie Wonder, Carole Bayer Sager, Tom Bahler, and David Foster. They also brought in some exceptional musicians: "virtuoso keyboardist," Greg Phillinganes, a friend of the Jacksons who worked closely with Michael on the rhythm tracks; "monster trumpeter and arranger" Jerry Hey and the talented Seawind Horns; Grammy-Award-winning composer/arranger Johnny Mandel on strings; Louis Johnson (of the Brothers Johnson) on fender bass; David Jones and Melvin "Wah Wah Watson" Ragin on guitar; John Robinson and Jeff Porcaro (of Toto) on drums; and Brazilian Paulinho Da Costa on percussion. Quincy Jones affectionately referred to this remarkable collection of talent as the "A-Team."

In retrospect, coordinating this diverse group in such a seamless way was an extraordinary act of artistic collaboration. "It was the smoothest album I have ever been involved in," Jackson said in a 1979 interview. "There was so much love, it was incredible. Everybody worked together so easily." It was an atmosphere of openness and trust Quincy Jones helped to foster and that Jackson would learn from and implement as executive producer on later projects. "We were just taking a lot of chances," recalls Jones. "We felt free."

This freedom, spontaneity, and collaborative spirit translated onto the tracks. "On a couple of tunes

After returning from *The Wiz*, Jackson was eager for independence—especially from his father.

the band was there while I sang and we were able to feel each other," Jackson said in a 1979 interview. "And it comes across on the record. I had never done that before—ever! It gives such a spontaneous feeling and reminds me of when R&B first started in the South and all the blacks would just get together in a shack and jam. That's what's missing today. Everything is so commercial and mechanical. Too many musicians today are into what they're doing for themselves and not with each other." As an artist, Jackson always believed in this communal energy as integral to creativity.

Quincy Jones's primary focus, meanwhile, was on Michael Jackson. "We tried all kinds of things I'd learned over the years to help him with his artistic growth," Jones recalled. "Dropping keys just a minor third to give him flexibility and a more mature range in the upper and lower registers, and more than a few tempo changes. I also tried to steer him to songs with more depth, some of them about relationships. Seth Riggs, a leading vocal coach, gave him vigorous warm-up exercises to expand his top and bottom range by at least a fourth, which I desperately needed to get the vocal drama going."

Michael Jackson and Quincy Jones, captured here in 1983, would form one of the most successful creative partnerships in popular music history.

A brooding Jackson on the set of his 1980 music video, *Can You Feel It*.

Jackson responded to the challenges, impressing his more experienced colleagues not only with his talent, but also with his preparation. Jones remembers him coming into studio sessions with all his parts completely memorized—lyrics, harmonies, timing. "He can come to a session and put down two lead vocals and three background parts in one day," Jones said in a 1982 interview. "Studio time is enormously expensive, and that's why someone like Michael Jackson is a producer's dream artist. He walks in prepared. We accomplish so much in a single session, it stuns me."

Quincy and Michael scoured through dozens of potential songs for *Off the Wall*, some of them written by Jackson and some brought in by Jones, Temperton, and others. They wanted just the right mix of sounds and styles and attempted to bring in tracks that would highlight Jackson's diverse skills. In the midst of making the record, Jackson also developed a healthy competition with fellow songwriter Rod Temperton. "[One day]," Jackson recalls, "he comes in the studio with this killer [groove], 'doop, dakka dakka doop, dakka dakka dakka doop,' this whole melody and chorus, 'Rock With You.' I go, 'Wow!' So when I heard that I said, 'Okay, I really have to work now.' So every time Rod would present something, I would present something, and we'd form a little friendly competition." Jackson compared it to the way Walt Disney brought in different artists to compete for animating a film. "Whoever had the most stylized effect that Walt liked, he would pick that.... It was like a friendly thing, but it was competition.... So whenever Rod would bring something, I would bring something.... We created this wonderful thing." Temperton and Jackson would not only end up composing the majority of the songs on *Off the Wall*, but on *Thriller* as well.

Eventually, Jackson and Jones whittled the long list of potential tracks down to ten songs: Three ("Don't Stop 'Til You Get Enough," "Workin' Day and Night," and "Get on the Floor") were Jackson compositions. Three others ("Rock With You," "Off the Wall," and "Burn This Disco Out") were contributed by Rod Temperton. Finally, "Girlfriend" came from Paul McCartney, "She's Out of My Life" came from Tom Bahler (who worked with Jackson on *The Wiz*), Carol Bayer Sager brought in "It's the Falling In Love," and Stevie Wonder contributed "I Can't Help It."

While the finishing touches were being made on the songs at Westlake and Cherokee studios, attention was also paid to the album cover and the artist's new image. For many people, in spite of the recent success of *Destiny*, Michael Jackson remained stigmatized as the cherubic child star of the Jackson 5. "Until now," wrote Stephen

Jackson, pictured here in tuxedo, wanted to present a new, more mature image to the public.

Holden for *Rolling Stone* in 1979, "[Jackson has] understandably clung to the remnants of his original Peter Pan of Motown image while cautiously considering the role of the young prince." One of the primary goals of *Off the Wall* from a marketing perspective, then, was to take this symbolic step forward and introduce the adult Michael Jackson as mature, polished, sophisticated, and sexual. Before one even played the record, this new image was conveyed on the album cover with Jackson presented as the "black Frank Sinatra," wearing a stylish (for the time) tuxedo and flashing his megawatt smile. It looked like "a photo taken at a graduation or a wedding, or any other rite of passage," observes *Rolling Stone*'s Anthony DeCurtis. Jackson's manager at the time, Ron Weisner, claimed credit for this imaging game plan—with the exception of the white socks, not surprisingly, Jackson's idea. (As a performer, Jackson had a keen eye for iconic imagery; he also loved the sharp color contrast that heightened the perception of movement in dance. Later covers for *Off the Wall* would show only Jackson's bottom half, highlighting the glowing socks and loafers.) In both its packaging and content, then, the album served as Jackson's metamorphosis into a new, young, hip, adult persona.

Off the Wall was completed in just six months. "Michael's approach is very dramatic," recalls Quincy Jones. "Very concise. When he commits to an idea he goes all the way with it. He has the presence of mind to feel something, conceive it and then bring it to life. It's a long way from idea to execution. Everybody wants to go to heaven and nobody wants to die. It's ass power, man. You have to be emotionally ready to put as much energy into it as it takes to make it right." After all the work and energy invested in the album, both Jones and Jackson were justifiably proud of the final product. *Off the Wall* was a tight, rich, multifaceted album in which every track counted. "[Quincy and I] share the same philosophy about making albums," Jackson later wrote. "We don't believe in B-sides or album songs. Every song should be able to stand on its own as a single, and we always push for this." The Jackson–Jones approach also meant a diverse but balanced lineup of songs. They wanted it to contain something for everyone but still feel like it all belonged together.

The album was released on August 10, 1979, to a curious public. The lead single, "Don't Stop 'Til You Get Enough," had already shot to #1 on the *Billboard* charts in July and was being played in dance clubs throughout the country. However, it wasn't until the album was heard in its entirety that people began to realize something special had been formed in the partnership of Michael Jackson and Quincy Jones. "Fans and industry peers alike were left with their mouths agape when [it] was issued to the public," wrote biographer J. Randy Taraborreli. Indeed, it is difficult now to fully imagine people's experience playing the record or cassette tape for the first time and hearing its cascading rhythms, its colorful textures, and unbridled ecstasy.

In addition to its two #1 hits ("Don't Stop 'Til You Get Enough" and "Rock With You"), two others ("Off the Wall" and "She's Out of My Life") reached the Top Ten in 1980. Meanwhile, the album stayed in the Top 20 for an incredible forty-eight weeks. By 1982, it had already sold close to seven million copies in the United States alone, making it the best-selling album ever by a black artist.

It signaled an important cultural milestone, to be sure. For many listeners and critics, however, the music itself was just as revolutionary. *Off the Wall* was a new breed of album, a unique synthesis of genres and sounds. In its 1979 review, *Rolling Stone* called it "a slick, sophisticated R&B-pop showcase"; *All Music* described it as "an intoxicating blend of strong melodies, rhythmic hooks, and indelible construction ... that is utterly thrilling in its utter joy"; *Blender* claimed "[it] looked beyond funk to the future of dance music, and beyond soul ballads to the future of heart-tuggers—in fact, beyond R&B to color-blind pop."

While not overtly message-driven, its implicit themes were important as well. *Off the Wall* was ultimately a celebration of difference and excitement, of emotion and immediacy, of liberation and transformation. It was a temporary escape from the "real world" of soul-deadening monotony and conformity, an invitation to feel alive, young, unique, and free. If Pink Floyd's famous "wall" was a symbol of its narrator's isolation, Michael Jackson's was a barrier that must be leapt from, even if the exhilarating freedom was transient. As Jackson sings in the title track, "Let the madness in the music get to you.... Life ain't so bad at all/If you live it off the wall." Lyrics like these not only resonated with Jackson on a personal level, but also they spoke to millions of others in the late seventies who flocked

With *Off the Wall*, Jackson not only reinvented himself, but revolutionized the genre of R&B.

to dance floors and disco clubs, experimenting openly with identity and sexuality.

Perhaps *Off the Wall*'s greatest achievement, however, is in its sonic adventurousness. "[It] is a dance album released at the height of disco fever, but it indulges none of the genre's clichés," observes music critic Anthony DeCurtis. "Its rhythms are smooth but propulsive, charged but gracefully syncopated; the melodies are light as air but immediate and unforgettable." *NME*'s Barney Hoskyns describes it as the "most intricately timed, fully textured, glossily sensual dance music ever made."

The layers of instruments complement but never overwhelm Jackson's alternately playful, sensual, and sublime vocals. "Jackson brought to *Off the Wall* vocal tricks that no pop singer, before or after, could have imagined," writes music critic Jimmy Gutterman. "His tenor flies all over the place (even semi-rapping a bit on 'Get on the Floor'), but the most expressive vocal moments here are wordless—cries, shouts, exultations, sighs that speak volumes."

Considering its enormous commercial success and critical acclaim upon release, it is no wonder Jackson felt so devastated when the album was snubbed at the Grammy Awards in 1980 (receiving only one nomination for Best Male R&B Vocal Performance). "I remember where I was when I got the news," Jackson recalled. "I felt ignored by my peers and it hurt." Family members remember him sobbing inconsolably. "Jackson felt that the music industry was trying to keep him in his place as a niche artist," observed *Rolling Stone*, "a black singer making dance music." Jackson, however, refused to accept this fate. "That experience lit a fire in my soul," he later wrote. "All I could think about was the next album and what I would do with it. I wanted it to be truly great."

Regardless of being snubbed for Grammys, *Off the Wall* has stood the test of time. For many who came of age in the seventies it is the defining album of their young lives. "If you asked me to choose between *Off the Wall* and the entire back catalog of The Sex Pistols and The Beatles," writes music critic Mark Fisher, "there would be no contest. I respect The Beatles and the Pistols, but they had already calcified into newsreel heritage before I even took heed of them; whereas *Off the Wall* is still vivid, irresistible, sumptuous, teeming with Technicolor detail."

Indeed, more than thirty years since its release, listeners and critics alike are nearly unanimous in its praise. In a VH1 poll of more than seven hundred musicians, songwriters, disc jockeys, radio programmers, and critics in 2003, *Off the Wall* was ranked the thirty-sixth greatest album of all time. *Rolling Stone* rated it number 68 on its list of the 500 Greatest Albums of All Time. In 1999, the United Kingdom's *Q Magazine* called it "one of the greatest albums ever made ... [with] some of the best melodies in the history of pop."

Off the Wall would also inspire several generations of artists to come—including Prince, Janet Jackson, Usher, Justin Timberlake, Alicia Keys, Jay-Z, Kanye West, Ne-Yo, and Beyoncé, among hundreds of others—serving as what music critic John Lewis has called the "Rosetta Stone for all subsequent R&B."

Jackson, glittering with sequins on the set of his music video for the #1 hit, *Rock With You*.

mystery to most. When he wasn't working, he was usually alone or with his family. In other ways, however, he had experienced far more than most young men his age. Before he had even reached puberty, he was performing with his brothers in nightclubs featuring strippers and cross-dressers and dealing with the constant presence of groupies. In addition, he had recently returned from New York (where he was working on the musical film, *The Wiz*) and witnessed the city's decadent night scene, including the infamous Studio 54. The display of sex, drugs, and theatrics fell in sharp contrast to the lessons of morality and purity he was taught by his mother and his religion (Jehovah's Witness), yet Jackson observed it with a keen if detached curiosity. Jackson constantly struggled to reconcile these disparate worlds, frequently feeling isolated and confused about who or what he should be.

From a young age, therefore, music became his escape and catharsis. It allowed him to temporarily drop his inhibitions, confusions, fear, and guilt and find the confidence, intimacy, expression, and connection he lacked in real life. It was his drug, lover, and religion all wrapped into one. With this context in mind, "Don't Stop" is more than just a catchy dance song. It is a sonic marvel that is also one of the earliest intimations of Jackson's complex and evolving identity. With that now-signature "Oooooh!" he breaks through numerous barriers—personal, cultural, artistic—and becomes fully possessed with the "force" of his music.

The song's music video—Jackson's first as a solo artist—showcased the "new" Michael Jackson in all his radiance and vitality. "[It] captures [him] the way the world fell in love with him," wrote *Rolling Stone*. "The boy next door living out his glammiest disco dreams, putting on a tux and strutting his stuff. You can't help getting swept away by his joy and exuberance."

A #1 hit in 1979, "Don't Stop" remains one of Jackson's most enduring dance songs today.

2. ROCK WITH YOU

(Written and composed by Rod Temperton; produced by Quincy Jones. Lead and background vocals: Michael Jackson. Horns arranged by Jerry Hey. Rhythm and vocal arrangements by Rod Temperton. String arrangement by Ben Wright. Bass: Bobby Watson. Drums: John Robinson. Guitar: David Williams and Marlo Henderson. Synthesizer: Greg Phillinganes and Michael Boddicker. Electric piano: David "Hawk" Wolinski. Horns: The Seawind Horns. Concert master: Gerald Vinci)

"Rock With You" is smooth disco-pop-soul perfection. From the opening drum roll, Jackson locks into its vintage groove, singing effortlessly over a subtle background of percussion (including hand-claps and finger-snaps). "What's remarkable about 'Rock With You' is how unobtrusive it is," writes *Rolling Stone*'s J. Edward Keyes, "a silky string section and barely-there twitch of guitar—Michael doesn't even hit the word 'rock' all that hard—he just glides over it, preferring to charm with a wink and a smile rather than with aggression or ferocity."

Composed by Rod Temperton, the song was different than anything Jackson had sung with his brothers, which pleased him. "It was perfect for me to sing, and move to," he recalled. The alluring track had an intoxicating effect on many listeners. "[It] manages the amazing feat of simultaneously bringing a tear to the eye and a shuffle to your feet," writes music critic Mark Fisher. "Jackson comes on as disco-Svengali, so he can seduce the listener-girl that the song turns us all into: 'Girl, close your eyes/Let that rhythm get into you/Don't try to fight it'—and who would want to fight it? Listen to the way the synths and strings suggest starlight seen by starstruck lovers' eyes."

Indeed, the mood it conjures with its tempo, melody, and texture became the blueprint for thousands of subsequent R&B singers, from R. Kelly to Ne-Yo. However, it is Jackson's utterly unique voice that carries the song. "The part where Michael sings, '*Girrrrrrl*, when you dance, there's a magic that *must* be love,' is the most purely joyful moment I've ever heard in a pop song," writes music critic Steven Hyden.

As with "Don't Stop," the lyrics to "Rock With You" are sensual and suggestive. "Relax your mind," Jackson sings. "Lay back and groove with mine." If "Don't Stop" hadn't driven home the impression, "Rock With You" confirmed it: Michael Jackson had moved beyond the bubblegum material of "ABC" and "Rockin' Robin." Yet, unlike much disco material, Jackson's work had a subtlety to it that captured not only the passion, but also the innocence and magic of being in love. "Is there any record," writes Mark Fisher, "which better captures the cosmic vertigo of falling in love than 'Rock With You'? That headlong synesthetic rush in which music, dancing and love feed each other in a reflexive virtuous circle which, even though it seems miraculous, unbelievable ('Girl, when you dance/ there's a magic that must be love'), at the same time seems like it couldn't possibly end ('And when the groove is dead and gone/you know that love survives/and we can rock forever'). This was soul to sell your soul for."

The song's music video, directed by Bruce Gowers, featured twenty-one-year-old Jackson in a vintage, sparkling sequin suit, dancing amid smoke, lights, and lasers. It was a far cry from the big-budget short films to come, but Jackson's youthful charm and energy still shine forth from the screen.

Like "Don't Stop," "Rock With You" shot to #1 on the *Billboard* Hot 100 in early 1980, making it the first time Jackson had sung back-to-back chart-toppers since his early days with the Jackson 5.

3. WORKIN' DAY AND NIGHT

(Written and composed by Michael Jackson; produced by Quincy Jones, coproduced by Michael Jackson. Rhythm arrangement by Greg Phillinganes and Michael Jackson. Vocal and percussion arrangements by Michael Jackson. Horns arranged by Jerry Hey. Lead and background vocals: Michael Jackson. Bass: Louis Johnson. Drums: John Robinson. Guitar: David Williams and Phil Upchurch. Electric piano: Greg Phillinganes. Percussion: Paulinho Da Costa, Michael Jackson, and John Robinson. Horns: The Seawind Horns)

The second of three Jackson compositions on *Off the Wall*, "Workin' Day and Night" continues the frenetic pace established in "Don't Stop 'Til You Get Enough," while once again showcasing his rhythmic genius. He begins the song with his own voice as percussion (Jackson possessed an uncanny ability to mimic instruments and often put it to work in demos as well as the final recordings). From the near-tribal beatboxing, the song gradually builds up the layers of sound: Greg Phillinganes' keyboard-driven bass, David Williams's funky guitar licks, and Jerry Hey's blazing array of horns. However, the song is driven by the propulsive rhythm of the percussion, arranged by Jackson and Paulinho Da Costa. Along with "Don't Stop," the song demonstrates Jackson's early instinctual talent for composing music, particularly rhythmically driven tracks. The funk is undeniable, combining James Brown-esque grunts, gasps, and exclamations with Ghana-style rhythmic drumming. "He has never, ever been funkier," writes music critic Ben Werner. "Dig it out, put it on. Speaks for itself. On fire. You can keep the rest. I have to have this one."

The song's subject matter is also illuminating. No doubt inspired by his own life of working incessantly since childhood, Jackson sings of simply being worn out and wanting a release. It is his version of the Beatles' "A Hard Day's Night," a playful plea that becomes its own catharsis. "Scratch my shoulder," he sings. "It's aching, make it feel alright/When this is over, lovin' you will be so right." As with most Jackson-penned tracks about relationships, however, the song is not as straightforward as one might initially assume. The final few stanzas introduce the singer's anxiety about infidelity ("You must be seein' some other guy instead of me"). Speaking from the perspective of a husband, he worries that a life of constant work is not only unfulfilling (in one verse he sings of being tired "of thinkin' of what my life's supposed to be"), but damaging to his marriage (something Jackson hadn't experienced personally but was certainly familiar observing in the fraught marriages of his parents and brothers). "You say that workin' is what a man's supposed to do," Jackson sings, "But I say it ain't right if I can't give sweet love to you." Work may be what "a man's supposed to do," yet the song playfully suggests a desire for freedom and real human connection instead.

4. GET ON THE FLOOR

(Written and composed by Michael Jackson and Louis Johnson; produced by Quincy Jones. Horns arranged by Jerry Hey. Rhythm arrangement by Louis Johnson and Quincy Jones. String arrangement by Ben Wright. Vocal arrangement by Michael Jackson. Lead and background vocals: Michael Jackson. Bass: Louis Johnson. Drums: John Robinson. Clavinet: Greg Phillinganes. Percussion: Paulinho Da Costa. Guitar: Melvin "Wah Wah Watson" Ragin. Horns: The Seawind Horns. Concert master: Gerald Vinci)

Perhaps as partial response to "Workin' Day and Night," Jackson offers "Get On The Floor," a song that celebrates the joyful release of music and dance. An early version of the song was originally penned by Louis Johnson of the Brothers Johnson for their disco album, *Light Up the Night*. Johnson, however, ultimately decided to rework the song with Michael Jackson. The result was a dance-inciting extravaganza. "Jackson lets loose over a slap-bass disco riff," writes music critic David Abravanel, "making an infectiously energetic dance track that nevertheless pulsates with . . . tension."

Jackson enjoyed recording the song. "It was particularly satisfying," he later wrote, "because [bassist] Louis Johnson gave me a smooth enough bottom to ride in the verses and let me come back stronger and stronger with each chorus." Indeed, it is possible that Jackson has never sounded more blissfully joyful and uninhibited than on this disco-funk gem. Surrounded by effervescent strings, big brass, and a relentless beat, Jackson's voice soars with infectious energy. "Not a lot of people give 'Get On The Floor' any credit," writes music critic Andre Grindle. "But the fact is it's one of *the toughest* slices of hard disco-funk of 1979: the rhythms, the bass, and of course [Jackson's] hot n' heavy breathing at the song's breakdown is just raw sweat, energy and drive."

Indeed, after building to the climax with the "Get up, won't you g'on down" chant (a sort of primal buildup Jackson would similarly use in the video to "Smooth Criminal"), Jackson begins to ad-lib as if reveling in his newfound freedom, playfully changing voices, experimenting with inflections, laughing, and letting out his now-signature "oooooh"s and "heeee"s. The song is, quite simply, a celebration of life, music, and dance.

5. OFF THE WALL

(Written and composed by Rod Temperton; produced by Quincy Jones. Horns arranged by Jerry Hey. Rhythm and vocal arrangements by Rod Temperton. Lead and background vocals: Michael Jackson. Bass: Louis Johnson. Drums: John Robinson. Guitar: David Williams and Marlo Henderson. Electric piano and synthesizer: Greg Phillinganes. Synthesizer programming by Michael Boddicker and George Duke. Percussion: Paulinho Da Costa. Horns: The Seawind Horns)

The second of three Rod Temperton contributions, "Off the Wall" is the perfect theme song for the album, celebrating the "strangeness" of living with passion and originality ("living crazy/That's the only way") over the "normalcy" of conformity and mind-numbing routine. The song, in this way, is actually a reverse indictment of "straight" society, calling into question its expectations while flaunting an alternative vision of fulfillment. Temperton intentionally aimed the track's content at Jackson, believing its celebration of being different and "living crazy" would resonate with the eccentric singer. "I knew he liked Charlie Chaplin, and I thought 'Off the Wall' would be a nice thing for Michael," Temperton recalled. "Off the Wall" also foreshadowed some of the horror-motif theatrics of "Thriller," with its eerie opening and cackling ghouls. Along with "This Place Hotel," it represents one of the earliest examples of Jackson's forays into Gothic themes and sounds.

The song is an excellent example of Jackson's brilliant rhythm, timing, and vocal versatility. Rod Temperton intentionally crafted the song to highlight these strengths. Listen to the shifting tempo, the complex arrangement, the superb harmonies. "At one point," notes Timothy Pernell, "you can hear Michael's baritone, tenor and falsetto clash into each other during the bridge ("do what you wanna do/there ain't no rules it's up to you").

Meanwhile, the lyrics combine the themes of the previous two tracks: the alienation of modern "work" and the joy of "escaping" via music and dance. "When the world is on your shoulders," Jackson sings, "leave that nine to five upon the shelf." Society's expectations and obligations are tossed aside in favor of spontaneity, excitement, and passion. "Let the madness in the music get to you," Jackson sings. "Life ain't so bad at all if you live it off the wall." With its funky groove and Jackson's vibrant vocals, the title track is one of the highlights of the album.

6. GIRLFRIEND

(Written and composed by Paul McCartney; produced by Quincy Jones. Horns arranged by Jerry Hey. Rhythm arrangement by Quincy Jones, Tom Bahler and Greg Phillinganes. Vocal arrangement by Michael Jackson and Quincy Jones. Lead and background vocals: Michael Jackson. Bass: Louis Johnson. Drums: John Robinson. Electric piano: Greg Phillinganes. Synthesizer: David Foster. Synthesizer programming by George Duke. Guitar: Wah Wah Watson and Marlo Henderson. Horns: The Seawind Horns)

Depending on one's tastes, "Girlfriend" is either a charmingly innocent love song or a regrettably saccharine Wings cover. Most critics tend to side with the latter. Generally regarded as the weakest track on *Off the Wall*, it simply lacks the sonic excitement and adventurism of the album's dance tracks and the emotional depth of its ballads.

The song was composed by Paul McCartney and originally included on his 1978 Wings album, *London Town*. Jackson remembers McCartney offering him the song at a party and being taken by its "engaging melody." It is indeed a catchy tune, even if its lyrics are on the sappy side. McCartney, of course, had long been criticized for writing such "silly love songs" since parting with the Beatles. Jackson, however, was genuinely flattered to be offered a song by a legend whose music he deeply admired.

A playful, teasing confession of a love triangle, "Girlfriend" is not without redeeming qualities. For many listeners who grew up with the album, the simple melody and Jackson's pure, unaffected vocals still conjure up a nostalgic warmth and innocence.

7. SHE'S OUT OF MY LIFE

(Written and composed by Tom Bahler; produced by Quincy Jones. String arrangement by Johnny Mandel. Lead and background vocals: Michael Jackson. Bass: Louis Johnson. Guitar: Larry Carlton. Electric piano: Greg Phillinganes. Concert master: Gerald Vinci)

In sharp contrast to the lightweight "Girlfriend" is "She's Out of My Life," a landmark Jackson track that gave *Off the Wall* a different dimension. Quincy Jones initially intended the song for Frank Sinatra and hesitated to give it to a young Michael Jackson. "It's a very mature emotion," Jones recalled. "You can feel the pain in it." The song was a departure from most of the upbeat, feel-good material Jackson had done with his brothers, and Jones wasn't quite sure Jackson was ready for it. Jackson, however, had long demonstrated his ability to communicate powerful emotions, even as a young boy (including songs such as "Who's Lovin' You," "I'll Be There," and "Ben"). Still, his connection to "She's Out of My Life" surprised everyone, including himself.

The song begins with an atmospheric, orchestral prelude, before Jackson comes in with his pure, melancholy vocals: "She's out of my life ..." Located in the midst of an otherwise celebratory dance album, the effect is even more piercing. With disarming authenticity, he makes the listener feel every word of Tom Bahler's heartbreaking Broadway-soul ballad. It forced skeptical critics to recognize *Off the Wall* as more than a shallow disco album. Music critic Larry Carlton described it as a "hauntingly beautiful ballad." "[Jackson] takes huge emotional risks," added Stephen Holden in his 1979 *Rolling Stone* review, "and wins every time." Indeed, his voice had perhaps never sounded more vulnerable. "I don't know whether to laugh or cry," he sings. "I don't know whether to live or die." It was the first time as an adult that Jackson seemed to bare a part of his soul. "[It] became a Jackson signature, similar to the way 'My Life' served Frank Sinatra," observed music critic Nelson George. "The vulnerability, verging on fragility that would become embedded in Michael's persona found, perhaps, its richest expression in this wistful ballad."

While recording the song, the words and music had such a strong effect on Jackson that he couldn't finish without crying. "I had been letting so much build up inside me," he recalled. "I was twenty-one, and I was so rich in some experiences while being poor in moments of true joy.... I remember burying my face in my hands, and hearing only the hum of the machinery as my sobs echoed in the room." Quincy Jones and Bruce Swedien, who were in the studio with Jackson, were surprised he felt the song so deeply. "He cried at the end of every take," Jones recalled. "We recorded about 8 or 11 takes, and every one, at the end, he's crying. So finally I said, hey, it's supposed to be—leave it on there." They eventually stuck with the first recording.

To this point, Jackson's only real public relationship had been with Oscar-winning child actress Tatum O'Neal, and it is possible that his strong emotional reaction to the song was partially with her in mind. She was, in his words, his "first love," but the relationship didn't last. (In an interview with *Vibe* magazine, Tatum later acknowledged, "He asked me to go to the premiere of *The Wiz* with him, and my agent at the time said it wasn't a good idea, maybe because they felt he wasn't a big enough star yet. He never talked to me after that. I think he thought I just canceled, but it wasn't me at all. I was a child doing what I was told. I want you to print that, because I don't think he ever knew that. I lost touch with him because of it, so I don't really know him anymore. But I love him; he's one of the nicest, most innocent people I've ever met. I love 'She's Out of My Life' because I think it describes our friendship at that time."

Yet for Jackson, the song's emotional resonance went beyond one relationship. At this time, in his own words, he was "one of the loneliest people in the world." Having grown up in a fish bowl of fame, the only people he really knew were his family and the people he worked with professionally. Real intimacy was something he longed for, but simply didn't know how to realize. He kept it "locked deep inside," as the song's lyrics put it, until it was "too late." "She's Out of My Life," Jackson would later reflect, is "about knowing that the barriers that have separated me from others are temptingly low and seemingly easy to jump over and yet they remain standing while what I really desire disappears from my sight."

8. I CAN'T HELP IT

(Written and composed by Stevie Wonder; produced by Quincy Jones. Horns arranged by Jerry Hey. Rhythm arrangement by Greg Phillinganes and Stevie Wonder. String arrangement by Johnny Mandel. Synthesizer programming by Michael Boddicker. Lead and background vocals: Michael Jackson. Bass: Louis Johnson. Drums: John Robinson. Electric piano and synthesizer: Greg Phillinganes. Percussion: Paulinho Da Costa. Horns: The Seawind Horns. Concert master: Gerald Vinci)

The emotional ending to "She's Out of My Life" sets the stage for the lush disco-jazz odyssey that is "I Can't Help It." Composed by friend and mentor Stevie Wonder, some feel it is not only one of the most underrated tracks from *Off the Wall*, but from Jackson's entire catalog. The otherworldly ambience it conjures is exotic and enchanting. "I just love the bass line and chords of that song," says singer Alicia Keys. "It just puts you in an immediate zone—that yearning and that desire in [Michael's] voice . . . it's just a beautiful culmination of the emotion of music."

Stevie Wonder himself was blown away by Jackson's interpretation of the song: the flawlessly smooth delivery, brilliant harmonies, and variety of vocal twists, syncopation, and scatting. The jazz-rooted Quincy Jones ensured the production was equal to Jackson's talent. From its bubbling opening chords, the song moves with the fluidity of a dream. "Floating just above a lush bed of organ and bass," writes *Rolling Stone*'s J. Edward Keyes, "[Jackson] takes his time on this one, making its pleasures simple but irresistible." Indeed, as in the title track, Jackson's rhythmic timing is uncanny as he narrates the feeling of being in love. "Looking in my mirror," he sings, "Took me by surprise/I can't help but see you/Running often through my mind." Jackson allows the endings of words to take off, as if soaring through the imagination.

The song is about a mysterious lover ("an angel in disguise") who has enchanted the singer. "Love to run my fingers/Softly while you sigh," Jackson tells her. The understated but sensual lyrics float on the melody, rendering the weightless feel of being in love. Finally, toward the end of the song, the lyrical descriptions dissolve into wordless exultations, perhaps signifying the joy of intimacy that simply can't be expressed in language.

A simple, but sublime musical poem, "I Can't Help It" is the result of three singular talents—Wonder, Jones, and Jackson—operating at the top of their games.

9. IT'S THE FALLING IN LOVE

(Written and composed by Carole Bayer Sager and David Foster; produced by Quincy Jones. Horns arranged by Jerry Hey. Rhythm arrangement by Quincy Jones and David Foster. Synthesizer programming by Steve Porcaro. Vocal arrangement by Quincy Jones and Tom Bahler. Lead and background vocals: Michael Jackson and Patti Austin. Bass: Louis Johnson. Drums: John Robinson. Guitar: Wah Wah Watson and Marlo Henderson. Electric piano: Greg Phillinganes. Synthesizer: David Foster. Horns: The Seawind Horns)

The album's final ballad, "It's the Falling in Love," is a mid-tempo duet with Jazz singer Patti Austin. The song was written by Carole Bayer Sager and originally included on her 1978 album, *Too*. Quincy Jones brought in David Foster and Tom Bahler to adapt and arrange the song for Jackson. The result is a melodic light pop showcase featuring two lovers conversing about their fears of getting closer. The tension is achieved in this state of unknowing anticipation.

While they are deeply in love, they worry about the pain that might result from making themselves vulnerable. "Though I'm trying not to look in your eyes," Austin sings, "Each time I do they kind of burn right through me." The song captures the anxiety and excitement of young love, the mixture of fear and hope. As Jackson sings: "A web of mystery/A possibility of more to come."

The song rides along a cheerful beat backed by Wah Wah Watson's funky guitar licks and David Foster and Steve Porcaro's experimental synthesizer effects. The highlight is in the joyful vocals and deftly arranged harmonies that evoke the turbulent, reckless emotions of falling in love.

10. BURN THIS DISCO OUT

(Written and composed by Rod Temperton; produced by Quincy Jones. Horns arranged by Jerry Hey. Rhythm and vocal arrangements by Rod Temperton. Lead and background vocals: Michael Jackson. Bass: Louis Johnson. Drums: John Robinson. Guitar: David Williams and Marlo Henderson. Electric piano: Greg Phillinganes. Percussion: Paulinho Da Costa. Horns: The Seawind Horns)

The album ends with the appropriately titled "Burn This Disco Out," which would essentially signal the end of the disco era. *Off the Wall* was the last great album—and many argue the best—of the genre's approximately five-year reign over dance music (1975–1980). Beginning in the early eighties, a more spare, synth-pop revolution would take over the radio, epitomized by songs like The Knack's "My Sharona," Prince's "1999," Queen and David Bowie's "Under Pressure," and of course, Michael Jackson's entire album *Thriller*. (Indeed, if you listen to this conclusion to *Off the Wall*, followed by the opener on *Thriller*, the vast difference in sound and production is striking.)

Still, "Burn This Disco Out" feels perfectly at home in the context of the album. The final song of three contributed by Heatwave's Rod Temperton, it concludes *Off the Wall* with the same relentless energy that began the record: combining disco, funk, and R&B to create yet another blistering dance classic. Some felt that it contained the most excitment on the album with its thick beat, jubilant horns, and soaring vocals.

Along with several other songs on the album, "Burn This Disco Out" became a big club hit, inspiring DJs to do exactly what the lyrics demand ("spin the sounds"). For listeners, the energy, passion, and pure joy of the song (and album) provided exactly the escapism and liberation Jackson intended. It is a moment of pure sonic ecstasy that continues to shine through thirty years later.

OTHER NOTABLE *OFF THE WALL*-ERA SONGS

BLAME IT ON THE BOOGIE (from *Destiny*, 1978)
A melodic, mid-tempo dance track, "Blame It on the Boogie" served as the lead single for *Destiny*. The song peaked at just #54 on the charts, but became a big club hit with its breezy harmonics and Jackson's confident, playful vocals singing over a background of brass. It has since become a classic of the disco era.

CAN YOU FEEL IT (from *Triumph*, 1980)
Written by Michael and older brother Jackie, "Can You Feel It" is a message song about the power of music to bring love and unity to the world. "Spread the word and try to teach the man/Who is hating his brother/When hate won't do," Jackson sings. "Cuz we're all the same/Yes the blood inside of me is inside of you." It is an early example of the socially conscious, massive pop anthems ("We Are the World," "Earth Song") Jackson would write later in his career. The song also featured one of Jackson's first music videos, a cutting-edge (for the time) cosmic spectacular, featuring the Jacksons as black superheroes sprinkling gold dust on a futuristic cityscape.

DESTINY (from *Destiny*, 1978)
A beautiful, aching ballad about finding one's place in the world. The song builds into a soaring resolution to live life deliberately, culminating with Tito's fantastic guitar solo.

EASE ON DOWN THE ROAD (from *The Wiz: Original Soundtrack*, 1978)
A spirited soul duet with Diana Ross, performed by Dorothy and the Scarecrow in *The Wiz*. The song is notable for being the first Jackson track produced by Quincy Jones and the first to win a Grammy nomination. It reached #41 on the *Billboard* Hot 100 in 1979.

THIS PLACE HOTEL (from *Triumph*, 1980)
"This Place Hotel" (originally titled "Heartbreak Hotel," but renamed due to copyright on Elvis Presley's famous song by the same name) was a watershed track for Jackson. Written, arranged, and composed entirely by Michael, it revealed his rapidly emerging talent as a songwriter. In contrast to the mostly celebratory tone of *Off the Wall*, "This Place Hotel" is a dark, psychological song about regret, revenge, and fear that anticipated later classics like "Billie Jean" and "Dirty Diana." The number opens with a foreboding instrumental prelude, before a piercing scream unleashes the song's menacing Gothic funk. "The scream was the kind that normally shatters a bad dream," Jackson later wrote, "but our intention was to have the dream only begin, to make the listener wonder whether it was a dream or reality." In the song's narrative, Jackson's pained voice sings of "faces staring, glaring, tearing through me." He speaks of "yearning," of "sin" and "concealing gloom." The song also experiments with new sounds. "This is the first example," observes Nelson George, "of a cinematic use of sound effects, horror film motifs, and vocal trickery to convey a sense of danger in his work." Jackson was justifiably proud of the song's depth and scope. "['This Place Hotel'] was the most ambitious song I had composed," he wrote in his 1988 autobiography. Many critics and listeners took note. The single reached #22 on the pop charts (and #2 on the Black Singles chart).

LOVE NEVER FELT SO GOOD (recorded 1980, unreleased)
A charming, piano-based demo written with Paul Anka and Kathy Wakefield in 1980, "Love Never Felt So Good" features Jackson's signature finger-snapping and a wonderful vocal.

LOVELY ONE (from *Triumph*, 1980)
A disco-funk floor burner, "Lovely One" gave *Triumph* a big dance hit in the spirit of "Shake Your Body (Down to the Ground)." The song was *Triumph*'s biggest single, reaching #12 on the *Billboard* Hot 100 and #2 on the Black Singles chart.

SHAKE YOUR BODY (DOWN TO THE GROUND) (from *Destiny*, 1978)
Cowritten by Jackson and younger brother Randy, "Shake Your Body" is considered one of the finest dance tracks of the era. In 1978, it reached #7 on the charts and sold more than two million copies. Beginning with a "piano rumble, a cymbal glide, [and the] bass zooming from side to side," the track is more than eight minutes of relentless energy. The song's killer bass line is surrounded by deft guitar work (played by brother Tito), blazing horns, and, of course, Jackson's impressive vocal versatility. "It's appropriate to see 'Shake Your Body' as the true start to the adult Michael Jackson's solo career," observes music critic Nelson George.

SUNSET DRIVER (recorded 1979; released on *Michael Jackson: The Ultimate Collection*, 2004)
A funky outtake from the *Off the Wall* sessions, later released on *The Ultimate Collection*.

THIS IS IT (recorded 1980; released on *This Is It* soundtrack in 2009)
A demo cowritten with Jackson and Paul Anka, this yearning, nostalgic soft pop ballad was resurrected as Jackson's first posthumously released song, due to its fitting title (the same as Jackson's ill-fated concert series in London). It was rerecorded in 2009 with backing vocals from Jackson's brothers and produced by John McClain.

WALK RIGHT NOW (from *Triumph*, 1980)
A high-energy, Earth, Wind, and Fire-esque disco-prog-rock-funk track, "Walk Right Now" is one of the standouts of *Triumph*.

YOU CAN'T WIN (from *The Wiz: Original Soundtrack*, 1978)
Jackson's only solo from *The Wiz*, "You Can't Win" is one of his early hidden gems. It was written by Charlie Smalls at Quincy Jones's behest for Jackson's character, the Scarecrow. The highlight is Jackson's ad-libs in the second half. The seven-minute soul workout was rereleased on *The Ultimate Collection* in 2004. Jackson said the song addressed "humiliation and helplessness."

Jackson performs in his signature white socks and black loafers in 1980.

"I love to create magic—to put together something that's so unusual, so unexpected that it blows people's heads off. Something ahead of the times. Five steps ahead of what people are thinking. So people see it and say, 'Whoa, I wasn't expecting that.'"

MICHAEL JACKSON, INTERVIEW, 1982

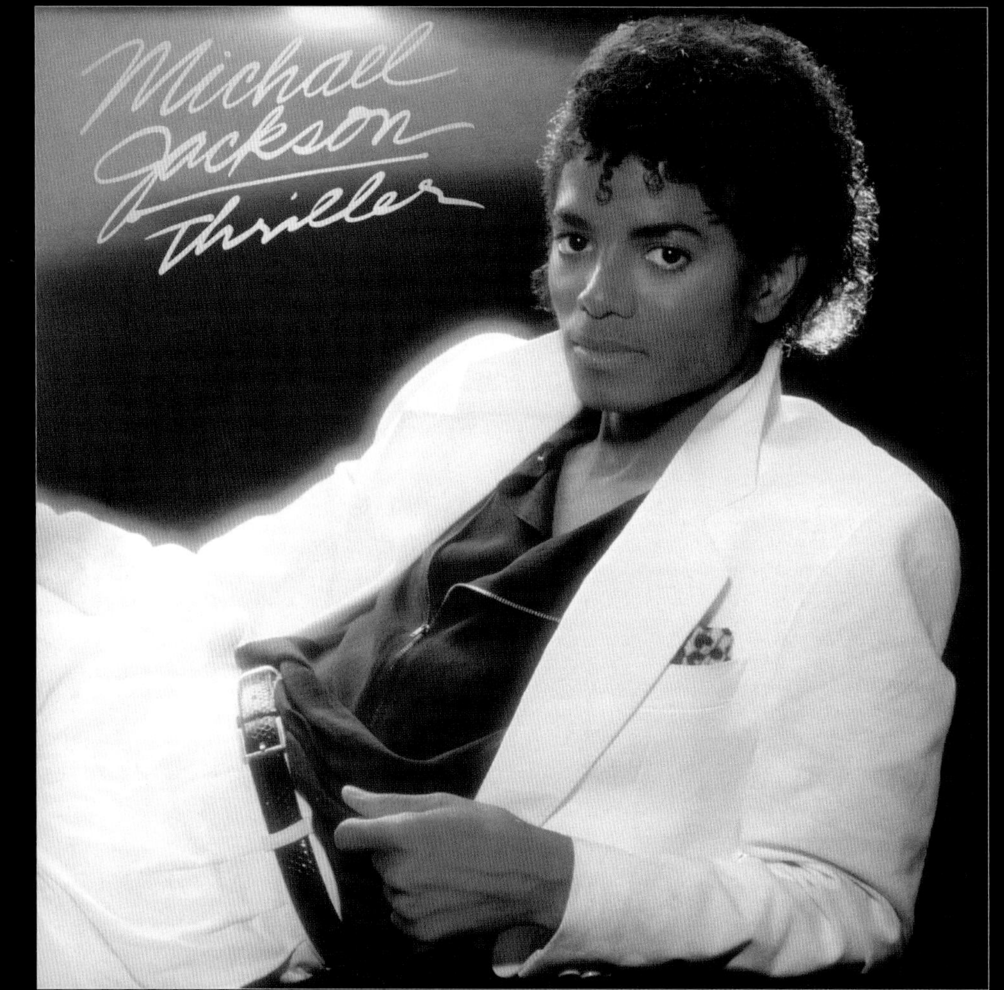

CHAPTER 2 THRILLER

Thriller was more than just an album; it was a mass-cultural, multimedia phenomenon that hasn't been matched in scope before or since. It marked the arrival of a new sound, a new musical era, and a new kind of pop star and pop album. "In today's world of declining sales and fragmented audiences," writes music critic Alan Light, "it is almost impossible to imagine how much this one album dominated and united the culture." At its peak—1982 to 1984—*Thriller* crossed every barrier imaginable: it reached young and old, black and white, middle-class and poor; it reached fans of rock as well as R&B; it reached beyond America to the Soviet Union, Europe, Asia, Africa, and just about everywhere in between.

The album itself contained just nine songs. Yet seven of those nine became Top Ten hits, three became revolutionary music videos, and one, the most significant pop performance since the Beatles appeared on the *Ed Sullivan Show* in 1964. In addition to being the best-selling album of all time—with recent estimates putting it at more than 110 million—it was also perhaps the most visually ubiquitous, establishing an elaborate iconography that is now irrevocably woven into the fabric of the music. The songs themselves formed the ultimate crossover album, fusing elements of R&B, disco, rock, funk, soul, world music, jazz, and gospel as they express the tensions and paradoxes of Jackson's conflicted psyche.

Although the nickname would come later, *Thriller* was the album that officially elevated Michael Jackson to the "King of Pop, Rock, and Soul." At the beginning of the decade he was a rising talent with an enormously successful, but still overlooked, first solo album. By 1984, he was without question the

---

RELEASED: *November 30, 1982*

PRODUCER: *Quincy Jones*

NOTABLE CONTRIBUTORS: Rod Temperton *(songwriting/arrangements)*, Bruce Swedien *(recording engineer)*, Matt Forger *(technical engineer)*, Steve Porcaro *(songwriting/synthesizer)*, David Paich *(synthesizer)*, Jeff Porcaro *(drums/arrangements)*, Greg Phillinganes *(keyboard/synthesizer), Paulinho Da Costa (percussion)*, N'dugu Chancler *(drums)*, David Williams *(guitar)*, Jerry Hey *(strings/horns)*, Paul McCartney *(vocals)*, Eddie Van Halen *(guitar)*, Vincent Price *(voice rap)*

SINGLES: *"The Girl Is Mine," "Billie Jean," "Beat It," "Wanna Be Startin' Somethin," "Human Nature," "P.Y.T.," "Thriller"*

ESTIMATED COPIES SOLD: *110 million*

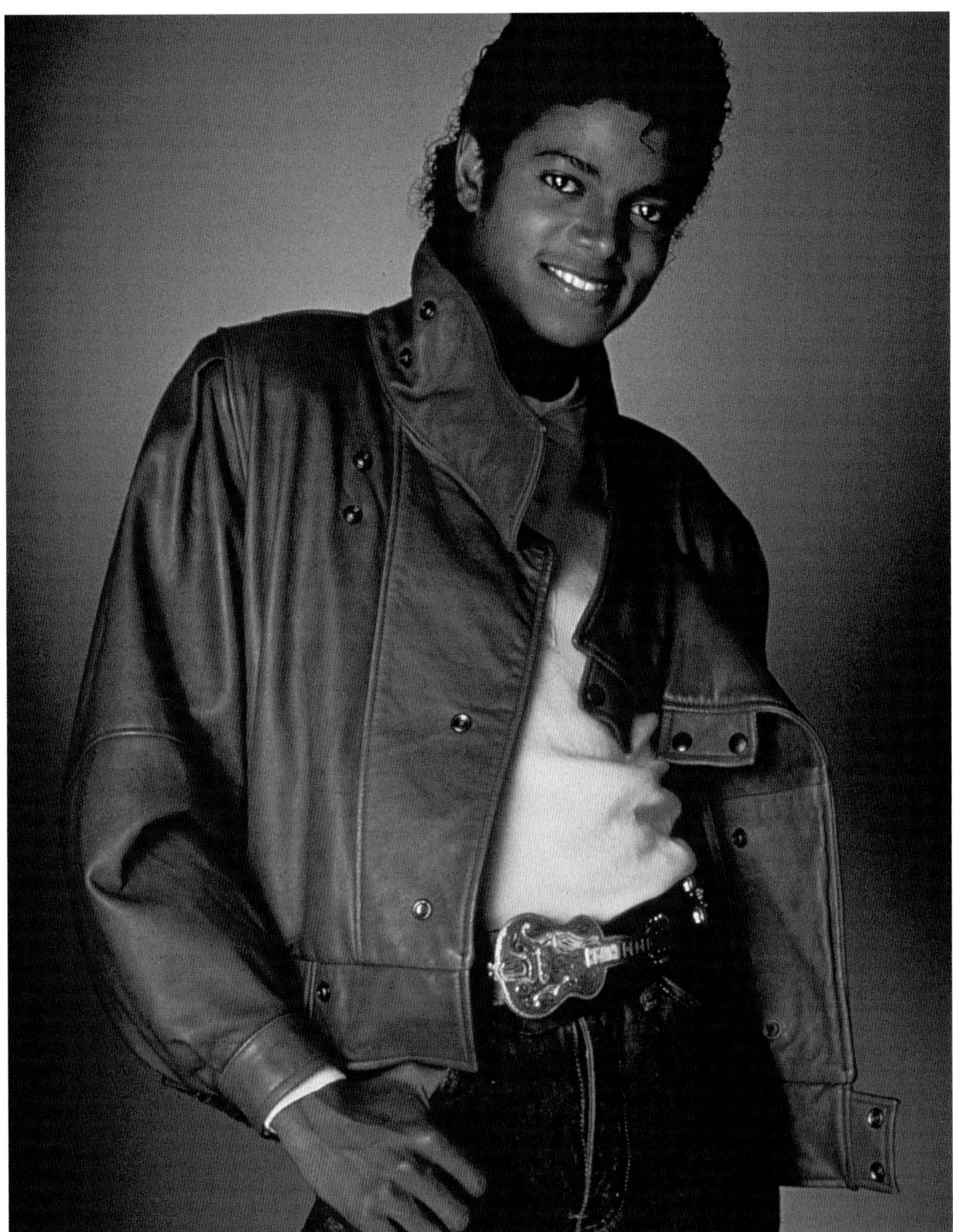

biggest entertainer in the world. "We live now in the world of the 'long tail,'" proclaimed music critic Tom Ewing. "*Thriller* was the big head."

The 1980s saw profound transformations in America. Often referred to as the "Me Decade," it was an era of political and ideological conservatism: Reaganomics and corporate growth, mass consumption, malls, and yuppies. "You can have it all!" and "Shop 'til you drop!" were common catchphrases as the country transitioned from recession to boom. The eighties heralded an era of optimism and patriotism, even as it witnessed the rise of AIDS and unemployment. While the official motto was "Just Say No" to drugs, the use of cocaine and particularly crack reached epidemic proportions (which led to increased crime and gang violence). Meanwhile, Cold War tensions continued as Reagan launched a revitalized defense program (nicknamed Star Wars) to counter the Soviet Union (nicknamed the Evil Empire).

Yet there was another side to the eighties. Its commercials and cartoons (*Smurfs*, *Transformers*, *Alvin and the Chipmunks*), its sitcoms (*The Cosby Show*, *Who's the Boss?*, *Cheers*) and movies (*E.T.*, *Goonies*, *The Breakfast Club*, *Back to the Future*), its crazes (Rubik's Cube, Pac-Man, MTV) and technologies (cable TV, computers, video games), were all part of a pop culture explosion that was as compulsive as it was unifying. Due largely to this kaleidoscopic web of collective experiences, there is a unique nostalgia for the decade. Its vast array of cultural phenomena became deeply ingrained in people's lives and memories. And featured prominently in that collage was Michael Jackson, the coolest, smoothest, most electrifying star since Elvis Presley.

When Michael Jackson died in the summer of 2009, some cultural observers saw the enormous emotional outpouring as a collective grieving for the decade itself and the time it represented in people's lives. In a way, it was quite similar to the emotional outpouring following the death of John Lennon and its association with the 1960s.

Part of *Thriller*'s legacy, then, is its connection with a particular moment in history. While timeless, it is both a product of and helped to produce the decade it now represents. For many, it is about personal experiences: watching the moonwalk on *Motown 25* or the premier of the *Thriller* video on MTV, attending a Victory concert with friends, or listening to "Beat It" on one's new Walkman or boom box. These memories, for many, were just as important as the music itself.

***Thriller* was released** in the midst of a severe recession both for the music industry and the United States as a whole. By November 1982, the month *Thriller* was released, unemployment hit a four-decade high (10.8 percent), while record companies such as Epic, Atlantic, Capitol, Columbia, and Warner Bros. all laid off employees due to the worst record sales in history.

Signed under the Epic label, Michael Jackson and his team were well aware of these challenges. "In the late '70s," recalls recording engineer Bruce Swedien, "I heard some people say that recorded popular music couldn't possibly survive the attention that young people were paying to video

For many, Michael Jackson (and *Thriller*) defined pop culture in the 1980s.

arcades and home video games." Others pointed to blank cassette tapes that allowed people to share music and record it from the radio for free. Still others felt that music was simply in a creative lull; if it became more compelling and exciting, people would buy it. It was, in this way, a time not unlike the present, when technological changes, formulaic music, and a slow-to-adapt corporate music industry created widespread pessimism about future prospects.

"In the summer of 1982, however, no one could have imagined all Thriller *would accomplish."*

In spite of the recession, however, the moment, in many ways, was ripe for a musical revival. The inception of music videos offered artists a new platform to promote records and connect with fans. By the middle of the decade, "I want my MTV" was a household phrase as young people across the country tuned in to see the latest styles and sounds. "Rock videos are firing up a musical revolution," observed *Time* in 1983. "Increasingly, and perhaps irreversibly, audiences for American mainstream music will depend, even insist, on each song's being a full audiovisual confrontation."

The early eighties also saw new technologies like the Sony Walkman, the boom box, and the car stereo become rapidly integrated into society. Each of these media changed the way music was listened to and experienced. It was now increasingly transportable, bringing with it a greater sense of freedom, privacy, and choice. Music could be listened to while working out, driving, or on headphones that blocked out parents. The introduction of cassette tapes (which outsold records by 1983), and soon after, CDs (put on the market, incidentally, the year *Thriller* was released) likewise increased portability, functionality, and sound performance.

The technological advances, of course, also extended into how music was made. In the studio, synthesizers largely replaced traditional instruments, creating a dramatic shift in sound (Van Halen's eventual use of synth in their music was viewed by rock purists as almost as blasphemous as Bob Dylan plugging in an electric guitar).

When *Thriller* was released in 1982, disco was on the wane as synth pop, New Wave, and "big hair" rock took root. In 1983, *Time* called this genreless sound "New Music": "a diverse but irresistible mix of sounds... a blend of soul, rock, reggae and disco set to a synthesized, whipcrack beat." REO Speedwagon's *Hi Infidelity* became 1981's best-selling album, with other ballad-based rock groups such as Survivor, Journey, and Chicago joining them on the charts. Lionel Richie, Hall and Oates, Cyndi Lauper, and Billy Joel enjoyed immense popularity in America, while Brit-pop bands Duran Duran and Depeche Mode ushered in the "New Romantic" movement.

It was *Thriller*, however, that really opened the floodgates for popular music in the eighties. "For a record industry stuck on the border between the ruins of punk and the chic regions of synthesizer pop," wrote *Time*'s Jay Cocks in 1984, "*Thriller* was a thorough restoration of confidence, a rejuvenation. Its effect on listeners, especially younger ones, was nearer to a revelation. *Thriller* brought black

At twenty-four years of age, Jackson already had his sights set on the biggest selling record of all time.

music back to mainstream radio, from which it had been effectively banished after 'restrictive special-format programming' was introduced in the mid-seventies. Listeners could put more carbonation in the pop and cut their heavy-metal diet with a dose of the fleetest soul around."

Indeed, with Jackson leading the way, 1983 and 1984 became watershed years in popular music history. It saw black-and-white musical integration as never before (led by "Beat It"). It saw the emergence of Prince and Madonna, two superstars who would join Jackson as the defining icons of the eighties. And, it saw the birth of a new generation of compelling rock: R.E.M. released *Murmur*, U2 released *Sunday Bloody Sunday*, Bruce Springsteen released *Born in the U.S.A.*, and the Police released *Synchronicity* (which included the biggest-selling single of 1983, "Every Breath You Take").

In two years, the music industry had gone from recession to boom. "After four years of slumping sales and stagnating sounds," wrote J. D. Reed in 1983, "the pop music industry is once again experiencing a welcome artistic and financial bonanza, one that is making this rock 'n' roll's headiest season of the decade." Indeed, by 1984, the number of albums certified gold was up twenty-five percent while Epic celebrated a five hundred percent increase in profits.

"There is no question that *Thriller* was the driving force behind what became the hottest span in Epic's history," Epic V.P. Dan Beck says. It wasn't, of course, the only force. Yet there is no question, as recording engineer Matt Forger notes, "the quality of [*Thriller*] inspired many people in the music industry.... People were revitalized in believing that music could achieve great results."

In the summer of 1982, however, no one could have imagined all *Thriller* would accomplish. Indeed, people often forget that before Michael Jackson had to live up to the success of *Thriller* with every new album, he first had to live up to *Off the Wall*. With nearly ten million albums sold by 1982 and four top ten hits, it wasn't an easy task. Just about everyone besides Jackson didn't think it was possible. "In general, record companies never believe a new album will do considerably better than the last one you did," Jackson later wrote. "They figure you either got lucky last time or the number you last sold is the size of your audience." Even Jackson's colleagues tried to temper expectations, reminding Jackson that they were in the midst of a recession, and the record industry had declined since *Off the Wall*.

"I remember being in the studio with Quincy and Rod Temperton while we were working on *Thriller*," Jackson recalled. "One of them asked me, 'If this album doesn't do as well as *Off the Wall*, will you be disappointed?' I remember feeling upset—hurt that the question was even raised. I told them *Thriller* had to do better than *Off the Wall*. I admitted that I wanted this album to be the biggest-selling album of all time. They started laughing. It was a seemingly unrealistic thing to want. There were times during the *Thriller* project when I would get emotional and upset because I couldn't get the people working with me to see what I saw. That still happens to me sometimes. Often people just don't see what I see."

Members of *Thriller*'s A-team: Quincy Jones, Matt Forger, and Bruce Swedien.

What Jackson envisioned with *Thriller* was much more than numbers. He wanted an album that would "blow people away." He wanted it to surprise, to seduce, to invigorate and inspire. He wanted every song to be "a killer." To twenty-four-year-old Jackson, the formula was simple: if he made a great album, people would buy it.

To this end, Jackson and Quincy Jones reassembled the A-Team of *Off the Wall*, including Rod Temperton and Bruce Swedien. As talented as Jackson was, *Thriller*, like all his albums, was a collaborative effort by a dedicated and dynamic creative group. The trio of Jones, Swedien, and Temperton were not only seasoned professionals, but also close friends who had the utmost respect for what each brought to the table. As producer, Jones oversaw the project and production, helped select songs, and pushed for every ounce of creativity and delivery Jackson possessed. Temperton was a songwriter who created demos tailored specifically for Jackson (both in content and rhythm), yet was also open and flexible enough to adapt them if something wasn't working. As recording engineer, Swedien was the sonic magician who maximized the quality and richness of sound for each song. Significantly, even though all of these men were decades older than Jackson and enormously talented in their own right, they had total respect for twenty-four-year-old Michael Jackson. They knew it was his artistry that ignited the whole project and were completely dedicated to actualizing his creative vision to the fullest.

For *Thriller*, there was also another important addition to the A-Team: Matt Forger. Forger had begun working with Quincy Jones and Bruce Swedien on a couple of their earlier projects, including Donna Summer's self-titled 1982 album. On *Thriller*, he was the technical engineer, which meant he was in charge of coordinating all the complex studio technology they were using at what was probably the "pinnacle of analog tape production." Like many others at the time, Forger and Swedien were working with twenty-four–track analog, which was still state-of-the-art technology for recording. The key difference, however, was in how they were using it. When more tracks were recorded than could fit, they would synchronize multiple analog twenty-four-tracks together (this revolutionary method was referred to as the Acusonic Recording Process in the album's liner notes).

For each potential song for *Thriller*, then, Forger, Swedien, and Jones, working in the new Studio A at Westlake Audio in Hollywood, would generate multiple tapes with different sections—a synth part, a horn part, a string part, etc. Synthesizers at the time were still fairly rudimentary (Quincy Jones often said recording with synthesizers was like "painting 747s with a Q-tip"). However, all these disparate synth sounds and instrumental parts were layered for texture in premixing. "Quincy wants his arrangements and his recordings to be thick and lush," says Forger. "He loves creating these textures and colors; and the way he creates them is layering sounds that are sometimes similar and sometimes dissimilar. But when they combine they create the unique character."

Quincy Jones had a deep repository from which to draw. Not only had he worked with numerous American jazz legends, but he also studied composition in Paris with legends such as Nadia Boulanger and Olivier Messiaen. After *Off the Wall* and *Thriller*, when others in the industry heard the richness and vibrancy of Michael Jackson's albums, they tried to imitate this texturing by simply stacking parts. "There was a misconception," says Forger, "that 'Oh, if I play the same guitar part six times it will make it thick and rich.'" Instead, the result was often mushy and overproduced. "We didn't use all these tracks just to record over and over again," says Forger. "We used them so that Quincy could layer different sound characters together very strategically so that the textures that were created had this richness and depth." *Thriller* also exudes a natural warmth that is often missing in digitally produced music. Swedien attributes some of this warmth to his Dave Harrison–designed mixing desk. "I heard something in his wonderful 3232c series music mixing desk that I haven't heard since. Perhaps it is due in part to the simplicity of its signal path. The equalizer of this warm-sounding desk is legendary."

It has often been said that groups such as the Beach Boys and the Beatles were the first to use the studio as an instrument. "What we did on *Thriller*," says Forger, "was the extension of that. We were able to warp the technology and stretch it to such an extent that we were able to make the technology adapt to whatever it was Michael or Quincy creatively wanted to achieve." (Interestingly, there was a sort of symbolic passing of the torch when Beatles' producer George Martin and recording engineer Geoff Emerick met with Quincy Jones, Bruce Swedien, and Matt Forger to record Jackson and McCartney's duet "The Girl Is Mine.") For Jackson, as with the Beatles, the studio technology always followed the lead of the music. "It was all about the emotional content. Not just what they hear, but what they feel. This is the power of music."

This emotional depth and sonic innovation were the goals when work began on *Thriller* at Westlake Studios. "It has to give you goose bumps," Quincy Jones often said. And for everyone involved with the project, there were numerous "goose bumps" moments. Each time Jackson brought in a new demo he had worked out at his home studio or on his tape recorder, his collaborators were amazed. According to Quincy Jones, Jackson was "writing music like a machine" during this period. He had

Jackson with Quincy Jones at the 1984 Grammy Awards, where he would collect a record eight Grammys.

begun composing new songs as soon as *Off the Wall* was finished. In fact, *Thriller*'s first track, "Wanna Be Startin' Somethin'" had been written and recorded *during* the *Off the Wall* sessions in Jackson's home studio, but he decided to hold on to it. Over the next two years, he continued to come up with new track after new track, many of which never made it onto the album's final lineup. Because he wasn't trained to write the music on paper, he would dictate it into a tape recorder, inventing beats and rhythms, imitating instruments and humming melodies. Then he would flesh it out further in the studio, sometimes with musicians or engineers or sometimes with the assistance of his sisters or brothers. Listening to his demos from this period is fascinating. Any misconceptions that Jackson was simply a "singer" are quickly dispelled. By the time songs like "Billie Jean" and "Beat It" made it to Westlake, they were already fully composed (and partially produced) by Jackson.

While Jackson was creating his own material, Quincy Jones went through nearly six hundred potential songs and song ideas that might work for the album. He referred to this process as "Polaroids." Each song was examined quickly to see if it contained qualities—tempo, key, and mood—that would work well with Jackson's abilities and vision for the album. The best of these were brought to the studio and tested on Jackson. Rod Temperton wrote more than thirty potential songs for *Thriller* "with complete bass lines, counter lines, and all, recorded [along with]...ten to twenty-five alternate titles for each song, with the beginnings of lyric schemes." According to Swedien, when Jackson received the songs he would go home, "stay up all night, and memorize every one of his demos" so that he "never had a piece of paper in front of him" in the studio. Of Temperton's thirty plus songs, many of which might have been the lead singles for other artists, only three—"Baby Be Mine," "The Lady in My Life," and the title track—made the final cut.

"The producer's main job is to find the right tunes," Quincy Jones explained. "After we go through all of these songs and tear it down, [we] then go back through the nine main songs and take out what you consider the four weakest, and try to replace that with the four stronger than anything else on the album. It turns the axis completely around. So we took out some great songs, really good songs. But we replaced them with 'The Lady in My Life,' 'Pretty Young Thing,' 'Human Nature,' and 'Beat It.'"

By the spring of 1982, the album was gradually beginning to take shape. The early tracks—"Wanna Be Startin' Somethin'," "Baby Be Mine," and "The Girl Is Mine"—were all mostly completed by this time. The latter song, written by Jackson, was first recorded in his home studio. He later brought the demo to Paul and Linda McCartney's ranch in Tucson, Arizona. "That was a very magical night," recalls keyboardist David Paich. "In between takes, me, [guitarist Steve] Lukather, [and drummer] Jeff Porcaro were jamming...[with] Paul McCartney and Michael Jackson, singing all these Stevie Wonder songs." The track was finally completed at Westlake Studios. "The Girl Is Mine," however, was hardly indicative of the material to come.

The inspiration for Jackson's masterpiece, "Billie Jean," came in late 1981. In a demo Jackson recorded in his Hayvenhurst studio, one can hear how fleshed out it already was at this point. Still, he and the A-Team meticulously worked on every detail of it over the next several months. While about half of the songs had been selected and recorded by the end of summer, however, plenty of work remained. Due to numerous distractions, including Jackson finishing the *E.T. Extra Terrestrial* storybook for Steven Spielberg, the bulk of recording for *Thriller* didn't begin in earnest until September of 1982. This left just eight weeks to finish the album on time.

Unsatisfied with the tentative title track, "Starlight," Jones challenged Temperton to come up with something new. "Michael had already written fantastic songs for the album, which we knew would be cornerstones of the album," recalled Temperton. "["Starlight"] did not meet the chemistry and the atmosphere of strong titles like 'Billie Jean' or 'Startin' Somethin'...[So] I went home and wrote down 200 to 300 titles with the favorite being 'Midnight Man,' and then went to bed. In the morning I woke up and said this word—'Thriller.'"

Jackson and Jones loved the new title and concept. It made the album edgier and more exciting. Jones quickly enlisted legendary actor Vincent Price to provide the spoken rap for the title track. Price nailed it in just two takes. Things seemed to be falling into place. As Quincy put it, there was no time for "paralysis from analysis."

Around this time, Jones also discovered a demo of the stunning ballad "Human Nature." Steve Porcaro and John Bettis, from the popular musical group Toto, had been sending in potential demos for Jackson. One day, while one of their tapes was running, Jones heard an early instrumental version of the song. He immediately fell in love with it and brought the song to Jackson. "He and I both agreed that the song had the prettiest melody we'd heard in a long time," recalled Jackson. The song replaced "Carousel" in the final lineup.

Still, Jones felt one track was missing. He wanted something with a rock edge, something to really put the album over the top. For weeks, he pestered Jackson about coming up with something, challenging him to compose something similar to but better than the Knack's hit, "My Sharona." Jackson had something he had been working on, but was initially reluctant to present it. "I like my songs," he reflected, "but initially I'm shy about playing them for people, because I'm afraid they won't like them and that's a painful experience. He finally convinced me to let him hear what I had. I brought out 'Beat It' and played it for him and he went crazy. I felt on top of the world."

Later, according to myth, while recording the song in the studio, one of the speakers burst into flames. With the inclusion of "Beat It," the final lineup of *Thriller* was complete. Still, Jackson, Jones, and company worked to the last minute to add the final touches. "We did the final mixes and fixes and overdubs up until nine o'clock in the morning of the deadline for the reference copy," remembers Jones. "We had three studios going at once. We put final touches on Michael's vocals on 'Billie Jean.'… I took Eddie Van Halen to another small studio with two huge Gibson speakers and two six-packs of beer to do his classic guitar solo, dubbing the bass line on 'Beat It' with Greg on mini Moog.… In the meantime, I took Michael to my place, laid him out on the couch in my den, and covered him with a blanket for a three-hour nap at 9 a.m. By twelve o'clock we had to be back to hear the test pressing that was going out to the world."

Everyone was anxious to hear the final product. Finally, after several whirlwind months of planning, creating, rehearsing, recording, and polishing, the album was done. Everyone gathered at the studio to listen: Jackson, Jones, Temperton, Swedien, and Michael's managers, Freddy DeMann and Ron Weisner. It was the moment they had been waiting for.

"It was a disaster," Jones recalled. "After all the great songs and the great performances and great mixes and a great tune stack, we had 24-karat sonic doo-doo. There was total silence in the studio. One by one we crept across the hall for some privacy: more silence ensued."

Tears streamed down Jackson's face. "I felt devastated," he remembered. "All this pent-up emotion came out. I got angry and left the room. I told my people, 'That's it, we're not releasing it. Call CBS and tell them they are not getting this album. We are not releasing it.' Because I knew it was wrong. If we hadn't stopped the process and examined what we were doing, the record would have been terrible. It never would have been reviewed the way it was because, as we learned, you can ruin a great album in the mix. It's like taking a great movie and ruining it in the editing."

Jones knew what the problem was: "We'd put too much material on the record.… You need

Jackson and Beatles legend Paul McCartney pose for a picture during a break in recording "The Girl Is Mine."

big fat grooves to make a big fat sound. If you squeeze it into thin grooves, you get tinny sound. We had twenty-eight minutes of sound on each side.... With vinyl you had to be realistic; it had to be under nineteen minutes of music per side.... Deep down inside we must have all known this all along as we were working, but chose not to deal with reality in our fatigue and musical euphoria."

By this time, the first single from the album, "The Girl Is Mine," had already been released as a single on radio and surged to #2 on the charts. The album was supposed to be ready within the month, and Jackson and Jones were feeling the heat from Epic. Ultimately, they were able to convince executives that a little more time was needed.

At Quincy's recommendation, everyone took a couple of days off to take a step back and clear their head, before returning to remix the entire album again in two weeks. "We put it dead in the pockets," Quincy recalled, "mixing one tune per day."

The result was well worth it. This time Jackson was satisfied. "When it was done—boom—it hit us hard," Jackson recalled. "CBS could hear the difference too... It felt so good when we finished. I was so excited I couldn't wait for it to come out." It was now almost Thanksgiving, and *Thriller* was finally ready to be unveiled.

The album hit stores around the globe on November 30, 1982. "From the beginning," writes *Billboard's* Gail Mitchell, "Epic intended to live up to its name. The label made *Thriller* the first major release to debut worldwide simultaneously, the first album to be worked for close to two years instead of the usual six or eight months and the first album to spin off seven singles to radio—more than double the normal number." Still, while *Thriller* sold well from the beginning, it was more a growing avalanche than an instant sensation.

The cover, featuring the now iconic portrait of a lounging Jackson in white tuxedo, simultaneously projected innocence and sophistication. Like *Off the Wall*, it was intended to present the singer as a youthful but mature artist. However, this was clearly a different version of Jackson than the one that appeared on *Off the Wall*. Everything about him had been polished and fine-tuned: his features were flawlessly sculpted, his caramel skin radiant, his entire body glowing with an aura of otherworldly beauty. *GQ Magazine* said he looked like an "iconic sun-god relaxing after quitting time." Indeed, just as *Thriller's* songs would set a new standard for music, the cover symbolized a new cross-racial, cross-gender ideal of beauty. Jackson's features were soft and feminine, and neither stereotypically Caucasian nor African. He represented a new androgyny that appealed not only to black and white, but also to Asian, Latino, Middle Eastern, and Indian people. The *Thriller* album portrait not only hung in lockers and on bedroom walls across America, but also around the world. This new image aligned perfectly with the record itself, which demolished traditional genres and barriers.

"*Thriller* is a wonderful pop record," wrote the *New York Times* in 1982, "the latest statement by one of the great singers in popular music today. It is as hopeful a sign as we have had yet that the destructive barriers that spring up regularly between white and black music—and between whites and blacks—in this culture may be breached once again."

In its 1982 review, *Rolling Stone* called it a "watershed" in Jackson's creative development, particularly with its lyrics. Where *Off the Wall* was primarily an expression of youthful sensuality and exuberance, *Thriller* goes deeper and broader. It is by turns frenetic ("Wanna Be Startin' Somethin'"), smooth ("Baby Be Mine"), moralistic ("Beat It"), mysterious ("Billie Jean"), funky ("P.Y.T."), evocative ("Human Nature"),

The iconic *Thriller* cover in full, with a luminous Michael Jackson holding a baby tiger.

and intimate ("Lady in My Life"). Jackson's unique and versatile delivery was also praised. Wrote *Newsweek*'s Jim Miller in 1983: "On ballads he is hushed, reverent, trembling, his tenor arching into a supple, pure falsetto. On up-tempo dance tunes he's hoarse, ecstatic, possessed—his singing an awesome repertoire of pops, clicks, squeaks, gurgles, moans, almost any sound that can be juggled rhythmically. Michael's voice haunts these songs, gives them heart. It transcends all the electronic gimmickry. It is what will make this music endure."

No one would have guessed the album's range and depth, however, by its first single. Released a month ahead of the record, Jackson's duet with Paul McCartney, "The Girl Is Mine," seemed for many as tame and sentimental as the latest Lionel Richie ballad. According to Jackson, because of the international appeal of the duo they had no choice but to "get it out of the way." "When you have two strong names like that together on a song," Jackson explained. "It has to come out first." The song was indeed a big hit, reaching #2 on the *Billboard* Hot 100 in the United States and receiving ample airplay on the radio. However, it also caused some to wonder if Jackson was already backtracking from the innovative spirit of *Off the Wall*. "From Prince to Marvin Gaye, from rap to Rick James, black artists have incorporated increasingly mature and adventurous themes—culture, sex, politics—into grittier, gutsier music," wrote *Rolling Stone* at the time. "So when Jackson's first solo single since 1979 turned out to be a wimpoid MOR ballad with the refrain 'the doggone girl is mine,' sung with a tame Paul McCartney, it looked like the train had left the station without him."

The concern, however, wouldn't last long. Quincy Jones called the song their "red herring." Following "The Girl Is Mine" came "Billie Jean" and "Beat It." Both songs, written by Jackson, established the tone and ambition of the album and quickly soared to #1 on the charts. In fact, at the behest of new manager Frank DiLeo, Jackson released "Beat It" while "Billie Jean" was still sitting at number one. "CBS screamed, 'You're crazy. This will kill 'Billie Jean,''" recalled Jackson. "But Frank told them not to worry, that both songs would be number one and both would be in the Top Ten at the same time. They were."

It wasn't long before *Thriller*, and Michael Jackson, exploded in a way never seen before or since. Over the course of the next two years (1982–1984), *Thriller* spent an astounding eighty weeks in the Top Ten in the United States. Thirty-seven of those weeks were at number one. Of its nine songs, a record seven became Top Ten singles. The album would go on to win a record eight Grammy Awards (an astounding achievement, particularly when fewer categories existed) and an unprecedented ten American Music Awards. It hit number one in just about every country in the world. With each new single, video, or performance, *Thriller* continued to fly off the shelves, sometimes selling more than a million copies a week. "At some point, *Thriller* stopped selling like a leisure item—like a magazine, a toy, tickets to a hit movie—and started selling like a household staple," writes biographer J. Randy Taraborrelli. Within the first year alone, it sold twenty-two million copies, more than double the sales of David Bowie, the Police, and Duran Duran—combined. By 1984, just two years after its release, the *Guinness World Records* declared

Thriller America's and the world's best-selling album of all time, a mantle it still holds today.

Indeed, while Jackson's artistic and cultural significance in relation to the Beatles and other music legends continues to be debated, one fact can't be denied: Michael Jackson's global reach was larger. Due in part to globalization and technology, his image, music, and style rapidly spread around the world. *Thriller* resonated in countries as diverse as Japan (where it stayed on the charts for sixty-five consecutive weeks), South Africa (where it became the racially segregated country's top seller), and the Soviet Union (where it was officially banned, but still "swapped and treasured" in the form of bootleg cassettes). Jackson's broad, trans-everything appeal seemed to be written into the very beats and melodies of *Thriller*. "The pulse of America and much of the rest of the world moves irregularly," observed *Time*'s Jay Cocks in 1984, "beating in time to the tough strut of 'Billie Jean,' the asphalt aria of 'Beat It,' the supremely cool chills of 'Thriller.'"

Indeed, the *Thriller* phenomenon wasn't just about Jackson's music sales; it was an entire cultural web of images, sounds, and events that became indelible to life in the eighties: The classic performance on "Motown 25" that captured the imagination of a generation; the groundbreaking music videos that revolutionized what was then a fledgling art form (and network); the burn accident while filming a Pepsi commercial that invoked such widespread concern the president of the United States wrote him a get-well card. The array of singular trademarks: the single glove, the fedora, the red leather jacket, the black pants and white socks; the kicks, spins, and toe-raises; the moonwalk; the choreographed dances; the sculpted face, the aviator sunglasses, and Jheri curl. In the early eighties, everywhere one looked, Jackson's presence seemed to be found in commercials, videos, magazines, posters, T-shirts, or even replica dolls.

The world had simply never witnessed someone like Michael Jackson.

Jackson's fascinating, enigmatic persona only added to his appeal. For fans, he seemed to carry an aura about him wherever he went, as if walking straight out of one of his music videos, fully-costumed and in character. The effect was startling to those that saw him in person, often inciting pandemonium bordering on hysteria. It was Beatlemania, only more concentrated, as Jackson was one person, not four, and rarely seen in public.

To the public and media alike, the singer was endlessly intriguing. He was the shy, childlike recluse who turned his Encino home into a miniature Disneyland; he was the mysterious young man who electrified audiences yet barely spoke above a whisper when accepting awards. He was the sexually ambiguous Jehovah's Witness, whose moral purity was in constant tension with his passionate, pulsating dancing.

Perhaps one of the greatest of Jackson's cultural achievements, however, was in breaking down still-pervasive racial barriers. By the early eighties, black artists had more opportunities than ever before, thanks to the efforts of pioneers such as Chuck Berry, Little Richard, Ray Charles, Aretha Franklin, Sammy Davis Jr., James Brown,

Jackson is mobbed outside Madame Tussauds in London. By 1984, Jackson-mania was at its height.

Jackie Wilson, Stevie Wonder, and Marvin Gaye, among others. However, when *Thriller* was released in 1982, numerous walls still existed. Black artists were often pigeonholed and denied the full recognition and audience of their white contemporaries. This "cultural apartheid" was sometimes subtle and sometimes not so subtle. One could perhaps explain away something arbitrary like a denied magazine cover or Grammy Award. Yet it was more difficult to rationalize leaving the number one song in the country off "mainstream" radio because it was "R&B" (often used as a euphemism for black music). Even more of a stretch was the justification for refusing to play videos by black artists on a station called Music Television (MTV) because it wasn't "rock" (often used as a euphemism for white music).

Michael Jackson and Quincy Jones keenly understood these political realities. After *Off the Wall* became one of the most critically acclaimed and best-selling albums in years (including the first solo album ever to produce four Top Ten hits), it was denied a Grammy nomination and *Rolling Stone* cover.

Jackson's philosophy for overcoming racism was simple: he would make everything he did so good it simply couldn't be denied. "When *Thriller* came along, it really changed everything," observed Island Def Jam Chairman L. A. Reid. "Because all of a sudden music—for the first time ever—music didn't have a color. He was too good to be denied. He was too good to be put into any box and it didn't have a color. So whether it was rock, or whether it was pop, or whether it was R&B, whatever it was, Michael defied categorization with that album. And as a result of that he really broke the barrier."

Jackson would also refuse to be boxed in with labels. He despised the label "R&B" because he felt it limited him. "I don't categorize music," he told *Vibe Magazine*. "Music is music. They changed the word R&B [from] rock 'n' roll. It's always been [the same]."

Indeed, if *Off the Wall* hadn't sent the message, *Thriller* broke out the megaphone. How could white radio stations deny a duet featuring beloved former Beatle Paul McCartney and budding superstar Michael Jackson? While "The Girl Is Mine" certainly wasn't the best song on the album, it did challenge racial norms by featuring a black man and a white man bantering over the same woman on mainstream radio. It clearly couldn't be labeled R&B.

"Beat It" pushed the conundrum even further. "The sound of 'Beat It' was simply outrageous, for both R&B and rock listeners," writes *Rolling Stone*. The music was undeniably great, it was a rock song (albeit a new kind of rock), and it featured the most famous guitarist in the world, Eddie Van Halen. Long before Run DMC and Aerosmith brought down walls on "Walk This Way," Michael Jackson helped demolish the longstanding segregation between black and white music with "Beat It." It wasn't that Jackson was pandering to a white audience either; he was bending and reinventing genres to fit his unique aesthetic vision. "Today we do things called mash-ups, right?" observes L. A. Reid. "Take Linkin Park and Jay-Z and put it together, and it's certainly unique, but it's not unusual. At that time, Eddie Van Halen was at the top of his game and fit right in with 'Beat It.' It didn't feel like a guitar solo over some R&B track. It was very organic. The idea of it was really unusual, but the results weren't strained at all."

Crossover songs like these opened the door for more exotic tracks like the African-rooted "Wanna Be Startin' Somethin'" and the dark rhythm and blues of "Billie Jean." Before Michael Jackson, the fruits of black innovation were often reaped by white artists. However, Jackson's music and style were so dynamic and singular they simply couldn't be appropriated in any other form. No one could do what he did better, and the world was finally ready to fully embrace an artist of color.

Perhaps Michael Jackson's most significant racial trailblazing came with music videos. "MTV was arguably the best example of cultural apartheid in the United States [in 1982]," observes cultural critic Mark Anthony Neal. While the color barrier was not an official company policy, it was understood that only playing "rock" for all intents and purposes meant only playing white artists (the *Washington Post* called it "the subtle apartheid of pop"). "If you would have come out with a station called RMTV (rock music television), then you could make [the claim that it wasn't about race, but genre]," reasoned Ed Lover, former co-host of the groundbreaking *Yo! MTV Raps*. "But if you're saying music [MTV stands for Music Television], music is

Jackson, pictured here on his Victory Tour in 1984, shattered all barriers—racial and otherwise—with *Thriller*.

music. If you're going to show music videos, show all music videos." Disco, R&B, funk, rap, and soul—all predominantly African American genres—were consistently banned from the two-year-old cable station. Rick James was furious when MTV refused to play the video for his #1 hit, "Super Freak," in 1981. In 1983, David Bowie called MTV out on the air for its racist policy of exclusion.

As with magazine covers, Grammys, and radio, Michael Jackson's plan for hurdling the barrier was simply to make something so good MTV couldn't resist. When he first saw the channel and fledgling art form he was fascinated, but felt it wasn't near its potential. "At the time," he later wrote, "I would look at what people were doing with video, and I couldn't understand why so much of it seemed primitive and weak. I saw kids watching and accepting boring videos because they had no alternatives." Indeed, most music videos at the time were simply presented as promos or commercials. They usually either featured some kind of montage of images or a live performance. Jackson envisioned something different: he wanted to tell a story, to really entertain his audience, to treat the medium as a "short film" rather than a commercial.

Jackson's first opportunity to realize this vision came with *Billie Jean*. With a then-exorbitant $75,000 budget from CBS, Jackson and director Steve Baron created a short masterpiece. There were the dance moves, of course: the toe raises, spins, and gyrations. However, it was the overall mood of the cinematography and the mystery of the narrative that really complemented the inherent intrigue of the song. In the video, we see a pensive Jackson sauntering through a postmodern wasteland and eerily empty urban streets. Everywhere he goes he is stalked by an overeager paparazzo as the concrete tiles beneath him light up. In fact, everything he touches is illuminated (including a homeless man whose ragged clothes are transformed into a white tuxedo). The entire video plays out with the strangeness of a dream in which each detail can be alternately absurd and profound. In the end, as Jackson's character climbs hotel stairs and gets into bed with a woman (presumably Billie Jean), the paparazzo snaps a picture, but Jackson disappears underneath the sheets. The stalker

The music video for *Billie Jean* officially ended apartheid on MTV and began Jackson's reign as the defining visual artist of the era.

is left with nothing but his obsession while the audience is left to interpret its meaning.

MTV at first refused to play the video, citing its policy of only playing rock music. However, CBS Chairman Walter Yetnikoff, who had just shelled out huge money for the video, in addition to his interest in promoting *Thriller*, would not accept the denial of his biggest artist. "I said to MTV, 'I'm pulling everything we have off the air, all our product," Yetnikoff recalled. "'I'm not going to give you any more videos. And I'm going to go public and fucking tell them about the fact you don't want to play music by a black guy.'" MTV caved and soon put *Billie Jean* into heavy rotation due to audience demand. "Certain executives from MTV will deny it now," says Jackson's longtime attorney John Branca, "but it was absolutely the case that Walter forced that to happen." With that decision, the wall came tumbling down.

"He was MTV's Jackie Robinson," writes cultural critic Touré. Indeed, Jackson not only opened the door for himself, but also for a whole generation of black artists.

After the success of the *Billie Jean* video, Jackson upped the ante with *Beat It*. For this song, he had a specific concept in mind. He wanted its anti-violence message to be interpreted literally, but he didn't want it to be soft or didactic. To carry out his vision he hired talented commercial director Bob Giraldi and brilliant choreographer Michael Peters (whose background was in ballet and modern dance). He also insisted on filming the video on the streets of Los Angeles rather than a studio. When CBS refused to pay for the budget, Jackson fronted the money himself.

The result was the most revolutionary and influential music video MTV had ever aired to that point. Inspired partially by the Broadway musical *West Side Story*, *Beat It* displayed both grace and grit. Its group choreography with Jackson leading in his electric red jacket became the blueprint for hundreds of music videos to come. "His videos made a sensation in tandem with the rise of video as an art form," observes Quincy Jones. "He helped define the music video in terms of style, dance ensembles, and overall performances."

Shot on the streets of Los Angeles's infamous Skid Row and featuring more than eighty gang members, *Beat It* was approached with a level of realism and ambition that made it completely different than other music videos of the era. The finished product was original and edgy, innovative and exciting. MTV played the video even more than *Billie Jean* as ratings continued to soar. The short film would go on to win numerous awards and honors, including the Best Music Video of All Time by *Rolling Stone* readers and critics. It also put the final nail in the coffin of MTV's reluctance to play black artists. Michael Jackson had proved definitively that music had no boundary or color.

And then came the video for "Thriller." From the beginning it was treated more like a full-length film, with an unprecedented budget of $500,000 (a number that would ultimately balloon to closer to a million). Jackson lured horror-comedy director John Landis (best known then for *An American Werewolf in London*) to direct the video. At the time, Landis didn't know much about Michael Jackson but decided the project sounded intriguing enough to get onboard. Once work began, however, he soon realized he was part of an enormous phenomenon. "It was amazing working with Michael at the time," Landis recalls, "because it was at the height—it was like working with The Beatles at the height of Beatlemania or something, it was extraordinary being with him, because he was just ridiculously famous. It was like being with Jesus, I used to say, because people used to see him and go into hysterics."

Academy-Award-winning makeup artist Rick Baker was brought in for the elaborate prosthetic transformation of Jackson and the supporting cast into zombies, werewolves, and monsters. Finally, Michael Peters (who had also participated in *Beat It*) worked with Jackson on the choreography.

Jackson was thrilled to do film again. It had been nearly five years since his role in *The Wiz*. Similar to that film, *Thriller* allowed him to hide behind a mask, to metamorphose via makeup and costume and become absorbed in different characters. "I love it so much," he said in a 1983 interview. "It's escape. It's fun. It's just neat to become another thing, another person. Especially when you really believe it and its not like you're acting." Jackson was asked if that wasn't a bit frightening to believe it totally. "No, that's what I love about it," he replied. "I just like to really forget.... I just like jumping in other people's lives and exploring."

In the narrative of *Thriller*, Jackson plays several characters, beginning with a classic 1950s teenager on a date with his girlfriend (played by model Ola Ray). His true identity, however, is in constant flux.

> "I'm not like other guys," Jackson confesses to his date in the beginning.
>
> "Of course not," she responds. "That's why I love you."
>
> "No, I mean I'm different," he reasserts.

The telling exchange, of course, is loaded with deeper implications for audiences who are forced to confront Jackson's "difference," his abnormality. What makes him "not like other guys"? In the film, Jackson begins to transform into a werewolf. He grimaces with pain and begins to convulse as the evolution takes place. Suddenly, right before the previously infatuated girl's eyes, he is a monster. He looks up at her with diabolical eyes and she screams and runs.

Throughout the rest of the video, Jackson's character changes back and forth from protective,

A rare photo of Jackson standing in the graveyard on the set of *Thriller*.

playful boyfriend to hideous, frightening freak. Every time danger is imminent, every time the girl (and audience) seems most sure about his identity, it shifts again. Just as the werewolf Jackson pounces on her, they are suddenly watching the scene in a theater. "It's only a movie," he tells her.

As the couple leaves the theater, they begin their famous walk down a deserted street. Jackson, attired in vintage red-leather jacket and red pants, sings the opening lyrics as he flirtatiously circles his captivated date. Before long the couple reaches an old graveyard and the music fades and becomes more ominous. Ghouls and zombies are seen coming out of the mist and rising from the graves. Jackson and his date hold each other tight as the monsters press in from every side. Jackson's date turns to him for protection, but he's not there anymore. He has transformed again—he is one of the zombies.

The choreographed dancing that follows is the Michael Jackson that put the world under his spell. It is one of those collective pop-culture moments so many people remember seeing and experiencing for the first time. Michael Jackson at his absolute height, flanked by zombies, stomping, shaking, spinning, singing, "This is Thriller!"

In the final scene, the girl flees into a deserted mansion, where she hides in a room. The zombies begin to break in from the walls, the doors, the floors. Just as they are about to close in on her, however, the nightmare ends. We are back in the safe confines of a living room. "What's the problem?" Jackson says innocently. "Come on, I'll take you home." As he leads her out, he turns one more time to reveal yellow eyes and a nefarious smile.

The *Thriller* video worked on a number of levels. On the surface, it was riveting entertainment. The fourteen-minute short film had it all: humor, suspense, excitement, and of course, brilliant dancing. Yet lurking beneath the glitz, camp, and Hollywood flair, the video cleverly delves deeper, raising questions about our fascination with "horror" as well as our desire for cathartic (and often formulaic) resolution. As cultural critic Kobena Mercer recognizes, the video is essentially an extended parody of the horror genre itself, a self-conscious film within a film that teases many of its tropes while exploring issues of identity, abnormality, and the uneasy juxtaposition of reality and fantasy. Ultimately, the story—and Jackson's "true" identity—remains unresolved, suspended in tension. Who is he? The innocent fifties-revived mythical boyfriend, the terror-inducing werewolf, the eighties-cool boy next door, the zombie, the pop star? All of these at once? What can be considered "real" in a horror film (or any film)? What is artifice? What is projected, imagined, or constructed by the audience? In other words, what does it tell us about ourselves?

The response to *Thriller* was overwhelming. It premiered at the AVCO Theatre in Los Angeles in November 1983, where it sold out every night for two weeks. "I've been to the Oscars and I've been to the BAFTAs," said director John Landis, "I've been to the Emmys, I've been to the Golden Globes, and I've never been anywhere like this première. It was incredible. There was everyone from Diana Ross and Warren Beatty to Prince. It was nuts. [We] got a standing ovation and all that stuff and they're shouting, 'Encore, encore.' ... Then Eddie Murphy got up and shouted, 'Show the goddamn thing again!' So they sat and they watched *Thriller* again. Why not? It was just amazing, it was just amazing."

Soon after the premier, the video went to Showtime, MTV, and other stations, at which it was played repeatedly to captivated audiences. Watching *Thriller* was a cultural event for eighties youth. "If you were young then," writes Mike Celizic, "the *Thriller* video and Jackson's music became part of your DNA. But even if you were older, you knew when you turned on MTV and saw Jackson's breathtaking performance that you were seeing something that had never been seen before." Indeed, no other music video before or since has generated as much anticipation and excitement. Millions of people vividly remember sitting down with friends or family and watching it for the first time. After they'd seen it once, they wanted to see it again. "For the first time in the

Jackson, surrounded by zombies and ghouls. A devout Jehovah's Witness at the time, Jackson was almost pressured into throwing the horror-themed music video away before his attorney, John Branca, convinced him to add a disclaimer at the beginning.

history of MTV, we spotted big time rating spikes," says MTV's former director of programming Les Garland. "We were averaging back in those days like a twenty-four-hour rating of 1.2, but every time we would play *Thriller*, we'd jump up to an 8 or 10. We learned a lot about programming."

To offset the huge costs of making the short film, Jackson's lawyer John Branca worked out a $1.2 million dollar deal with Showtime for a "making of" documentary—"the first making of documentary of its kind." *The Making of Thriller* VHS was subsequently released by Vestron Video, selling an astounding 500,000 copies in its first month. *The Making of Thriller* became the best-selling VHS—music or movie—of all time.

Ironically, all of this might have never happened had Jackson's attorney, John Branca, done what Jackson asked him to and "destroy the tapes of the video." Jackson was still a devout Jehovah's Witness at the time and came under the condemnation of church elders for the content of *Thriller*. Jackson was so distraught and scared he felt his only choice was to do as the Witnesses said and burn it before it was released. "When they chastised me, it really hurt me. It almost destroyed it," Jackson later said. Fortunately, Branca held onto the tapes and convinced Jackson that a "disclaimer" at the beginning of the video saying that he "in no way endorses a belief in the occult" would suffice. Jackson relented and the rest is history.

The fourteen-minute video is now almost universally recognized as the most successful, influential, and culturally significant music video of all time. MTV, VH1, and *TV Guide*, among numerous other publications and polls, have recognized it as the best music video ever made. In 2006, *The Guinness World Records* listed *Thriller* as the most successful music video in history, with sales of more than nine million units.

As significant as Michael Jackson's videos were, however, his performance at the "Motown 25 Anniversary Special" perhaps outdid them all. There were only two comparable "pop culture" precedents: Elvis Presley on the *Ed Sullivan Show* in 1956 and the Beatles on the same show in 1964. Like those era-defining moments, there was a build-up, a collective anticipation to what was about to happen. *Thriller* remained #1 on the charts, where it had already reigned for several weeks. "Beat It" and "Billie Jean" were two of the hottest songs in the country. Their music videos dominated MTV. Jackson was singing duets with Paul McCartney and narrating a soundtrack for Steven Spielberg. He was on the cover of *Rolling Stone*. He was being called the "new Sinatra" and as "exciting as Elvis."

Yet for many who didn't get cable or watch MTV, it was the first time they had seen Michael Jackson on television as an adult. "Motown 25" was his coming-out party, the visual revelation of his metamorphosis. "[It] was the unveiling of a marvelous, mature Jackson," writes Stephen Thomas Erlewine, "a musician whose growth seemed sudden, swift, staggering."

Indeed, with nearly fifty million viewers, it was the largest audience ever to view a musical special. There were, of course, other incredible Motown legends on the bill: Stevie Wonder, Marvin Gaye, Smokey Robinson. However, on this night, they were all warm-up acts surrounding the main event. For a show primarily dedicated to nostalgia, the country was anxious to see the future.

Jackson mesmerizes with his "Billie Jean" routine at the "Motown 25 Anniversary Special" in 1983. It is widely considered his best live performance and one of the most significant moments in popular music history.

The stage, then, was set. People tuning in that night—May 16, 1983 (it was taped two months earlier)—would see a "new" Michael Jackson. "You know, I have to say, those were the good old days," he reminisces in a soft, feminine voice. After performing a medley of Jackson 5 hits with his brothers, he is alone, pacing the stage.

Visually, he is striking: the sequined black jacket that shimmers with every movement, the sculpted face, ethereal and exquisite, the single white glove with twelve-hundred hand-sewn rhinestones, the haunting doe eyes. There is a magical aura about him, an otherworldly quality that transfixes and intrigues.

"You know, those were good songs—I like those songs a lot," he continues. "Those were magic moments with my brothers, including Jermaine." He pauses and puts the microphone on the stand. "But especially I like . . ."—the live audience is now groaning and screaming in anticipation—"the new songs."

With that, he picks up a black fedora, strikes a Bob Fosse-like pose, and pulses with the bass line of all bass lines. From there, he is constant movement, expression, energy. "It was like watching quicksilver in motion," filmmaker Martin Scorsese later said. "Every step he took was absolutely precise and fluid at the same time."

Indeed, while the performance is often remembered as a cultural event, or the moment Jackson first showed off the "moonwalk," it is its total artistic quality that sets it apart. Stylistically, it draws from a range of influences: Fred Astaire, Sammy Davis Jr., Bob Fosse, and Charlie Chaplin, among others. In addition, there are elements of

minstrelsy, miming, jazz, and street dancing in his routine. According to Quincy Jones, Jackson would also "watch tapes of gazelles and cheetahs and panthers to imitate the natural grace of their movements." He practiced these movements for hours in his home studio, not simply imitating or "choreographing," but letting the music "speak to him" and dictate its own creation. "Once the music plays, it creates me," he explained. "The instruments move me, through me, they control me. Sometimes I'm uncontrollable and it just happens."

Yet as Jackson kicks, mimes, locks, and gyrates to "Billie Jean," the live audience seems stunned. "I'm pretty blasé about crowd response," writes Christopher Smith, "but this was different. It wasn't a roar; more the sound of simultaneous shrieks from all over the auditorium, like everyone being scared at once. A couple rows in front of me, two women in my sight line were violently hugging, almost tackling each other, while riveted on the stage, as though they were unconsciously trying to hold onto the moment more than each other."

As Jackson performs the song, he almost seems unaware of the audience. He is completely absorbed in the rhythm and story of the track, interpreting its mystery, passion, tension, and pain. While previous landmark performances like Presley's "Hound Dog" or the Beatles' "She Loves You" were joyful expressions of youthful exuberance, "Billie Jean" is darker. Its narrative is about entrapment, deception, distrust, and fear. At twenty-five, Jackson has obviously experienced

Jackson, pictured here in concert in 1984, broke every record imaginable with *Thriller*. While the cultural phenomenon was undeniable, the success began with the music.

more than most his age. These are certainly not typical pop sentiments. While Jackson conveys complex emotions in his performance, however, there is also a sense of wonder and liberation to his movement. The moonwalk is an expression that not only seems to defy the laws of physics, but all repressive restraints. It is, as philosopher Alain Badiou once wrote of dancing, a "body that forgets its fetters, its weight... free[ing it] from all social mimicry, from all gravity and conformity."

As the music to "Billie Jean" begins to fade, Jackson seems reluctant to let the performance end, still moving to the rhythm of the song. Finally, he looks up, as if waking from a dream. The crowd erupts in applause. He doesn't smile but bows and raises his arm in acknowledgment.

In the days following the show, Jackson gradually began to realize the impact his performance made. Not only were ratings for the show through the roof, copies of *Thriller* were once again flying out of stores at a pace of one million copies per week.

Overnight, Jackson also reached millions of new admirers—including dance legends Gene Kelly and Fred Astaire. Astaire was so amazed by Jackson's performance he called to praise him the very next day. "You're a hell of a mover," he said. "Man, you really put them on their asses last night.... You're an angry dancer. I'm the same way."

Jackson, who had felt frustrated with a couple "mistakes" in the performance, finally felt validated. "It was the greatest compliment I had ever received in my life," he confessed.

All of these moments—breaking the MTV apartheid, the *Thriller* video, the "Motown 25" performance—are a part of *Thriller*'s enormous legacy. Beyond the performances, however, beyond the videos, awards, records, and cultural significance, beyond the "phenomenon" of *Thriller*, there is still the music itself, which is sometimes lost. "There are great rewards to be had in diving into these songs as, well, songs," writes music critic Nelson George. "Forget the red jacket and sparkling glove and moonwalking. Listen, instead, to the deep foghorn that opens 'Beat It,' listen to the intricate keyboards (arranged by Michael) and strings (arranged by Jerry Hey) that add danger to 'Billie Jean.' Or just focus on the playful tone Michael uses to sing the James Ingram–Quincy Jones penned 'P.Y.T.'"

Indeed, while some critics have written *Thriller* off as a "commercial album," Jackson's originality, creativity, and talent are imprinted on every track. "*Thriller*'s parts added up to the most improbable kind of art," writes music critic Jody Rosen "[It was] a work of personal revelation that was also a mass-market masterpiece. It's an achievement that will likely never be topped."

In 2009 alone, *Thriller* sold more than a million copies, repropelling it over the *Eagles Greatest Hits* as the best-selling album ever in the United States. Globally, it more than triples the sales of any other album. In 2008, *Thriller* was inducted into the Grammy Hall of Fame. The same year it was also selected as one of twenty-five albums preserved by the Library of Congress for being "culturally significant." For nearly thirty years, it has served as the holy grail of pop, perpetually dazzling and beckoning new generations of listeners and artists. With just nine songs, three videos, and one magical performance, it changed popular music forever.

THE SONGS

1. WANNA BE STARTIN' SOMETHIN'

(Written and composed by Michael Jackson; produced by Michael Jackson and Quincy Jones; rhythm arranged by Michael Jackson and Quincy Jones. Lead and background vocals: Michael Jackson. Horns arranged by Jerry Hey and Michael Jackson. Trumpet and flugelhorn: Gary Grant and Jerry Hey. Saxophone, flute: Larry Williams. Trombone: William Reichenbach. Backing vocals: James Ingram, Becky Lopez, Bunny Hull, Julia Waters, Maxine Waters, and Oren Waters. Bass: Louis Johnson. Electric piano and synthesizer: Greg Phillinganes. Guitar: David Williams. Percussion: Paulinho Da Costa. Synthesizer: Bill Wolfer and Michael Boddicker)

It doesn't take long for listeners to hear just about everything that makes *Thriller* so exhilarating and compelling. A complex, frenetic, unabashedly eccentric six-minute workout, "Wanna Be Startin' Somethin'" is an appropriate beginning to the world's best-selling album. Like Jackson himself, the song eludes easy characterization: it is by turns a timeless dance hit, a psychological confession, an unflinching social critique, "a subtle black-pride anthem," and an ecstatic spiritual breakthrough. The result is what music critic Mark Anthony Neal has argued is the "purest form of genius on *Thriller*." While that distinction is debatable for a record that contains "Billie Jean," there can be no doubt that it deserves consideration as one of Jackson's finest artistic achievements.

In 1982, the unusual track certainly made for a bold—and, to many, surprising—opening statement. "Hot as Jackson was after the quantum leap that 1979's *Off the Wall* brought his solo career, few expected him to match, much less dramatically surpass, those heights so quickly," wrote music critic Randy Lewis. "But *Thriller*'s lead-off track immediately established the new album as another giant step forward. It connected to *Off the Wall* with an irresistible Afro-Caribbean funk dance-floor pulse and peppery horn accents akin to 'Don't Stop 'Til You Get Enough,' then rocketed to new heights with even more sinewy bass and guitar lines propelling his impossibly nimble vocals. If *Off the Wall* demonstrated that Jackson was a kid no more, 'Startin' Somethin'" signaled the full maturity of his musical acumen. All the more impressive for a song built on just two chords."

"Startin' Somethin'" was originally composed during the *Off the Wall* sessions, but Jackson intelligently saved it for *Thriller*, in which both sonically and lyrically it better fit. The song begins with three synth-drumbeats, followed by an array of layered hooks, rhythms, and cross-rhythms. Once the song takes off, sounds seems to ricochet off each other like a pinball machine, with keyboards, snare drums, and horns complementing Jackson's layered vocals. "It's a giddy and glamorous sound," wrote *Newsweek* in 1983. "Hands clap, horns blare. A carnival of percussion erupts. Electric guitars chatter like a corps of African talking drums. A voice gasps and then chants a chorus. So go the first few seconds of 'Wanna Be Startin' Somethin', six minutes of musical frenzy." Yet the song's arrangement is anything but random sound. It is an expertly layered rhythmic symphony that essentially bridges African and Western musical styles.

Matching the diverse array of sounds are the idiosyncratic lyrics, which Jackson twists and contorts like a vocal acrobat. In suggestive fragments, he sings of the madness and hysteria of modern life: of ignored illness, mental breakdowns, unplanned pregnancies causing unfed babies, tongues like razors, and being eaten off of like a buffet or a vegetable. Needless to say, the song was far removed from the worn clichés of a typical pop song. While it contained a similar energy and abandon to "Don't Stop 'Til You Get Enough," its provocative material was strikingly new—and challenging—territory for Jackson.

"It's too high to get over/Too low to get under," Jackson laments in the chorus. "You're stuck in the middle/And the pain is thunder." The lyrics suggest Jackson's growing feelings of unease and anxiety with the world, his sense of isolation and claustrophobia—and his difficulty in finding a way out.

At approximately the 4:30 mark in the song, however, Jackson begins to break through this imprisonment, achieving at least temporary freedom through the communal energy of the music. "Jackson seemingly summons the gods," observes Mark Anthony Neal, "delivering a sermonic spectacle worthy of the greatest black preachers ('Lift your head up high and scream out to the world/I know I am someone and let the truth unfurl/No one can hurt you now, because you know what's true/Yes I believe in me, So you believe in you'). The song soars when Jackson yelps (literally, out of breath) 'help me sing it' at which point the legendary backing group the Waters (Julia, Maxine and Oren) chime in rhythmically 'ma ma se, ma ma sa, ma ma coo sa.'... Jackson ad-libs behind the Waters when suddenly the bottom drops out, and listeners are left with Jackson (damn near orgasmic), the still frenzied Waters, the punctuating lines of the horn section (including veteran studio trumpeter Jerry Hey), and a shout-clap rhythm worthy of the Ring Shout tradition."

The culminating Swahili chant, borrowed from Cameroonian saxophonist Manu Dibango, gave the song a transcontinental flavor, while also demonstrating pride in Jackson's (and music's) African roots. "These are the ... moments that most casual listeners of Jackson's music continue to miss," continues Neal. "For those who read Jackson's ever devolving facial features as some evidence of racial self-hatred, 'Wanna Be Startin' Somethin'" is Jackson's unspoken retort, as he summoned the Orishas in a way never before experienced in American pop music."

One of seven Top Ten singles on *Thriller*, "Wanna Be Startin' Somethin'" peaked at #5 on the *Billboard* Hot 100 in 1983. Jackson performed the song on every tour—often as the lead—after the Victory Tour in 1984. It remains one of his most popular and critically acclaimed songs.

2. BABY BE MINE

(Written and composed by Rod Temperton; produced by Quincy Jones. Synthesizer programming by Anthony Marinelli, Brian Banks, and Steve Porcaro. Horns arranged by Jerry Hey. Lead and background vocals: Michael Jackson. Keyboards: Greg Phillinganes. Synthesizer: Greg Phillinganes, David Paich, and Michael Boddicker. Drums: Ndugu Chancler. Guitar: David Williams. Saxophone and flute: Larry Williams. Trombone: William Reichenback. Trumpet and flugelhorn: Gary Grant and Jerry Hey)

The first of three songs contributed by Rod Temperton, "Baby Be Mine" slows the pace after the high-energy opener, easing the listener into its smooth soulfulness. Reminiscent of *Off the Wall*'s "Rock With You," this understated (and often overlooked) funk-soul groove is a testament to the consistent quality of the album, even on the so-called "filler." "Imagine if this weren't the better of the two non-singles from a monster album but a one-shot single by an unknown artist," writes music critic Michelangelo Matos. "The sweet midtempo glide of 'Baby Be Mine' would have likely bubbled into the R&B Top 20 and gotten lots of roller-skate play, been included on recent mix CDs by cutting-edge European DJs and been remade as a slow jam at least three times. We'd have wondered at the bionic singer, the effervescent synth arrangements, the popping groove. In short, it would sound like the hidden classic it remains, even in plain sight."

One of the earliest tracks recorded for the album, "Baby Be Mine" contains a soft disco flavor: its bouncy synth-driven bass is accompanied by David Williams's subtle guitar licks and Jerry Hey's expansive horns. It also has some jazz influence. Quincy Jones described the melody as similar to a "John Coltrane-style progressive jazz line."

Thematically, in contrast to the manic anxiety and ecstasy of "Startin' Somethin'," "Baby Be Mine" is an airy love song, as Jackson gently offers his promises to a girl. "I don't need no dreams when I'm by your side," he sings. "Every moment takes me to paradise." The frustrations and fears of life are temporarily melted by the warmth of love, as Jackson confides, "You're everything this world could be/The reason that I live."

In the broader context of the album, lighter material like this stands in stark relief from its darker tracks. Interestingly, most of the songs Jackson wrote fall in the latter category. Yet the contrast works to great effect on *Thriller*. The side-by-side perspectives illuminate Jackson's (and the listener's) "contrary states," allowing dreams and fantasies to occupy the same space as nightmares and fears. *All Music Guide*'s Stephen Thomas Erlewine calls the track "positively incandescent, perhaps because it isn't as familiar, but more likely because it is a brilliantly crafted piece."

3. THE GIRL IS MINE

(Written and composed by Michael Jackson; produced by Quincy Jones; vocals arranged by Michael Jackson and Quincy Jones. Rhythm arranged by David Paich and Quincy Jones. Synthesizer programmed by Steve Porcaro. Synthesizer arranged by David Foster. Strings arranged by Jerry Hey. Vocals: Michael Jackson and Paul McCartney. Concert master: Gerald Vinci. Bass: Louis Johnson. Drums: Jeff Porcaro. Electric piano: Greg Phillinganes. Piano: David Paich. Guitar: Dean Parks and Steve Lukather)

"The Girl Is Mine" is generally considered the weakest track on the album. With its mawkish lyrics and pedestrian production (which actually sounds much better on Jackson's demos), it simply doesn't have the verve or depth of many of the other tracks. Of course, its relative shortcomings are magnified because: (a) it happens to find itself on the best-selling album of all time, and (b) it features two of the most significant talents in the history of modern music.

Yet there is a playful charm to "The Girl Is Mine": the breezy melody, the "doggone" chorus, the memorable one-liners ("Paul, I think I told you, I'm a lover not a fighter"). Decades later its corniness seems to contain a wink and a smile, while its simple fun invokes an innocent nostalgia. It also has a simple but beautiful rhythm and melody. As Paul McCartney explained in 1982: "The song I've just done with Michael Jackson, you could say that it's shallow. There was even a word—'doggone'—that I wouldn't have put in it. When I checked it out with Michael, he explained that he wasn't going for depth—he was going for rhythm, he was going for feel. And he was right. It's not the lyrics that are important on this particular song—it's much more the noise, the performance, my voice, his voice." Indeed, years later, critics continue to praise Jackson's effortless vocal. "The lift Jackson gives the word 'endlessly' midsong can still make a listener feel like she's swimming in a sea of Love's Baby Soft," writes music critic Ann Powers.

But "The Girl Is Mine" is perhaps most significant for what it represents. In 1982, with the tragic passing of John Lennon two years previously, Paul McCartney was arguably popular music's most renowned singer. Collaborating with music's most promising young star, Michael Jackson, sent a message about where music was heading. Eventually the pair recorded three songs together, two of which (the #1 hit "Say Say Say" and "The Man") were included on Paul McCartney's 1983 album *Pipes of Peace*. At the time, Jackson considered the experience one of the highlights of his young recording career. In this way, "The Girl Is Mine" was a sort of symbolic passing of the torch from the legendary Beatles singer to the soon-to-be King of Pop.

The song was also significant because of race. Musical segregation on the radio was still the norm in the early eighties with rock and R&B occupying, for the most part, separate worlds. With "The Girl Is Mine"—a song featuring the most famous black and white artists in the world—many radio stations were finally forced to reconsider their obsolete categories for programming. That Jackson and McCartney are openly competing for the same girl made it even more taboo. Observed *Newsweek*'s Jim Miller in 1983: "[The Girl Is Mine] sounds very pretty and perfectly innocuous—until you begin to think about the lyrics. Have American radio stations ever before played a song about two men, one black and the other white, quarreling over the same woman?" It was a new concept indeed (one that is taken for granted today). But "The Girl Is Mine" helped pave the way for interracial love on the radio.

4. THRILLER

(Written and composed by Rod Temperton; produced by Quincy Jones. Synthesizer programmed by Anthony Marinelli. Horns arranged by Jerry Hey. Lead and background vocals by Michael Jackson. Effects: Bruce Swedien and Bruce Cannon. Rap: Vincent Price. Synthesizer: Brian Banks, Greg Phillinganes, and Rod Temperton. Guitar: David Williams. Saxophone and flute: Larry Williams. Trombone: William Reichenbach. Trumpet and flugelhorn: Gary Grant and Jerry Hey)

It is difficult to think of another song in popular music history that conjures its visual presentation as thoroughly as "Thriller." "If ever a video killed the radio star," writes Baz Dreisinger, "'Thriller' was it." Far from killing the music, however, *Thriller* brought it new life. Album sales tripled after its appearance on MTV. The video lured people to the music and the music lured people back to the video. They soon became inextricably intertwined. The common thread, of course, was Michael Jackson. Even today, when one hears the famous chorus, the instant mental image is of a young, radiant Jackson in electric red jacket and pants, flirtatiously circling Ola Ray, morphing into alter-egos, dancing with effortless grace and funk alongside zombies, while projecting an energy and magnetism that still pushes through the screen. The revolutionary fourteen-minute *Thriller* video essentially reinvented the medium. Music videos had been done before. But, not like this. *Thriller* was the *Citizen Kane* of short films.

Written for Jackson by Rod Temperton, "Thriller" was always meant to be "seen" as well as heard. It gave the album a dramatic entryway and theatrical narrative that could be as literal or figurative as the listener wanted. Some critics felt the horror theme was too campy and over-the-top. This, however, was Jackson's very intent. With its spectacular Gothic motifs, including doors opening, floors creaking, wolves howling, and the ghoulish rap of the legendary Vincent Price, "Thriller" was Old Hollywood revived. Yet as *Rolling Stone* notes, this "camp charm" makes it "easy to overlook the song's inherent, cheeky darkness. This is, after all, a song that begins with something evil lurking in the dark, [and] makes a brief stop at demon possession before ending with an army of zombies descending on their prey."

Sonically, the track offers it all: drama, funk, a brass-exploding signature riff that one-ups Prince's "1999," and one of the most famous choruses ever sung ("'Cause this is thriller!"). "'Thriller' is about as epic as a pop song gets," writes music critic Tyler Fisher. "The song draws from Tower of Power horn licks and Funkadelic pop sensibility. The huge brass statement that leads the song into its main groove simply states that 'Thriller' plans to go beyond the normal limits of a pop song."

For all its grandiosity, there are some less noticeable nuances to be appreciated as well. "On the intro," reveals recording engineer Bruce Swedien, "there's a little rhythm track that commences the music, and I purposely limited the bandwidth on it so that as you listen to it your ear adjusts to that spectral response. Then, all of a sudden, the real bass and kick drum come in and the effect is really startling."

In the verses, Jackson carefully builds the tension, stretching the vivid descriptions slowly over a cross current of synth lines and guitar licks, before bursting into the chorus. The lyrics begin to form a frighteningly grotesque scenario in which evil is constantly "lurking in the dark." The narrator feels trapped with "nowhere left to run" and has visions of the living dead "walking in their masquerade." Just as in the video, the narrator has a split identity: the other part of him takes on the persona of the "thriller," the "monster" that threatens to "terrorize y'alls neighborhood." "And whosoever shall be found," narrates Vincent Price, "Without the soul for getting down/Must stand and face the hounds of hell/And rot inside a corpse's shell."

For most listeners, however, as music critic J. Edward Keyes notes, the lyrics are surrounded by "such spectacular robo-funk—that simple six-note synth riff rolling over and over, unmistakable and unforgettable—that it's easy to miss the skeletons crouching in its shadows." The song perfectly encapsulates the paradoxical genius of the album: It is both a massively popular and entertaining spectacle as well as a humorously dark mirror that reflects society's fascinations and fears.

"Thriller" was the seventh and final single released from the album, peaking at #4 on the *Billboard* Hot 100 in 1984. Its landmark short film is widely considered the greatest music video of all time. In 2009, *Thriller* became the first music video ever to be inducted into the National Film Registry of the Library of Congress.

5. BEAT IT

(Written and composed by Michael Jackson; produced by Quincy Jones. Synthesizer programming by Steve Porcaro. Rhythm arrangement by Michael Jackson and Quincy Jones. Lead and background vocals by Michael Jackson. Guitar solo: Eddie Van Halen. Guitar: Paul Jackson Jr.. Electric bass: Steve Lukather. Drums: Jeff Porcaro. Drum case beater: Michael Jackson. Electric piano and synthesizer: Greg Phillinganes. Keyboards: Bill Wolfer. Synclavier: Tom Bahler)

"Beat It" made just about every song before it sound old-fashioned by comparison. It was the "Johnny B. Goode" of the eighties, breaking aesthetic and racial barriers as it signaled a new era of music. The sound was so fresh, vibrant, and ahead of the curve, many music critics at the time simply didn't know how to characterize it. It was a hard rock song that had people dancing in the clubs, an anti-macho plea that still managed to be tough and cool. Some called it "black rock," others called it "dance metal." *Time* described it as an "asphalt aria." The commonality among all descriptions was its fusion of seemingly disparate elements. It was the ultimate "crossover," bridging black and white, rock and R&B, pacifism and grit.

Listeners, however, didn't care what genre or label it fell under (or the race of its singer). From America to the Soviet Union, "Beat It" played on boom boxes and Walkmans, on dance floors and in gyms. It epitomized, for many, the "new sound" of music. Listeners in the early eighties described it as "electrifying" and "invigorating" as they "hip-hopped to it in clubs and break-danced to it in the streets," *Time* reported.

"Beat It" was the third of four compositions by Michael Jackson and the final song written for *Thriller*. Challenged to create something edgy and rock-driven by Quincy Jones, Jackson went to work on the song, determined to surprise. "I wanted to write the type of rock song that I would go out and buy," he recalled, "but also something totally different from the rock music I was hearing on Top Forty radio." Just weeks later, he came back with "Beat It." Jones and the rest of the team were blown away. "We knew he'd come up with the nitroglycerin," Jones said.

Indeed, from the opening gong (created on the Synclavier) to its strutting percussion to the world-famous guitar riff, "Beat It" explodes from the speakers with attitude. In its 1982 review, *Rolling Stone* called it a "this-ain't-no-disco AOR track. . . . Jackson's voice soars all over the melody, Eddie Van Halen checks in with a blistering guitar solo, you could build a convention center on the backbeat, and the result is one nifty dance song."

Nifty was a polite way of describing it; *revolutionary* is more apt. In terms of overcoming barriers (racial and otherwise), while "The Girl Is Mine" charmed with a bouquet of flowers, "Beat It" knocked the door down and demanded its due. (One can literally hear a knocking sound, in fact, before Eddie

Van Halen enters with his famous guitar solo.) Radio and MTV could no longer resist. The song soared to #1 on the *Billboard* Hot 100 while the video played nearly every hour on television.

Often lost in the song's exciting sound, however, is its countercultural message. In a time of escalating gang warfare and inflammatory Cold War rhetoric, "Beat It" was a plea for pacifism over violence. It defied the "macho" posturing of traditional rock, offering instead a warning against ego-inspired conflict. The alternative Jackson offers is to resist the vicious cycle of socially induced retribution, to "beat it," and thus, choose life over death.

To emphasize the serious intent of the song Jackson used real gang members from the Crips and Bloods for the music video. It subsequently became an easy target for criticism and parody, however, as some claimed Jackson's "solution" of dancing away gang violence was overly simplistic and unrealistic. Yet, this interpretation is too literal-minded. Jackson never saw his role as an artist as being "political" in the prescriptive, didactic sense. Rather, it was about demonstrating more generally the transformative role he felt music and dance could play in overcoming social problems. If his music could be appreciated by blacks and whites, Americans and Soviets, perhaps, he felt, that might have a more salutary effect on the world than the policies of Reagan.

"Beat It" made the Rock and Roll Hall of Fame's list of 500 Songs That Shaped Rock and Roll. It has been covered numerous times since its release, most notably by punk band Fall Out Boy (featuring John Mayer on guitar) and Fergie of the Black Eyed Peas.

6. BILLIE JEAN

(Written, arranged, and composed by Michael Jackson. Produced by Michael Jackson and Quincy Jones. Vocal, rhythm, and synthesizer arrangement by Michael Jackson. String arrangement by Jerry Hey. Strings conducted by Jeremy Lubbock. Synthesizer programming by Bill Wolfer. Engineered and mixed by Bruce Swedien. Lead and background vocals by Michael Jackson. Drums: Leon Ndugu Chancler. Bass guitar: Louis Johnson. Guitar: David Williams. Emulator: Michael Boddicker. Rhodes piano: Greg Phillinganes. Synthesizer: Greg Phillinganes, Greg Smith, and Bill Wolfer)

If one were to pick a single song that defines Michael Jackson as an artist, it would have to be "Billie Jean." With its instantly identifiable bass line and dark, mysterious narrative, it contains all the fascinating tensions and paradoxes of its creator. It is intriguing and disturbing, explicit and enigmatic, confession and concealment. Jackson's visual interpretations—first, in the form of its captivating music video, and second, via his legendary "Motown 25" performance—only add to its artistic aura.

As with other popular "classics," however, there is a tendency to praise its "greatness" without paying much attention to why or how it achieved this status. "But let it play," writes music critic Mark Fisher, "and you're soon bewitched by its drama, seduced into its sonic fictional space." Fisher goes on to argue that such a close listen will reveal "'Billie Jean' is not only one of the best singles ever recorded, it is one of the greatest art works of the twentieth century, a multileveled sound sculpture whose slinky, synthetic panther sheen still yields up previously unnoticed details and nuance nearly thirty years on."

Fisher isn't alone in this assessment. The BBC proclaimed the track the "greatest dance record of all time." In 2005, in a list compiled by *Blender* of the top 500 singles of our lifetime, "Billie Jean" ranked #1. *The Guardian* called it "one of the most revolutionary songs in the history of popular music."

"It's been said before," reaffirmed *Rolling Stone* in 2009, "but it's worth repeating: 'Billie Jean' is a masterpiece, and one that doesn't lose its strange, dark power, no matter how many times you hear it.... Sinuous, paranoid and omnipresent [it is] the single that made Jackson the biggest star since Elvis."

Jackson first conceived of the song in 1981 while driving on the Ventura freeway in Los Angeles. "I wanted to write a song with a great bass line," he recalled, "and a few days later, this bass line and this melody crept over me." According to Jackson, he was so consumed by constructing the song, he didn't even realize smoke was coming out of his car until a motorcyclist drove by and mouthed that his car was on fire. "Even while we were getting help and finding an alternate way to get where we were going," Jackson recalled, "I was silently composing additional material."

Jackson quickly put the song onto tape, vocally dictating all the instruments, chords and parts (which had become his standard practice), before recording a more fleshed out demo in his home studio at Hayvenhurst. The creation of "Billie Jean" is a perfect demonstration of how Jackson operated, not just as a singer, but also as a writer, arranger, and producer. Early demos of the song reveal a twenty-four-year-old with astounding musical instincts, creativity, and craftsmanship. One can hear Jackson making up lyrics as he goes along and experimenting with ad-libs, but all the parts were in place before it was even brought to Quincy Jones and Bruce Swedien.

When Jackson brought the song to Quincy Jones in 1982, he also demonstrated a newfound independence and confidence in his creative vision. When Jones pushed to cut the extended bass line intro and rename the song "Not My Lover" (so as not to be confused with tennis player, Billie Jean King), Jackson stuck to his guns. "The intro to 'Billie Jean' was so long you could shave during it," recalled Quincy Jones. "I said we had to get to the melody sooner, but Michael said that was what made him want to dance. And when Michael Jackson says something makes him want to dance, you don't argue, so he won."

From demo to final product, however, the song did go through a fascinating collaborative evolution. Jackson and his creative team were determined to create a track with "the most unique sonic personality" they had ever recorded. To this end, they went to elaborate lengths to achieve the polish and nuance that listeners now enjoy. Recording engineer Bruce Swedien had Jackson sing vocal overdubs through a five-foot-long cardboard tube; Quincy Jones brought in jazz saxophonist Tom Scott to play "a very unusual instrument, the lyricon, a wind-controlled analog synthesizer whose unique, trumpet-like lines are subtly woven through the track." The song's ominous strings were arranged by Jerry Hey, while bass guitarist Louis Johnson "ran through his part on every guitar he owned before Jackson settled on a Yamaha bass with an ideally thick and buzzing sound."

After receiving instruction from Quincy Jones and Jackson about the sound they wanted in the bass line, Swedien went to work trying to capture "drums with as tight, and powerful a drum sound as I could come up with." It wasn't as easy as it might be today, however. This was before the technology of samplers and loops. Ndugu Chancler, therefore, played his drums for the entire take rather than sampling a couple of bars. "Michael always knew how he wanted it to sound," recalls Chancler. "There was originally just a drum-machine track on it. I came in and cut a live-drum track over the overdub." Swedien then had a special plywood drum platform constructed with a kick drum mic zipped in to capture the fullness of the sound. Finally, using a twelve-channel mixing console, he recorded the rhythm section. "I recorded the bass, drums, and guitars on my analog 16-track," Swedien recalls, "with no noise reduction equipment in the way of that fantastic sound!"

Still, the song wasn't completely finished. "I had been mixing 'Billie Jean' for only two days," recalls Bruce Swedien. "I was up to mix number two and I thought it was killer! I called Michael, Quincy, and Rod into the control room and played [it] for them. They loved it! They were all dancing and carrying on like crazy. Then Michael slipped out of the control room, turned around and motioned for me to follow him. Then he whispered to me, 'Please, Bruce, it's perfect, but turn the bass up just a tiny bit, and do one more mix, please.' I said to him, 'OK, Smelly, no problem.'

"Then I went back into the control room to add this tiny bit of bass to my mix. Quincy pulled me over into the corner and said, 'Add a little garlic salt to the snare and the kick. Just a squirt!' So I went back into the control room and added a little garlic salt to the snare and the kick. Now I was up to mix #20 on 'Billie Jean.' Well, this went on for about a week. Soon I was up to mix #91! I played [it] for the boys and everybody smiled. But Quincy said, 'You know, just for the fun of it, can we listen to one of your earlier mixes?' My heart jumped because I knew that the earlier mixes were dynamite. We listened to mix #2 again and it was slammin'! Everyone was grooving and dancing. Mix #2 was the final decision and that is exactly what you hear on the record.... See if you can think of any other piece of music where you can hear the first three drum beats and know what the song is," Swedien has said. "That's what I call sonic personality."

The result of Jackson and his team's commitment and craftsmanship was a stunningly original tour de force that rewards close (and repeated) listens. "If you can manage to keep focused as the track crawls up your spine and down to your feet," writes Mark Fisher, "check the way that the first string stabs shadow the track like a stalker's footsteps, disappearing into the wind like mist and rumor. Feel the tension building in your teeth as the bridge hurtles toward the chorus, begging for a release ("the smell of sweet perfume/This happened much too soon") that you know will only end in regret, recrimination, and humiliation, but which you can't help but want anyway, desire so intense it threatens to fragment the psyche, or expose the way that the psyche is always-already split into antagonistic agencies: 'just remember to always think twice.'"

Fellow musicians are as complimentary as critics. "'Billie Jean' is hot on every level," says keyboardist Greg Phillinganes (who played Rhodes piano and synthesizer on the track). "It's hot rhythmically. It's hot sonically, because the instrumentation is so minimal, you can really hear everything. It's hot melodically. It's hot lyrically. It's hot vocally. It affects you physically, emotionally, even spiritually."

Upon its release, of course, "Billie Jean" became a huge hit (especially after the "Motown 25" performance). However, in many ways it was a strange song to dominate the pop charts. *Blender* describes it as "one of the most sonically eccentric, psychologically fraught, downright bizarre things ever to land on Top 40 radio." Indeed, "Billie Jean" is miles from the prototypical love songs that generally permeate the airwaves and dance clubs (in 1983, Lionel Richie's "All Night Long" and Patti Austin and James Ingram's "Come To Me" were representative of what one might hear next to Jackson's piece).

The song tells the story of a woman who stalks the narrator with paternity accusations. "Billie Jean is not my lover," he insists in the chorus, "She's just a girl who claims that I am the one/But the kid is not my son." Jackson has said that the song was inspired by overzealous "groupies," including several who did, in fact, claim he was the father of their children. One girl purportedly even threatened to kill herself and her unborn child if Jackson didn't marry her. For Jackson, then, part of the emotional energy of the song emanates from these very personal—and very disturbing—experiences.

Yet beyond its literal narrative and background, "Billie Jean" is a symbol for many things: She represents fear, distrust, and deception; she represents the seductions and trappings of fame; she represents "lies becoming the truth."

In both Jackson's vocal and dance interpretations, he juxtaposes pain and anger, passion and denial. The song is a sort of exorcism, a release of the demons that haunt him. In the end, there is no resolution; he remains trapped in a vulnerable state. "This happened much too soon," he sings. "She called me to her room." Does he respond? Does he enter the room? Is she telling the truth? How has she managed to consume his attention (and life)? All of these questions are left unanswered, hovering provocatively for the listener to untangle. "Twenty-five years later," writes Richard Cromelin, "*Thriller*'s central chamber has lost none of its fevered mystery. This is where the album's material plane gives way to a haunted interior.... Jackson finds a new voice here, a victim's voice that shudders in the shadows of this remarkable sonic space, lashing at his own naiveté and at the false accusers who were just starting to gather at his door."

Jackson's masterpiece remains one of the most popular dance songs in the world, in addition to being one of the most critically acclaimed.

7. HUMAN NATURE

(Written by John Bettis and Steve Porcaro; arranged by David Paich, Steve Lukather, and Steve Porcaro. Produced by Quincy Jones. Synthesizer programming by Steve Porcaro. Lead and background vocals by Michael Jackson. Synthesizer: David Paich. Drums: Jeff Porcaro. Guitar: Steve Lukather. Percussion: Paulinho Da Costa)

Michael Jackson once described "Human Nature" as "music with wings." The metaphor was apt. A gorgeous synth-ballad, "Human Nature" glides effortlessly over shimmering strings and sparkling scenery. A song about desire, youth, and yearning, it evokes a vibrant cityscape in which the narrator wanders in the twilight between reality and dream. Music critic David Stubbs describes the track as "a thing of unnatural beauty, with Jackson's vocal shiver arousing an electric frisson across the skin of the song and the sheen of the '80's production triggering [a] sort of ecstatic, self-perpetuating, hall of mirrors effect." In its 1982 review. the *New York Times* called "Human Nature" *Thriller*'s most "striking" song: "This is a haunting, brooding ballad by Steve Porcaro and John Bettis, with an irresistible chorus, and it should be an enormous hit." More than twenty years later, *Slant*'s Eric Henderson concurred, calling the track "probably the best musical composition on the album and surely one of the only A/C ballads of its era worth remembering."

An early demo of the song was sent, with a handful of others, to Quincy Jones by the musical group Toto. Jones left the tape running until it reached an instrumental version of "Human Nature" (then untitled), which he loved immediately and brought to Jackson. Steve Porcaro had composed the original demo, but it still lacked a title and lyrics. Jones asked John Bettis to complete the task, which he did magnificently (Steve Lukather and David Paich both contributed to the arrangement). The finished product was a beautiful, evocative ballad that tapped into Jackson's complex mixture of innocence and sensuality.

Jackson's brilliant vocal interpretation, though, is what fully realized the song. "The way his voice tumbles down the notes in the chorus is a master class in vocal delivery," observes J. Edward Keyes, "and his pleading repetition of 'Why? Why?' is the sound of quiet heartbreak." Indeed, while the song pulses with the aching intoxication of possibility, "a rich seam of melancholy" also runs through it. The subtle, suggestive lyrics convey a Gatsby-esque yearning. "Looking out/Across the nighttime," Jackson sings, "The city winks a sleepless eye/Hear her voice/Shake my window/Sweet seducing sigh." The imagery throughout conjures the magic of a night in the city. The narrator is both observed (by "electric eyes") and observes ("She likes the way I stare") as he makes his way through the neon streets.

One can imagine Jackson drew from his personal experience leaving the sheltered confines of his parents' home and experiencing the nightlife of New York while working on *The Wiz* in 1978. His vocals convey both wonder and a curious detachment, as he dreams of the intimacy and connection that eludes him. "If this town is just an apple," he tells himself, "Then let me take a bite." In the final coda, Jackson delivers some of the most sublime strains of his career as he lets out a wordless falsetto cry.

Jazz legend Miles Davis covered the song for his 1985 album *You're Under Arrest*. It has been sampled or covered by numerous other artists including Boyz II Men, Ne-Yo, John Mayer, and SWV. "Human Nature" was the last song included on *Thriller*, replacing "Carousel." It reached #7 on the *Billboard* Hot 100 in 1983.

8. P.Y.T.

(Written and arranged by James Ingram and Quincy Jones; produced by Quincy Jones. Synthesizer programmed by Greg Phillinganes. Lead and background vocals by Michael Jackson. Additional backing vocals: Howard Hewitt and James Ingram. Backing vocals (P.Y.T.s): Janet Jackson, LaToya Jackson, Becky Lopez, and Bunny Hull. Vocoder: Michael Boddicker. Drums: Ndugu Chancler. Electric bass: Louis Johnson. Guitar: Paul Jackson Jr. Handclaps: Greg Phillinganes, James Ingram, Louis Johnson, and Michael Jackson. Keyboards [Portasound]: James Ingram)

Michael Jackson originally wrote a slower, more melodic version of "P.Y.T." with Greg Phillinganes (this version was eventually included on *Michael Jackson: The Ultimate Collection* in 2004). Quincy Jones, however, felt the album had too many slow jams and reworked the track with James Ingram to give it more funk and flair. Interestingly, in spite of (or perhaps partly because of) the song's dated phraseology ("tenderoni," "sugar fly," "take you to the max," etc.), "P.Y.T." has aged as well as anything on *Thriller*. A Top Ten hit in 1983, it has since become an MJ staple. In addition to being sampled or covered by numerous contemporary artists, including Kanye West and Monica, it has also been sung on shows like *American Idol* and is one of Jackson's most downloaded singles on iTunes.

Why has the "frizzy funk" workout—widely considered "filler" by critics in 1982—become such a classic in Jackson's vast catalog? "It's all about the chipmunk," jokes Oliver Wang. "The production has a compelling charm already; it's not as forceful as 'Beat It' or as slick as 'Human Nature,' but those squiggly synths and chewy bass lines do their work well. But besides the robo-accented 'P.Y.T.' hook, what seals the deal is that helium-pitched voice after the bridge."

Whether the "chipmunk theory" holds up or not, there is no doubt that the song's playful elements are a large part of its lasting appeal. With its vocoder vocals (programmed by Jackson and James Ingram), giddy verses, and "na na na na" chants (sung by sisters Janet and LaToya), the fun and energy of "P.Y.T." is simply infectious. Jackson's vocals slide fluidly along the bouncy bass line (recorded on a Mini-Moog), as he flirtatiously charms and seduces. "The breakdown in 'P.Y.T.,'" writes *Pitchfork*'s Rob Mitchum, "with its ecstatic call-and-response and sultry panting, remains the funkiest goddamn thing since James Brown's 'Hot Pants.'" *Rolling Stone* describes it as "MJ at his breathiest and most salacious."

"P.Y.T." was the final single released from *Thriller*. It reached #10 on the *Billboard* Hot 100.

9. THE LADY IN MY LIFE

(Written and composed by Rod Temperton; produced by Quincy Jones. Lead and background vocals by Michael Jackson. Bass: Louis Johnson. Drums: Jeff Porcaro. Electric piano: Greg Phillinganes. Guitar: Paul Jackson Jr. Synthesizer: David Paich and Steve Porcaro)

"The Lady in My Life" was one of only two songs from *Thriller* not released as a single. Yet the album's closer is anything but filler, revealing a subtlety and depth of emotion that adds yet another dimension to a remarkably versatile record. "'Lady' shines for its classic simplicity and nuanced craft," writes music critic Steve Hochman, "[It is] a verse melody straight from vintage Burt Bacharach (the muted trumpet early on leaves no doubt) topped with a chorus that's almost a Stevie Wonder homage."

The final one of three songs penned by Rod Temperton, "Lady" challenged Jackson in a similar way to "She's Out of My Life" from *Off the Wall*. "[It] was one of the most difficult tracks to cut," Temperton recalled. "We were used to doing a lot of takes in order to get a vocal as nearly perfect as possible, but Quincy wasn't satisfied with my work on that song, even after literally dozens of takes. Finally, he took me aside late one session and told me he wanted me to beg. That's what he said. He wanted me to go back to the studio and literally beg for it. So I went back in and had them turn off the studio lights and close the curtain between the studio and the control room so I wouldn't feel self-conscious. Q started the tape and I begged. The result is what you hear in the grooves."

The Sinatra-meets-Marvin Gaye feel of "The Lady in My Life" proved that Jackson, at just twenty-four years old, could excel in any genre, including a classy but soulful ballad. For students of the craft, "Lady" served as a blueprint. "Jackson's closing minute-and-a-half ad-lib should be required listening for anybody needing a lesson in the Soul Man tradition," observes Mark Anthony Neal. "Even those folks who tired of Jackson's over-the-top antics in the years following the release of *Thriller* continued to give him dap for what remains, alongside 'She's Out of My Life,' one of his most sophisticated and nuanced vocal performances."

OTHER NOTABLE *THRILLER*-ERA SONGS

BEHIND THE MASK (recorded 1982, unreleased)
(See Appendix)

BE NOT ALWAYS (recorded 1984, released on the Jackson's 1984 *Victory* album)
An obscure but haunting ballad written by Jackson, "Be Not Always" is an expression of alienation in Cold War America. "We turn our backs on life," he sings, "How can we claim to stand for peace/When the race is armed in strife."

CAROUSEL (recorded 1982, released on *Thriller*, Special Edition, 2001)
A light midtempo ballad written by Michael Sembello, "Carousel" almost made the final cut for *Thriller* but was replaced by "Human Nature."

CENTIPEDE (recorded 1984, released on *Rebbie Jackson*, 1985)
A quirky Jackson-penned tune given to his sister Rebbie Jackson. Michael sings background vocals and the chorus for this vibrant, colorful track.

GOT THE HOTS (recorded 1982, released as bonus track on some versions of *Thriller 25* in 2008)
A funky "Thriller"-sounding track with great harmonies. Written by Michael and Quincy Jones, it was left off the final lineup.

HOT STREET (recorded 1982, unreleased)
A catchy synth-pop song written by Rod Temperton, it features cowbell, funky guitar licks, a nice chorus, and *Thriller*-era sound and production.

NIGHTLINE (recorded 1982, unreleased)
This fun, four-and-a-half-minute piece contains strains of soul, R&B, and gospel. It was written by Glen Ballard (who would later cowrite "Man in the Mirror") and recorded at Westlake Studios in 1982.

SAY SAY SAY (recorded in 1981/1983 and released on Paul McCartney's 1983 album, *Pipes of Peace*)
"Say Say Say" was a #1 hit in November of 1983. The song was cowritten by Jackson and Paul McCartney and recorded at Abbey Roads studio with George Martin, the legendary "fifth Beatle," as producer. Martin said of Jackson, "He actually does radiate an aura when he comes into the studio." Work began on the track in 1981 but was completed two years later following the release of *Thriller*. McCartney and Jackson made a popular video for the track, directed by Bob Giraldi,

which was filmed in the Santa Ynez Valley where Jackson would later buy his Neverland Ranch. The upbeat, infectious pop song is probably the best of the Macca-Jackson duets.

SHE'S TROUBLE (recorded 1982, unreleased)
Another synth-pop rhythm track left off the final lineup for*Thriller*. It was written by Terry Britten, Bill Livsey, and Sue Shifrin.

SOMEBODY'S WATCHING ME (recorded 1983, released on Rockwell's 1984 album, *Somebody's Watching Me*)
A classic eighties track that reached #2 on the *Billboard* Hot 100. Jackson loved the paranoid anthem when he heard it in the studio and eventually provided vocals for the chorus (though he was intentionally uncredited to avoid label disputes). Rockwell is Berry Gordy's son and released the album on the Motown label.

SOMEONE IN THE DARK (recorded 1982, released on the 1982 *E.T. Extra Terrestrial* storybook album; later included on *Michael Jackson: The Ultimate Collection* in 2004)
A pretty, plaintive ballad Jackson recorded for Steven Spielberg's E.T. storybook in the midst of the *Thriller* sessions.

STATE OF SHOCK (recorded 1983, released on the Jackson's 1984 *Victory* album)
A rock–pop fusion featuring Jackson and Rolling Stones' lead singer Mick Jagger that reached #3 on the *Billboard* Hot 100 in 1984. Jackson also recorded a demo of the song with Freddie Mercury.

THE MAN (recorded 1981/1983 and released on Paul McCartney 1983 album, *Pipes of Peace*)
A duet with Paul McCartney about an enigmatic man "who everyone thought they knew." It was blocked as a single by Jackson's label to avoid competing with singles from *Thriller*.

THERE MUST BE MORE TO LIFE THAN THIS (recorded 1983, unreleased)
An unfinished, but fantastic anthemic duet with Queen lead singer, Freddie Mercury. The demo was recorded along with two other songs—"Victory" and "State of Shock"—in the summer of 1983. On one version, Jackson sings the entire song; on the other, he is accompanied by Mercury, who plays piano.

The *Thriller* era generated dozens of Jackson songs that were not on the actual album, including work with Paul McCartney, Freddie Mercury, and Mick Jagger.

We worked on Bad *for a long time. Years. In the end, it was worth it because we were satisfied with what we had achieved, but it was difficult too.... You can always say, 'Aw, forget* Thriller,*' but no one ever will."*

MICHAEL JACKSON, *MOONWALK*, 1988

CHAPTER 3 BAD

The initial backlash to *Bad* was predictable. Nothing could match the phenomenon of *Thriller*. In the early to mid-eighties, Michael Jackson reached the pinnacle of success as a recording artist and entertainer, achieving every honor, record, and award imaginable. By 1987, he was already being labeled "Wacko Jacko" as people speculated wildly about his changing skin color, plastic surgery, hyperbaric chambers, and the Elephant Man's bones. This shift in public perception had a huge impact on the way *Bad* was received. Many critics and consumers simply couldn't separate the music from the new image and sensational stories.

In spite of the controversy, however, *Bad* became a massive worldwide hit, producing a record five #1 hits. While it wouldn't reach the gaudy sales numbers of *Thriller*, it sold more than thirty million copies (two-thirds of which were outside the United States), making it one of the best-selling albums of the 1980s.

Similar to Prince's 1984 classic, *Purple Rain*—to which *Bad* can be viewed as a partial response—*Bad* is a fantastical, thematically eclectic, sonically innovative musical odyssey. The songs work like cinematic dream capsules, taking listeners from an urban subway station ("Bad") to a speeding car ("Speed Demon"), from the jungles of Africa ("Liberian Girl") to the murder scene of a young girl ("Smooth Criminal"). "Jackson's free-form language keeps us aware that we are on the edge of several realities," observes *Rolling Stone*'s Davitt Sigerson, "the film, the dream it inspires, the waking world it

---

RELEASED: *August 31, 1987*

PRODUCERS: *Michael Jackson and Quincy Jones*

NOTABLE CONTRIBUTORS: Bruce Swedien *(recording engineer)*, Matt Forger *(technical engineer)*, John Barnes *(rhythm/synth/drum arrangement)*, Christopher Currell *(Synclavier/synth/keyboard arrangement)*, Larry Williams *(synth programming/sax)*, Greg Phillinganes *(synth/arrangement)*, Stevie Wonder *(vocals)*, Siedah Garret *(vocals, songwriting)*, Glen Ballard *(songwriting)*, The Andraé Crouch Choir *(vocals)*, Steve Stevens *(guitar)*

SINGLES: *"I Just Can't Stop Loving You," "Bad," "The Way You Make Me Feel," "Man in the Mirror," "Dirty Diana," "Another Part of Me," "Smooth Criminal," "Leave Me Alone," "Liberian Girl"*

ESTIMATED COPIES SOLD: *35 million*

illuminates." Sonically, *Bad* expands on the sounds of *Thriller*, using "a combination of digital drum sounds, fat keyboard created bass lines and other percussive elements that pulse like heartbeats and slam like fists."

As Jackson's final album with producer Quincy Jones, *Bad* contains some of the artist's most enduring work. It wasn't the commercial juggernaut of *Thriller* (as no album by any artist has been), but creatively, it was certainly a worthy sequel.

As Michael Jackson was preparing to release *Bad* in 1987, the Reagan era was nearing its end. While the president would leave with a more than sixty percent approval rating, his legacy was mixed: conservatives saw him as a strong, charismatic leader who revived American pride and power, reinvigorated the economy, and helped end the Cold War. Others felt he was an intellectually challenged fill-in for corporations, who oversaw ballooning deficits, social regression, and an increased gap between the rich and the poor.

Jackson, flanked by Ronald and Nancy Reagan, visits the White House in 1984. He received an award for his participation in a campaign to discourage drunk driving.

Regardless of one's perspective, Reagan was a powerful cultural presence whose soft-spoken voice, cowboy/actor image, and grandfatherly aura reminded people of an imagined "golden age" in America. His famous "Morning in America" campaign ad spoke to people's nostalgia for a pre-1960s stability and simplicity.

If Ronald Reagan represented conservative America's yearning for the past, however, the decade's other major icon, Michael Jackson, represented something quite different. Indeed, when the two met in 1984, the contrast couldn't have been more striking. Reagan was old and white; Jackson was young and black; Reagan was stolid and masculine, Jackson was sleek and feminine; Reagan wore a dark corporate suit and tie, Jackson wore a sparkly blue Sgt. Pepper-style military jacket with gold trim, sequined socks, aviator sunglasses, and a sequined white glove. "Was there ever a more surreal meeting of opposites," asked cultural critic Paul Lester, "than the one between the world's most eccentric pop star and the … ex-actor President?"

That was in 1984. By 1987, Jackson had assumed a far more eccentric, countercultural persona. The

soundtrack, *Purple Rain*, a masterful cinematic fusion of funk, rock, and R&B that Jackson viewed competitively and sought to surpass with *Bad*. In 1987, Prince released the experimental critical favorite *Sign o' the Times*. Both records represented an edgier version of pop, with liberal experiments in sound and provocative themes (especially dealing with sex). A song from *Purple Rain* ("Darling Nikki"), in fact, led Tipper Gore, wife of then-Tennessee senator Al Gore, to ensure that "Parental Advisory" stickers be placed on all music that was deemed offensive.

He wanted Bad *to be tougher and edgier than* Thriller.

Madonna, similarly, led pop into new territory, creating an accessible but provocative image that pushed the boundaries of acceptability. From her landmark albums *Like a Virgin* (1984) and *True Blue* (1986) came controversial classics such as "Material Girl" and "Papa Don't Preach" that helped make her, along with Jackson, the defining pop icon of the decade. Like Prince, her sexuality was blunt and often raunchy, creating an edgy brand of pop that threatened to make Michael Jackson look tame by comparison.

Jackson was well aware of these musical trends and responded accordingly. He wanted *Bad* to be tougher and edgier than *Thriller*. In 1986, Quincy Jones arranged a meeting with Run DMC. At the time, the brash, blunt hip-hop trio was at the height of their popularity and still had major street credibility. "We are the Michael Jackson of now," boasted Darryl McDaniels to *Rolling Stone* in 1986. "Prince was it when *Purple Rain* came out. But we are what's going on right now. We are the music. We are what's hot."

Before meeting Jackson in person, the group from Queens was skeptical about working with the pop star. They felt he was too detached from the real world to even comprehend what happened on the streets. After meeting and discussing a demo called "Crack Kills," however, Run DMC's concerns (or posturing) dissipated. "He's the best man in the world," Rev Run gushed. "He's an incredible human being. We ate soul food at Michael's studio last night, and it seemed like he was in touch with God. He's so calm, so content, and I'm going to go into the studio to do a tape with him. It'll be an anti-crack song. The guy who did *Mean Streets* and *Taxi Driver* [director Martin Scorsese] is going to make the video. The whole thing was just great. Michael kept asking me about rap. I asked him about record sales. And when the fried chicken came, I knew he was cool."

Unfortunately, the collaboration between the Kings of Hip-Hop and the King of Pop was never realized for the album, though there are existing demos. Some claimed there was a falling out, though publicly Run DMC has maintained a respect and admiration for Jackson since their meeting. Quincy Jones has claimed that Jackson wasn't sold on hip-hop as a legitimate force in music at this point, feeling it might simply be another fad. Others, however, including Jackson, have said that he was indeed very interested in rap

Jackson, pictured here in 1987, generated questions and controversy with his increasingly ambiguous physical appearance. Evidence of Jackson's skin disorder, vitiligo, can already be seen in this photo.

Jackson's performances become more provocative on his *Bad* World Tour as he attempted to shed his image of being innocent and naive.

but felt it needed an injection of melody (which, incidentally, would soon happen in the 1990s). Accordingly Jackson liked the concept of "Crack" but didn't feel it was quite right for the album. (Jackson did eventually sample Run DMC in the intro to "2Bad" on *HIStory*.)

Jackson also extended an invitation to rival Prince (via Quincy Jones) to appear in a duel for the title track. For arguably the two biggest artists of the decade—who shared much in common but were also fierce competitors—to perform together at the height of their powers, would have been something to behold. "As Michael planned it," writes biographer J. Randy Taraborrelli, "he and Prince would square off against one another [in the video], taking turns vocalizing and dancing, in order to determine, once and for all, who was *'bad.*'"

Michael Jackson and Prince had been following each other's careers since the early eighties and grudgingly admired each other's work, though both felt they were artistically superior. "It was a strange summit," remembered journalist Quincy Troupe of one of the meetings between the artists. "They're so competitive with each other that neither would give anything up. They kind of sat there, checking each other out, but saying very little. It was a fascinating stalemate between two very powerful dudes."

Ultimately, Prince decided to pass on the project, feeling it was set up for Jackson to look better. "I was there for a couple of the meetings with Prince and Michael," recalls Jackson's longtime recording engineer Bruce Swedien. "Personally I think that after meeting with Michael, Quincy, and John Branca, Prince realized that he couldn't win this duet/duel with MJ, artistically or otherwise . . . and pulled out."

"Bad," of course, still ended up a number one hit (which Prince predicted would be the case), though it also generated a lot of criticism. Many felt Jackson's tough new image was too contrived. While Prince and Madonna could easily get away with being "bad," Jackson still struggled to move beyond his alternately "innocent" and "eccentric" persona. As Jay Cocks wrote for *Time* in 1984, "Many observers find in the ascendancy of Michael Jackson the ultimate personification of the androgynous rock star. His high-flying tenor makes him sound like the lead in some funked-up boys choir, even as the sexual dynamism irradiating from the arch of his dancing body challenges government standards for a nuclear meltdown. His lithe frame, five-fathom eyes, long lashes might be threatening if Jackson gave, even for a second, the impression that he is obtainable. However, the audience's sense of his sensuality becomes quite deliberately tangled with the mirror image of his life: the good boy, the God-fearing Jehovah's Witness, the adamant vegetarian, the resolute non-indulger in smoke, strong drink, or dope of any kind, the impossibly insulated innocent. Undeniably sexy. Absolutely safe. Eroticism at arm's length."

Some argued this "safeness" stemmed from a lifetime of insulation and privilege that made it impossible for him to understand real-world issues. What did he know about drugs, poverty, or gang violence? (Interestingly, this entire dilemma was played out in the Martin Scorcese-directed short film for "Bad.") While it was true Jackson hadn't lived on the "streets" since he was a boy in Gary—and, therefore, couldn't convincingly convey that reality the way a hip-hop group like Run DMC could—he had his own experiences to draw from. He had experienced isolation, abuse, exploitation, betrayal, loneliness, fear, discrimination, objectification, and a host of other challenges. He also tended to deeply internalize the suffering and injustice experienced by others. Many of these experiences and emotions surfaced in his work, though often in subtle or metaphorical ways. With *Bad*, they would be blended into an eclectic, edgy fantasia that provided both an escape and a window into his unique inner world.

Before work on *Bad* began in earnest, however, Jackson took part in a project that, for all the accusations of his insulation and fantasy, was decidedly outward looking.

Michael Jackson was first introduced to the USA for Africa concept in late 1984. The brainchild of musician and social activist Harry Belafonte, the goal was to bring together some of the biggest stars in the music industry to create an anthem (à la Band Aid's "Do They Know It's Christmas?") to raise funds and awareness for African famine. The circumstances in parts of Africa, including Ethiopia and the Sudan, were dire: hundreds of thousands of people desperately needed food, medical relief, and other essentials. When Quincy Jones was contacted to direct the recording of the song, he suggested that Michael Jackson, who had previously expressed interest in helping, cowrite the anthem with Stevie Wonder and Lionel Richie. (Wonder ultimately wasn't able to contribute to its writing, though he did provide vocals for the recording.)

For years before the "We Are the World" project, Jackson had been involved in humanitarian work. Increasingly, he considered it one of the most fulfilling and important aspects of his life. Following his burn accident while filming a Pepsi commercial in 1984, he donated all the money he received

($1.5 million) to set up the Michael Jackson Burn Center for Children. In 1986, he donated another $1.5 million to the United Negro College Fund to give young underprivileged African Americans the opportunity to receive an education. He frequently visited hospitals and met with children who were suffering, including some who were on the verge of death. "He's not afraid to look into the worst suffering and find the smallest part that's positive and beautiful," said then-manager Frank DiLeo.

Throughout the entire *Bad* World Tour Jackson donated tickets and gifts to underprivileged and sick children. "Every night the kids would come in on stretchers, so sick they could hardly hold their heads up," recalled Jackson's voice coach Seth Riggs, who often traveled with the singer on tour. "Michael would kneel down at the stretchers and put his face right down beside theirs so that he could have his picture taken with them, and then give them a copy to remember the moment. I'm a sixty-year-old man, and I couldn't take it. I'd be in the bathroom crying. But Michael could take it, and right before going on stage no less. The kids would perk right up in his presence. If it gave them a couple days' more energy, to Michael that was worth it." With "We Are the World," however, Jackson was beginning to see new and powerful possibilities for fusing his music with large-scale social action.

Jackson and Lionel Richie got to work on the song in late 1984. After coming up with just a few lines in their sessions together, they received some gentle prodding from Quincy Jones—"My dear brothers, we have forty-six stars coming in less than three weeks and we need a damn song." Jackson responded to the pressure by taking a couple of the melodies he and Richie had come up with and locking himself in his house until he had fleshed the song out. "Around this time," he recalled, "I used to ask my sister Janet to follow me into a room with interesting acoustics, like a closet or the bathroom, and I'd sing to her, just a note, a rhythm of a note. It wouldn't be a lyric or anything; I'd just hum from the bottom of my throat. I'd say, 'Janet, what do you see? What do you see when you hear this sound?' This time, she responded, 'Dying children in Africa.'"

Piece by piece, he created an entire rough demo in the studio at his Hayvenhurst home. "I love working quickly," he said. "I went ahead without even Lionel knowing, I couldn't wait. I went in and came out the same night with the song completed—drums, piano, strings, and words to the chorus."

When the day came for recording the song, Quincy Jones put a sign above the entrance that read: Check your egos at the door. "I wanted to remind them that this project was bigger than all of us," he said. On the evening of January 28, 1985, the most prominent musicians in the industry began filing in: Stevie Wonder, Diana Ross, Cyndi Lauper, Bruce Springsteen, Billy Joel, Ray Charles, Tina Turner, Bob Dylan, and Paul Simon, among others. "I have never before or since experienced the joy I felt that night working with this rich, complex human tapestry of love, talent, and grace," Quincy Jones later wrote.

"We Are the World" was released, along with its accompanying video, in March 1985, and the initial shipment of 800,000 copies sold out within three days. It would eventually become the best-selling single of all time (selling an estimated twenty million copies), and raise more than $60 million for the relief effort in Africa.

"Man in the Mirror" to "Heal the World," "Earth Song" to "What More Can I Give?"

Twenty-five years after its initial release, "We Are the World" has proven durable. In 2010, the song was put to humanitarian use again, this time on behalf of relief efforts following a devastating earthquake in Haiti. Featuring an entirely new generation of recording artists, including Jennifer Hudson, Pink, Usher, and Haitian-born Wyclef Jean, the song and video once again surged to the top of the charts while providing millions of dollars for relief and development.

"Pioneering new ideas is exciting to me and the movie industry seems to be suffering from a dearth of ideas," he explained.

Soon after "We Are the World," Jackson fulfilled another dream: he became his own feature attraction at Disneyland. Having already conquered the music industry, he was anxious to become more involved in film, a medium he loved and felt held enormous untapped potential. His revolutionary music videos (which he preferred to call "short films") had already given him a platform in which to blend his talents of dancing and singing. He had also received critical praise for his acting in *The Wiz*. Yet Jackson wanted to do more. He wanted to really innovate, to create something people had never seen or experienced before. "Pioneering new ideas is exciting to me and the movie industry seems to be suffering from a dearth of ideas," he explained. "So many people are doing the same things. The big studios remind me of the way Motown was acting when we were having disagreements with them: They want easy answers, they want their people to do formula stuff—sure bets—only the public gets bored, of course."

Jackson's attempted antidote was *Captain EO*, a futuristic full-immersion 4-D music film that took more than a year to create. At the time, the seventeen-minute multisensory experience was the most expensive film ever made on a per-minute basis. Jackson assembled a veritable dream team to work on the project: George Lucas produced the film, Francis Ford Coppola directed it, and James Horner wrote the score. The attraction was a testament to Jackson's unparalleled star power in the mid-eighties. In 1985, there were few people or entities that didn't want to work with him, including family-friendly Disney (this near-universal appeal, of course, began to rapidly change around this time, putting Disney in the uncomfortable position of deciding whether to keep an attraction that was still popular but increasingly controversial).

Captain EO premiered at Epcot's Imagination Pavilion on September 12, 1986 (and soon after at Disneyland in Anaheim) to huge crowds and anticipation. While the film's plot was rather simplistic—Jackson leads a rag-tag team of Star Wars-like characters to confront the evil Supreme Leader (played by Anjelica Huston) and save the galaxy—the special effects were ahead of their time and the musical numbers riveting. By combining 3-D film with such physical effects, *Captain EO* became the first "4-D" film ever made.

Jackson in a rare photo shoot for his music video, *The Way You Make Me Feel*, in 1987.

"It was great, exciting stuff," recalls Matt Forger, who worked on the project with Jackson from its infancy and later with the people at Disney's Imagineering and George Lucas's THX. "It was the first discreet 5.1 film in continuous playback. The Disney people developed the equipment. It didn't exist before. It was full bandwidth with six digital tracks of audio." Forger helped with setup at all four theaters, each of which had audio specifically designed for the acoustics of the respective room. Of all the premiers, however, he was most impressed with the experience at Tokyo. "Tokyo was just kickass," he recalls. "They had a playback system that just totally rocked. It was like being at a rock concert. The room, physically, just shook. It sounded phenomenal. All the theaters sounded great, but Tokyo was just incredible." For children, especially, the experience was magical. Michael Jackson was the coolest, smoothest, funkiest superhero in the galaxy.

The film also delivered a simple but, to Jackson, important message, about using song and dance to bring peace and harmony to the universe. "[*Captain EO* is] about transformation and the way music can help change the world," he explained. *Captain EO* remained a feature attraction at Disneyland for more than a decade. It was re-instituted by popular demand in February 2010, months after Jackson's death.

In the mid-1980s, it seemed everything Jackson touched turned to gold. As he began preparing the follow-up to *Thriller*, however, things would begin to change. In 1987, *Spin Magazine* described it as "the most powerful backlash in the history of popular entertainment." Indeed, reading news and magazine articles from this period, the transformation is striking. Suddenly,

Jackson on the set of his 1988 music video, *Leave Me Alone*, with his chimpanzee (Bubbles) and python (Muscles).

the eccentricities that were alternately intriguing or overlooked just months earlier were now characterized as weird, bizarre, and strange. "In record time," wrote journalist Quincy Troupe, "he went from being one of the most admired of celebrities to one of the most absurd." For Jackson, the relentless attacks, intrusions, questions, and attention became difficult to manage.

Jackson's unprecedented fame and success had led to a nearly impossible existence. More than ever, he was insulated and isolated. He couldn't leave home without being mobbed by fans and paparazzi. The rise of *Thriller* had converged with a new, voracious tabloid media to create a type of celebrity and celebrity obsession that had never been seen before. Every single aspect of his life was held under a microscope. People wanted to know everything about him: Why was his voice so high? Was he taking hormones? Did he have a sex change? Was he gay? Was he asexual? Why the seclusion and fantasy? Why the obsession with animals and children? Why the masks and costumes? Was he in tune with reality? Was he even human?

By 1987, Jackson the human being no longer seemed to exist to a public fed on sensationalism and hype.

Already shy and given to isolation, Jackson almost completely stopped giving interviews and rarely went out in public or to social events. "The year 1985," wrote Gerri Hirshey, "has been a black hole for Michael watchers, who witnessed the most spectacular disappearing act since Halley's comet headed for the far side of the solar system in 1910." The year 1986 was much the same. People began referring to him as Howard Hughes; when he wasn't seen for a period of time, he was said to be in hiding. In the vacuum of his absence, speculation ran wild. The "Wacko Jacko" stigma soon took hold, and the floodgates were opened. Some of the stories seemed harmless if unusual: about his supposed "shrine" to Elizabeth Taylor, about his chimpanzee, Bubbles, even about buying the Elephant Man's bones.

Jackson was, in fact, deeply interested in the story of the Elephant Man, John Merrick—a Victorian-era "freak," who was misunderstood and ostracized by society because of his physical deformities yet yearned for love and acceptance. He watched the classic 1980 film, directed by David Lynch, over and over, crying every time. As the stories about Jackson became more vicious and intrusive, the story became more personal; he understood what it felt like to be a public spectacle and object of derision and scorn. "I visited John Merrick's remains [and] I feel a closeness to [him]," Jackson confessed in a 1988 interview, "I love the story.... It's a very sad story."

The parallels between Jackson and John Merrick also reveal insights about the cultures they lived in. As author James Baldwin once put it: "Freaks are called freaks and are treated as they are treated—in the main, abominably—because they are human beings who cause to echo, deep within us, our most profound terrors and desires."

In Jackson's case, those terrors and desires were multiple: they had to do with race, sexuality, aging, technology, fame, and money, among numerous other issues. They also had to do with America's ritual of elevating and then crucifying its own creations. Jackson could only be the talented, eccentric man-child for so long; the next phase was enfreakment.

By 1987, Jackson the human being no longer seemed to exist to a public fed on sensationalism and hype. He had become whatever people projected him to be. Even those to whom he seemed most "normal" began to see the effects. "Once I saw Michael sitting on the bathroom countertop in the lounge behind the control room [in the studio]," recalls assistant engineer Russ Ragsdale. "His feet were on the counter, knees bent, shoulder against the mirror; he was almost in a trance, like a caged animal."

Later that year, in the midst of his *Bad* World Tour, Jackson scribbled a desperate letter to the press from his hotel room, which read in part: "Like the old Indian proverb says, do not judge a man until you've walked 2 moons in his moccosins [sic]. Most people don't know me, that is why they write such things in wich [sic] most is not true. I cry very often because it hurts.... Animals strike not from malice, but because they want to live, it is the same with those who criticize, they desire our blood, not our pain.... But have mercy for I've been bleeding a long time now."

Of course, Jackson wasn't a mere victim of the media. "It's a great paradox about Michael," observes biographer J. Randy Taraborrelli, "that he is as much a public show-off as he is a recluse." Indeed, as much as he genuinely felt frightened of the "outside world," he was also an entertainer by nature and training. As the eighties progressed, he carefully cultivated a persona that kept people guessing (and talking). He liked the idea of being mysterious and elusive. He was fascinated with masks, costumes, and metamorphosis. Around this time, he even began to embrace and perpetuate the public perception of his strangeness and eccentricity.

In 1986, Jackson told his attorney, John Branca, and manager, Frank Dileo, that he wanted his "whole career to be the greatest show on earth." He handed out copies of P. T. Barnum's autobiography (which he had read numerous times) and began devising plans to win the world's attention. "This is going to be my bible and I want it to be yours," he said. Barnum, of course, was the consummate showman and promoter. He was also the self-titled "prince of humbugs," which, in today's parlance, essentially means publicity stunts. Barnum explained it this way: "As generally understood, 'humbug' consists in putting on *glittering appearances*—outside show—novel expedients, by which to suddenly arrest public attention, and attract the public eye and ear." This idea thrilled Jackson. He was already the master of stage performances; but now it could be extended outside the "show." His entire life would be performance art. It was a way to turn the tables on an intrusive media and public that felt they owned him. He would be in control; they were subject to his directions and imagination.

Perhaps the most famous of these publicity stunts was the hyperbaric chamber story, orchestrated by Jackson and then-manager Frank DiLeo. The photograph and story, which initially ran in the *National Enquirer*, captured people's imaginations and made headlines around the globe. Even credible news organizations covered the story, ruminating about whether such an item actually existed and if Michael Jackson could really live to be 150 years old by sleeping in it. Like a child who had just executed the perfect prank, Jackson was ecstatic about the response. "It's like I can tell the press anything about me and they'll buy it," he said. "We can actually *control* the press."

Of course, when the media didn't cooperate with his game and turned malicious, Jackson retreated and felt angry and hurt. He felt there should be a tacit agreement: he would give them entertainment ("stories"), but they couldn't get too personal. Jackson was particularly sensitive about speculations concerning his cosmetic surgery, skin color, and sexuality. These were "private" issues on which he felt the public had no right to intrude. He also hated the label Wacko Jacko.

However, he loved what Barnum called "glittering appearances": he loved to entertain, to surprise, to provoke fascination. He was good at it, too. "It's rhythm and timing," he once explained as if speaking of a literal performance. "You have to know what you're doing.... It's like a fever, they're waiting, they're waiting. It's important to wait... to conserve and preserve.... If you remain mysterious people will be more interested." In many ways, his plan worked. The press and public couldn't get enough.

Jackson had been an entertainer since he was a young boy. It was all he knew. Now the impulse to "perform" was almost constant. His identity was becoming inextricably wrapped into the persona, the character. He was the strange, magical, mysterious, eccentric pop star: "Michael Jackson, the greatest show on earth."

Michael and Matt Forger in the studio.

When manager Frank DiLeo was asked in 1987 about scaling back on the publicity because of the price of fame on his client, he responded: "It's too late, anyway. He won't have a normal life even if I stop."

It was toward the beginning of this new phase that Jackson began work on what would become *Bad* in 1985. Three years had lapsed since the release of *Thriller*, and fans were waiting anxiously for the sequel. Following the most successful record in the history of the music industry, however, was not an enviable task.

Jackson added to the pressure, taping a piece of paper to his mirror that said simply: "100 million." That was his goal for *Bad*—more than double the sales (at the time) of *Thriller*. With this ambitious goal in the back of his mind, he went to work.

In the early stages, he would simply go into his home studio with musicians and engineers such as Matt Forger, John Barnes, or Bill Bottrell and work on ideas. Jackson called it "the laboratory." Here, he would record numerous 48-track demos in a variety of styles and themes. It was a space that allowed him more freedom and spontaneity to pursue creative ideas.

Eventually, however, a bit of a rift developed between what become known as the B-Team working with Jackson at his home studio and Quincy Jones's crew at Westlake Studios. "Michael was growing and wanted to experiment free of the restrictions of the Westlake scene," explained producer Bill Bottrell. "That's why he got me and John Barnes to work at his home studio for a year and a half, on and off. We would program, twiddle, and build the tracks for much of that album, send the results on two-inch down to Westlake and they would, at their discretion, rerecord, and add things like strings and brass. This is how MJ started to express his creative independence, like a teenager leaving the nest."

Many of the songs the B-Team worked on were practically finished before they reached Westlake. "He was able to take some finished demos into the 'real' studio with Quincy and that was his way of getting more say [in how they were produced]," recalls Bill Bottrell.

In late 1986, recording finally began in earnest at brand new Studio D at Westlake, where Jackson continued to work with many of the same key players from *Off the Wall* and *Thriller*, including recording engineer Bruce Swedien, keyboardist Greg Phillinganes, and horns specialist Jerry Hey. Quincy Jones also brought in some fresh, new talent, including jazz organist Jimmy Smith and talented songwriters such as Glen Ballard and Siedah Garrett. The brilliant Andraé Crouch Choir was tapped for "Man in the Mirror," a choir he would include on every subsequent album.

Quincy Jones, meanwhile, continued to act as producer, though he and Jackson didn't always work together as smoothly as they had in the past. It was clear to everyone around Jackson that he was evolving and gaining more and more creative confidence and control as an artist (he would

Jackson poses with gang members on the set of his *Bad* video in Brooklyn, New York.

write nine of the eleven songs included on *Bad*, plus numerous others that didn't make it onto the record). This led to some collisions on production and song choices, as well as on the album's overall aesthetic vision.

"[Quincy and I] disagreed on some things," Jackson later recalled. "There was a lot of tension because we felt we were competing with ourselves. It's very hard to create something when you feel like you're in competition with yourself." Those participating in the project sometimes felt this pressure as well. "There was so much stress," remembered guitarist David Williams. "I was doing the exact same part at least five times on each song." For Jackson, of course, that perfectionism was simply the way he was trained since his days at Motown to get the best results.

In spite of the pressure and high expectations, most who worked on the album remember the atmosphere in the studio as one of "love" and "camaraderie"—a creative climate attributed to both Jones and Jackson. Bruce Swedien recalls a tradition Jackson started called "Family Night," in which all the family members and friends of the studio crew were invited on Fridays to dinner in the studio prepared by Jackson's cooks, Catherine Ballard and Laura Raynor (affectionately nicknamed the "slam-dunk sisters"). Assistant engineer Russ Ragsdale remembers Jackson doodling all the time in the studio; he also remembers him enjoying getting out for a break. "On a few occasions," recalls Ragsdale, "Michael would want to get out of the studio for a bit. At the time I had a big full-sized Ford pickup truck with tinted windows. Michael loved riding in that truck and got real excited because he was able to sit so much higher off the ground than in his Mercedes."

In 1987, *Spin* magazine described a typical day in the studio like this: Jackson walks in with sunglasses, a brown fedora, and a red corduroy shirt accompanied by his chimpanzee, Bubbles (Jackson would also sometimes bring in his python, Muscles). Quincy Jones is sitting on the floor taking notes, while eating; "walrus-mustached" Bruce Swedien is in the control room along with Jackson's manager Frank DiLeo, who is "sending long streams of cigar smoke curling toward the ceiling." On the other end of the studio, there is a "spread of fried chicken, potato salad, greens, and coleslaw." On other days, Jackson would show up wearing a parka with a fur-lined hood in the middle of August because he didn't care for the air-conditioning. "We tried our best to just treat Michael like a regular guy," recalls Russ Ragsdale, "We didn't go out of our way too much."

Once the recording started, Jackson was completely in his element. Journalist Quincy Troupe, who was given access to a studio session for one day in 1986, described it like this: "Alone in the semidarkness, illuminated softly by a single spotlight, he starts to sing. This, finally, is what it's about.... There are no problems, no merchandise deals, no deadlines, no family rivalries. It's just Michael and the song. Suddenly, he is no longer the dreamy, whispering recluse. He is no longer soft. He attacks the song, dancing, waving his hands, moving with unexpected power. He is in his own world.... For these few moments, at least, he is neither a joke nor an icon, just a very, very talented singer."

As with *Thriller*, hundreds of songs were considered for *Bad*. From these, Jackson and Jones whittled down the list. "Fifty percent of the battle is trying to figure out which songs to record," Jones remarked.

"It's total instinct. You have to go with the songs that touch you, that get the goose bumps going."

"It took over 800 multitrack tapes to create Bad."

According to *Rolling Stone*, "Jackson had 62 songs written and wanted to release 33 of them as a triple album, until [Quincy] Jones talked him down." This trimming down led to some excellent tracks being left on the cutting room floor, including "Streetwalker" (which Jackson preferred, but was talked out of by Jones in favor of "Another Part of Me"), "Fly Away" (a beautiful, melodic mid-tempo ballad), and "Cheater" (a funky, gritty track about infidelity), among others.

Once the songs were chosen for recording, it was about creating sounds the "ear hadn't heard." Jackson didn't want to duplicate *Thriller*, or other music on the radio, for that matter. He wanted to innovate sonically. "Michael's vision [is] to start making a record by creating totally new fresh sounds that have never been heard before," explained assistant engineer Russ Ragsdale. "For *Bad* this was achieved by [musicians] Michael Boddicker and Greg Phillinganes, with synth stacks filling up the entire large tracking room taking up every available space, as well as the largest Synclavier in the world at the time operated by Chris Currell.... It took over 800 multitrack tapes to create *Bad*; each song was a few hundred tracks of audio." For the rhythm tracks in particular, Jackson wanted fresh drum sounds that would really hit. Swedien recorded them on 16-track tape like on *Thriller*, but then transferred them to digital to get that mechanical but "fat, analog rhythm, sound" Jackson loved. Jones called it "big legs and tight skirts."

In the end, Jackson and Jones were in the studio for more than a year. "A lot of people are so used to just seeing the outcome of work," Jackson said in a 1987 interview. "They never see the side of the work you go through to produce the outcome." As deadlines came and passed, however, frustration mounted. Quincy Jones reportedly walked away from the project for a time when he discovered Jackson had snuck into the studio and altered his work. Epic executives kept pushing to wrap up the record, but Jackson couldn't bring himself to release the album until it was "ready." "A perfectionist has to take his time," he explained. "He shapes and molds and sculpts that thing until it's perfect. He can't let it go before he's satisfied; he can't."

Finally, around mid-summer 1987, a firm deadline was set for the release of *Bad*. "You need a dramatic deadline," Quincy Jones explained to *Rolling Stone*. "I swear to God, we would have been in the studio another year without that deadline." As with *Thriller*, Jackson and Jones worked all the way to the finish line, putting the final touches on until the album was mastered on July 10.

Originally, the cover for the *Bad* album was a close-up of Jackson's face superimposed by black lace. Jackson loved the strangeness and mystery of the image, but executives at Epic were horrified, fearing it would reinforce his "weird," feminine persona. The cover was ultimately scrapped in July in favor of a photo shoot from the *Bad* video, which featured the singer in black leather and buckles, with fists clenched and the title spray-painted in

In 1988, Michael Jackson remained the most electrifying entertainer in the world.

red. Since they were going for a "tougher" album, this seemed to be a better fit.

To celebrate *Bad*'s release, Michael Jackson hosted a party at his Encino home for those who had helped with the album, as well as Epic executives and other people in the music industry. While Jackson remained mostly aloof, he was relieved and rejuvenated to finally be finished. "It's a jubilation, is what it is," he told *Ebony*. Still, after years of putting his heart and soul into the album, he was anxious to see how the public would receive it. "I can't answer whether or not I like being famous," he would later write in his autobiography, "but I do love achieving goals. I love not only reaching a mark I've set for myself but exceeding it. Doing more than I thought I could, that's a great feeling."

Jackson, and the world, for that matter, had set a high bar for *Bad*—and now the time had finally come for its unveiling.

***Bad* was released** worldwide in August 1987 and immediately went to #1 on the *Billboard* chart and around the world. The reception from critics varied: some had a hard time separating the strange stories they had been hearing for the past couple of years from the actual music. "Jackson the singer can get bushwhacked by Jackson the persona," wrote *Time*'s Jay Cocks. "The Man in the Mirror most people will see is not the conscience-racked singer ('I'm starting with the man in the mirror/I'm asking him to change his ways . . .'), but the Captain EO of theme-park fantasies or the peekaboo celebrity, recumbent in his isolation tank or cornered by paparazzi flashes, wearing his Elephant Man surgical mask and upping his bid for the remains of John Merrick."

In nearly every other contemporaneous review of *Bad*, Jackson's tabloid image was prominent. Many critics engaged in pseudo-psychoanalysis, pontificating about Jackson's eccentricities as if artists or rock stars were supposed to be the poster children for normalcy.

Jackson defies gravity in his music video for *Smooth Criminal*. The video showcased the intentionally cinematic and fantastical nature of the album.

When the album's lead single was released, the Jackson-penned ballad, "I Just Can't Stop Loving You," one might have assumed from the reviews that it was the single worst piece of music ever created. "With a face as plastic as the disc it covers," wrote one reviewer, "Wacko Jacko steps back into the limelight . . . even more of a girlie than before." "Jackson might have telephoned these vocals through," wrote another, while a third assessment described it as an "ocean-sized drip of blustering sentiment." Such critiques were absurdly hyperbolic. While the song didn't represent the album's best material (just as *Thriller*'s lead single, "The Girl Is Mine," didn't), it was also clear from the beginning that regardless of merit, *Bad* had no chance of topping *Thriller*. Many people simply weren't capable of looking past the sensationalism and giving it an open and objective listen.

In a 1988 *Rolling Stone* poll, this reality was confirmed as Jackson was voted "Worst Male Singer," while *Bad* was voted "Worst Album." "The backlash has more to do with the singer's quirky personality than his music," reasoned *Rolling Stone* music editor David Wild. "People are responding negatively to his image and to the hype. The category he should have won is 'worst image' or 'least understood.'"

Yet in spite of the backlash (and the comparisons to *Thriller*), *Bad* became an enormously successful record. In its first few months, it sold briskly, staying at #1 for six consecutive weeks in the United States and outselling the rest of the Top 40 combined. *Bad* also demonstrated Jackson's increasing global popularity, reaching the top of the charts in a record twenty-five countries. (*Bad* is Jackson's best-selling album in the United Kingdom. It is also one of the top-ten selling albums of all time in that country.) Indeed, when Jackson traveled to countries such as Japan, Australia, and the United Kingdom later that year for his *Bad* World Tour he was greeted with Beatle-esque pandemonium (Japan dubbed his visit "Typhoon Michael"). To build excitement for the shows, Jackson would enter from the side of stadiums (captured on film), jogging or marching with a few dozen police officers. The massive audiences, already whipped into feverish anticipation, would be flooded with bright white lights until Jackson appeared frozen on stage, before exploding into the opening number. "The word 'superstar' became meaningless compared with the power and grace pouring from the stage," wrote Gregory Sandow, a reviewer for the *Los Angeles Herald Examiner*. In 1988, in spite of everything, Michael Jackson remained, without question, the biggest recording artist in the world.

This commercial success, however, was another common point of criticism in the aftermath of *Thriller*. Jackson's stated goal of wanting to outsell the biggest selling album didn't sit well with critics. Was Jackson interested in making meaningful music, or was he simply trying to win sales records and awards? Said biographer J. Randy Taraborrelli, "[Michael Jackson] couldn't imagine recording an album for any purpose other than for it to be the biggest and best, ever. He needed to have his work acknowledged in a huge way, or he simply was not going to be satisfied. Perhaps such determination can be traced back to his days as a youngster when The Jackson 5 competed on talent shows in which the only goal was to be the winner. That forum was Michael's original training ground."

Certainly, there was some truth to this. From his earliest days performing, Jackson was expected to be the best—and being the best meant validation from an audience. Whether that meant pleasing a raucous crowd at the Apollo Theater in Harlem or recording a hit at Motown, Jackson grew up with the idea that if people didn't buy your music, it was a failure. (Later in life, Jackson would at least theoretically understand that great art isn't always immediately popular.) Throughout his career, though, he was determined to be both artistically and commercially successful. He wanted to be the biggest entertainer in the world and sell 100 million albums, but he also wanted to innovate artistically, to create music "the ear had never heard" and songs that changed people's consciousness. Most critics, however, had a difficult time comprehending this paradox and simply dismissed him as an entirely commercially minded entertainer.

Bad was also criticized for being lyrically shallow. In his 1987 review for the *New York Times*, Jon Pareles dismissed Jackson in such terms: "The albums that *Thriller* displaced as the world's best sellers—Carole King's *Tapestry*, Fleetwood Mac's *Rumours*, even the soundtrack to *Saturday Night Fever*—all offered something more than listenable or danceable hit singles although they were well-stocked with those. Ditto for albums in the next-lower rung of sales, such as Bruce Springsteen's *Born in the U.S.A.*, Prince's *Purple Rain*, and Pink Floyd's *Dark Side of the Moon*. They're all well-produced, rich-sounding collections of songs that stick in the ear. But they also have lyrics that try to go beyond typical pop sentiments, and those lyrics found a response outside the usual pop audience."

For Pareles, then, Michael Jackson could create songs that "stick in the ear" but that ultimately lacked the depth of artists such as Carole King and Fleetwood Mac. While this claim gained some journalistic currency beginning in the late eighties, however, it doesn't hold up well to scrutiny. "Many of the attacks [on Jackson's artistry]," observed *Spin*'s Quincy Troupe, "came from white rock critics who suddenly seemed to resent his unparalleled success. Jackson didn't fit the model for rock-critic idolatry. Someone like Bruce Springsteen plays the guitar, writes songs that are subject to literary criticism, and dances like a white guy. Whereas Michael Jackson represents a black cultural heritage that white critics either don't know about or would rather appreciate nostalgically from someone who's dead."

The considerable artistic merits of *Bad*, of course, have been put in clearer perspective since these late-eighties reviews. Yet, many of the same assumptions about Jackson's music have persisted among critics. Whether this is due to his enormous commercial success, stereotypes about "dance music," his persona, his personal controversies, his race, or a combination of these things, has been, and will continue to be, debated. However, there is no question, beginning with *Bad*, rock critics like Pareles developed an excessively hostile and dismissive attitude toward his music.

For *Bad*, the key in critical reappraisals is in understanding its artistic framework. Comparing Michael Jackson to Bruce Springsteen is like comparing Madonna to Janis Joplin or James Brown to Bob Dylan. They are simply operating on different paradigms and aesthetic models. Michael Jackson writing songs about rural America would be as disingenuous as Springsteen singing "Smooth Criminal." In truth, *Bad* is no shallower in its lyrics than a classic rock album like *Born in the U.S.A.* It simply contains different styles and themes.

On *Bad*, Jackson's music is largely about creating moods, visceral emotions, and fantastical scenarios. The funky, engine-revving car chase of "Speed Demon" leads fluidly into the lush, earthy intonations of "Liberian Girl." The tense, sensual narrative of "Dirty Diana" gives way to a mysterious crime scene in "Smooth Criminal." Each song works as a dream capsule, inviting the listener into a vivid new sound, story, and space. It is meant to mesmerize, to transport, to awe, and also to explore and reveal. In this way, it is more comparable to a cinematic soundtrack (with elements of blues, jazz, and R&B).

Experienced on its own terms, then, *Bad* is a compelling, phantasmagorical album, which a handful of critics recognized from the beginning. "Anybody who charges studio hackery is too narrow-minded to be able to hear pros out-doing themselves," wrote music critic Robert Christgau. "Studio mastery is more like it, the strongest and most consistent black pop album in years, defining Jam & Lewis's revamp of Baby Sis as the mainstream and then inundating it in rhythmic and vocal power." *Time* magazine called it "a state-of-the-art dance record. Jackson's lyrics combine sometimes glancing felicity ('Your talk is cheap/You're not a man/You're throwin' stones/To hide your hands') with scat-style facility." *Rolling Stone* felt, as a whole, it was even better than *Thriller*. "*Bad* is not only a product but also a cohesive anthology of its maker's perceptions," wrote Davitt Sigerson. "Comparisons with *Thriller* are unimportant, except this one: even without a milestone recording like 'Billie Jean,' *Bad* is a better record.... Leaving the muddy banks of conjecture—as to sales, as to facial surgery, as to religion, as to, Is he getting it, and if so, from whom or what?—we can soar into the heart of a nifty piece of work."

Indeed, that work included what recording engineer Bruce Swedien describes as the "widest variety of soundfields" of any album Jackson had created. The layers of dynamic synth and drum programming meshed not only with electric guitars, organs, and horns, but also with car engines, heartbeats, birdsong, and crowd noise. "*Bad*... cranks up the music's intensity," writes *Rolling Stone*'s Jon Dolan. "The beats have wicked pistol pop, the rock guitars are torrid, and its synth textures are shadowy and sleek." The album also prominently featured many of Jackson's vocal signatures: the hee hees, oooohs, and awwws, the grunts, gasps, and *shamones* (the latter of which is now featured in the Urban Dictionary). From the infectious energy of "The Way You Make Me Feel" to the throaty rapping of "Speed Demon" and "Smooth Criminal," from the rich harmonies of "Liberian Girl" to the sublime entreaties of "Man in the Mirror," Jackson's vocals on *Bad* are completely unique, and completely brilliant.

In terms of its legacy, *Bad* now stands firmly with *Thriller* as one of the best and most influential pop albums of the decade. Balancing memorable hooks with unique and innovative sounds and visuals, it is one of Jackson's most imaginative and successful records. Not only did it contain an unprecedented five #1 hits ("I Just Can't Stop Loving You," "Bad," "The Way You Make Me Feel," "Man in the Mirror," and "Dirty Diana"), three others—"Smooth Criminal," "Another Part of Me," and "Leave Me Alone"—would crack the Top 15. These songs remain staples in Jackson's vast catalog. "It's interesting to me to reflect on the album *Bad*," writes Jackson's longtime recording engineer Bruce Swedien, "and realize that I have more favorite songs on this album than any of the others." Many fans can say the same. The Rock and Roll Hall of Fame calls it "some of the sharpest black pop ever recorded" with its "canny use of urban beats, smooth jazz-funk and rock guitar." *Rolling Stone* ranked it #202 in its list of the 500 Greatest Albums of All Time.

Decades later, Jackson's famous question on the title track—"Who's bad?"—is as rhetorical as ever.

***Bad* was an album loaded with memorable videos and hits. It was also Jackson's first to sell more copies outside the United States than within the United States.**

THE SONGS

1. BAD

(Written and composed by Michael Jackson; produced by Quincy Jones; rhythm arrangement by Michael Jackson, Christopher Currell, and Quincy Jones. Horn arrangement by Jerry Hey. Vocal arrangement by Michael Jackson. Drum programming: Douglas Getschal. Solo and background vocals: Michael Jackson. Hammond B3 Midi organ solo: Jimmy Smith. Synthesizer solo: Greg Phillinganes. Drums: John Robinson. Guitar: David Williams. Saxophones: Kim Hutchcroft and Larry Williams. Trumpets: Gary Grant and Jerry Hey. Percussion: Paulinho Da Costa. Synclavier keyboards, digital guitar, and rubboard: Christopher Currell. Synthesizers: John Barnes, Michael Boddicker, and Greg Phillinganes)

The smooth, slinky opening riff of "Bad" is one of the more memorable grooves of the 1980s. Where the opener to *Thriller* was sonically playful and loose, "Bad" is cooler, moodier. Its tight mechanical beat snakes forward relentlessly as Jackson delivers his provocative challenges. "'Bad' needs no defense," recognized *Rolling Stone*'s Davitt Sigerson in his 1987 review. "Jackson revives the 'Hit the Road, Jack' progression and proves (with a lyric beginning with 'Your butt is mine' and ending with 'Who's bad?') that he can outfunk anybody any time."

The production and arrangement on the track are phenomenal, juxtaposing sleek synthesized drum sounds with rich organ parts, declarative horns, and tight harmonies. The darker tone of the song is matched by Jackson's aggressive vocals. "Your talk is cheap," he challenges. "You're not a man/ You're throwin' stones/To hide your hands." Originally intended as a standoff piece with musical rival Prince, the confrontational lyrics instead direct outward. "When Jackson declares that the 'whole world has to answer right now,'" observed Davitt Sigerson, "he is not boasting but making a statement of fact regarding his extraordinary stardom. If anything, he is scorning the self-coronation of lesser funk royals and inviting his fickle public to spurn him if it dare. Not since the 'Is it good, ya?' of Godfather Brown has a more rhetorical question been posed in funk."

Following a bold B3 Midi organ solo by Jimmy Smith in the bridge, Jackson ad-libs, grunts, and soars over the chorus and trumpets, before ending with the famous quip, "Who's bad?"

While the song is now considered a classic in Jackson's catalog, however, it experienced a significant backlash upon its release in 1987. This response was largely a reaction to the song's music video, an ambitious seventeen-minute short film directed by acclaimed filmmaker Martin Scorsese. The video—based on the true story of tragically killed African American student, Edmund Perry—was shot primarily in a Brooklyn subway station and featured Jackson (dressed in black leather and buckles) leading a group of gang members in flawlessly choreographed dances. While Jackson's moves would inspire endless imitation, the video's concept came under scrutiny. Some argued, based mostly on his changing physical appearance, that he was losing touch with his "black roots," while others felt he simply didn't understand "real world" issues. "Michael's concept of what really is bad—as in 'tough' and 'streetwise'—seemed wildly distorted and exaggerated," wrote biographer J. Randy Taraborrelli. "[He] shouted; he stamped his feet; he flicked his fingers and shook his groin. He tugged at his crotch repeatedly. Is *this* what Michael Jackson sees from the tinted window of his limousine?" Defenders of Jackson argued that the video actually addresses this very tension (Jackson's character, Daryl, plays an out of place prep-schooler returning home to the skepticism of his former friends), and that, like most musicals, the concept is intentionally "exaggerated" or dramatized. "The film is this year's most ideologically complex," wrote film critic Armond White. "Scorsese brings proficient craft to Jackson's old-fashioned (*West Side Story*-derived) fantasy about gangs. . . . Daryl is Jackson's attempt at solidarity. He brings the Edmund Perry story to the world by identifying with it. He sees himself as facing the same choices as other young black men but is able (lucky) to make his decision through art. . . . It's a completely serious, but *stylized*, musical film."

Regardless of the initial backlash, the short film for "Bad" has aged well, and is now considered one of his more memorable and influential videos. In 2009, Armond White called it "Scorsese's best post-'70s film." Others have praised Jackson's acting in the largely unseen prelude. "This is going to sound strange," director Allen Hughes told MTV News, "but Michael Jackson was an incredible actor and no one knew that. If you look at the nuances of *The Wiz*, when he played the Scarecrow. Or if you look at the short film Scorsese directed before 'Bad,' where he's going head to head with Wesley Snipes. The acting he was doing? Oh my god it was good. I know actors and he was an incredible actor."

Scorsese himself was deeply impressed by Jackson's talent, calling him "extraordinary." "When we worked together on 'Bad,'" he recalled, "I was in awe of his absolute mastery of movement on the one hand, and of the music on the other. . . . He was wonderful to work with, an absolute professional at all times, and—it really goes without saying—a true artist."

"Bad" became one of a record five #1 hits from the album. The song and video announced a new version of Jackson, which, whether one liked it or not, certainly wasn't a repeat of *Thriller*.

2. THE WAY YOU MAKE ME FEEL

(Written and composed by Michael Jackson; produced by Quincy Jones. Drum programming: Douglas Getschal. Synthesizer programming: Larry Williams. Rhythm and vocal arrangement by Michael Jackson. Horn arrangement by Jerry Hey. Solo and background vocals by Michael Jackson. Finger snaps: Michael Jackson. Drums: John Robinson. Saxophones: Kim Hutchcroft and Larry Williams. Trumpets: Gary Grant and Jerry Hey. Percussion: Ollie E. Brown and Paulinho Da Costa. Synclavier and finger snaps: Christopher Currell. Synthesizers: John Barnes, Michael Boddicker, and Greg Phillinganes)

Jackson follows "Bad" with one of the most durable dance tracks in his catalog—the high-energy blockbuster, "The Way You Make Me Feel." With its signature shuffle rhythm, the song leaps out of the speakers. Music critic Sam Chennault calls it "ecstatic dance pop that's permanently engrained into our mind's jukebox." *Rolling Stone* describes it as "four and a half minutes of unadulterated bliss." More than twenty years after it became a #1 hit, it remains one of Jackson's most popular songs, played perhaps more regularly on radio than any song he wrote beside "Billie Jean."

The shuffle rhythm on the track was actually suggested to Jackson by his mother. After trying to convey the sound to her son, Michael replied, "I think I know what you mean." Two weeks later, he had written a demo of the song, resulting in his first and only known "collaboration" with his mother. Jackson subsequently took the song, originally titled "Hot Fever," to his A-Team of producers and engineers, who brilliantly helped bring out the song's organic energy and elasticity. "It's a really intense shuffle," says keyboardist Greg Phillinganes. "I remember how much fun I had laying down those offbeat parts, the bass line, all that stuff, and watching the expression on Michael's face—he'd get that big grin that meant you had it." Bruce Swedien recalls Jackson dancing in the studio as he recorded the song. Rather than take out the sounds of stomping, spinning, finger snapping, and beatboxing, he decided to leave it in as part of the "overall sonic picture." "I would hate to record Michael with what I would call the clinical approach," he explained. "If I were to try to have Michael's sound antiseptically clean, I think it would lose a lot of its earthy charm."

Indeed, much of the song's charm lay in such idiosyncrasies, in its raw spontaneity and unbridled exclamations of joy—"hee hee," "whooo," and "gawn girl!"—that so perfectly encapsulate the excitement and thrill of being in love. These natural elements provide textures and colors that complement the machine-driven motion of the bass line. "Amid the modern electronics, there's a taste of older soul music, with the rolling groove and blues harmonies," observed Jon Pareles in 1987. These features come through even more clearly in a slowed-down version of the song Jackson often used in performances—including his acclaimed 1988 Grammy Awards rendition—which allowed the song's blues harmonies to build mood and anticipation (Jackson referred to it as letting it "simmer"), before the song explodes into the signature bass line.

"Hey pretty baby with the high heels on," Jackson sings in the opening. "You give me fever like I've never ever known." The lyrics throughout are playful and flirtatious and Jackson delivers them effortlessly. "Every piece of this song is in perfect place," notes *Rolling Stone*, "the big brass punctuating each of Jackson's heartfelt demonstrations of affection."

Jackson's visual rendering of the song, meanwhile, wonderfully complements the track's sonic personality. Directed by Joe Pytka (award-winning director of iconic commercials like "This Is Your Brain on Drugs" and music videos like the Beatles' *Free As a Bird*), the nine-minute short film features Jackson on a smoky urban neighborhood street, playfully pursuing a love interest (played by model Tatianna Thumbtzen). The chemistry between Jackson and Thumbtzen comes across as genuine and self-deprecating, as he makes exaggerated sexual advances and she counters by mocking his moves and bravado. Indeed, the majority of the video is driven by a combination of humor (beginning with the pithy wisdom from an old man on the street: "you don't know about women, you don't have that kind of knowledge," to Jackson's head-first dive into a car) and sexual tension (if *Bad* hadn't made it clear, Jackson wasn't holding back on the erotic bluntness). The video also brilliantly uses lighting, shadows, and textures to establish mood and atmosphere and accentuate Jackson's stellar dance moves (the concluding group routine in silhouette is the video's highlight). With its memorable imagery, energy, and dancing, the music video is as classic as the song itself. Both showcase Jackson in his prime, operating with confidence, charm, and vitality.

3. SPEED DEMON

(Written and composed by Michael Jackson; produced by Quincy Jones; sounds engineered by Ken Caillat and Tom Jones. Rhythm arrangement by Michael Jackson and Quincy Jones. Vocal arrangement by Michael Jackson. Synthesizer and horn arrangements by Jerry Hey. Drum programming: Douglas Getschal. Solo and background vocals and vocal synthesizer: Michael Jackson. Synthesizer programming: Eric Persing. Midi saxophone solo: Larry Williams. Drums: Miko Brando, Ollie E. Brown, and John Robinson. Guitars: Bill Bottrell and David Williams. Saxophone: Kim Hutchcroft. Trumpets: Gary Grant and Jerry Hey. Percussion: Ollie E. Brown and Paulinho Da Costa. Synclavier and effects: Christopher Currell. Synthesizers: John Barnes, Michael Boddicker, and Greg Phillinganes)

"Speed Demon" perfectly illustrates the dream-capsule concept of the *Bad* album. The song depicts a thrilling car chase in which Jackson's character seeks to outpace an officer "hot on his tracks." It is a song about escaping the restricting confines of society, and entering a world of excitement, freedom, and imagination. Some critics pointed to the track as an example of Jackson's supposed penchant on the album for shallow, naïve escapism (*All Music Guide* reduced it to mechanical "studiocraft" while *Rolling Stone* dismissed it as a "fun little power tale"). It is actually one of the album's most telling artistic expressions, revealing subtle but profound hints about what he wants his music to accomplish, while experimenting boldly with sounds.

Sonically, the song uses a revving engine, steady rhythm, and quick lines to simulate the experience of speeding in a car. To the attentive listener, the song's intricate beat divisions generate a crescendo/diminuendo effect to highlight the feeling of movement and power. "In a year in which Whitney Houston's 'I Wanna Dance With Somebody' and Dirty Dancing's '(I've Had) The Time of My Life' ruled the airwaves," observed *The Vine*'s Andy Roberts, 'Speed Demon' sounded positively avant-garde . . . as drum patterns and synths brilliantly communicate the sound of shifting through the gears of a sexually motivated motorbike." Jackson's vocal performance—shifting from gritty in the verses to plaintive falsetto in the bridge—drew praise as well: "There is a great singer at work here," observed *Time*'s Jay Cocks, "doing vocal stunts . . . that are as nimble and fanciful as any of his dance steps."

Jackson reportedly wrote the song after getting a speeding ticket on the way to the studio. Quincy Jones challenged him to turn the experience into music. Jackson's creative response not only offers an energizing car chase scenario, but also a window into the nature of "escapism" itself. The car becomes a symbol for the imagination, while the officer represents repressive authority. The world he is leaving behind is one in which he feels trapped, targeted, profiled, and stifled. "You're preaching 'bout my life like you're the law," Jackson sings before denouncing this socialization, and shifting into high gear. "Go! Go! Go!" he yells as he leaves the officer in the dust.

Throughout the song, however, the policeman repeatedly attempts to punish the speeding narrator, saying "Pull over boy/And get your ticket right." The diminutive terminology clearly carries racial connotations. Indeed, the entire scenario—a (presumably) white officer pulling over a black man, while condescendingly calling him "boy"—carries deep implications that only start with racial profiling. Jackson seems to be hinting at an entire social system of constraint and limitation.

In the satirical video for the song, directed by Oscar-winning director and claymation inventor Will Vinton, Jackson is written up by the officer, not for speeding, but for dancing. In other words, a seemingly harmless act of self-expression is punished. In several other places, the video levels social critiques as Jackson transforms into an alter ego (a rabbit) and flees from mobs of crazed tourists, paparazzi, and police. At one point, as he hides behind an animated Statue of Liberty, she remarks on the frenzied scene: "Land of the free, home of the weird."

In the song, then, when Jackson's character says he is "heading for the border," he is speaking of crossing a figurative threshold, of leaving society's insanity and authority behind and entering an alternative world of uninhibited expression and imagination. "Mind is like a compass," Jackson sings, "I'm stoppin' at nothin.'" Once in this vehicle, he is liberated to roam wherever his mind takes him.

4. LIBERIAN GIRL

(Written and composed by Michael Jackson; produced by Quincy Jones. Drum programming: Douglas Getschal. Synthesizer programming: Steve Porcaro. Rhythm arrangement by Michael Jackson, John Barnes, and Quincy Jones. Synthesizer arrangement by Jerry Hey, John Barnes, and Quincy Jones. Vocal arrangement by Michael Jackson and John Barnes. Swahili chant arrangement by Caiphus Semenya. Solo and background vocals: Michael Jackson. Drums: Miko Brando, Ollie E. Brown, and John Robinson. Percussion: Ollie E. Brown and Paulinho Da Costa. Synclavier and effects: Christopher Currell. Synthesizers: John Barnes, Michael Boddicker, David Paich, and Larry Williams. Swahili chant: Letta Mbulu)

Once Jackson has successfully sped the listener out of "civilized society's" world of control and limitations, we are suddenly transported into the faraway, primal jungles of Africa (Jackson makes a similar move in the video for "Black or White"). The juxtaposition is striking. The sounds shift from mechanical to natural as the noises of engines dissolve into the distant cries of birds and animals. For Jackson, this imagined Africa seems to represent a purer, richer, more connected world. The "Liberian Girl" in the song is the exact opposite of the white police officer: while he is hyper-masculine, domineering, moralistic, and threatening, she is feminine, mysterious, sensitive, and loving. "Liberian Girl," Jackson sings to her, "You know that you came and you changed my world." She frees him from his previous state of fear and repression, and opens up a more fluid, expressive world of music and love.

Both Quincy Jones and Bruce Swedien have pointed to "Liberian Girl" as an example of Jackson's unique and vivid artistic imagination. "All of his stuff is so different," Quincy Jones explained. "I mean, 'Liberian Girl,' who would think of a thing like that? It's amazing. The imagery and everything else. It's [an] amazing fantasy." Bruce Swedien has called it "one of my absolute favorites of all the music I have done with Michael."

The song begins with an intimate Swahili intro (spoken by Letta Mbulu), "Naku penda piya, naku taka piya—mpenziwe (which translates to: "I love you too, I want you too—my love"), followed by deep, exotic drums and lush instrumentation. The *Los Angeles Times* described the track as the album's best ballad, conjuring a "dusky, tropical atmosphere, jazz shadings and less mawkish lyrics [than 'I Just Can't Stop Loving You']." Jackson's vocals are exquisite, beautifully conveying the song's passion and yearning. "The lead, and the big, block background harmonies . . . are absolutely stellar," notes Bruce Swedien. The result is an intoxicating and unusual love song that forced a primarily white audience to consider the beauty and vitality of an African woman.

The final single released from the album, "Liberian Girl" is one of *Bad*'s hidden gems, often overlooked on an album packed with well-known hits. The song is yet another dream capsule in which Jackson transports the listener to a vivid paradise of possibility.

5. JUST GOOD FRIENDS

(Written and composed by Terry Britten and Graham Lyle. Produced by Quincy Jones. Rhythm, synthesizer, and vocal arrangements by Terry Britten, Graham Lyle, and Quincy Jones. Horn arrangement by Jerry Hey. Drum programming: Cornelius Mims. Vocal duet: Michael Jackson and Stevie Wonder. Synthesizer solo: Stevie Wonder. Drums: Ollie E. Brown, Humberto Gatica, and Bruce Swedien. Guitar: Michael Landau. Saxophones: Kim Hutchcroft and Larry Williams. Trumpets: Gary Grant and Jerry Hey. Percussion: Paulinho Da Costa. Synclavier: Christopher Currell. Synthesizers: Michael Boddicker, Rhett Lawrence, Greg Phillinganes, and Larry Williams)

One of just two songs on the album not written by Jackson, "Just Good Friends" is a synth-funk duel featuring two of music's most famous voices. Jackson and Stevie Wonder had been close friends since their days at Motown and held a deep mutual respect for each other's ability. Jackson, in fact, learned a great deal about what he called the "anatomy" of constructing a song by watching Stevie at work in the studio in the seventies. Wonder, meanwhile, considered Jackson a natural genius.

On "Just Good Friends," the pair playfully banter over a girl à la *Thriller*'s "The Girl Is Mine" (it even features a "doggone lover" reference). However, "Just Good Friends" is a cut above "The Girl Is Mine," if not for being one of the album's standouts, then at least for bringing the energy and vocal fireworks. While recording the song together, the two legends ended up providing quite a show for an unexpected visitor. "During the vocal session," recalls assistant engineer Russ Ragsdale, "we had apparently left the studio door unlocked and a homeless man wandered into the tracking room and looked on in awe.... Michael and Stevie were singing together, facing each other. This was the one song on the album that was recorded with the lights on. I remember this like yesterday. The man remained standing against the wall until he was discovered and escorted back outside."

Ragsdale also remembers Stevie laying down "the most ripping synth solo" for the song's bridge. There is no question the song contains its share of charm and energy. Considering the talent involved, however, some listeners viewed the song as a bit of a letdown. Many critics felt Jackson and Wonder—both first-rate songwriters—should have crafted their own song rather than outsourcing it to Terry Britten and Graham Lyle. With such a rare opportunity, they argued, why not attempt something more challenging and innovative rather than coasting on a relatively lightweight vocal workout?

Yet as it stands, the track still features Michael Jackson and Stevie Wonder, and their sheer talent, chemistry, and dynamism make it worth the price of admission.

6. ANOTHER PART OF ME

(Written and composed by Michael Jackson; produced by Quincy Jones. Rhythm and vocal arrangements by Michael Jackson and John Barnes. Horn arrangement by Jerry Hey. Solo and background vocals: Michael Jackson. Guitars: Paul Jackson Jr. and David Williams. Saxophones: Kim Hutchcroft and Larry Williams. Trumpets: Gary Grant and Jerry Hey. Synclavier: Christopher Currell. Synthesizers: Rhett Lawrence and John Barnes)

"Another Part of Me" was originally featured on Jackson's 1986 4-D film attraction, *Captain EO*, at Disneyland. The spacey synth-driven groove is about the cosmic power of music to bring global peace and harmony. "We're takin' over," Jackson sings. "We have the truth/This is the mission/To see it through." Lyrically, it is a sequel to "Can You Feel It," a sincere if simple message song that reflects the good-versus-evil mythology of eighties sci-fi films like *Star Wars*. While the lyrics may have worked in the context of the Tomorrowland attraction, however, critics felt the track revealed a Reagan-esque, messianic naïveté about the world. Unless one reads the song as a satire of Cold-War imperialism, there is some merit to this critique. Certainly many of Jackson's later political songs—"Jam," "They Don't Care About Us," etc.—are much more sophisticated and compelling social statements. While Jackson was a gifted songwriter from the beginning of his solo career, he did grow and mature in many areas, perhaps nowhere more clearly than his "socially-conscious" tracks.

Interestingly, while "Another Part of Me" was one of the first songs written and recorded for *Bad*, it was one of the last to be chosen for inclusion. Jackson leaned toward the edgier, bluesy groove, "Streetwalker" (produced by Bill Bottrell). Quincy Jones, however, favored "Another Part of Me" and ultimately convinced Jackson to keep it on the album. Since *Bad* was primarily a fantasy-themed album, this made some sense (though "Streetwalker" would have added to the edgier concept).

Sonically, "Another Part of Me" offered a taut, mechanical rhythm with sharp horn parts and deft harmonies. The *Los Angeles Times* called it a "heavy R&B riffer ... [with] a timely salute to harmonic convergence." The song reached #1 on the R&B charts in the United States, but was the first Jackson single unable to break the top ten on the *Billboard* Hot 100, peaking at #11.

7. MAN IN THE MIRROR

(Written and composed by Siedah Garrett and Glen Ballard; produced by Quincy Jones. Rhythm arrangements by Glen Ballard and Quincy Jones. Synthesizer arrangement by Glen Ballard, Quincy Jones, and Jerry Hey. Vocal arrangement by Andraé Crouch. Solo and background vocals: Michael Jackson, featuring Siedah Garrett, the Winans (Carvin, Marvin, Michael, and Ronald), and the Andraé Crouch Choir. Clap: Ollie E. Brown. Guitar: Dan Huff. Keyboards: Stefan Stefanovic. Synthesizers: Glen Ballard and Randy Kerber)

While some critics have been slow to recognize its rightful place among popular music's elite recordings, "Man in the Mirror" stands with classics such as John Lennon's "Imagine," Marvin Gaye's "What's Goin' On," and the Beatles' "Let It Be" as one of the great social anthems of the modern age. A passionate, inspirational gospel-fused call for individual and social change, it is not only the centerpiece of *Bad*, but also one of the crowning achievements of Jackson's career. *Time* magazine called it "one of [his] most powerful vocals and accessible social statements, not to mention the best-ever use of a gospel choir in a pop song." Following Jackson's untimely death in the summer of 2009, it was "Man in the Mirror" (similar to Lennon's "Imagine") that people turned to most. More than twenty years after its initial release, it shot to #1 on iTunes and other music sites around the world. "This, more than any other," observed Paul Lester, "was the song that was given a new lease on life through his death, by public demand."

"Man in the Mirror" was written during the late sessions of *Bad*. "Siedah [Garrett] and I wrote it for him directly," recalled Glen Ballard. "Quincy said, 'Don't you have anything for us?' So Siedah wrote 'Man in the Mirror' on a Saturday night at my house in Encino. We didn't have a chance to dress it up, so I didn't feel like it had a chance, but Quincy played it for Michael, and he said, 'Make a track.'"

Jackson took to the song immediately; in rehearsals, he began feeling his way into its rhythm, words, and meaning, intuitively shaping and molding it. "The song was this really magical moment, and it had everything to do with Michael's vocal interpretation," recalls Ballard. "In the last two minutes, [he] started doing these incantations: all the 'shamons' and 'oohs.' He went to that place on his own. We certainly couldn't have written that.... There were all these strange intervals in the vocal harmonies we'd written, and Michael totally got it.... He felt music at its core.... He was so soulful and rhythmically sophisticated.... He knew how to sing flawlessly."

The song begins as a quiet confession: with minimal accompaniment, Jackson snaps his fingers and sings near a cappella. "I'm gonna make a change, for once in my life." "Here," observes Thom Duffy, "the fantasies found elsewhere on *Bad* give way to realism and a call for self-reflection and social action." Gradually, with each verse and chorus, the momentum builds as he looks out at the world's problems and then back at himself. "I've been a victim of a selfish/Kind of love," he sings.

It's time that I realize
That there are some with no home
Not a nickel to loan
Could it be really me
Pretending that they're not alone.

The lyrics convey a stark acknowledgment of his—and by extension, the listener's—passive complicity in other people's poverty and suffering. By "pretending that they're not alone" or ignoring their reality, he feels alienated from his own identity. The mirror serves, ironically, as a reflection not only of the self, but also of the ways the self has been distorted and deceived by misplaced cultural values. It is a bold and timely statement in the midst of the so-called Me Decade of greed, solipsism, and materialism.

Indeed, while some critics have derided the song for being too inward looking (the *New York Times'* Jon Pareles wrote it off as "activism for hermits"), this interpretation seems to willingly ignore both the lyrics and the point of the gospel call-and-response. "Affirmations," writes cultural critic Armond White, "are easy fodder, but Jackson ingeniously sings the song as a challenge.... [The choir is] not coddling the listener, but singing with a joyous communal strength." The use of the choir, in other words, symbolizes solidarity and action; that action, however, first requires an individual awareness and resolve. "No one since Dylan," argued *Rolling Stone*'s Davitt Sigerson, "has written an anthem of community action that has moved so many as Michael's (and Lionel's) 'We Are The World.' And no such grandiose plans can succeed without the first, private steps that Jackson describes here."

Indeed, Jackson sings of homelessness, poverty, and injustice; he sings of "washed out dreams"; he sings of looking outward, then inward, then outward again. Once we see things as they are, once change is internalized, he suggests, we have a chance to change the world. As the song progresses, his guilt (and the listeners') transforms into resolve, conviction, and determination. "I'm starting with the man in the mirror," he sings, "and I'm asking him to change his ways."

The climax of the song is Jackson at his finest: the passionate ad-libbing, the call and response with the brilliant Andraé Crouch Choir, the ecstatic exultations. "It is a remarkable dramatic performance," observed *Time*'s Jay Cocks "—intense, direct and unadorned, one of the best things Jackson has ever done." The intensity came through particularly strong when Jackson performed the anthem live. The song seemed to utterly possess him as he transmitted its energy, urgency, and passion. In his legendary 1988 Grammy performance at Radio City Music Hall in New York, he improvised a nearly three-minute coda that left the audience stunned. "The white man's gotta make a change," he belted, "the black man's gotta make a change." *Rolling Stone* described it as one of his most "amazing performances ... Jackson took the song to church, with a full blown gospel production that stands as one of his most stunning vocal workouts. [He] didn't win a single award that evening, but in a way, this was as majestic and definitive as the *Motown 25* moonwalk."

8. I JUST CAN'T STOP LOVING YOU

(Written and composed by Michael Jackson; produced by Quincy Jones. Vocal duet with Michael Jackson and Siedah Garrett. Bass: Nathan East. Drums: N'dugu Chancler. Guitar: Dan Huff. Percussion: Paulinho Da Costa. Piano: John Barnes. Synclavier: Christopher Currell. Synthesizers: David Paich and Greg Phillinganes. Synthesizer programming: Steve Porcaro. Rhythm arrangement by Quincy Jones. Synthesizer arrangement by David Paich and Quincy Jones. Vocal arrangement by Michael Jackson and John Barnes)

The first single released from *Bad*, "I Just Can't Stop Loving You" was the highest debuting song of 1987. Within weeks, it soared to #1 on the *Billboard* Hot 100, the first of a record five songs on the album to do so. While it was highly anticipated and successful with listeners, however, it was perhaps the most castigated song on the album by critics. A large part of this negative response was due to its position as the lead single. The backlash against Jackson was in full force before *Bad* was even released. Many detractors were simply waiting in the wings, ready to pounce on the first song. In this context, the track was a strange choice to lead with in terms of declaring the album as a whole. To critics, "I Just Can't Stop Loving You" was a safe, sentimental AC ballad that offered no hints about sonic marvels like "Smooth Criminal" or social statements like "Man in the Mirror." Like *Thriller*'s "The Girl Is Mine," then, it made for an easy target—particularly with its original, slightly awkward spoken intro (this intro was taken out of all subsequent editions).

However, without the baggage of its initial context, "I Just Can't Stop Loving You" is actually a fine pop ballad, comparable to the better work of Whitney Houston, Barbra Streisand, and Céline Dion. " Churls may bemoan . . . Jackson's duet," wrote one of few objective critics in 1987, *Rolling Stone*'s Davitt Sigerson, "[But] without descending to musical McCarthyism and questioning the honor of anyone who can fault a record with both finger snaps and timpani, it need only be asked, Who, having heard the song at least twice, can fail to remember that chorus?"

The song was originally intended as a duet with Barbra Streisand. When she declined, the spot was offered to Whitney Houston, who passed as well. Quincy Jones then decided to enlist young R&B protégé (and cowriter of "Man in the Mirror") Siedah Garrett, who wasn't made aware of her new role until the day of the recording. The vocal chemistry, however, was natural, and the song has become one of Jackson's most enduring ballads.

9. DIRTY DIANA

(Written and composed by Michael Jackson; produced by Quincy Jones. Rhythm arrangement by Michael Jackson, John Barnes, and Jerry Hey. Synthesizer arrangement by Michael Jackson, Quincy Jones, and John Barnes. String arrangement by John Barnes. Vocal arrangement by Michael Jackson. Drum programming: Douglas Getschal. Solo and background vocals and clave clapstick: Michael Jackson. Guitar solo: Steve Stevens. Drums: John Robinson. Guitar: Paul Jackson Jr. and David Williams. Synclavier: Christopher Currell. Synclavier synthesis: Denny Jaeger. Synthesizers: John Barnes, Michael Boddicker, and Randy Waldman)

With "Dirty Diana" Jackson is back in cinematic territory. From the opening sound effects, the mood is tense, coiled, dramatic. The music video (directed by Joe Pytka) perfectly captures the drama of the song as Jackson, singing to a live audience, looks anxiously off to the side of the stage where a woman is seen in silhouette, stepping out of a limousine. It is a song about guilt, fame, and seduction.

Jackson wanted a song on the album with a hard-edged rock feel, something that would take the sound a notch higher than "Beat It." To this end, he enlisted the services of Billy Idol's former guitarist, Steve Stevens, who performs a blistering guitar solo. He and Quincy Jones also decided to add crowd noise to give the track a live, raw feel, while John Barnes's string arrangement provided atmosphere. It all set the stage perfectly for Jackson's tense narrative, which Quincy Jones described as an updated version of "Killing Me Softly" (a song Jones produced).

Like that classic and Jackson's "Billie Jean," "Dirty Diana" is a song about a predatory "groupie." Unlike in "Billie Jean," Jackson's character is no longer denying interest or culpability. Rather, in vivid detail, he paints a picture of a woman "who waits at backstage doors for those who have prestige" and a man who is both intrigued and afraid. The song is structured as a dramatic dialogue of seduction and rationalization. Jackson's character is married, which further heightens the situational tension. When Diana says, "I hate sleepin' alone/Why don't you come home with me," Jackson responds that his "baby's at home/She's probably worried tonight/I didn't call on the phone to/Say that I'm alright."

Jackson executes the internal conflict of temptation to perfection, capturing the frustration, guilt, excitement, anger, and pain of an affair. The song's sexuality is by far his most explicit to date; yet like all of Jackson's best songwriting about relationships, the story is subtle and suggestive enough to remain open to interpretation.

Sonically, the song was jolting to those expecting the melodic R&B of *Off the Wall* or even most of *Thriller*. At its dizzying climax, Jackson repeatedly yells, "Come on!" as Steve Stevens's guitar solo soars with abandon amid lasers and screaming fans. "Dirty Diana" became Jackson's fifth single from the album to reach #1 on the *Billboard* Hot 100.

10. SMOOTH CRIMINAL

(Written and composed by Michael Jackson; produced by Quincy Jones. Rhythm arrangement by Michael Jackson and John Barnes. Horn arrangement by Jerry Hey. Vocal arrangement by Michael Jackson. Solo and background vocals and clap: Michael Jackson. Drums: Bill Bottrell, John Robinson, and Bruce Swedien. Guitar: David Williams. Saxophones: Kim Hutchcroft and Larry Williams. Trumpets: Gary Grant and Jerry Hey. Muted Steinway: Kevin Maloney. Synclavier: Christopher Currell. Certain Synclavier effects by Denny Jaeger and Michael Rubini. Synthesizers: John Barnes and Michael Boddicker. Chief of Police announcement by Bruce Swedien. Michael Jackson's heartbeat recording by Dr. Eric Chevlan, digitally processed in the Synclavier)

The album's final dream capsule is the dark, film-noir epic, "Smooth Criminal," a song more attached to its video than perhaps any other Jackson track besides "Thriller." It is another testament to Jackson's unique and vivid imagination that in a time when most music videos continued to offer predictable representations in prosaic settings, Jackson gives us yet another strange and memorable story, taking us deep into the alternative world of 1930s underground Chicago. Here, in a tense nightclub, with the flick of a coin into a jukebox, the scene comes alive with music and dance as Jackson unveils some of his most jaw-dropping moves since "Billie Jean."

Originally conceived as a Western, the ten-minute short for "Smooth Criminal," directed by Colin Chilvers and choreographed by Vincent Paterson, became the centerpiece of Jackson's 1989 film, *Moonwalker* (which eventually surpassed *The Making of Thriller* as the best-selling home music video of all time). The concept was inspired by the musical number, "The Girl Hunt Ballet," from the classic 1952 MGM film, *The Band Wagon* (featuring Fred Astaire). Dressed in his signature white pin-striped suit, suspenders, and hat, Jackson moves about the club with the grace and fluidity of Astaire but a style uniquely his own. "What really makes 'Smooth Criminal' stand out," writes critic Christopher Sunami, "is the choreography as a whole. The advance over the similarly themed 'Beat It' is clear. In 'Beat It' the indelible image is of the gang members gradually joining together with Michael, as their individual chaos is transformed into a massive production number. But in 'Smooth Criminal' the entire speakeasy is alive from beginning to end with motion, choreography encompassing everything from the tango-like dance floor to the gamblers playing craps. Through it all glides Michael, moving sometimes in unison, sometimes in counterpoint, and sometimes in a complex relationship with the other dancers not easily summarized (but reminiscent of the choreography of 'high-art' dancers like Alvin Ailey)."

"None of the signature moves that appear in the video," continues Sunami, "—the moonwalk, the lean, the circular rotation—is sustained for more than a few seconds. Rather, Michael's performance is mercurial, shifting instant by instant through movement vocabularies that other performers might spend years to develop and perfect. This lends a unique quality to his motion. He's not so much dancing to the music as an ordinary person would. Rather, his dancing floats on the top of the music, a dizzying progression of technological virtuosity."

Considered by many to be Jackson's best music video, *Smooth Criminal* is a multisensory masterpiece. Owen Gleiberman describes it as "brilliant," containing "some of [Jackson's] most slashingly visionary dance moves." Jay Ziegler praises it as not only "awesome for its dancing, cinematography, mood, lighting, costume design," but for "rais[ing] the standards of music and filmmaking, specifically for music videos."

The song has become one of Jackson's most memorable rhythm tracks, used for endless dance routines, and covered by numerous artists (most notably by American rock band Alien Ant Farm, who rode the song to #1 on the charts in 2001). Written and arranged by Jackson, "Smooth Criminal" combines elements of film noir, horror, and mystery. The track begins with frightened breathing and the sound of a pounding heartbeat (actually Jackson's heartbeat, recorded by Dr. Eric Chevlan and digitally processed in the Synclavier). The suspense gradually builds until the song explodes into the signature opening bass line. As in "Speed Demon," Jackson's vocals are more throaty and rough as he describes the disturbing murder (and possibly rape) of a fictional girl named Annie.

"As he came into the window," Jackson recounts as witness, "It was the sound of a crescendo/He came into her apartment/He left the bloodstains on the carpet." Listeners of the song often overlook the song's dark subject matter. Once again, Jackson proves that a pop song can explore unexpected (even uncomfortable) territory. In the final chorus, he conveys a profound sense of desperation and sadness over the still body of the victim as he answers the track's recurring question, "Annie, are you okay?" with the resigned, "I don't know! I don't know!" over multiple layers of rhythmic vocals.

Music critic Owen Gleiberman describes the song as "gorgeously, ominously intoxicating" and the sequel to "Billie Jean." "It's a song that remains, after more than twenty years, Michael's single most under-celebrated masterpiece.... One listen to its two-step heartbeat, its percolating syncopated bass line, and you can hear that it's 'Billie Jean' shot through with more anxiety.... 'Smooth Criminal' mourns the death of Annie, but at the same time, the song is a violent rock-and-roll fantasia in which the innocent Annie must die to atone for Billie Jean's sin. It's a song that glistens like a dagger in the night, because it reflects the ecstatic anger in Michael Jackson's soul."

11. LEAVE ME ALONE

(Written and composed by Michael Jackson. Rhythm and vocal arrangement by Michael Jackson. Solo and background vocals and vocal synthesizer: Michael Jackson. Drum programming and synthesizers: Larry Williams. Guitar: Paul Jackson Jr. Synclavier and synthesizer programming: Casey Young. Synthesizer: Greg Phillinganes)

Because of space constraints, "Leave Me Alone" appeared only on the CD version of *Bad*. Yet this intricately arranged song is yet another audiovisual tour de force, with the satirical, Grammy-Award winning video further illuminating the song's blunt message. "I worked hard on the song," Jackson recalled, "stacking vocals on top of each other like layers of clouds." He also worked hard on the video, which took twenty-five people more than six months to realize to the singer's satisfaction. *Rolling Stone* called the song "vintage Michael" with "a batch of thick chords for Jackson to vamp over" creating a "darker inversion of 'The Way You Make Me Feel.'" *All Music Guide*'s Stephen Thomas Erlewine proclaimed it the album's best song.

While that distinction is debatable, "Leave Me Alone" was certainly Jackson's boldest response to date to his legions of critics. For years, the press—mainstream and tabloid alike—fed on Michael Jackson like no other pop star in history. "Leave Me Alone" is his expression of exasperation at a media and public that had grown insatiable.

In the music video, Jackson shrewdly opts for humor and satire instead of self-pity. Directed (with input by Jackson) by the revolutionary Jim Blashfield, the short film presents Jackson's complex life in the form of an amusement park ride. "While poking fun at the wildest tabloid rumors about the star's life," writes critic Jim Farber, "Blashfield offers unexpected insight into Jackson's psychology. He constructs two Jacksons here—one an impish child, the other a Gulliver-style giant, trapped in a labyrinth of roller coasters and log flumes. With wit and empathy, he portrays him as an adult enslaved to a child's fantasies."

Yet Jackson is not merely portrayed as a slave to his *own* fantasies. Throughout the film, he sings from various representations of capitalist consumption: newspapers, dollar bills, and reenactments of tabloid stories (including sleeping in a hyperbaric chamber and dancing with the Elephant Man's bones). It is a knowing critique of crass exploitation, of a postmodern funhouse of distraction and deception in which Jackson is paradoxically victim and participant. He is the goldfish trapped in the fishbowl and the sideshow entertainer who nonetheless wants to entertain.

By the video's end, a literally larger-than-life Jackson has been pinned down among the numerous carnival attractions (à la Jonathan Swift's *Gulliver's Travels*), as dogs in corporate suits relentlessly pound pegs into the ground to tie the singer down. Finally, however, he has had enough. He begins to realize what he has become (or at least how he is being perceived and exploited) and breaks through the ropes that have bound him. As he stands up, he crushes the roller coaster and other nearby rides and looks around pensively at the circus scene that surrounds him. The video ends here, leaving Jackson's next step intentionally ambiguous. It is unknown whether he will, or can, ever completely escape the circus that has become his reality.

A fascinating exploration of contemporary culture, identity, celebrity, and media, *Leave Me Alone* is one of Jackson's keenest and most provocative videos. It was also a revealing glimpse into what lay ahead.

OTHER NOTABLE *BAD*-ERA SONGS

BUFFALO BILL (recorded 1984, unreleased)
Jackson worked on the song with John Barnes during the early *Bad* sessions. It had "a big symphonic opening and a charming melody," according to Bruce Swedien. "That song went through such contortions and changes and green writes and variations," recalls Matt Forger. "But an amazing song . . . " The track was inspired by Wild Bill Hickock, a poker player who was shot in the back and became a dime-novel hero.

CHEATER (recorded 1987, released on *Michael Jackson: The Ultimate Collection*, 2004)
A fantastic organ-driven track about infidelity. Jackson worked on the song with keyboardist Greg Phillinganes. An almost-finished demo, with Jackson's signature finger-snapping and gritty vocals, was released on *The Ultimate Collection* in 2004.

EATEN ALIVE (recorded 1985, unreleased)
A provocative rhythm track Jackson co-wrote with the Bee Gees. Jackson later allowed Diana Ross to record the song, providing vocals for the chorus. Ross's version was released on her 1985 album by the same title.

FLY AWAY (recorded 1987, released on *Bad, Special Edition*, 2001)
A gorgeous song featuring sublime vocals and a catchy chorus. Jackson wrote the song during the *Bad* sessions, but it failed to make the final lineup. He later gave it to his sister Rebbie to re-record with his background vocals.

GET IT (recorded 1986, released on *Characters* by Stevie Wonder, 1987)
A funky, late-eighties-sounding duet by Jackson and Stevie Wonder.

GROOVE OF MIDNIGHT (recorded 1987, unreleased)
One of the final songs Jackson worked on with Rod Temperton. Nice R&B feel with rich harmonies. It was later recorded by Siedah Garrett and released on her 1988 album, *Kiss of Life*.

MAKE OR BREAK (recorded 1986, unreleased)
Jackson worked on this dance track with John Barnes and Matt Forger. "Very driving, terrific hook, but never got finished," recalls Matt Forger.

SCARED OF THE MOON (recorded 1984. released on *Michael Jackson: The Ultimate Collection*, 2004)
A haunting, poetic song about a young girl's childhood fears and isolation. While what haunts the girl at night (abuse? neglect?) isn't fully revealed, what is tragically clear is that she faces it alone, where it "terrorizes" and "twists her soul" every night. The Blakean narrative traces the "fearful toll" it takes on her psyche, even into adulthood. The final stanza depicts a group of similarly-scarred childhood victims ("Together they gather/Their lunacy shared/ Not knowing just why they're scared"). The song, composed by Jackson and the talented Buz Kohan (who later wrote "Gone Too Soon"), was based on a story Jackson learned from Brooke Shields about her sister. The story resonated deeply for Jackson. He wrote it down in detail in a notebook and, soon after, came up with the song's mournful melody..

STREETWALKER (recorded 1988, released on *Bad: Special Edition*, 2001)
An outstanding, invigorating track featuring harmonica by Jasun Martz, smooth harmonies, and a fat, synthesized, boogie-woogie bass line. Jackson worked on the song with Bill Bottrell. While it was left off *Bad* in favor of "Another Part of Me," it feels right at home with the album, and has since become one of Jackson's most popular non-album tracks. Jackson mentioned the song in a 1994 court deposition as a precursor to the song "Dangerous," which features a variation of the track's driving bass line.

WE ARE HERE TO CHANGE THE WORLD (recorded 1986; released on *Michael Jackson: The Ultimate Collection*, 2004)
A funky rhythm track recorded with John Barnes during the early *Bad* sessions and featured on the 4-D film attraction, *Captain EO*, along with "Another Part of Me."

Jackson on the set of his 1987 short film *Bad*, directed by Martin Scorsese. Jackson was hoping to achieve a tougher, edgier image with his new album.

CHAPTER 4 DANGEROUS

Dangerous was a new kind of album for Michael Jackson. After a remarkable run with Quincy Jones that resulted in three of the most successful and influential albums in modern music history, Jackson refused to simply rest on his laurels or repeat proven formulas. He was ready for a new challenge, a new sound, and a new vision.

Acting for the first time as executive producer, Jackson boldly sought out fresh talent, including new jack-swing mastermind Teddy Riley. However, this wasn't simply a "new jack" album, as it has often been characterized. *Dangerous* sampled Beethoven's Ninth Symphony; it featured talents as diverse as the Andraé Crouch Singers Choir, Slash, and Heavy D; it explored issues of race, identity, alienation, and God. It was an eclectic, maximalist collection as audacious as anything pop music had seen. Having already achieved the pinnacle of commercial success, Jackson wanted to create something for the ages—something that wouldn't just entertain but also provoke and inspire.

At seventy-seven minutes, *Dangerous* fulfilled Jackson's lofty vision. By turns, gritty, haunting, and transcendent, it not only became the singer's most socially conscious album to date, but also his most personally revealing. Its very cover—an intricate, circus-like mask from which piercing eyes gaze out at the world—signifies a new self-awareness and depth. A dazzling musical odyssey, *Dangerous* is Michael Jackson's *Songs in the Key of Life*: the work of an artist engaging with the world around him—and inside him—as never before.

RELEASED: *November 26, 1991*

EXECUTIVE PRODUCER: *Michael Jackson*

KEY CONTRIBUTORS: Teddy Riley *(producing/songwriting)*, Bill Bottrell *(producing/songwriting)*, Bruce Swedien *(recording/mixing/songwriting)*, Matt Forger *(recording/mixing/technical director)*, Brad Sundberg *(technical director)*, Brad Buxer *(arrangement/keyboard)*, Steve Porcaro and David Paich *(synth/arrangement)*, Andraé Crouch Singers Choir *(vocals)*, Glen Ballard *(songwriting)*, Siedah Garret *(songwriting)*, Buz Kohan *(songwriting)*, Slash *(guitar)*, Heavy D *(rap)*, Johnny Mandel *(orchestra)*

SINGLES: *"Black or White," "Remember the Time," "In the Closet," "Jam," "Who Is It," "Heal the World," "Give Into Me," "Will You Be There," "Dangerous"*

ESTIMATED COPIES SOLD: *40 million*

Much had changed in the world since the release of *Bad* in 1987. Politically, it was a time of volatility and transition. In 1988, George Bush Sr. defeated Democratic nominee Michael Dukakis in a landslide to become the forty-first president of the United States. The campaign, however, brought the specter of racism to the surface with the infamous Willie Horton ad reinforcing stereotypes and fears of black men. A few years later, in 1991, racial tensions boiled over again following the brutal beating of Rodney King and the ensuing riots in Los Angeles. On *Dangerous*, in response to this climate, Jackson would explicitly confront racism for the first time in his career.

Meanwhile, the AIDS epidemic loomed larger than ever with the deaths of high-profile figures like Ryan White, who Jackson had befriended in 1989, and Queen frontman Freddie Mercury, who Jackson had collaborated with in the early eighties. In November 1991, basketball star Magic Johnson shocked the world when he announced in a press conference that he too had contracted the HIV virus and would retire from basketball immediately. The next year, he was in Michael Jackson's video for "Remember the Time."

Overseas, the world saw both signs of hope and destruction. In 1989, joyous images of the Berlin Wall being taken down with sledgehammers were tempered with the picture of a young man standing in front of a tank at Tiananmen Square. Likewise, in 1990, the long-awaited prison release of South African antiapartheid icon Nelson Mandela was contrasted with Saddam Hussein's invasion of Kuwait and the subsequent Persian Gulf War.

For many, however, these were distant events that played out like movies on TV. Closer to home, families dealt with neglect, divorce, and dysfunction (as depicted in popular shows such as *Married with Children* and *The Simpsons*). In school and on the streets, the zeitgeist was shifting from the optimism and materialism of the eighties to a restless anxiety and alienation that came to define Generation X. These were the children of the baby boomers: they had grown up with Cold War propaganda, Reagan, MTV, and video games. By the end of the decade, they were beginning to reassess the "material world" they had been raised in.

Of course, throughout the eighties, this alternative undercurrent was present, as represented by revolutionary hip-hop groups such as Run DMC and Public Enemy and alternative acts such as R.E.M. and the Pixies. However, by late 1991—the year Michael Jackson's *Dangerous* was released—grunge and gangsta rap were beginning to take the country by storm. It was January 1992, when Nirvana's seminal album, *Nevermind*, replaced Jackson's *Dangerous* at the top of the charts. Many saw it as a symbolic moment that officially ended the reign of pop and ushered in the grunge era with bands such as Nirvana, Pearl Jam, Soundgarden, and Smashing Pumpkins taking over the airwaves and MTV.

In our tendency to simplify history, however, we often forget that in music and culture there are always multiple currents. Before Jackson's *Dangerous* was replaced by Nirvana's *Nevermind* on the *Billboard* charts, it had likewise knocked off U2's *Achtung Baby*, which had previously knocked off Guns N' Roses multi-platinum–

Jackson, pictured here in his *In the Closet* video, reinvented himself again to begin the new decade.

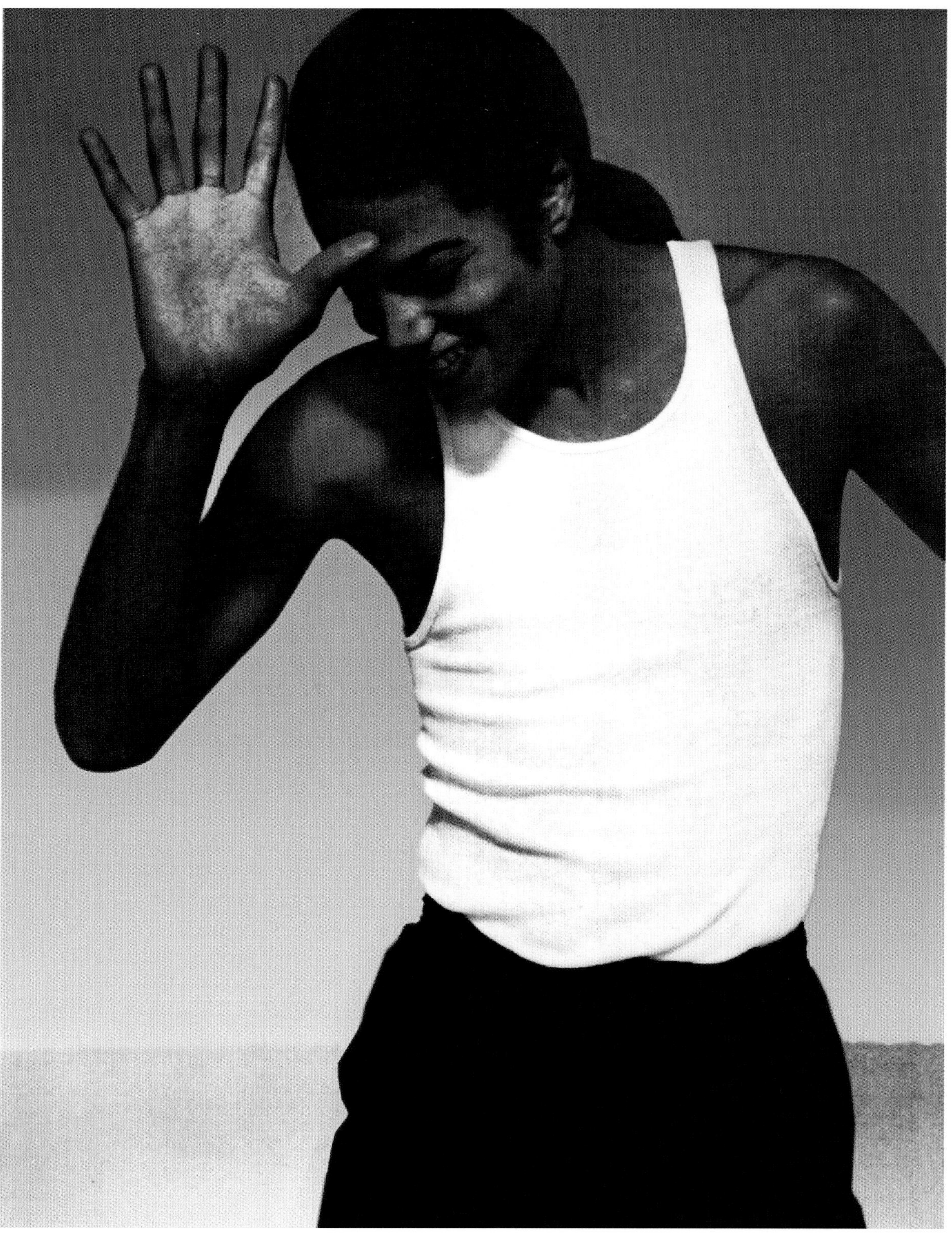

selling *Use Your Illusion I and II*. The best-selling album of 1992, interestingly, was the soundtrack for *The Bodyguard*, featuring six songs by Whitney Houston.

Grunge certainly made its presence felt in the early nineties, but it was also an era that saw the popularity of everything from the pop-country of Garth Brooks to the pop-rap of MC Hammer and Vanilla Ice. Perennial stars such as Madonna, Prince, and Janet Jackson competed on the charts with newcomers Paula Abdul, Mariah Carey, and Sinead O'Connor. In rock, the diverse styles of Guns N' Roses, U2, and R.E.M. still enjoyed massive success even as the Seattle wave began to rise. While *Nevermind* was the CD of choice for angst-filled teens in the suburbs (and among predominantly white critics), the streets were splintering in different directions. More cerebral acts such as Living Colour and Arrested Development provided a counterpoint to the rising movement of gangsta rap, whose blunt expressions about sex, drugs, and gang violence inspired a decade-long takeover of hip-hop (which really exploded in late 1992 with the release of Dr. Dre's *The Chronic*).

The late eighties/early nineties also saw the rise of another street-inspired movement: new jack swing. The brainchild of hip producer-artists such as Teddy Riley, L. A. Reid, and Babyface, the new jack sound "galvanized pop music" in the late eighties. New jack was "a tight, jazz-inflected variation on hip-hop" that also incorporated elements of funk, R&B, and soul. "Classic rap assaults your guts with its maxed-out, sloppy bass," wrote music critic Robert Doerschuk in 1992. "Under similar circumstances, new jack swing goes for your feet and your brain. It's as tidy as it is tight."

Indeed, using "a hybrid of rhythms and drum machine wizardry" it was a forward-looking sound that became the foundation of much contemporary R&B. It also paid homage to its roots, carrying echoes of Motown soul, James Brown funk, and Stevie Wonder studio mastery. Journalist and filmmaker Barry Michael Cooper coined the term new jack swing in a feature about Teddy Riley for *The Village Voice* in 1988. It quickly caught on. "Three words in one capsule," wrote Doerschuk in 1992, "fashioned to slip smoothly down the media's throat—snap, crackle, pop for the '90s. It's the hook of the season, the je ne sais quoi that everyone wants in their rhythm tracks."

". . . fashioned to slip smoothly down the media's throat—snap, crackle, pop for the '90s."

New jack's primary godfather was Teddy Riley, a young musical prodigy from the projects of Harlem who began producing and singing professionally before he could drive a car. In 1987 (the same year *Bad* was released), he arrived on the national scene, producing Keith Sweat's *Make It Last Forever* and one year later, Guy's self-titled multi-platinum album. His major breakout, however, came with the Grammy-Award winning 1989 hit, "My Prerogative," by New Edition's Bobby Brown. The song showcased the possibilities of blending the street-sensibilities of hip-hop with the smoothness of R&B. In fact, sonically it was not far from what Jackson was doing with the song "Bad."

Riley, then, was one of the hottest young R&B producers in the industry as the decade transitioned. When he met Michael Jackson in

1991, he was just twenty-five years old. It was a big risk for the much more established Jackson, who had almost single-handedly defined the sound of dance music in the eighties. However, Jackson wanted something "new" and "fresh" for *Dangerous* and he liked what he heard in the rhythms, beats, and textures of new jack swing.

Jackson had barely returned from his record-setting sixteen-month, one hundred and twenty three-concert *Bad* World Tour in early 1989 before he was back in the studio, working on new material. The big change was that he was no longer working with Quincy Jones. Before *Off the Wall*, the pair had worked out a three-album contract. Now that it had been fulfilled, Jackson made the decision not to renew. Some read this as Jackson stiffing Jones or speculated about a falling out. Certainly there were some strains in the final years. After a decade of work together, Jackson felt anxious to branch out on his own. His desire for more independence was already apparent with the two largely separate creative teams he assembled for *Bad*. The truth was, however, that Jackson retained an enormous amount of love and respect for Quincy Jones.

"Michael was not angry with Quincy," says songwriter/musician Brad Buxer. "He has always had an admiration for him and an immense respect. But with *Dangerous*, Michael wanted to control the creative process from A to Z. Simply put, he wanted to be his own boss. Michael was always very independent, and he also wanted to show that his success was not because of one man, namely Quincy."

For Jackson, this full autonomy was invigorating and liberating. He began working on a range of experimental tracks with people such as Bill Bottrell, Brad Buxer, and Matt Forger at Westlake Studios. Many of the resulting songs from these sessions—including demos of "Black or White," "Who Is It," "Monkey Business," "Dangerous," and "Earth Song"—were unlike anything Jackson had done before. Not only were the sounds and styles evolving, but the material was becoming more challenging. By the end of 1989, a planned double-disc greatest-hits package called *Decade*, which would feature four new songs in addition to the classics, was canned due to the influx of new material. Jackson was already reluctant to do a project that looked backward, but once Sony executives heard some of the early tracks for *Dangerous*, they were convinced it would be worth the wait.

Recording engineer Matt Forger, who had worked with Jackson since *Thriller*, remembers the years between *Bad* and *Dangerous* as a constant flow of creativity: "With Michael, he never stopped creating. He wasn't an artist who said, 'Oh, I've got an album coming up, I better start writing songs.' The songs were constantly flowing from him, and if it wasn't a song it was a poem, it was an idea for a story or short film.... It was a constant creative process."

In 1989, Bill Bottrell brought in talented keyboardist, Brad Buxer, who had previously worked with Stevie Wonder. Buxer joined a studio session of "Heal the World" and the chemistry with Jackson was immediate. "It was pretty unbelievable really," recalls Buxer. "I will never forget my first encounter with him. A current immediately passed between us. Musically speaking, we were on the same wavelength; we spoke the same language."

Jackson valued Buxer's instincts as well as his classical training and versatility. The pair would work closely together over the next twenty years. "He was always open to my suggestions and ideas," says Buxer. "He gave me full confidence. . . . From a musical point of view, Michael was a genius; he knew he could not do everything and he had the intelligence to delegate some things. Sometimes he knew exactly what he wanted to hear, all the parts of a song. Other times, he let me play until he heard something he liked."

Jackson had a similar relationship with Bill Bottrell, who became one of the key contributors to *Dangerous*. Bottrell had been working with Jackson since the early *Bad* sessions in 1985. "I was an engineer when he first hired me," recalls Bottrell. "I worked by the hour all around L.A. Michael just started asking me, unlike many of my other clients, to take more responsibility." By 1989, Bottrell had established himself as a respected and in-demand songwriter/producer/engineer who earned a Grammy and a #1 hit for engineering Madonna's seminal track, "Like a Prayer" (a few years later he would produce Sheryl Crow's multi-platinum debut album).

Bottrell brought a different musical sensibility from Quincy Jones or Teddy Riley. He could do pop, but he infused it with elements of rock, blues, folk, and country. Jackson not only liked the alternative sound Bottrell provided, but he also felt they challenged each other. Bottrell could bring out regions of Jackson's artistry he hadn't explored before, which excited Jackson. The respect was mutual. "It was Michael who actually drew me out as a musician," acknowledges Bottrell. "He would hum me things and go away, and I'd be there alone for two weeks, working on a track. I was used to sampling, but he needed music; guitars, keyboards, you name it. That's what he expected of me. He assumed I could do it, and since I had been a musician before going into engineering I just followed his lead."

Jackson and Bottrell worked together in spurts over the next three years as individual tracks and the album as a whole began to coalesce. "Michael was always prepared to listen and put his trust in me," Bottrell recalls, "but he was also a sort of guide all the time. He knew why I was there and, among all the songs he was recording, what he needed from me. I was an influence that he didn't otherwise have. I was the rock guy and also the country guy, which nobody else was. He has precise musical instincts. He has an entire record in his head and he tries to make people deliver it to him. Sometimes those people surprise him and augment what he hears, but really his job is to extract from musicians and producers and engineers what he hears when he wakes up in the morning." Three Jackson-Bottrell collaborations—"Black or White," "Give In To Me," and "Who Is It"—would end up on the album, while several others—including "Earth Song" and "Monkey Business"—surfaced on subsequent releases.

While it took more than a year to coordinate, Jackson was also able to enlist the most popular guitarist in the world at the time, Guns N' Roses' Slash, for two of those tracks. It seemed an unlikely pairing but speaks to the respect Jackson elicited in all areas of the music industry. "He's a fucking brilliant entertainer," Slash would later say, "a complete natural. He's the only guy I've ever met that's real—for that kind of music. I grew up listening to the Jackson 5. I used to love 'Dancing Machine.' We've been friends for a while, so he just lets me do what I want to do. I get a basic framework, and I just make up my part and they edit it. I wonder sometimes what it's gonna sound like, [laughs] but every time, they do a great job. He's very shrewd. He's got a great, sarcastic sense of humor. People always ask me, 'Is he weird?' Well, he's different. But I know what it's like to be weird, growing up in the music business. I have to admit working with Michael Jackson is different than working with your basic, gritty rock 'n' roll band. One time when I went to play for Michael, he walked in with Brooke Shields, and there I am with a cigarette in one hand, a bottle of Jack Daniel's in the other, and my guitar hanging low around my neck. And he doesn't care. That's not the way he is, but I don't have to change for him. He accepts me for what I am."

Meanwhile, for the gospel-based songs Jackson tapped talented songwriters Glen Ballard and Siedah Garrett (who had cowritten "Man in the Mirror") and the Andraé Crouch Singers Choir (who performed on both "Will You Be There" and "Keep the Faith").

By 1990, recording on *Dangerous* had shifted from Westlake to Record One at the Ocean Way facilities. The material kept coming as Jackson tested out new collaborators, including R&B big shots, L. A. Reid and Babyface (none of their work made it onto *Dangerous*). Jackson also recorded several songs with Bryan Loren and Richard Cottrell, including funky tracks such as "Work That Body" and "Superfly Sister" (the latter of which surfaced on *Blood on the Dance Floor*). Loren was deeply disappointed when he learned that none of his tracks would make the *Dangerous* album. "We recorded some twenty-plus tracks together," recalls Loren. "Sadly, many of these we never finished. But when we did do vocals, beyond his lead work it was always a pleasure to listen to this man lay background harmonies. His voice was truly unique. Really pure tone, and great intonation."

A lighter moment between an unlikely pair: Michael Jackson and Slash, preparing for a performance in 1991.

While much of this work was very good, Jackson was still searching. He wanted something edgier and grittier for the dance tracks. "Michael loved finding new sounds that the human ear had never heard," recalls Brad Buxer. "Often, he [would say], 'Brad, get me a sound that hurts really bad.' That meant he wanted something that shakes him inside." Buxer and Matt Forger remember going out and recording "organic" percussion sounds. They would hit on things like glass, metal, or trash cans (occasionally with baseball bats), and Teddy Riley recorded samples from Jackson's zoo at Neverland. Jackson simply heard "music" in everything and asked his collaborators to record it and store it for potential use.

Teddy Riley finally came to the project toward the end of 1990. By this time, Jackson had worked on more than seventy potential songs for the album but still wanted more. Riley, he determined, could be the missing ingredient. When he called to ask the young producer if he wanted to help out, Riley didn't hesitate. Working with the King of Pop was the opportunity of a lifetime; he was ecstatic to get the call. He wasn't oblivious, however, to the big shoes he was stepping into. "There was more pressure," he says. "I didn't want to be the one to fail Michael." Yet he also knew Jackson didn't want or expect him to be Quincy Jones.

When Riley arrived at Neverland, Jackson took him on a tour of the grounds as they talked about life and music. Riley remembers Jackson asking him specifically about a song he had recorded with Guy called "Spend the Night." "He started scatting and beatboxing different parts of it," recalls Riley, "wanting to know where I'd gotten certain sounds. He told me [it] was his favorite of my songs and wanted me to give him something stronger than that."

That night Jackson had a helicopter fly Riley to a nearby Universal Hilton. "I didn't check out until a year and two months later," recalls Riley. Indeed, Riley spent about half the time sleeping at Larrabee Studios as he worked on track after track for *Dangerous*.

Still, when he first arrived, Riley was understandably a bit intimidated to be working with Michael Jackson. At one point, Jackson confronted him, saying, "Listen, you're going to have to really produce me.... I need you to talk to me, I need you to criticize me, I need you to comment, I need you to give me all of you."

Jackson not only worked with Riley on new songs, but also on some he had recorded versions of before, including "Jam" and "Dangerous." "Teddy was very professional," said Jackson's longtime recording engineer Bruce Swedien. "No problems. He'd come in with a groove, we'd say it wasn't exactly right, and there would be no complaining. He'd just go back and then come back in and blow us away with something like 'Dangerous.'"

Riley learned Jackson's likes and dislikes early on and was quick to adapt new jack's signature sound. "I was using a lot of vintage stuff to get the sound we needed," Riley recalls. "Reeds and SSL XLs were mainly the boards we used—I always loved vintage better than digital. It's way better ... much warmer." Of one particular exchange, Riley remembers Jackson saying, "'You know what I'd like to have overlaid to new jack swing? I'd still like to have my strings. I want the strings to be really wide.' So that's what we did, even on 'Dangerous.'" Jackson also refused to use stock sounds—he wanted everything to sound original—so when they didn't use live instruments, they manipulated the sound in the studio.

Once they were in the creative zone, Jackson and Riley began working feverishly, coming up with incredible song after incredible song. To get a feel for a track in progress, Jackson would characteristically crank up the volume in the studio. "Michael likes to listen [to music] even louder than me," said Riley. "His volume is past twelve. I'm maybe nine or ten. His volume is twelve-plus. Oh, man, he loves loud music. And he jams! Only way you know your music is right is if he's dancing all over the studio."

As the making of the album unfolded, Riley admittedly learned just as much as he directed. "He always pushed me to be different and innovative and strong. He was demanding and we'd work on songs for a long time; we always had to get the mix right. We had the elements, but we had to get the mix right."

He wanted Dangerous *to be his best work yet. He wanted to prove he could make a great album without Quincy Jones.*

In the end, however, the hard work paid off. Exactly half of the album's fourteen songs were Jackson-Riley products. It was a fortuitous choice on Jackson's part—requiring patience, risk, and some luck—but it paid huge dividends. When Jackson told Riley the good news—that seven of their collaborations would make the album—Riley was over the moon. "I felt confident 'Remember the Time' would make the cut but I was blown away when he mentioned the names of six other songs we'd done together. 'These are all great!' he said."

With so many new faces on board, the major standby for Jackson was Bruce Swedien, who joined the new team in 1990. Swedien was not only the consummate professional and brilliant at bringing out the vitality of Jackson's performances, but he was also someone Jackson could count on. While singing "Keep the Faith" during the stressful final weeks of recording, Swedien remembers Jackson's suddenly leaving in the middle of the take. He found him standing in the corner of an office, "crying his eyes out." His perfectionism and anxiety about the song (and album as a whole) had finally caught up to him. Swedien eventually calmed Jackson down, and the two went back to work on the song. It was already very late in the night, but Swedien told Jackson, "We're not going home until you've sung this all the way through." They didn't leave the studio till dawn, but Jackson went home satisfied with the result.

With this diverse, talented creative team, Jackson tackled *Dangerous* with all the energy, imagination, and hard work he possessed. Recording would take place, on and off, for nearly three years, which tested everyone's patience. However, Jackson was on a creative high and his passion was infectious. He wanted *Dangerous* to be his best work yet. He wanted to prove he could make a great album without Quincy Jones. He wanted it to sell one hundred million copies. He wanted the quality to be so high the music "would live forever." These were lofty goals, but then, Jackson was never one to aim low.

It was an exciting, rejuvenating time in many ways for Jackson. In addition to a new creative team, he had also purchased a new home in 1988: a secluded ranch in the beautiful Santa Ynez Valley (located about one hundred miles north of Los Angeles). He would call it Neverland.

Jackson first fell in love with the area back in 1982 while filming the music video for "Say Say Say" with Paul McCartney. Neverland was then called Sycamore Ranch, a 2,700-acre estate that featured an English-style country house with beautiful wood detailing, seventeen rooms, and a wine cellar. The property was just outside of Los Olivos, a quaint village of one thousand residents known for its art galleries, wine, and antiques. Far away from the bustle and smog of Los Angeles, the Santa Ynez Valley was a quiet, private place with picturesque vistas, rolling hills, and sprawling ranches. It seemed to be the perfect escape for the incessantly hounded superstar.

Over the following months and years, Jackson would invest the same creative energy he gave to his music into his new home. Jackson had already transformed his shared home in Encino into a kind of Disney-esque fantasyland, complete with exotic animals, a mini-version of Main Street, U.S.A., and a small theater. "I put this stuff in here, so I'll never have to go out there," he reasoned. Jackson had an even greater vision for his new estate.

Neverland was a child's paradise: There was a C. P. Huntington–style train (similar to the one at Disneyland) that circled around much of the grounds. There were teepees and forts and barricades for water balloon fights. There was an amusement park complete with bumpers cars, a flying ride, and a large Ferris wheel; a recreation building and an arcade; and a five-acre lake with a bridge crossing over it and a waterfall. A zoo held giraffes and deer, zebras and llamas, lions and chimpanzees. A beautiful theater was furnished with lush crimson seats, a full-size stage, and a movie screen. Just outside the theater—past the concession stands filled with candy, drinks, and popcorn—a sign announced which movie was playing that night. There were statues of blissful children everywhere, and throughout the grounds, speakers played classical music from composers such as Debussy and Tchaikovsky.

Neverland Ranch was an imagined world made real, a gated Utopia, a hiding place apart from screaming fans, reporters and photographers, lawyers, managers, and music executives. Apart even from his father and family. It was a place of which he'd secretly always dreamed.

Secluded in Neverland, Jackson, now thirty-one, felt free to explore regions of his identity, worldview, and purpose that he never had before. When he wasn't creating, he was reading voraciously: everything from the verses of Emerson and Wordsworth, to the biographies of Michelangelo and Beethoven, from the psychology of Freud and Jung, to Sufi poetry (Jackson's personal library grew to more than twenty thousand titles, including numerous first editions of his favorite classics). Jackson also began meditating. In 1988, he became close friends with Indian physician and spiritualist, Deepak Chopra, who encouraged Jackson to develop and express his intuitions about the world. "I sat with him for hours," Chopra recalled, "while he dreamily wove Aesop-like tales about animals, mixed with words about music and his love of all things musical. This project became *Dancing the Dream* [published by Doubleday in 1992] after I pulled the text together for him, acting strictly as a friend. It was this time together that convinced me of the modus vivendi Michael had devised for himself: to counter the tidal wave of stress that accompanies megastardom, he built a private retreat in a fantasy world where pink clouds veiled inner anguish and Peter Pan was a hero, not a pathology."

For Jackson, this was an important time of self-discovery. Spiritually, he had largely grown out of the exclusive, apocalyptic worldview of his childhood religion, the Jehovah's Witnesses (in 1987, he officially withdrew his membership). The God of the Jehovah's Witnesses was too angry and cruel for the sensitive Jackson to understand. The God of his childhood wouldn't allow birthdays or Christmases. He was vengeful

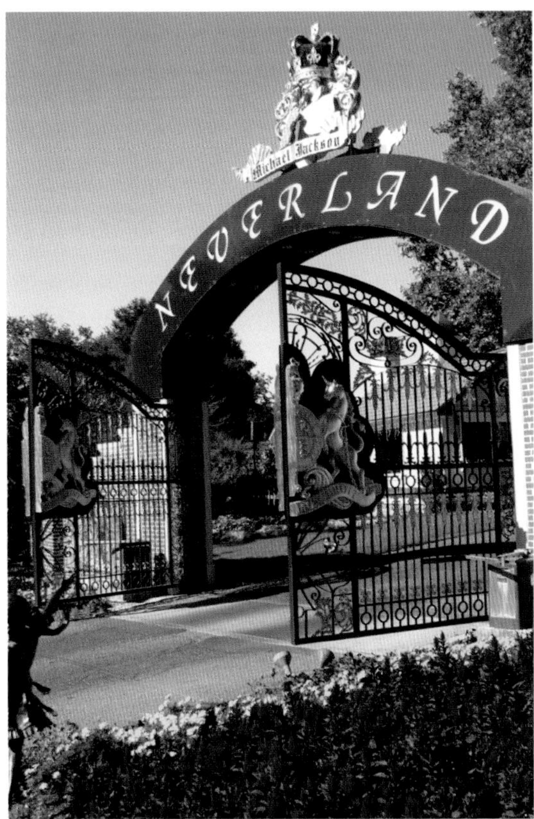

The gate to Jackson's mythical home, Neverland Ranch. Jackson bought the property in 1988 and lived there until 2005.

and demanding. He was too much like Jackson's father. Jackson remembered the Jehovah's Witness elders calling his "Motown 25" performance "dirty burlesque dancing" and the *Thriller* video "demonic." "When I did certain things in the past that I didn't realize were against the religion and I was reprimanded for it, it almost destroyed me," Jackson confessed. "Certain things that I did as an artist in my music I didn't realize I was crossing a line with them and when they chastised me, it really hurt me. It almost destroyed it. My mother saw it."

In place of this strict fundamentalism, Jackson was developing a more naturalistic, inclusive worldview, which in turn had an impact on his art. In a piece called "God" in *Dancing the Dream* he writes: "It's strange that God doesn't mind expressing Himself/Herself in all the religions of the world, while people still cling to the notion that their way is the only right way. . . . For me the form God takes is not the most important thing. What's most important is the essence. My songs and dances are outlines for Him to come in and fill. I hold out the form, She puts in the sweetness. . . . I've looked up at the night sky and beheld the stars so intimately close, it was as if my grandmother had made them for me. . . . But for me the sweetest contact with God has no form. I close my eyes, look within, and enter a deep soft silence. The infinity of God's creation embraces me. We are one."

Jackson still appreciated many of the rituals, morals, and community of religion. Now, however, he saw God less as an authority figure and more as a creative energy.

Much of the rest of *Dancing the Dream* provides glimpses into Jackson's romantic, wonder-filled vision of "the world around us and the universe within each of us." It is a book that has received little attention; yet years after its publication, Jackson said it was a better representation of him than his autobiography.

In "Planet Earth" he speaks to it as a lover, asking: "Do you care, have you a part/In the deepest emotions of my own heart/Tender with breezes, caressing and whole/Alive with music, haunting my soul." Jackson's poem "Magical Child" carries echoes of the English poet William Wordsworth, with its message of wisdom, truth, and ecstasy found in the innocence and purity of children. "And while they whispered and conspired," writes Jackson, "Through endless rumors to get him tired/To kill his wonder, trample him near/ Burn his courage, fuel his fear/The child remained just simple, sincere." In other works, Jackson writes of the grace and joy of dolphins, the freedom of hawks, and the majesty of elephants.

"The whole world abounds in magic," Jackson exclaims in one piece. "When a whale plunges out of the sea like a newborn mountain, you gasp in unexpected delight... But a toddler who sees his first tadpole flashing in a mud puddle feels the same thrill. Wonder fills his heart, because he has glimpsed for an instant the playfulness of life.... Every time the sun rises Nature is repeating one command: 'Behold!' Her magic is infinitely lavish and in return all we have to do is appreciate it."

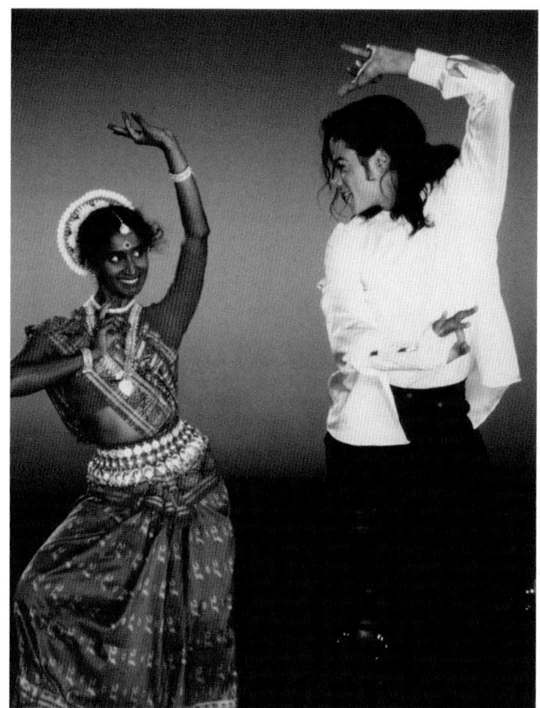

Jackson poses with an Indian dancer on the set of his *Black or White* video. His worldview and creative ambition were expanding dramatically as the 1990s began.

Jackson's language vividly conjures the ecstasy and thrill of creation: "What delight nature must feel when she makes stars out of swirling gas and empty space," he writes. "She flings them like spangles from a velvet cape, a billion reasons for us to awaken in pure joy. When we open our hearts and appreciate all she has given us, Nature finds her reward. The sound of applause rolls across the universe, and she bows."

The book was mostly overlooked or scoffed at by critics; Jackson's sincerity made him an easy target. Yet the book provides a fascinating window into an artist who had an uncanny ability to experience (and convey in his performances) what Deepak Chopra describes as the "God feeling"—a transcendent, "ecstatic state" that dissolves hard lines, barriers, and ideologies and recognizes instead the unity in existence—between different races, cultures, and religions, between mind and body, between human beings, nature and animals. "All of life is in me," he writes in one of the final pieces. "The children and their pain; the children and their joy. The ocean swelling under the sun; the ocean weeping with black oil. The animals hunted in fear; the animals bursting with the sheer joy of being alive."

It was a philosophy that didn't see problems as "out there." "You and I were never separate," Jackson says, "It's just an illusion." He similarly collapses the space between humans and the divine/

universe: "This world we live in is the dance of the creator. Dancers come and go in the twinkling of an eye but the dance lives on. On many occasions when I'm dancing, I've felt touched by something sacred. In those moments I've felt my spirit soar and become one with everything that exists. I become the stars and the moon. I become the lover and the beloved. I become the victor and the vanquished. I become the master and the slave. I become the singer and the song. I become the knower and the known. I keep on dancing and then, it is the eternal dance of creation. The creator and the creation merge into one wholeness of joy. I keep on dancing and dancing... and dancing, until there is only... the dance."

With such a vision of life and creativity, Jackson also had a clearer vision of what he hoped to accomplish with his music. "I really believe that God chooses people to do certain things," Jackson explained to *Ebony* magazine in 1992. "The way Michelangelo or Leonardo da Vinci or Mozart or Muhammad Ali or Martin Luther King Jr. is chosen. And that is their mission to do that thing. And I think I haven't scratched the surface yet of what my real purpose is for being here. I'm committed to my art. I believe that all art has as its ultimate goal the union between the material and the spiritual, the human and the divine. And I believe that that is the very reason for the existence of art and what I do. And I feel fortunate in being that instrument through which music flows."

In quotes like this, one could sense a new confidence in Jackson, a deeper awareness of what he wanted to achieve beyond fame and commercial success. Gone, it seemed, were the circus-show publicity stunts and distractions (whether willful or not) that too often defined him during the *Bad* era. Jackson wanted the focus—his own as well as his audience's—back on his art. With a new home, new management, and new creative partners he had a fresh palette with which to work. He wanted to show the world something different from what he had ever done before—something that would resonate on a deeper level, a work of art, something that would live.

In total, Michael Jackson worked on *Dangerous* for more than three years. With several studios reserved at all times—primarily at Record One and Larrabee (both in Los Angeles)—the album cost an estimated $10 million, an unheard of amount in the music industry (then and now). Jackson recorded an estimated one hundred songs in various states of completion for *Dangerous*. Many brilliant tracks, for a variety of reasons, didn't make the final cut (including standouts such as "Earth Song," "Blood on the Dance Floor," "Someone Put Your Hand Out," and "Do You Know Where Your Children Are").

Jackson's perfectionism meant he refused to release anything until it was as close to that mark as possible. "I'm never satisfied with anything," he later confessed, "After I've cut a track, I'll come home and say 'oh no, that's not right,' and you just go back and back and back." While he was mostly competing with himself, he was also motivated by the artistic breakthrough of his sister Janet's 1990 album, *Rhythm Nation 1814*. The album and its videos were both cutting edge and praised by critics. The beats were sharp, angular, and mechanical; the imagery, bleak, urban, militaristic and sexual. Michael loved it, especially the title track. It was one of the reasons he sought out Teddy Riley to replace the airier funk of Bryan Loren. He wanted the dance tracks on *Dangerous* to really hit the listener, and he wanted the material to be more street-conscious.

Finally, in the late summer/early fall of 1991, under pressure from his manager, Sony, and fans alike, Jackson realized, despite the constant influx of new ideas and material, it was time to set a definitive date and finish the project. Over the final two months, Jackson and Bruce Swedien stayed at a hotel just minutes away from the studio so they could get back to work as soon as possible. "We'd drive to the studio and work until we couldn't work anymore," recalled Swedien. "Then we'd drive back to the hotel, go to sleep and then go back in the morning and hit it again."

The final week of October was an all-out sprint to the finish. "The last three days of the project, Michael and I got about four hours sleep," recalls Bruce Swedien.

Dangerous was finally completed early in the morning of October 31, 1991. A still-hesitant Jackson, however, wanted one more opinion: that of his longtime mentor, Quincy Jones. After sending the CD, Jackson anxiously awaited the response. Not long after, he got word back: Quincy felt *Dangerous* was "a masterpiece." Jackson was elated. He finally felt ready to release his work to the public.

For the media, every Michael Jackson album after *Thriller* was measured against its impossibly high commercial standard. If the new record didn't sell more copies than the best-selling album of all time, it was considered a flop. In 1991, a headline for the *New York Times* ran: 'THRILLER'—CAN MICHAEL JACKSON BEAT IT? "This is the challenge Jackson is up against," echoed *Rolling Stone*. While it made for good media fodder, however, it tended to obscure focus on the album's actual quality.

Jackson himself, of course, played into these expectations. From the outset, he made it clear to his producers and collaborators, he not only wanted to top *Thriller*, but also he wanted *Dangerous* to sell one hundred million copies.

Jackson certainly got off to a good start. Before the album was even released, its first single and accompanying video, *Black or White*, made history. Broadcast simultaneously on FOX (which earned its highest ratings ever), BET, VH1, and MTV, the *Black or White* video was watched in more than twenty-seven countries by an estimated five hundred million viewers. The response was overwhelming. *Black or White* became the most watched video in the history of MTV, even surpassing *Thriller*.

The single, meanwhile, dominated the airwaves. One New York station played it for ninety minutes straight to satisfy audience demand. Within twenty-four hours, the song had been added to ninety-six percent of play lists on American radio stations. Within weeks, "Black or White" hit #1 on the charts, the fastest chart topper since the Beatles' "Get Back" in 1969, where it would stay for six weeks, becoming Jackson's most successful single since "Billie Jean." It also hit #1 in nineteen other countries including the United Kingdom, Israel, and Zimbabwe.

MTV dedicated an entire weekend exclusively to Michael Jackson material, referring to him repeatedly as "the King of Pop" (a marketing ploy worked out by Jackson's management years before). The claim to pop royalty, which some considered egotistical, could hardly be disputed: "Black or White" gave Jackson a #1 hit in each of the last three decades, a mark never before achieved by a solo artist and a testament to his staying power.

While the song and video, in many ways, met with unprecedented success, however, it wasn't without its detractors. The final sequence of the video, often referred to as the "panther coda," generated a firestorm of controversy for being too violent and sexual. Some described it as a "betrayal" to his longtime fans. A cover story for *Entertainment Weekly* called it Jackson's "video nightmare." "It's like using bathroom talk to get attention," said Peggy Charren of Action for Children's Television (ACT). "I'd like to know if any of the people involved with this have had their storefronts bashed up or their car windows smashed."

In response to the frenzy, Jackson issued a statement saying that he simply meant to portray the animalistic instincts of a panther and show the destructiveness of discrimination. "It upsets me to think that 'Black or White' could influence any child or adult to destructive behavior, either sexual or violent," he said. In spite of his explanations, however, "offended" viewers prevailed, and television networks subsequently censored the final segment. (According to Bill Bottrell, some radio stations also censored the rap segment of "Black or White," feeling it wasn't appropriate for traditional pop/rock radio.)

Like other controversial videos of the time (Madonna's *Like a Prayer* and Pearl Jam's *Jeremy*), the video struck a sensitive nerve, posing uncomfortable questions about racism, violence, and sexuality. It also increased the already visceral buzz surrounding Jackson's new album. Jackson had been customarily quiet since the release of *Bad* and its ensuing world tour. Now, with a new single soaring up the charts and a video stirring controversy and debate, it was clear many were anxious for the reappearance of Michael Jackson. The anticipation was so high, in fact, that armed robbers stole thirty thousand copies of the new album at a Los Angeles air terminal days before its official release. By late November, fans around the world were lining up to get their copy of *Dangerous*.

***Black or White* is Jackson's most watched—and controversial—video to date.**

Before people even heard the music, they were confronted with the fascinating album cover. An acrylic glaze painting created (with input by Jackson) by pop surrealist Mark Ryden, it was described by one critic as a "sleeve so symbol-laden it could provide grist for an entire symposium of pop psychiatrists." Indeed, not since the Beatles' cover for *Sgt. Pepper's Lonely*

Hearts Club Band has an album contained such mysterious and intricate packaging (a 1992 special edition of the album was packaged as a large box, which folded open as a diorama). At first glance, the cover looks like a display for the circus with Michael Jackson being promoted as "the greatest show on earth." Near the bottom, dressed in a tuxedo, in fact, is none other than P. T. Barnum, the legendary showman with whom Jackson became fascinated in the mid-1980s. Circuses, of course, are public spectacles, and Jackson seems to be recognizing, for better or worse, this is what "Michael Jackson," the persona has become.

The painting also seems to playfully resist this characterization. Jackson is aware of the way he is perceived, and sometimes deliberately plays the part. In this way, he is responsible for designing and erecting the mask that draws so much attention. However, for all the attention, he also attempts to conceal a part of himself behind the façade. Jackson's piercing eyes stare out from society's postmodern funhouse just as it stares back at him. It becomes, in this way, a sort of mirror. Like T. J. Eckleberg's famously brooding billboard in *The Great Gatsby*, it comes to "mean" what we interpret in its gaze: an illusory reality, a circus, a deity, a work of art.

The mask itself contains all of these things, revealing a fascinating maze of symbols. Flanked to Jackson's right is a "Dog King" sitting on a throne, clothed in a crimson robe, and holding a scepter. The image is derived from an 1806 painting by Jean Auguste Dominique Ingres titled *Napoleon On His Imperial Throne* and signifies power, authority, and domination. (Jackson famously used dogs in his 1989 video, *Leave Me Alone*, to represent corporate power and greed.) To the Dog King's opposite is the "Bird Queen," who wears purple, holds a compass, and is connected to a gear-driven machine that pumps life into a bubble-like globe containing a naked man and woman. Derived from an elaborate painting by eccentric fifteenth-century artist Hieronymus Bosch (*The Garden of Earthly Delights*), the queen seems to represent life, creativity, and love.

Freud would have a field day with such loaded symbols (though, it should be noted, Jackson's psychologist of choice was Jung). In the picture, the animus/anima archetypes are presented as parts of a whole identity; yet like Jung, creativity more often comes from the feminine. Thus, just below the Bird Queen a child-version of Jackson exits a Disney-esque theme ride, which might represent the simple, uninhibited joys of childhood associated with the mother.

Meanwhile, just beneath Jackson's eyes is an industrial factory that seems to be inspired by the opening sounds of the title track, "Dangerous." (Ryden acknowledged that he did indeed take inspiration from the songs on *Dangerous*, and from other well-known aspects of the singer's life.) Like the Bird Queen's gear-driven "machine," the factory seems to represent the artist's industrious inner life of creativity, which pumps directly into a miniature globe, representing the world. Straight through the middle of the cover is a track, suggesting that by following it inside, one might go beyond the mask and enter into the creative

A 1991 photo of Jackson experimenting with a new look. With *Dangerous*, he was determined to present a new image to the public.

precedent of Jackson's wordless hiccups, which were similarly utilized to great effect by the likes of Little Richard, James Brown, and Jackie Wilson and sometimes intended to convey the very anxiety and claustrophobia Pareles notes.

Pareles goes on to describe *Dangerous* as Jackson's "least confident album since he became a solo superstar. . . . He sounds so eager to reclaim his popularity that he has ruled out taking chances." Pareles, however, fails to offer a compelling explanation for how a seventy-seven-minute pop album featuring all new producers and collaborators, cutting-edge sounds, socially conscious and personally revealing lyrics, music ranging from R&B to rock, hip-hop to gospel, soul to classical (including an orchestral prelude from Beethoven's Ninth Symphony) qualifies as unconfident and safe. Rather, he is content to speak of Jackson's "freakishness" and speculate about built-in marketing ploys.

While the critical response was mixed, however, *Dangerous* became Jackson's fastest-selling album since *Thriller*, shifting six hundred thousand copies in the United States in the first week alone and more than two million globally. By the end of December, just a month after its release, it had sold an impressive four million copies in the United States and ten million worldwide. It also hit #1 in nearly every country in the world, including Japan, Australia, and France.

Over the next two years, *Dangerous* would spend 117 weeks in the *Billboard* Hot 200. In addition to "Black or White," three other singles—"Remember the Time," "In the Closet," and "Will You Be There"—would break into the Top Ten in the United States while songs such as "Heal the World," "Jam," "Who Is It," and "Dangerous" became big global hits. *Dangerous* became Jackson's most successful album internationally and his second-most successful in total worldwide sales, behind only *Thriller*.

In 1993, when it seemed like the album had finally run its course, it caught fire again after Jackson performed to a record-setting 120 million viewers on the Super Bowl halftime show. Less than a week later, Jackson appeared live with Oprah Winfrey from his Neverland Ranch for the "television event of the year." Excluding Super Bowls, it was the fourth-most-watched program in TV history, with more than eighty-five million viewers tuning in. The two appearances propelled *Dangerous* back into the Top Ten nearly sixteen months after its original release.

At the Grammy Awards that February, Jackson—presented with a Living Legend Award by his sister Janet—seemed as high as he had been since *Thriller*. He had released a successful album, completed the first leg of his world tour, opened up publicly in a way he never had before, and redefined his image. "The last few weeks," he said in his Grammy acceptance speech, "I have been cleansing myself and it's been a rebirth for myself. It's like a cleansing spirit." Everything seemed to be coming together for Jackson. Just five months later, however, in the midst of the second leg of his *Dangerous* World Tour, news of allegations of child molestation broke. His life would never be the same.

As an album, then, *Dangerous* represents a period in-between for Jackson. It is a transitional album, released at a transitional moment in his life and popular music history. Indeed, one of the ironies of *Dangerous* being symbolically toppled by Nirvana's *Nevermind* on the charts—thereby, according to many narratives, signaling the "death of pop" and ushering in the "alt-rock era"—is how similar they are in certain respects. As music critic Jon Dolan notes, "Jackson's dread, depression and wounded-child sense of good and evil have more in common with Kurt Cobain than anyone took the time to notice."

While one certainly wouldn't find "Keep the Faith" or "Heal the World" on a Nirvana album, many songs similarly confront Jackson's discomfort and estrangement with the world he inhabits. "Jam" speaks of being "conditioned by the system," of "confusions" and "contradictions." "Who Is It" is a devastating expression of loneliness and isolation. In "Black or White," a song many critics wrote off as a postracial platitude, Jackson preempts society's duplicity, singing, "Don't tell me you agree with me when I saw you kicking dirt in my eye."

With time, however, reassessments of the album are putting its substantial achievement into better focus. Many critics and fans alike now feel it is one of his best albums. In a 2009 review, *The Guardian*'s Ben Beaumont-Thomas calls it Jackson's "career high": "In all the swooning at *Thriller*'s album sales and Jackson's pre-surgery beatitude," he writes, "*Dangerous* risks becoming even more underrated than it is now. That would be a tragedy—for me, it's his finest hour."

Rolling Stone had it right from the beginning praising the Jackson/Riley tracks in its 1991 review as "reminiscent of Jackson's solo album *Off the Wall* and that record's distillation of disco to its perfect pop essence." Just as *Off the Wall* perfected, enhanced, and elaborated on disco, *Dangerous* did the same for new jack swing. Comparing it to other popular new jack records reveals an enormous gulf in terms of richness, depth, and quality.

It is the second half of *Dangerous*, however, that really takes the album to another level. The brilliant trio of "Black or White," "Who Is It," and "Give In To Me" is followed by the majestic classical strains of "Will You Be There" and the fiery gospel force of "Keep the Faith." Finally, the quiet fragility of "Gone Too Soon" merges slowly into the industrial furnaces of "Dangerous." It is a sweeping survey of musical styles and themes, showcasing a vision, intelligence, and agility rarely seen in pop music.

It is, of course, impossible to say definitively which album is Jackson's finest. Each contains its own unique virtues. Fan rationales are often more personal than objective, while critics often bend with the cultural and commercial wind. *Dangerous* isn't without its flaws either. However, if it isn't Michael Jackson's best album, it certainly belongs in the conversation. Culturally, it lacks the impact of *Off the Wall* and *Thriller* (particularly in America), but the music is what ultimately matters, and as Quincy Jones relayed to Michael before its release: musically, *Dangerous* is a masterpiece.

By early 1993, Jackson, seen here in concert, was experiencing his greatest success since *Thriller*.

THE SONGS

1. JAM

(Music by René Moore, Bruce Swedien, Michael Jackson, and Teddy Riley. Song and lyrics by Michael Jackson. Produced by Michael Jackson, Teddy Riley, and Bruce Swedien. Recorded and mixed by Bruce Swedien, Teddy Riley, and Dave Way. Solo and background vocals: Michael Jackson. Arrangement by Michael Jackson, Bruce Swedien, Teddy Riley, and René Moore. Vocal arrangement by Michael Jackson. Rap performed by Heavy D. Keyboards: Rene Moore, Teddy Riley, Bruce Swedien, and Brad Buxer. Synthesizers: Teddy Riley, Rhett Lawrence, Michael Boddicker, and Brad Buxer. Drums: Teddy Riley and Bruce Swedien. Guitar: Teddy Riley)

"Jam" is the perfect representative opener for *Dangerous*. Bold, ominous, and revealing, it marks a transition point in his career (the opening sound of shattering glass appropriately signals this breakthrough). Gone are the pristine, Quincy Jones–produced cinematic fantasies of *Bad*; in its place, is something grittier, something more attuned to the street, yet still true to the essence of Michael Jackson.

With its staccato lyrics and stinging social commentary, some have called "Jam" a Gen-X version of James Brown. *Rolling Stone* reviewer Alan Light describes the song as "a dense, swirling [Teddy] Riley track, propelled by horn samples and a subtle scratch effect, includ[ing] a fleet rap by Riley favorite Heavy D. Though it initially sounds like a simple, funky dance vehicle, Jackson's voice bites into each phrase with a desperation that urges us to look deeper."

Indeed, with the track's powerful rhythmic tension and vocal urgency, Jackson sings of profound inner turmoil ("confusions, contradictions") and a world on the verge of apocalypse. "I have to find my peace 'cause/No one seems to let me be," he sings. "False prophets cry of doom/What are the possibilities." In lyrics like these, a connection is drawn between his personal fears and anxieties and the broader social context that stokes them. The world according to Jackson is filled with such hypocrisy, exploitation, greed, and manipulation that he can't help but wonder what its fate (along with his) will be. "I'm conditioned by/The system," he confesses. "Don't talk to me/Don't scream and shout." This is the kind of angst and self-reflexivity one might expect more readily from a band like Nirvana or Radiohead. Yet Jackson evokes the condition convincingly.

Jackson was shown an early version of "Jam" by Bruce Swedien, who was working on the track with René Moore for his album. "We had been experimenting with the 'looping' of old, but extremely high-energy drum and rhythm tracks," recalls Swedien. "Our idea was to take the fantastic feel of these vintage drum performances, and then layer them with new, very contemporary sounds on parallel tracks to bring the sonic value of the groove up to date." Swedien and Moore worked on it for some time before giving Michael a listen. "[He] absolutely loved the concept!" recalls Swedien. They decided to give the track to Michael, who subsequently worked it over with Teddy Riley and wrote the lyrics.

"Jam" became Jackson's most socially aware and psychologically candid track since *Thriller*'s opener, "Wanna Be Startin' Somethin'." The tone was now darker, Jackson more brooding. He spits out clichés ("The world must get together," "We'll work it out") with a knowing irony. The reality, he understands, is much bleaker. "The world keeps changing, rearranging minds," he observes, before questioning, "Do we know right from wrong." Family, politics, and religion all seem to let him down and leave him searching. He has to "find [his] peace," but he is weary of other people's formulas. "Don't you preach to me/ Don't scream and shout."

In the chorus, however, Jackson finds some hope and resolve, declaring resiliently, "It ain't too much for me." Indeed, if there is redemption, finally, for the singer, it comes in the music itself. *Jamming* means a temporary escape from an often suffocating world. It means becoming absorbed in a creative community, allowing the music to somehow "work it out."

2. WHY YOU WANNA TRIP ON ME

(Written and composed by Teddy Riley and Bernard Belle. Produced by Teddy Riley and Michael Jackson. Recorded and mixed by Bruce Swedien, Teddy Riley, Dave Way, and Jean-Marie Horvat. Sequencing and programming: Wayne Cobham. Vocal arrangement by Michael Jackson. Rhythm arrangement by Teddy Riley. Solo and background vocals: Michael Jackson. Keyboards, synthesizers, and guitar: Teddy Riley. Guitar intro: Paul Jackson Jr.)

"Why You Wanna Trip On Me" continues the social commentary of "Jam." In this more developed lyrical sequel to "Leave Me Alone," Jackson is no longer simply decrying his critics for "dogging [him] around"; he is directing their gaze to more pressing issues: poverty, world hunger, AIDS, and gang violence, among others. With "more problems than we'll ever need," he sings, "there's really no time to be trippin' on me."

The song begins with a blistering guitar intro by Paul Jackson Jr. before the hard rock fuses into a driving new jack funk. As in "Jam," Jackson sings in a "clipped, breathy up tempo voice" while a funky guitar lick (played by Teddy Riley) and "stacked layers of keyboards . . . shift and percolate, varying textures over [an] insistent, thumping rhythm track."

Brilliantly arranged by Riley and Michael Jackson, the track balances rhythmic intensity with exquisite vocal harmonies. "By keeping the beat straight-ahead," observes Robert Doerschuk, "giving the snare extra pop, and leaving the bass out . . . [Riley] brings Jackson's vocals out more than Quincy Jones did on some earlier cuts, and gives more exposure to the dotted eighth-note hi-hat pattern that essentially defines new jack swing." In the chorus, Jackson repeats the refrain, "Why you wanna trip on me?" as the question is echoed by beautifully layered falsetto vocals.

Jackson's criticism of the mass media's misguided focus and tendency toward sensationalism would become an increasingly prominent theme in his later work ("Scream," "Tabloid Junkie," etc.). With so many other pressing issues to cover, being "different," he argues here, shouldn't be real "news."

3. IN THE CLOSET

(Written and composed by Michael Jackson and Teddy Riley. Produced by Teddy Riley and Michael Jackson. Recorded and mixed by Bruce Swedien, Teddy Riley, Jean-Marie Horvat, and Dave Way. Sequencing and programming: Wayne Cobham. Rhythm arrangement by Teddy Riley. Synthesizer arrangement by Teddy Riley. Vocal arrangement by Michael Jackson. Duet: Michael Jackson and Princess Stephanie of Monaco. Solo and background vocals: Michael Jackson. Keyboards and synthesizers: Teddy Riley)

The sexual tension is palpable on this lesser-known Top Ten hit (the song peaked at #6 in the United States in 1992). The track was initially planned as a duet with Madonna, but she passed after Jackson didn't take to her lyrics. Still, Jackson was able to achieve the suggestive ambiguity for which he hoped. From its intentionally provocative title, "In the Closet" plays with expectations about identity and sexuality. ("Only Jackson would use that title for a heterosexual love song that opens by saying, 'Don't hide our love/ Woman to man,'" quips Jon Pareles.) Featuring a fluid, thumping beat and the sensual entreaties of a mystery girl (performed by Princess Stephanie of Monaco), Jackson sings longingly about a secret love affair.

In its 1991 review, the *New York Times* described the track as the "best song on the album": "It's the kind of song that made Jackson a megastar as the age of AIDS began," observes Jon Pareles, "all about desire and denial, risk and repression, solitude and connection, privacy and revelation. Once again, Jackson faces a temptress, embodied by a girlish voice saying things like 'If it's aching, you have to rub it.' Not only does she want to seduce him, she wants to 'open the door,' while he insists (contrary to his introduction) that they 'keep it in the closet.' The singer is torn, wanting 'to give it to you' but holding back; his final whispered words are 'Dare me,' followed by the sound of a door—shutting, or being thrown open."

It is one of numerous well-executed sonic effects. Beginning with an elegant piano and string prelude, the song proceeds to experiment with all kinds of percussive sounds: glass breaking, doors slamming, fingers snapping, and a variety of industrial noises. Jackson also uses an array of grunts and groans to convey the song's sensuality. The persistent, gyrating beat, however, is the song's most memorable feature. Originally conceived of by Jackson on his Dictaphone, it was enhanced in the studio with coproducer Teddy Riley. "We used a variety of drum machines, but we compressed all our snares to make 'em pop," recalled Riley. "[It] was something Michael came up with, and it came out exactly as he wanted."

The video for "In the Closet," directed by renowned photographer Herb Ritts and set on a balmy, deserted ranch in California, features Jackson and supermodel Naomi Campbell capturing every ounce of the song's elegance, passion, and sexual tension. It also shows off his extraordinary ability as a dancer as he first plays seducer (à la "The Way You Make Me Feel") and closes with a riveting series of moves in silhouette in the space of a doorway.

4. SHE DRIVES ME WILD

(Written and composed by Michael Jackson and Teddy Riley. Produced by Teddy Riley and Michael Jackson. Recorded and mixed by Bruce Swedien, Teddy Riley, Dave Way, and Jean-Marie Horvat. Sequencing and programming: Wayne Cobham. Rhythm arrangement by Teddy Riley. Synthesizer arrangement by Teddy Riley. Rap lyrics by Aqil Davidson. Solo and background vocals: Michael Jackson. Keyboards and synthesizers: Teddy Riley. Rap performed by Wreckx-N-Effect)

"Speed Demon" demonstrated Jackson's canny use of everyday sounds to create compelling music; "She Drives Me Wild" further extends this interest, turning *Dangerous* into a sort of updated, urban-inspired *Pet Sounds*. In place of traditional instruments, Jackson develops an entire rhythm track from car horns, engines, sirens, slamming doors, and other "noises" from the street. "Even the bass is a car horn," says Teddy Riley.

Often stigmatized as an artist only concerned about commercial viability, Jackson's songs like these demonstrate his interest in experimenting and innovating. As the *Village Voice*'s Chuck Eddy wrote in a 1991 review, "If there's nothing new happening on this record, as certain fools have claimed (as some of the same fools claimed when *Bad*, which they now like, came out), how do they explain all this *noise*? Right after ['In the Closet'], ['She Drives Me Wild'] opens with musique concrète 'Summer in the City'/'Expressway to Your Heart' traffic clatter.... Exactly what 'trend' is he trying to 'keep up with' here?"

Indeed, the track not only utilizes an array of interesting sound effects, but also expertly juxtaposes the funky, hard-hitting verses with smooth, textured harmonies in the chorus. Throughout the song, Jackson's strings provide a cinematic tension, capturing the feel of driving down a dark city street. It anticipates some of the West Coast sound of hip-hop artists such as Tupac and Dr. Dre. In the bridge, Aqil Davidson of Wreckx-N-Effect offers a rap solo that Jackson caps with a perfectly-timed percussive "hoooo!"

On *Bad*, Jackson was still reluctant to insert hip-hop into his work, but here—and on a handful of other *Dangerous* tracks—he sets the blueprint for rap-pop fusion.

5. REMEMBER THE TIME

(Written and composed by Teddy Riley, Michael Jackson, and Bernard Belle. Produced by Teddy Riley and Michael Jackson. Recorded and mixed by Bruce Swedien, Teddy Riley, and Dave Way. Sequencing and programming: Wayne Cobham. Rhythm arrangement by Teddy Riley. Synthesizer arrangement by Teddy Riley. Vocal arrangement by Michael Jackson. Solo and background vocals: Michael Jackson. Keyboards and synthesizers: Teddy Riley)

Like previous classics ("Rock With You" and "The Way You Make Me Feel"), "Remember the Time" is pure unadulterated pop bliss. It is also, arguably, the culmination of the new jack swing sound: smooth, meticulously crafted R&B built on a punchy backbeat with soulful vocals. Teddy Riley calls it his favorite collaborative effort with Michael Jackson. The song shot to #1 on the R&B charts and #3 on the Hot 100 in 1992. With its strong analog feel and vintage organ groove, "Remember the Time" expertly conveys the warmth and nostalgia of the song's lyrics. Jackson sings in a notably lower register, a "smooth tenor [that] flutter[s] over exquisite background harmonies." He also hearkens back to the playful improvisation of *Off the Wall* with some scatting in the bridge.

"One of the biggest things Michael really surprised me with on the *Dangerous* album was his vocal delivery on 'Remember the Time,'" recalls Teddy Riley. "That really blew me away. I came to the project with this track. That was the sound I was thinking of for this album . . . and he loved it—loved it from the beginning." Jackson and Riley got to work on the track right away. "Michael asked if he could sing the hook," recalls recording engineer Dave Way, "which was all that was written of the lyrics at that point and he went out and sang the first chorus, first note (melody). Now, the producer (Teddy Riley) and I were in the habit of singing the chorus once with all its parts and then flying it in to the other choruses. So when the first chorus was finished I stopped the tape and Michael, startled by this, said 'Why'd you stop?' to which we explained the flying in, etc. He said, 'Well, I'd just like to sing each part all the way through.' So we went back, started the song from the beginning and watched Michael sing each note and harmony, double it, triple it and then maybe quadruple—each time singing it perfectly, vibratos perfectly matched, perfectly in tune, rhythmically dead on, knowing exactly what he wanted to do the whole time. We were done with all the hooks faster than if I'd have flown them in. Flawless. That was day one."

Jackson and Riley continued to sculpt the song from there, creating a thick, lush sound that was almost an homage to both Motown and Quincy Jones. The final result had Jackson dancing all over the studio. It remains one of his most popular post-'90s grooves.

The song's music video, meanwhile, coming on the heels of *Black or White*, continued to show off Jackson's cinematic ambition. Directed by John Singleton (director of *Boyz n the Hood* and *Poetic Justice*), the nine-minute short film featured an all-star cast (including comedian Eddie Murphy, supermodel Iman, and basketball star Magic Johnson) and stunning special effects. Perhaps its boldest move was in its setting. In 1992, Jackson's racial identity remained an open topic of discussion. No one knew exactly why his skin had turned white (he had yet to reveal that he suffered from a skin disorder called vitiligo), but many assumed it was because he was ashamed, in some sense, of his race. In *Remember the Time*, Jackson directly challenges this assumption, setting the video in ancient Egypt with an all-black cast playing the part of royalty. "'Remember the Time' adopts an African heritage as a gesture of pride and a search for fulfillment," observed film critic Armond White in a 1992 review. "The line, 'Do you remember the time when we fell in love/[. . .]when we first met?' asks the queen to make a projection, to fantasize a liaison in her heart and mind, just as the video's context asks viewers to recall a past when black folks were not estranged from the African continent or their ancestral culture. Of course, Jackson aims this fantasy nostalgia toward a broad audience to make sense for non-blacks who can relate to Africa as the cradle of all civilization: 'Do you remember how it all began?'"

In the short film's storyline, Jackson acts as a sort of mysterious shaman who mesmerizes and seduces the queen in spite of his "outsider" status. "Their kiss characterizes the hyphen in African-American," writes Armond White. "Iman, the model-actress from Somalia with natural hauteur shares a rarefied delicate elegance with American-born Jackson. They look at each other in a cultural exchange between places of birth—a reunion between matriarch and exile." Indeed, while some try to chase and kill him for his advances, she sees him for who he is and loves him. The extended synchronized dance scene in the song's bridge—which incorporates elements of tribal dance and hieroglyphic poses with more contemporary hip-hop—further reinforces this idea of racial and cultural identification. Even though he is "different," as the video seems to suggest, he is one with them. The implicit message to viewers is that racial identity is much more than skin pigmentation: it is about shared dances, songs, narratives, and histories.

6. CAN'T LET HER GET AWAY

(Written and composed by Michael Jackson and Teddy Riley. Produced by Teddy Riley and Michael Jackson. Recorded and mixed by Bruce Swedien, Teddy Riley, Dave Way, and Jean-Marie Horvat. Sequencing and programming: Wayne Cobham. Rhythm arrangement by Teddy Riley. Synthesizer arrangement by Teddy Riley. Vocal arrangement by Michael Jackson. Solo and background vocals: Michael Jackson. Keyboards and synthesizers: Teddy Riley)

While Jackson's vocal performances in songs such as "Jam" and "She Drives Me Wild" show clear influence from the Godfather of Soul, "Can't Let Her Get Away" is perhaps as close as Jackson gets to paying direct homage to his longtime idol, James Brown. Generally considered one of the least memorable songs on the album, this breathy rhythm track is nonetheless an early, trailblazing experiment in merging early '60s-era funk with hip-hop. Music critic Ben Beaumont-Thomas praises it as "fiendishly intricate, loaded with scratching, multiple layers of drum programming, and shiny smashes of hyper-artificial brass. In its mechanic complexity and tautly funky precision, it mirrors and amplifies Jackson's corporeal and vocal exactitude."

When Jackson isn't grunting and gasping, he is singing in a high falsetto and even rapping. "Michael's ecstatic gasps and whoops are still wonders of nature," writes music critic Chuck Eddy. "'Can't Let Her Get Away,' a nonstop, nonlinear barrage of bopgun pops and bumblebeed beats, vamps and squeaks and gurgles, Cupid's arrows flying through space and what at one point could be a drippy faucet, has as much disco momentum as anything Jackson's waxed since *Off the Wall*."

The track concludes what is sometimes referred to as the new jack swing chamber of *Dangerous*, six songs produced or coproduced with Teddy Riley. The next eight songs, written mainly by Jackson himself, span the musical universe, from hymns to rock to classical and back to R&B.

7. HEAL THE WORLD

(Written and composed by Michael Jackson. Produced by Michael Jackson. Coproduced by Bruce Swedien. Recorded and mixed by Bruce Swedien and Matt Forger. Choir arrangement by John Bahler, featuring the John Bahler Singers. Orchestra arranged and conducted by Marty Paich. Prelude composed, arranged, and conducted by Marty Paich. Rhythm arrangement by Michael Jackson. Vocal arrangement by Michael Jackson and John Bahler. Solo and background vocals: Michael Jackson. Ending solo vocal: Christa Larson. Playground girl: Ashley Farell. Keyboards: David Paich and Brad Buxer. Synthesizers: Michael Boddicker, David Paich, and Steve Porcaro. Drums: Jeff Porcaro. Percussion: Bryan Loren)

Unlike "We Are The World," which was widely acclaimed for its humanitarian message and purpose, "Heal the World" was met with widespread cynicism, particularly in the United States. The *New York Times* called it "sticky-sweet" and "banal" while *All Music Guide* referred to it as "middle-class soft." This dramatic shift in response, however, seemed to be more an indicator of the cultural milieu (the general pessimism and disillusionment of grunge and rap dominated the music scene by 1992) than any real difference in the merits of the songs.

"Heal the World," like other anthems in its mold, can be viewed as sentimental and idealistic. However, for Jackson the point of a humanitarian anthem was pretty straightforward. He wanted a song with a simple message and a simple melody: something the whole world could sing, regardless of language, race, or culture. In particular, he wanted children to enjoy and benefit from it. "Heal the World" was the vehicle for these social aims.

The song was one of the first to be written and recorded during the *Dangerous* sessions. Jackson came up with the melody and lyrics in 1989 and began working on it in the studio with Matt Forger and Brad Buxer, among others. For the intro, he had Forger go out to "record children just being children." He wanted them to say something about the state of the world/planet/environment from a child's perspective, and he wanted it to be natural and unscripted. This turned out to be a much more challenging task than it seemed. "I must have recorded over a hundred kids," recalls Forger. "I called up every parent that I know. Finally, I interviewed the daughter of a friend of my wife's. I started asking her these questions about the earth, and she says this line, 'We have to think of our children, and our children's children . . . ' It was totally sincere. Without any pretense or coaching." Forger brought it to Michael and he thought it was perfect. "I started editing it to take out some of the stammering and Michael said, 'No, no, leave it in.' He loved that kind of spontaneity and innocence and that's what he wanted to capture."

"Heal the World," the song, launched the Heal the World Foundation, an organization dedicated to addressing poverty, world hunger, violence, and disease around the globe. In 1992, the nonprofit organization opened offices around the world and with Jackson's star-power, raised awareness and donated millions of dollars to less fortunate children from Los Angeles to Yugoslavia. The Heal the World Foundation's numerous activities in the early nineties included donating winter relief supplies to the children of Sarajevo, preparing and sending "shoe-box gifts" to impoverished children in Bosnia, airlifting doses of urgently needed children's vaccines to the Republic of Georgia, teaming with Toys "R" Us and AmeriCares to deliver thousands of dollars in toys, food, and supplies to two children's hospitals in Budapest and paying for a liver transplant for a young Hungarian boy.

It is no doubt because of the song's profound pragmatic impact all over the world that Jackson considered the song one of his greatest accomplishments. "'Heal the World' is one of my favorite[s] of anything I have ever recorded," he said in a 1996 interview, "because it is a public awareness song. It is something that I think will live in the hearts of people for a long time."

In January 1993, with the support of former president Jimmy Carter, Jackson also initiated Heal L.A., a Children's Relief Initiative providing "immediate action to help solve the pressing needs of America's inner-city children and youth." After performing "Heal the World" in front of a record audience at the halftime show of the 1993 Super Bowl, Jackson had his $100,000 compensation donated to Heal L.A.

"When an audience lights candles and sways to 'Heal the World,'" Jackson's longtime friend Deepak Chopra observes, "a space is created where nobody is unholy, no religion can exercise its imaginary exclusive patent on the true God. To the extent that Michael inspired such a feeling, he healed his own demons and ours, if only for an hour."

Indeed, at Jackson's 2009 memorial service in Los Angeles, a group-sing of "Heal the World" was the final number. Its melody and words were sung not only by friends, family, and colleagues in attendance, but also by millions watching on TV and online around the world. Perhaps most poignant, however, were his own children, front and center, earnestly singing the utopian dreams of their father.

8. BLACK OR WHITE

(Written and composed by Michael Jackson; produced by Michael Jackson and Bill Bottrell. Recorded and mixed by Bill Bottrell. Solo and background vocals: Michael Jackson. Drums: Bryan Loren. Rap lyrics by Bill Bottrell. Percussion: Brad Buxer and Bill Bottrell. Bass: Bryan Loren (moog) and Terry Jackson (bass guitar). Keyboards: Brad Buxer, John Barnes, and Jason Martz. Guitar: Bill Bottrell. Heavy metal guitar: Tim Pierce. Speed sequencer: Michael Boddicker and Kevin Gilbert. Rap performed by L.T.B.. "Intro": Special guitar performance by Slash. Directed by Michael Jackson. Composed by Bill Bottrell. Engineering and sound design: Matt Forger. Son played by Andres McKenzie. Father played by L.T.B.)

"Black or White" was Jackson's biggest single in America since "Billie Jean." It stayed at #1 on the *Billboard* Hot 100 for seven weeks and became the highest-selling rock single of the nineties. It was also his biggest global success, hitting the top of the charts in twenty countries, including the United Kingdom, Australia, Austria, Belgium, Cuba, Denmark, Finland, France, Israel, Italy, Japan, Mexico, Norway, Spain, Sweden, Switzerland, and Zimbabwe.

With its instantly identifiable guitar riff, "Black or White" was an explosive pop-rock-rap fusion with a message of racial harmony and an undercurrent of indignation. This was at a time when racial tensions were high following the police beating of Rodney King and subsequent riots in Los Angeles. The short film, meanwhile, is arguably the most compelling music video of Jackson's career. Film critic Armond White calls it "one of the best music videos ever made."

Like many Jackson songs, "Black or White" had a long gestation process. He had been tinkering with parts of it since the *Bad* sessions. "As soon as we got to Westlake [Studio], the first thing that Michael hummed to me was 'Black or White,'" recalls producer Bill Bottrell. "He sang me the main riff without specifying what instrument it would be played on." Bottrell ultimately selected a 1940s Gibson LG2 guitar to "put down this big, slamming, old sort of rock & roll acoustic guitar part." While Bottrell loved the sound, he wasn't sure what Jackson would think. Jackson loved it as well. "He just accepted it when he first heard it," said Bottrell, "and I was really happy to get that type of classic sound on a Michael Jackson album." It has been assumed by many that the song's famous guitar riff was played by Slash, but Slash's part was actually in the prelude (during the father-son fight, which, like "Heal the World" was orchestrated by Matt Forger).

Jackson and Bottrell continued to come back to the track over the next couple of years, constructing it piece by piece. "That's the sort of thing he does," recalls Bottrell. "It seems kind of random, but it's as if he makes things happen through omission. There's nobody else, and it's as if he knows that's what you're up against and challenges you to do it." Interestingly, while the track took years, Jackson (who often recorded vocals hundreds of times before he was satisfied) nailed the vocal on his first take. "The guy's an absolute natural," recalls Bottrell, "and for me the best thing about 'Black or White' was that his scratch vocal remained untouched throughout the next year [of work on *Dangerous*] and ended up being used on the finished song. . . . I thought the vocal was brilliant, and that the loose, imperfectly layered backgrounds were perfectly charming. As opposed to some of the other people who worked with Michael at the time, when I was allowed to produce I would consistently try to go for simpler vocals, comping them from two or three takes, with looser backgrounds and a more instinctive feel. In this case, he came in with such an endearing lead vocal and background track, I really resolved to try and keep it. Of course, it had to please him or he would have never let me get away with that."

Jackson liked the way the song was developing, but it still had some gaps, one of which he wanted filled with a rap solo. Jackson initially intended to bring in Heavy D or LL Cool J to do the job (both of whom rapped on other songs during this period), but after hearing Bill Bottrell's sample version, he felt it was perfect as it was. "For my part," jokes Bottrell, "I didn't think much of white rap . . . [but] I played it for Michael the next day and he went 'Ohhh, I love it, Bill, I love it. That should be the one.' I kept saying 'No, we've got to get a real rapper,' but as soon as he heard my performance he was committed to it and wouldn't consider using anybody else." The bridge, meanwhile, was filled in with Jackson's fiery vocal attack over surging guitar runs.

The finished recording was a seamless fusion of musical styles, containing elements of hip-hop, pop, classic rock, and even country. It was the musical equivalent of the song's inclusive theme. *Rolling Stone* described it as an "effervescent pop hit" that could "grab your heart with a line like 'I believe in miracles/ And a miracle has happened tonight,' but . . . also grab your body with those hyperactive guitar stutters and herky-jerky funky beats."

With its upbeat sound and catchy chorus, however, listeners often miss the song's darker undercurrent. Most have interpreted it as a straightforward call for racial harmony. While Jackson undoubtedly believed in music's power to bring people together, "Black or White" isn't merely a naïve expression of *kumbaya*. In one line, he preempts easy amity and hypocrisy, challenging: "Don't tell me you agree with me/When I saw you kickin' dirt in my eye." In the bridge, the buoyant verses suddenly give way to a burst of outrage: "I am tired of this devil/I am tired of this stuff/I am tired of this business . . . /I ain't scared of your brother/I ain't scared of no sheets/I ain't scared of nobody . . . "

It is a striking interjection, particularly for a chart-topping pop song. The lyrics remind that for all the aspirations for racial equality, the outrage of injustice remains. As one of the most powerful "black" voices in the world, Jackson openly defies victimization, contesting the intimidation of white supremacy. When he says, "I ain't scared of no sheets," he is not simply speaking of the KKK but of more subtle, structural forms of racism as well.

In the music video, this portion of the song comes directly after a shot of two babies (one black, one white), sitting on top of a globe. "Just before this saccharine image can pall, it turns apocalyptic," notes Armond White. "Jackson reappears walking through a wall of flames . . . images of war and misery haunt the background, but he keeps moving toward us . . . pushing aside a burning cross . . . [It] is reminiscent of the most audacious scene in Madonna's 'Like a Prayer,' but Jackson displays a more defiant indignation. And coming in the midst of the video's one-world idealism, Jackson's anger has a stronger effect." Indeed, part of the genius of the *Black or White* video is its sustained tension between oppositions: between idealism and realism, innocence and experience, satire and sincerity.

Directed by John Landis (who also directed *Thriller*), the eleven-minute short film begins in the sky, before zooming down on a typical white, suburban neighborhood. Here, the streets are immaculate, and the houses uniform. Even before we enter a house, we notice a certain sterility and emptiness to the neighborhood: it is clear that the citizens of this seemingly idyllic middle-class town are cut off from each other, consumed in their own private spaces. This idea is reinforced when we are granted a look inside a two-story home that symbolically divides a child (played by Macaulay Culkin) from his parents. While the child rocks out to a guitar solo in his room, his father is downstairs immersed in a baseball game and his mother is reading a tabloid newspaper. The music is so loud it finally drives the father upstairs to yell at his son ("I thought I told you to turn that noise down"). It is a play on the classic generational divide rock 'n' roll has provoked in American families (see the Twisted Sisters' video for "We're Not Gonna Take It"). However, it is also a parody of this trope. The suburban boy represents the primary demographic of rock bands in the nineties and his "rebellion" is almost laughably innocuous.

The whole opening scene is intentionally exaggerated for effect, suggesting the family's alienation—from each other as well as from the world they live in. Jackson, of course, knows that white middle-class America constitutes a big portion of his audience. What the video attempts to do then is to hold a mirror to this audience and provoke a moment of self-reflection.

Jackson transitions into the actual song by having the attention-starved boy come downstairs with guitar and amp and blast his father out of the house. Significantly, the father lands, recliner and all, in a field in Africa, a telling choice of relocation for the archetypal American father. Here, Jackson initiates the father's "reeducation" by stripping away his socialization and returning to the origins of music, song, and dance. "White America's proverbial resistance to the music of savages here meets its Afrocentric heritage," writes Armond White. "It's the proper beginning of the song, and Jackson's entrance here, among a group of spear-and-shield carrying warriors in black-and-white face paint doing a light-footed Watusi dance, denies the resistance by embracing the heritage."

As Jackson transports from culture to culture, he fluidly integrates and adapts his movements to the styles of various ethnicities: Native Americans, Indians, Russians, etc. In the famous "morphing" scene, the differences in national, racial, and sexual identity are easily dissolved in a celebration of diversity and hybridity. This adaptability and barrier crossing is meant to provide a contrast to the harsh divisions of the black-and-white world the father inhabited. This main portion is slickly produced, almost like a high-budget commercial.

The video could have easily ended there. On the surface, it was yet another Michael Jackson blockbuster: stunning visuals, cutting-edge special effects, a humorous, but socially conscious narrative. Jackson, however, wasn't finished. The "panther segment" that follows causes one to reinterpret everything that takes place before. "It is a fiercely jarring coda to a vision of folkloric global amity," writes cultural critic Margo Jefferson. It also made *Black or White* the most controversial video of Jackson's career—and his first to be openly censored.

This coda begins as the "official" video ends. We see the director come onto an elaborate Hollywood set. "That was perfect," he tells an actress. The camera scans back to show the entire crew, who all busily chat and begin to pack up, assuming, like the audience, that the video is over, that the story has been told. Then, the camera zooms back in on a mysterious black panther that lurks unseen by the crew, before creeping off the set. Once outside the building, the panther ominously walks down a set of stairs; when it reaches the street it gracefully morphs into Michael Jackson, who pauses, looks around, and picks up a black fedora. Then walking into a lone spotlight he turns and stares directly into the camera. His gaze is piercing, unsettling. Just as the image settles, Jackson bursts into a series of quick, staccato dance moves and poses. He is dressed in black loafers, white socks, black pants, white shirt, black overshirt, and white wrist guard. It is a striking visual of contrasts.

As Jackson walks down a vacant city street, there is no music, just the sound of his steps and the wind. He stares into the camera again—this time the gaze held a bit longer—before unleashing into a brilliant percussive dance routine. "It creates a strange tension," writes Margo Jefferson. "Partly because it's sinuous and elegant—the way soft-shoe tap is. And very much because every few beats he strokes, snatches at, caresses his phallus." This, of course, is part of what made the video controversial. It's not just that he grabs his crotch (he had done that in many videos before)—it is the disturbing aggression, the combination of pain, violence, and sexuality. "This is a film noir version of Gene Kelly's famous 'Singin' in the Rain,'" observes Armond White, "and Jackson's subversion of that cheerful archetype surely disturbed most people's notion of what show business is all about. But this coda is Michael's truth.... There's no music because Jackson, who's been performing since childhood, has no tradition for the musical expression of anger. This distemper ballet is done to internal rhythms; what he can't say in words comes out as a roar of a (that's right) black panther."

Indeed, one has to reimagine the original context to truly understand the artistic boldness and audacity. The video was airing on network television; all across America (and around the world), families were gathering, as if for the Super Bowl, to be entertained. Instead, many were left shocked and confused. In the final sequence, the video reaches its climax, as Jackson begins smashing in windows (the racist graffiti wasn't added until later), compulsively rubbing himself, and crying out. In perhaps the video's most powerful moment, Jackson spins like a tornado, before dropping to his knees into a puddle of water, ripping his shirt open, and wailing with agony.

Once the emotional outburst subsides, he seems to come to himself and looks out at the destruction with an expression of pain, remorse, and uncertainty. The video ends with Jackson morphing back into a panther, and slipping off into the dark, vacant street. Then, significantly, there is another sharp juxtaposition as we are back in a typical American home with another archetypal father (Homer Simpson) telling his son (Bart) to turn off what he has just seen. It is a way to lighten the built up tension with humor, but it also allows the video to come full circle and redeliver its point.

The final frame is one last close-up shot of Jackson's pained face and the words: "Prejudice is Ignorance."

The television networks, including MTV, immediately banned the full video for being too violent and sexual. Most critics at the time simply wrote it off as a desperate publicity stunt. Lost in the uproar, however, was the video's meaning. It is the censored coda, after all, that arguably makes "Black or White" the most significant music video Jackson ever created. The pain and rage Jackson conveys in his smashing of car and building windows actually anticipates the racially incited violence of the Los Angeles riots of 1992. Treated for so long like a second-class citizen, an animal, that is what Jackson's character in *Black or White* temporarily becomes. All that is pent up explodes in a furious burst of instinctual outrage. "I want[ed] to do a dance number where I [could] let out my frustration about injustice and prejudice and racism and bigotry," explained Jackson, "and within the dance I became upset and let go." In one of the few in-depth (and thoughtful) reviews of the time, film critic Armond White described it as a breakthrough. "I've gone on about it at length," he wrote in his award-winning 1991 piece, "because the video seems, to me, to be the most significant personal gesture any American artist has made in years.... He's already charmed the world; *Black or White* shows he has the courage to shake it up."

The song and video, of course, also reraised questions about Jackson's racial and sexual identity. *If it didn't matter if one was black or white*, as the lyrics said, *why had he changed his skin color?* some asked. In 1991, no one knew he had vitiligo (that revelation came two years later in his famous interview with Oprah Winfrey). The assumption, therefore, for many, was that he didn't like being black. The plastic surgery, of course, further complicated matters. For some, these cosmetic realities undermined his entire message; yet, as Mark Anthony Neal notes: "If you solely pay attention to Michael Jackson's physicality, you actually miss something that's much more complex.... Michael Jackson artistically and aesthetically never turned his back on blackness. His work was always in conversation with black culture both in the United States and more globally."

Indeed, in *Black or White* (and other videos from *Dangerous*), Jackson does exactly that, sending numerous signals that demonstrate his identification as a black man of African ancestry. Jackson also challenges traditional notions of identity. Race, he seems to argue, isn't merely about skin pigmentation ("I'm not gonna spend my life being a color"); likewise, being a man or a father isn't just drinking a beer, while sitting in a recliner watching sports on TV. Jackson is trying to upend traditional notions of race, gender, and sexuality that box people in and prevent communication and understanding.

The reassessment and tolerance Jackson is asking for, then, doesn't just concern black or white, but everything in between, all the variations, nuances, and hybrids of identity. This, after all, is what he represented. Because of this ambiguity, he was labeled a freak. Beneath this perceived atypical surface he is reminding us that even so-called freaks are humans rooted in a complex narrative that requires more than black or white labels.

9. WHO IS IT

(Written and composed by Michael Jackson. Produced by Michael Jackson and Bill Bottrell. Recorded and mixed by Bill Bottrell. Keyboard arrangement by Brad Buxer and David Paich. String arrangement by George del Barrio. Solo and background vocals: Michael Jackson. Arrangement by Michael Jackson. Drums: Bryan Loren and Bill Bottrell. Bass: Bill Bottrell (synthesizer) and Louis Johnson (bass guitar). Keyboard performance and programming: Brad Buxer, Michael Boddicker, David Paich, Steve Porcaro, and Jai Winding. Solo cello: Larry Corbett. Soprano voice: Michael Jackson and Linda Harmon. Concertmaster: Endre Granat)

"Who Is It" has often been linked to "Billie Jean," and it is easy to see why. Both songs are sonic marvels; both contain dark, tormented, enigmatic subjects; and both have killer bass lines. Yet while "Billie Jean" has been largely recognized as the masterpiece it is, "Who Is It" remains relatively overlooked. *Sputnikmusic*'s Adam Gilham describes it as a "criminally underrated song." Indeed, on an album full of remarkable songs, "Who Is It" makes a strong case for being the finest of all.

Jackson conceived of the track in 1989, not long after returning from his *Bad* World Tour. "I just remember him coming to me and singing it, singing me the bass line, and the mood he wanted," recalls Bill Bottrell. "And it sort of grew from there." Bottrell and Jackson worked with Brad Buxer and David Paich to get the sound and arrangement just right. "The parts came about instantly," recalls Buxer. "There was almost no thought process." Jackson's percussive opening and ending remained largely untouched. "The process is creating a vocal rhythm to a click track—which is a sound, a timed beat," Jackson explained of his beatboxing process. "And you're doing these mouth sounds to that beat. These sounds can be looped according to how you sample it in the computer again and again. This is your foundation for the entire track—everything plays off this. It's the rhythm. . . . Every song I've written since I was very little I've done that way. I still do it that way."

Jackson, in fact, demonstrated the foundation for the song in an impromptu a cappella performance in his 1993 interview with Oprah Winfrey. The moment elicited such a strong reaction that Sony decided to issue it as the album's next single (in place of the planned "Give In To Me"). (The *Village Voice*'s Greg Tate later wrote of the moment: "My official all-time-favorite Michael clip is the one of him on *Oprah* viciously beatboxing [his 808 kick sound could straight castrate even Rahzel's!] and freestyling a new jam into creation—instantaneously connecting Michael in a syncopating heartbeat to those spiritual tributaries that Langston Hughes described, the ones 'ancient as the world and older than the flow of human blood in human veins.' Bottom line: Anyone whose racial-litmus-test challenge to Michael came with a rhythm-and-blues battle royal event would have gotten their ass royally waxed.") "Who Is It" eventually reached #6 on the R&B charts (and #14 on the *Billboard* Hot 100) in 1993.

As with "Billie Jean," Jackson not only wrote the song, but also helped actualize all aspects of its intricately layered arrangement and instrumentation. A close listen reveals some superb touches: the haunting soprano vocals (by Jackson and Linda Harmon), the striking cello flourishes, the gorgeous flute solo in the bridge, and the melancholy strings throughout. Bill Bottrell remembers Jackson loving the extended "trance ending," which rhythmically repeats the chorus. The effect is such that the song hardly needs words. Everything is in the music, the ambience, the desperate gasps and cries. (While the album version powerfully conveys the song's psychological turmoil, some of its dark chaos is even more visceral in the IHS mix included on *The Ultimate Collection*.)

Yet the narrative Jackson paints only intensifies the song's anguish and mystery. "I gave her passion," he sings. "My very soul/I gave her promises/And secrets so untold." The lyrics, on the surface, are about a relationship torn apart by infidelity and betrayal. Yet the primary emotion Jackson conveys is loneliness. His desperate cry, "I can't take it 'cause I'm lonely!" is one of the most piercing moments in his entire catalog. "It doesn't seem to matter," he confesses in the chorus,

And it doesn't seem right
'Cause the will has brought no fortune
Still I cry alone at night
Don't you judge of my composure
'Cause I'm lying to myself
And the reason why she left me
Did she find in someone else.

It is this uncertainty and raw emotional urgency, as much as its sonic character that draws comparisons to "Billie Jean." Yet in certain ways, "Who Is It" represents an evolution in theme: the culprit of his despair is more ambiguous, more internalized. His subject is no longer a woman (and the dangers, seductions and traps she represents); it is his own psychological condition ("I am the dead/I am the damned/I am the agony inside this dying head"). These are powerful expressions of despair that rival the most penetrating work of poets such as Robert Lowell or Sylvia Plath. "Who Is It" is a desperate cry for human connection, a revelation wrapped in a six-and-a-half-minute exorcism.

10. GIVE IN TO ME

(Written and composed by Michael Jackson and Bill Bottrell. Produced by Michael Jackson and Bill Bottrell. Recorded and mixed by Bill Bottrell. Guitars recorded by Jim Mitchell, assisted by Craig Brock. Special guitar performance by Slash. Solo and background vocals: Michael Jackson. Bass, drums, mellotron, and guitar: Bill Bottrell. Guitar: Tim Pierce)

Like "Who Is It," "Give In To Me" comes from a place of deep internal conflict. It is a moody, mercurial track that begins with a droning Mellotron and slow-strumming guitar, before exploding into lightning bolts of pent-up aggression. Jackson had done rock before, but not like this. Songs like "Beat It" and "Dirty Diana" were more theatrical; "Give In To Me," in contrast, was raw and grungy, with elements ranging from the Rolling Stones and David Bowie to Guns N' Roses and Nirvana.

Jackson began developing the song with Bill Bottrell in 1990. "[Give In to Me"] was like a revelation," recalls Bottrell. "Michael walked through the room and I happened to have a guitar in my hand and I played the main riff to it and he said, 'Billy, that's a great song.' Then he hummed me the melody." The song evolved from there, though Bottrell now laments that they didn't stick with an earlier stripped down version. "We sat on two stools in Record One and we played that song," recalls Bottrell of the early version. "I should have left it alone. It was absolutely stunning."

Still, the song that evolved was stunning itself, retaining much of its original essence, including Jackson's "looser, more instinctive vocals." The main addition was the virtuosic guitar work of Slash. "He sent me a tape of the song that had no guitars other than some slow picking," Slash recalls. "I called him and sang over the phone what I wanted to do. . . . I was leaving for Africa. Our schedules were not in sync. So they were going to blow me off, but Michael managed to work it out so we could do it when I came back from Africa. I got off the plane and drove to the studio. I basically went in and started to play it—that was it. It was really spontaneous in that way. Michael just wanted whatever was in my style. He just wanted me to do that. No pressure. He was really in sync with me. I don't come from this heavy-metal school of guitar playing. All the stuff that I do or dig is from the same place that Michael Jackson comes from. We may go in separate directions or be on different sides of the fence, but when it comes down to it, it all comes from the same shit."

For Jackson, the track continued the soul-baring nature of the album. In the verses he is wounded and vulnerable, feeling betrayed by a former lover. Yet in the chorus, he transforms into someone more sensual and powerful, demanding submission from all that torments him ("Love is a feeling/Give it when I want it/Quench my desire/'Cause I'm on fire"). Fred Astaire famously commented with admiration that Jackson was an "angry dancer"; that same catharsis, of course, often found expression in his music. "Give In To Me" is an "angry" song emanating from a lifetime of pain and loneliness. "Don't try to understand me," he sings in one of his greatest lines. "Because your words just aren't enough." For someone as incessantly scrutinized and interrogated as Jackson, it is a powerful buttress. He can always push away what hurts him by hiding behind walls, masks, personas, by remaining elusive. As soon as he finishes the line, Slash comes slicing in on guitar while Jackson soars over the top—"Love is a feeling/Quench my desire/. . . Give into the feeling!"

"Michael Jackson was often at his best," observed *Rolling Stone*, "when he was indulging a dark streak, and this strange, sinister number about obsessive love . . . is all ice and shadows. Jackson sounds agonized on the chorus, and Slash's eerie descending arpeggios envelop the song like spider webs. [It is] one of Jackson's more masterfully ominous numbers."

11. WILL YOU BE THERE

(Written and composed by Michael Jackson. Produced by Michael Jackson. Coproduced by Bruce Swedien. Recorded and mixed by Bruce Swedien and Matt Forger. Choir arrangement by Andraé and Sandra Crouch, featuring the Andraé Crouch Choir. Orchestra arranged and conducted by Johnny Mandel. Rhythm arrangement by Michael Jackson and Greg Phillinganes. Vocal arrangement by Michael Jackson. Solo and background vocals: Michael Jackson. Keyboards: Greg Phillinganes and Brad Buxert. Synthesizers: Michael Boddickert. Synthesizers and synthesizer programming: Rhett Lawrencet. Drums and percussion: Brad Buxer and Bruce Swedien. Percussion: Paulinho Da Costa. Prelude: Beethoven Symphony No. 9 in D Minor, Opus 125. Performed by the Cleveland Orchestra Chorus, directed by Robert Shaw, and conducted by George Szell)

"Will You Be There" takes Michael Jackson into new artistic territory. The nearly eight-minute piece is essentially an epic film score, rooted in black gospel but fused with classical music and rhythm and blues. It is yet another example of Jackson's remarkable ability to draw from disparate musical styles and make them work together. Music critic John Kays calls it "one of the best efforts of his career . . . a moving spiritual that seems to be carved out of the pages of the Old Testament." Indeed, after the Job-like anguish and turmoil of the two previous tracks, "Will You Be There" tries to make sense of his suffering and transcend it.

The song begins with a sixty-five-second orchestral prelude taken from Beethoven's Symphony No. 9, as performed by the Cleveland Orchestra. It is an incredibly audacious move. The Ninth Symphony is considered one of the greatest pieces in the history of Western music. Jackson's canny use of such a renowned work (the first major orchestral symphony to use voices) gives an indication of the scope and ambition of his creative vision. While other pop artists of the time were singing standard, formulaic love songs, Jackson was drawing deep from the wells of art, history, and religion to create something that, in his words, "would live forever."

It is important to note, however, that he wasn't using the Ninth Symphony (or any other source) just for the sake of using it. The introduction is about establishing a mood, about taking the listener on an emotional journey. As the Cleveland Orchestra Choir's majestic strains reach their climax, the sound suddenly dissolves into the soothing descant of celestial voices (sung by the Andraé Crouch Choir). "He was brilliant with that stuff," says Brad Buxer. "Intros and outros were really important to him. The intros were almost as important as the song itself." With the appropriate mood set, the song proper begins with a purposeful piano hook and shuffling, *Chariots of Fire*-like percussion. "It was modeled after Michael's beatbox," says Buxer. "It was like *Chariots of Fire* but more aggressive. He'd say, 'It has to be dry and in your face,' meaning no reverb, no effects. Just raw. It has to be piercing."

Jackson sings in a calm, deep tenor, a stark contrast from when he was last heard on "Give In to Me." The music has transported him (and the listener) to a different place. "Hold me," he sings, "like the River Jordan. . ." Jackson had utilized elements of gospel before ("We Are the World," "Man in the Mirror"), but "Will You Be There" is the first time he fully explores its power. The song ebbs and flows, soars and sighs. Jackson is singing a prayer for comfort and strength, for the ability to overcome obstacles. However, he also confesses his weaknesses and doubts: "They told me," he sings, "a man should be faithful/And walk when not able/And fight till the end/But I'm only human." Later he pleads for guidance and clarity: "Everyone's taking control of me/Seems that the world's/Got a role for me/I'm so confused/Will you show it to me."

With each confession, Jackson is lifted by the momentum of the humming choir, by the sweeping rhythm of the percussion. At its climax, he ad-libs in an exhilarating call and response with the choir that nearly transports the singer (and his audience) on the spot. This is Jackson at peak performance. Part of his genius will always be his darker, more ominous tracks, but it is also found in the transcendent sublimity of his anthems. "Will You Be There" is a personal song about a universal condition. Whether the final words are directed at God, a loved one, or humanity as a whole, they communicate the simple human yearning for love and understanding.

12. KEEP THE FAITH

(Written and composed by Glen Ballard, Siedah Garrett, and Michael Jackson. Produced by Michael Jackson; coproduced by Bruce Swedien. Recorded and mixed by Bruce Swedien. Arrangement by Glen Ballard, Jerry Hey, and Rhett Lawrence. Choir arrangement by Andraé and Sandra Crouch, featuring the Andraé Crouch Choir. Solo and background vocals: Michael Jackson. Background vocals: Siedah Garret and Shanice Wilson. Piano and bass: Jai Winding. Drums, percussion, and synthesizer: Rhett Lawrence. Drums and percussion: Bruce Swedien. Synthesizers: Michael Boddicker. Guitar: David Williams)

"Keep the Faith" reunites the same team (minus Quincy Jones) that created "Man in the Mirror." Like its predecessor, it is a song about overcoming barriers and believing in one's ability to make a difference in the world. While the lyrics can be a bit clichéd, Jackson's spirited execution augments the track's motivational gospel fervor. Indeed, to fully appreciate the song, one must understand the role the black church—and gospel music—has played in American history as a force of solidarity, strength, and empowerment in the face of oppression and injustice. Rooted in the pain and pathos of spirituals and the blues, gospel songs tell stories of suffering and endurance. They connect the present with the past. As W.E.B. Du Bois wrote at the turn of the century: "The music of Negro religion still remains the most original and beautiful expression of human life and longing yet born on American soil. . . . Intensified by the tragic soul life of the slave . . . it became the one true expression of a people's sorrow, despair, and hope." Gospel-infused "freedom songs," of course, also played a key role in the civil rights movement.

Jackson, therefore, is tapping into a genre with a deep and rich past, his understanding of which began with his mother, who was raised in the South. He also grew up listening to artists like Sam Cooke, Ray Charles, and James Brown, all of whom were rooted in gospel, but blended it with soul and rhythm and blues and made it accessible to a wider "pop" audience.

On "Keep the Faith," Jackson follows in this tradition. Perhaps with his global, multi-cultural audience in mind he avoids religion-specific references in favor of something more universal. The highlight is the fiery call and response with the Andraé Crouch Choir, which mimics the dynamic between preacher and congregation. "The lyrics are like a proper sermon on Sunday by a spirited preacher trying to uplift his congregation to meet the challenges that life proposes," writes music critic John Kays. Indeed, what begins as a seemingly lightweight self-help number evolves into a rapturous, inspirational call for resilience and determination. "Sitting at a piano and having him sing . . . it's just a religious experience," recalls collaborator, Glen Ballard. "The guy is amazing. . . . He's expressive, has great pitch, does incredible backgrounds. His backgrounds are probably as good as anybody I've ever heard. They're textures unto themselves."

13. GONE TOO SOON

(Music by Larry Grossman; lyrics by Buz Kohan. Produced by Michael Jackson; coproduced by Bruce Swedien. Recorded and mixed by Bruce Swedien. Solo vocal: Michael Jackson. Orchestra arranged and conducted by Marty Paich. Prelude composed, arranged, and conducted by Marty Paich. Rhythm arrangement by David Paich. Keyboards: David Paich. Synthesizers: David Paich, Steve Porcaro, and Michael Boddicker. Bass: Abraham Laboriel. Percussion: Paulinho Da Costa)

Following Michael Jackson's untimely death, this quiet ballad was suddenly infused with new meaning. Its original inspiration was Ryan White, an American teenager from Kokomo, Indiana, who was diagnosed with HIV/AIDS in 1984 when he was just thirteen years old. White was often teased and threatened at school, and when the threats turned to violence, his family was forced to leave their hometown. White subsequently became a spokesperson for AIDS education (AIDS was deeply misunderstood and feared at the time).

Jackson befriended Ryan White in 1989. In the final years of White's short life, the two spent many days together at Neverland, forming a deep bond and friendship. "He didn't care what race you were, what color you were, what was your handicap, what was your disease," recalled White's mother, Jeanne. "Michael just loved all children."

White died in 1990 just before graduating from high school. "Gone Too Soon" and its accompanying video, a montage of White's life, was Jackson's tribute to him and his cause.

One of Jackson's most heartbreaking vocals, this simple song (written by Buz Kohan), in a string of metaphors, conveys the fragility and transience of life. "Born to amuse, to inspire, to delight/Here one day/ Gone one night." "One can never choose to forget how much vitriolic hate was spewed against AIDS patients at the height of the virus's transmission," writes Jason King. "Jackson released his tribute at a time in the 1990s when I can't recall many, if any, hip-hop artists willing to talk about or discuss AIDS publicly. "Gone Too Soon" may have been schmaltzy, but it was authentic, it was tender and terribly moving, a genuine expression of Jackson's passion and care for a young person who had been victimized."

Jackson rededicated the song to Princess Diana after her tragic death in 1997. Usher performed the song at Michael Jackson's memorial in 2009.

14. DANGEROUS

(Written and composed by Michael Jackson, Bill Bottrell, and Teddy Riley. Produced by Teddy Riley and Michael Jackson. Recorded by Jean-Marie Horvat, Bruce Swedien, Teddy Riley, and Thom Russo. Mixed by Bruce Swedien and Teddy Riley. Rhythm arrangement by Teddy Riley. Synthesizer arrangement by Teddy Riley. Vocal arrangement by Michael Jackson. Solo and background vocals: Michael Jackson. Synthesizers: Teddy Riley, Brad Buxer, and Rhett Lawrence)

The album closes with the new jack industrial funk of "Dangerous," one of Jackson's hardest-hitting and most impressively produced dance tracks. It was also used for one of his most memorable live performances at the 1995 MTV Music Awards.

Jackson recorded the first version with Bill Bottrell (a *Bad*-era, keyboard-driven mix that can be heard on *Michael Jackson: The Ultimate Collection*), but the singer felt something was missing. It didn't have the grit or contemporary feel he was trying to achieve. He subsequently decided to work on it with Teddy Riley. "I told Michael," recalled Riley, "'I like Billy. I like his producing, and everything about him. But this is your album, Michael. If this is the right tune, I can utilize what you have in your singing. Let me change that whole bottom and put a new floor in there.' He said, 'Try it. I guess we gotta use what we love.' And we did. I'm quite sure that if anyone else had come up with a better 'Dangerous,' [Michael] would have used that. So it's not actually about me or Billy [Bottrell]; it's about the music. I always say that the music is the star."

For his part, Bottrell agreed: "I never felt competition with Teddy, and when MJ suggested Teddy do a version, I had no problem. Hey, it's all about the writing. Teddy's version rocks and sounds like the '90s, where mine was stuck in the '80s."

Indeed, in retrospect, both versions of the song are excellent, but Riley's made more sense for the sound of the album. Riley gave the song a "taut, mechanical rhythm" in contrast to Bottrell's more spaced out, "moody" production. The result is a song that feels like it is being created in the depths of a furnace: the opening brilliantly builds up tension as the metallic pounding gradually increases intensity until the beat hits. The factory sounds are the sonic inspiration for the industrial center of the album cover.

The song's subject is a Michael Jackson staple: distrust and intrigue over a seductive woman ("The girl was persuasive/The girl I could not trust"). In so many of Jackson's best songs, he is positioned in this tension. "Deep in the darkness of passion's insanity," he sings, "I felt taken by lust's strange inhumanity." He is intrigued by the many possibilities represented in the woman; but he is also fearful of the repercussions and tries to restrain himself ("I have to pray to God/'Cause I know how/ Lust can blind"). This is perhaps the disciplining force of his religious education. Yet Jackson is clearly torn, simultaneously lashing out and indulging in the "danger."

The verses are narrated in a near-whisper, as if the listener is being let in on a secret. In the ladder, Jackson conveys his vulnerability and confusion, acknowledging, "I never knew but I was/Walking the line." He realizes he is in a precarious position: he can either hide and insulate himself from life or take a chance and risk being exploited and hurt. The tension of the situation builds until the chorus explodes into a one-word description: *dangerous*.

It is a nice, circular way to end the album. Jackson could have finished on the high, transcendent note of "Will You Be There" or "Keep the Faith," but instead chose to return to the ominous uncertainty and ambiguity of the first track, "Jam." The implication is that life for Jackson might contain glimpses of relief, even ecstasy; but the real world of disease and anxiety is never far removed; the "danger" is always encroaching, threatening his peace. The title track represents this danger in the form of a woman, but for Jackson it seems more about negotiating his fate in a world he fears.

OTHER NOTABLE *DANGEROUS*-ERA SONGS

DO YOU KNOW WHERE YOUR CHILDREN ARE (recorded 1990, unreleased)
"Do You Know Where Your Children Are" would have likely been a big hit had it been included on *Dangerous*. Jackson held on to it, thinking it wasn't quite ready, but having in mind to use it on a future album. The song features a fierce guitar riff and an instantly memorable chorus. Like other tracks on *Dangerous*, the song is keenly attuned to real-world issues, tackling neglect, exploitation, and sexual abuse.

FOR ALL TIME (recorded 1982, released on *Thriller 25* in 2008)
A pretty ballad originally written by Steve Porcaro, David Paich, and Michael Sherwood for *Thriller*. It was re-recorded during the *Dangerous* sessions, but left off the final cut for that album as well. It was finally released as a bonus track on *Thriller 25* in 2008.

IF YOU DON'T LOVE ME (recorded 1990, unreleased)
Written by Jackson and produced by Bill Bottrell, this infectious retro rock-soul number recalls the sound of sixties classics such as "Do You Love Me" and "It Takes Two." Jackson delivers an outstanding vocal performance on this fun, unique, yet-to-be-discovered gem.

MEN IN BLACK (recorded 1989, unreleased)
This track has long been the subject of speculation among fans. Jackson recorded a demo of the sleek rhythm track in 1990 with Bryan Loren, but it was left off the final lineup for *Dangerous*.

MIND IS THE MAGIC (recorded 1989, unreleased)
Jackson wrote "Mind is the Magic" with Bryan Loren for illusionists Siegfried and Roy.

MONKEY BUSINESS (recorded 1989, released on *Michael Jackson: The Ultimate Collection*, 2004)
"Monkey Business" didn't quite fit the sound of *Dangerous*. Its bluesy, southern feel made it more at home with the *Bad* album and its outtakes ("Streetwalker," etc.). It's a shame, because it is an outstanding track. Accompanied by a rich jazzy Wurlitzer piano, a crisp beat, and Jim Horn's soulful sax playing, Jackson sinks right into this one, narrating a tale of hypocrisy and deception. Jackson worked on the song with Bill Bottrell, primarily at Record One, in the early *Dangerous* sessions. The monkeys were recorded by Matt Forger.

SERIOUS EFFECT (recorded 1990, unreleased)
Cowritten by Jackson and Teddy Riley, "Serious Effect" is a smooth, swaggering new jack-hip hop fusion featuring LL Cool J.

SHE GOT IT (recorded 1990, unreleased)
A funk-rock groove reminiscent of eighties-era Prince. Cowritten with Bill Bottrell and Teddy Riley, it features a driving guitar riff and funky beat.

SOMEONE PUT YOUR HAND OUT (recorded 1992, released on *Michael Jackson: The Ultimate Collection*, 2004)
Originally written for *Bad*, Jackson re-recorded this beautiful falsetto ballad in 1992. Initially released as an exclusive Pepsi promo for Jackson's *Dangerous* World Tour, it was finally released to the public on *Michael Jackson: The Ultimate Collection* in 2004.

WORK THAT BODY (recorded 1990, unreleased)
A funky demo cowritten by Jackson and Bryan Loren during the early *Dangerous* sessions. Jackson sings the famous lines from the Jackson 5 hit, "ABC": "Sit down, girl! I think I love you! No! Get up, girl! Show me what you can do!"

YOU WERE THERE (recorded 1989, unreleased)
A gorgeous ballad written by Jackson and Buz Kohan. Jackson performed a stunning rendition of the song for Sammy Davis, Jr. at his 60th anniversary show at the Shrine Auditorium in 1989.

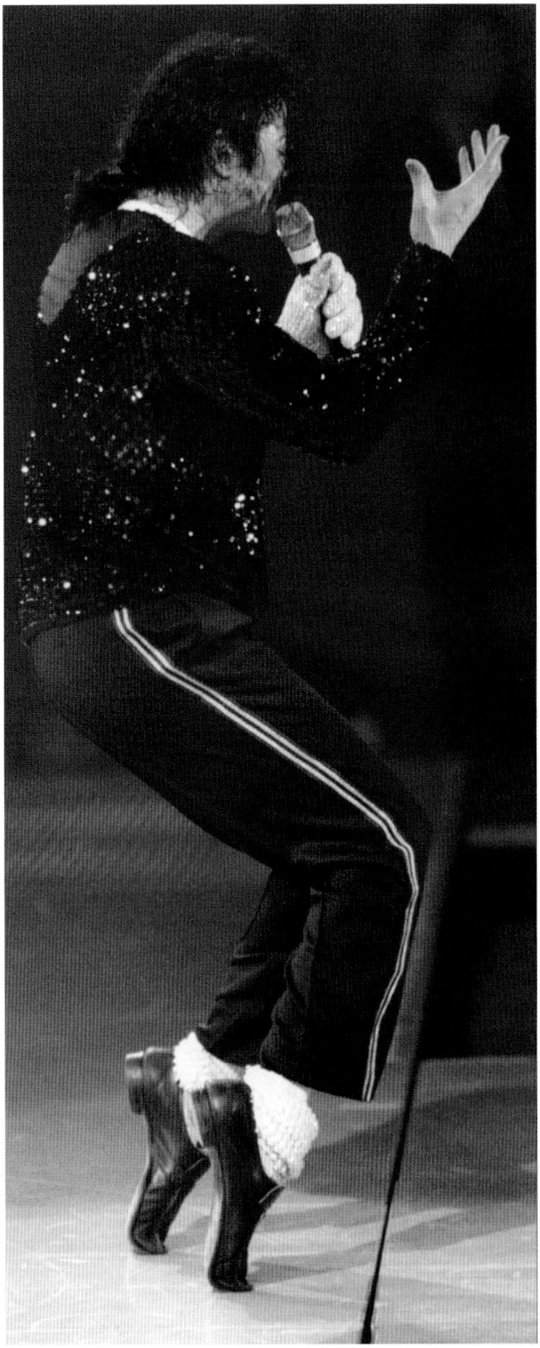

Jackson in a signature pose while on the first leg of his *Dangerous* World Tour in 1992. *Dangerous* signaled a new milestone in Jackson's creative development.

"I'm not planning to write another book anytime soon. If you want to know how I feel, you can check out HIStory. It's a musical book."

MICHAEL JACKSON, SIMULCHAT, 1995

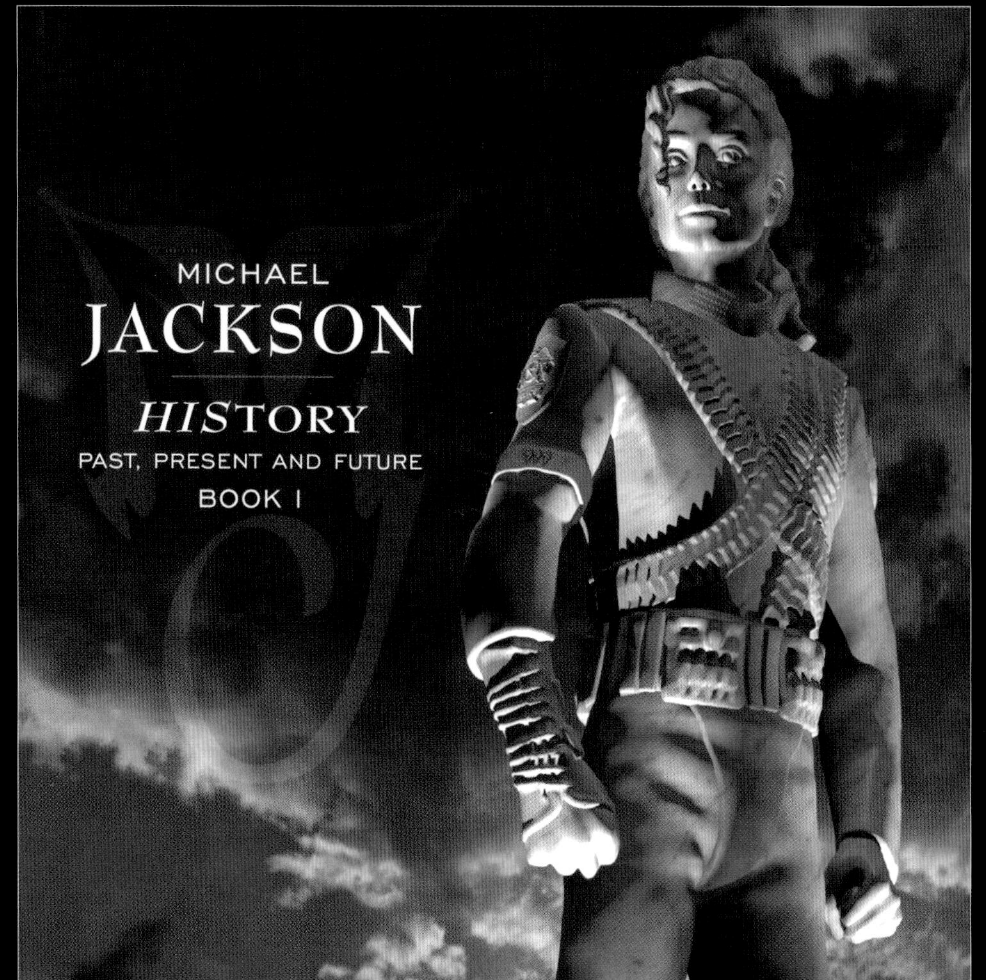

CHAPTER 5 *HIS*TORY: PAST, PRESENT AND FUTURE, BOOK I

HIStory is Michael Jackson's most personal album. From the impassioned rage of "Scream" to the pained vulnerability of "Childhood," the record was, in Jackson's words, "a musical book." It encompassed all the turbulent emotions and struggles of the previous few years: it was his journal, his canvas, his rebuttal.

The result, for some, was a bit jarring. They wanted the "old" Michael Jackson: the warm, breezy melodies and dance-invoking lyrics. *HIStory* openly defied these expectations. Sonically, it pressed forward as it continued to cross and mix genres (including hip-hop, industrial funk, and orchestral pop). Thematically, it confronted rather than evaded Jackson's complex emotional state. However, it also looked outward, tying his anguish and outrage to larger social issues such as media sensationalism, materialism, discrimination, and alienation.

While this approach produces some raw moments (and songs without the commercial viability of past albums), it also seems to liberate Jackson—and results in some of the most politically potent, emotionally honest, and artistically powerful tracks he ever made. "Jackson expresses hard experience and uneasy knowledge," observes cultural critic Armond White. "In his aggrieved voice, there's a place for everyone's desperate, urgent yearning." Indeed, though most critics have been slow to look past its immediate biographical context and recognize its artistic achievement, *HIStory* makes a strong case for being Michael Jackson's magnum opus. Never had the valleys been lower and the peaks been higher.

HIStory was created from a sort of cultural exile. By 1995, while he remained enormously popular throughout most of the rest of the world, Michael Jackson had lost much of his appeal in the United

---

RELEASED: *June 16, 1995*

EXECUTIVE PRODUCER: *Michael Jackson*

NOTABLE CONTRIBUTORS: Jimmy Jam *(producer)*, Terry Lewis *(producer)*, David Foster *(producer)*, Janet Jackson *(vocals)*, Bill Bottrell *(producer/songwriting)*, R. Kelly *(songwriting)*, Dallas Austin *(songwriting)*, Brad Buxer *(keyboard/arrangement)*, Bruce Swedien *(engineer)*, Eddie Delena *(assistant engineer)*, Andrew Scheps *(assistant engineer)*, Rob Hoffman *(assistant engineer)*, Johnny Mandel *(orchestration)*, The Andraé Crouch Singers Choir *(vocals)*, Slash *(guitar)*, Boyz II Men *(vocals)*, The Notorious B.I.G. *(rap)*, Shaquille O'Neal *(rap)*, Matt Forger *(technical coordinator)*

SINGLES: *"Scream," "You Are Not Alone," "Earth Song," "They Don't Care About Us," "Stranger in Moscow"*

ESTIMATED COPIES SOLD: *22 million*

States. The allegations of child molestation in 1993 were devastating to his image. Some felt it effectively ended his viability as a mainstream pop star. The lurid allegations, however, weren't the only reason for his waning relevance. It also had to do with the changing youth culture and musical zeitgeist. The cultural icons of the early to mid-nineties were artists like Kurt Cobain, Tupac Shakur, and Alanis Morissette. By comparison, Jackson's image and music seemed too theatrical and slick. "Black or White" and "Heal the World" simply didn't resonate with the cynicism and solipsism of Generation X. Dance pop and humanitarian anthems were scoffed at by flannel-wearing grungers and pant-sagging gangstas reacting against the perceived artificiality, flash, and optimism of the eighties.

The mid-nineties did see a resurrection of R&B with groups such as Boyz II Men and TLC and solo artists R. Kelly, Toni Braxton, and Michael's sister, Janet; but these were artists with more natural appeal to young people. Their songs were about sex and sentiment. Michael Jackson was now thirty-seven years old and mostly known to a new generation of music listeners as the subject of endless tabloid controversy. Because of this context, Jackson understood that *HIStory* would be the most challenging album of his career.

The cultural changes weren't just in musical tastes, of course. As Jackson returned to the studio in 1994, globalization and new information technology were revolutionizing the world in profound ways. It was the beginning of the digital age with the Internet changing the way people communicated, consumed, and received information. E-mail replaced "snail mail," chat rooms were the new bars, people began buying books, music, and clothes online, and entrepreneurs such as Steve Jobs and Bill Gates became multi-billionaires.

In the United States, the Clinton era was underway and along with it the dot-com boom that led to a decade of surging markets and prosperity. The nineties are now often recalled nostalgically as a pre-Bush, pre-9/11, pre-recession golden age. While Clinton's vision of a "bridge to the twenty-first century" inspired hope, however, before long it also generated some disillusionment and a severe countercultural backlash. While CEOs made record profits, it was also a time of outsourcing, downsizing, mergers, and corporate dominance. Citizen rage against globalization culminated in

Jackson on the set of his *Scream* video in 1995.

the chaos and violence of the 1999 Seattle protests against the World Trade Organization.

The nineties also witnessed an effective merger between twenty-four-hour cable news and entertainment news. The desire for celebrity coverage in particular became a sort of international obsession, fueled by an incessant chase for ratings and advertising dollars. The wall-to-wall coverage of two landmark events—the O. J. Simpson murder case (1994) and the death of Princess Diana (1996)—perfectly epitomized the new "infotainment" paradigm. Both cases featured celebrity drama, high-speed chases, and train-wreck tragedy that anticipated the shift to reality TV and set the new blueprint for what might be considered mainstream "news." Both instances also had a profound personal impact on Michael Jackson.

Jackson reportedly watched the infamous O. J. car chase from the Hit Factory studio in New York. As the circus trial unfolded over the next year, he could clearly see the ways courts, jurors, and the very idea of justice was being infected by parasitical media coverage. There were simply no guarantees the truth would prevail when trials were turned into TV shows and witnesses became celebrities in their own right.

The death of Diana, meanwhile—a more global media event—was devastating to Michael Jackson. While his relationship with her was limited (he met her once on his *Bad* World Tour and spoke with her on the phone a few times), he had long felt a kinship with the Princess of Wales. "She was very kind, very loving, very sweet," he said in a 1996 interview. When he found out about her death, he literally broke down. "I woke up," he recalled, "and my doctor gave me the news. And I fell back down in grief, and I started to cry. The pain… I felt inner pain, in my stomach, and in my chest. So, I said, 'I can't handle this… it's too much.' Just the message and the fact that I knew her personally." The message, of course, for Michael was that the tabloid media could not only mock you, stalk you, take away all privacy, manipulate the truth, and destroy your reputation, but they could also literally kill you. There were, of course, other factors in Princess Diana's car accident, but this was Jackson's takeaway. The paparazzi had hounded her all her life, and now, as her own brother said, they had "blood on their hands." "I've been living that kind of life all my life," Jackson said in an interview that year. "The tabloid press… that kind of press… I've been running for my life like that, hiding, getting away… You feel like you're in prison."

For Jackson, of course, it was just a few years earlier that he survived one of the biggest global-media feeding frenzies of the decade, following allegations that he had molested a young boy. In many ways, it was the prequel to the O. J. and Diana media spectacles. For the tabloids as well as for twenty-four-hour cable news, it was the perfect ratings grab. Michael Jackson was the biggest entertainer in the world. People remained fascinated by him. Now, after years of presenting stories of mere eccentricity or curiosity, the media had a scandal with much higher stakes that could be exploited for months, if not years.

The Sun, a notorious British tabloid, was the first to run the story. Others weren't far behind. Just days after the allegations broke, *Hard Copy* correspondent Diane Dimond (who would make a career off Jackson) obtained an illegally leaked copy of the abuse report from the Department of Child Services with all the salacious details of the allegations. Within hours, the document was being sold to other media outlets, which had converged in California from around the world. That night the allegations were reported as the lead story on several major news broadcasts.

From there, it was a slippery slope. Before anything was even checked beyond an allegation, the media ran wild. "Peter Pan or Pervert?" screamed a headline for the *New York Post*. "Scandal of the Decade," read the title of one of many similar shows by *A Current Affair*. Teasers were intentionally misleading and filled with paid "witnesses." Even more-respected media outlets compromised standards for ratings, joining in on the feeding frenzy. "Competition among news organizations became so fierce that stories weren't being checked out," recalled KNBC reporter Conan Nolan, "It was very unfortunate."

The press coverage, however, continued relentlessly. In an extensively researched piece for *GQ* magazine in 1995, journalist Mary Fisher described it as "a frenzy of hype and unsubstantiated rumor, with the line between tabloid and mainstream journalism virtually eliminated." The consequence for Jackson was a nearly year-long media witch hunt in which article after article and show after show offered speculation and innuendo but no supporting evidence or credible witnesses.

For Jackson, though, the injustice didn't end with the media. It extended to a police department and district attorney (Tom Sneddon) who spent an unprecedented amount of time, money, and energy fruitlessly pursuing an indictment. It was clear from the beginning—as more than seventy officers descended on Jackson's Neverland home in August 1993—this was no ordinary case. Doors were broken down, mattresses slashed open, and journals, books, videos, and photos taken away in box loads. Officers combed through every square foot of Jackson's property—looking under beds, in desks and closets, rummaging through his personal belongings. "Imagine having someone going through all of your stuff while you're a million miles away," Jackson later told biographer J. Randy Taraborrelli. "They took all kinds of things, stupid things like videotapes of me at Disneyland, pictures of my friends, boxes and boxes of personal things. And diaries! Imagine having some stranger reading your most private thoughts, his filthy hands turning all of those private pages, thoughts about [my] Mother and the way I feel about God. It was vicious. And we still haven't gotten back a lot of stuff. It makes me cry when I think about it. But in all of my private stuff, there wasn't one piece of evidence to prove I had done anything wrong."

The humiliation would also include a strip search in which photos were taken of his penis and buttocks. (It was later revealed that the search didn't match the accuser's description.) None of these facts, of course, made the same headlines as the initial allegations. "What became of the massive investigation of Jackson?" asked Mary Fisher in her 1995 study of the case. "After millions of dollars were spent by prosecutors and police departments in two jurisdictions, and after two grand juries questioned close to 200 witnesses, including 30 children who knew Jackson, not a single corroborating witness could be found." Ultimately, the accuser himself refused to testify as well—in 1993, and again in 2005. "The prosecutors tried to get him to show up and he wouldn't," explained Jackson's attorney, Thomas Mesereau. "If he had, I had witnesses who were going to come in and say he told them it never happened and that he would never talk to his parents again for what they made him say. It turned out he'd gone into court and got legal emancipation from his parents."

Indeed, Jackson never blamed the boy in question. Rather, he felt "betrayed" and manipulated by the parents. He was especially angry with the father (Evan Chandler), who was attempting to extort him for money for months before the allegations broke. In a recorded phone conversation, Chandler actually acknowledged that the welfare of his son was "irrelevant"; if he didn't get what he wanted there would be "a massacre." "There are other people involved that are waiting for my phone call that are in certain positions," Chandler threatened. "I've paid them to do it. Everything's going according to a certain plan that isn't just mine. Once I make that phone call, this guy [his attorney Barry Rothman] is going to destroy everybody in sight in any devious, nasty, cruel way that he can do it. And I've given him full authority to do that.... And if I go through with this, I win big-time. There's no way I lose. I've checked that inside out. I will get everything I want, and they will be destroyed forever.... Michael's career will be over.... This man is going to be humiliated beyond belief." Just a few weeks after this threat, when Chandler's attempts to arrange for Jackson-funded screenplays (Chandler was an aspiring screenwriter) failed, he carried through with his plan. Authorities were notified about the allegations, as was the press—and the "scandal of the decade" was underway.

Jackson, of course, maintained his innocence throughout his life. "I could never harm a child, or anyone. It's not in my heart, it's not who I am," he told Diane Sawyer in 1995. In another interview,

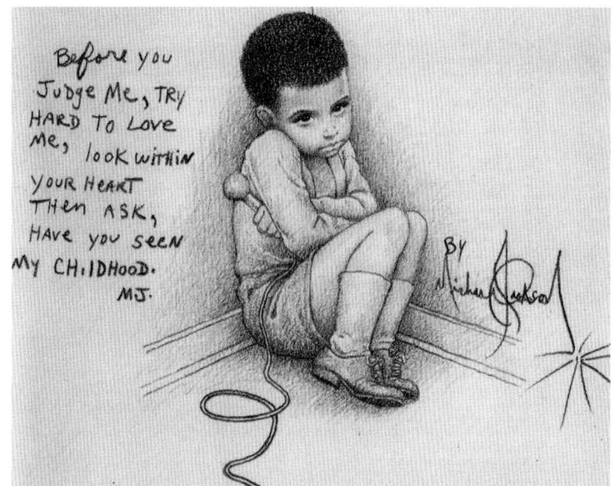

A revealing self-portrait Jackson included as part of the accompanying booklet to *HIStory*. To the left are lyrics from his song, "Childhood."

he said he would "slit his wrists" before he would hurt a child. The 1993 allegations, however, proved to be a traumatic experience with lasting effects, including a growing addiction to painkillers and further insulation from the outside world. After months of what he described as a "horrifying, horrifying nightmare"—including a complete demolition of his character by the press, the invasion of his home, and a dehumanizing strip search—Jackson decided he had had enough.

Once he learned from his attorneys that the "nightmare" could go on for years in public, drawn-out, humiliating court battles, Jackson instructed them to give in to Evan Chandler's demands and settle. "I talked to my lawyers," Jackson recalled, "and I said, 'Can you guarantee me that justice will prevail?' and they said, 'Michael we cannot guarantee you that a judge or a jury will do anything.' And with that I was like catatonic. I was outraged. Totally outraged. So what I said... I have got to do something to get out from under this nightmare.

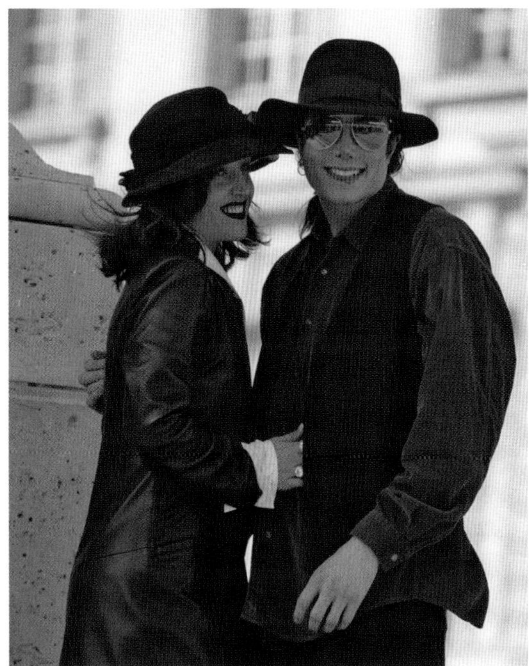

Jackson and Lisa Marie Presley smile for the cameras in Versailles, France, in 1995.

All these lies and all these people coming forth to get paid and all these tabloid shows, just lies, lies, lies. So what I did—we got together again with my advisors and they advised me, it was hands down, a unanimous decision—resolve the case. This could be something that could go on for seven years. We said let's get it behind us."

On January 26, 1994, that's exactly what they did. The settlement was officially announced, with Jackson maintaining his innocence. It was estimated that Evan Chandler and his family received up to $22 million in the settlement.

If there was anything positive to come from the crucible Jackson endured in 1993, it was the way he transfused the pain, anger, and disillusionment from the experience into astounding new music. Songs such as "Scream" and "Stranger in Moscow" likely would have never been written had Jackson not gone through this period of utter despair. "You have to have that tragedy, that pain to pull from," he later wrote of the paradoxical source of great art.

The original plan for *HIStory* was a greatest-hits collection with a few new songs tacked on. However, with an influx of promising new material, Jackson quickly opted to make it a double-disc album instead: one disc containing his classic hits and one, all new songs. "In truth, I really didn't want the album to be about old songs," Jackson acknowledged. "To me greatest hits albums are boring. And I wanted to keep creating." The new record, he determined, would be a powerful rebuttal to those who declared him dead: a record so strong, diverse, and bold that people would have no choice but to acknowledge it.

Helping with both his confidence and resilience was a new presence in his life, the daughter of rock royalty, Lisa Marie Presley. Jackson and Presley were introduced to each other by Jackson's longtime attorney, John Branca. For years, Jackson had prodded Branca (who once represented the Presley estate) about setting him up with Lisa. They grew close in the midst of the most difficult year of his life. "I was on tour," he recalled, "and it seemed like I was in Armageddon.... All these horrible stories were going around about me.... It was unbelievable. Lisa Marie would call. I could count my true friends on one hand. She was very, very supportive the whole time. That really impressed me. She would call and be crying."

Having lost her own father to drugs, Lisa was anxious to help Jackson recover from his addiction to painkillers. She was also sensitive to the exploitation he was experiencing at the hands of surrounding "vultures." When Jackson returned to the States in mid-December of 1993, the pair began seeing each other with more and more frequency. "The brilliant thing about us is that we were often together but did not let anybody know about it," said Michael. "We got to see each other that way.... We were really quiet and comfortable with each other. That's pretty much how the dating started happening.... We spent a lot of time on the ranch and just walked around and talked.... It happened, it unfolded all natural. We could feel the feeling we had for each other without even talking about it. It was all in the vibrations, the feelings and the look in our eyes."

"We fell in love," confessed Presley, acknowledging their courtship contained all the things one might expect—"flowers, calls, candies, you name it." Jackson proposed to Presley in his library at Neverland. A few months later, the couple snuck out of the States to the Dominican Republic, where they were married. The small and private ceremony lasted all of twelve minutes. By some miracle, the couple somehow managed to keep the marriage a secret for nearly two months after, as they honeymooned in Budapest, Hungary, and Disney World and settled in together at Neverland Ranch.

When the press finally got wind of the marriage, there was a predictable uproar and a great deal of skepticism. Many saw it as a "PR move," given that Jackson was less than a year out of his child abuse scandal. Others claimed Presley was using him to start her own singing career or to get Michael and his money into the Church of Scientology.

In multiple interviews (even after their divorce), however, Presley claimed that while she could understand the skepticism, the marriage was indeed real and intimate. "Our relationship was not 'a sham' as is being reported in the press," she later wrote on her blog shortly after Jackson died. "It was an unusual relationship yes, where two unusual people who did not live or know a 'normal life' found a connection.... Nonetheless, I do believe he loved me as much as he could love anyone and I loved him very much."

With her support and encouragement, Jackson was ready to start fresh and move on to a new phase of his life and artistry.

Not long after Jackson and Presley were married, the singer was back in the studio working on his new album, where Presley often accompanied him. "They acted like two kids in love," recalled assistant engineer Rob Hoffman. "Held hands all the time, and she [would] hang out for quite a while." Presley was deeply impressed by Jackson's talent, but she also wasn't afraid to be honest with him. She didn't want him to play victim on this album; she wanted him to fight back. Jackson agreed and was ready to release more than a year of pent-up rage and indignation.

Most of Jackson's early songs ("Stranger in Moscow," "Childhood," "Money," "Little Susie," etc.) were sketched out and recorded with songwriter/musician Brad Buxer, with whom Jackson had grown very close since the *Dangerous* sessions. Buxer was Jackson's musical director for the second leg of the *Dangerous* World Tour and they often worked together on new material in their hotel rooms. That material served as the foundation for *HIStory* when they returned to the United States.

Coincidentally, recording for *HIStory* was scheduled to begin the same day as the January

1994 Los Angeles earthquake (which resulted in seventy-two deaths and more than $20 billion in damage). Jackson was terrified by the quake and decided to move the entire team to New York. Recording began later that month at the legendary Hit Factory, at which the team often utilized all four studios, overseen primarily by production coordinator Matt Forger. During the early months of recording, Jackson lived in hotels in Manhattan, where he would often stay up late into the night developing lyrics and arrangements before traveling incognito to the studio. (Jackson primarily wrote and sang in Studio Three.)

After the nightmare that was 1993, Jackson was thrilled to be refocused on his work. The studio and stage, as always, were where he felt most at home. "When Michael walks into the recording area it becomes his," observed then-friend Uri Geller, who sat in on sessions at the Hit Factory in 1994. "He dominates the studio, a different kind of domination to the way he overwhelms a crowd.... Michael is utterly committed to his music. He works passionately at it, with a dedication that surprised me when I first saw it."

As with *Dangerous*, Jackson himself assumed the role of executive producer, assembling around him a fresh team of musicians, songwriters, and coproducers to help him carry out his creative vision. While he retained several longtime musical partners—Bruce Swedien, Rene Moore, and Steve Porcaro, among others—he also continued to look around for new talent. For *HIStory*, the main crew consisted of Brad Buxer, Eddie Delena, Andrew Scheps, and Rob Hoffman. After a positive experience working with Bill Bottrell and Teddy Riley on *Dangerous*, Jackson was also anxious to try out some new producers.

The new jack swing sound had evolved since *Dangerous*. Jackson did record a few new songs with Teddy Riley in the early sessions, but these failed to make the album. Jackson also recorded songs with Babyface (including "Why" and "On the Line"), but these also failed to make the final cut. (Two Bottrell collaborations, "Come Together" and "Earth Song," made *HIStory*, but these had already been written and recorded before—although "Earth Song" was slightly modified.)

In this early, feeling-out stage, Bruce Swedien remembers Jackson calling him into his room at the studio one day and asking if he "could think of anyone who was truly original in the crafting of synthesizer sounds and colors." Jackson emphasized, "And I mean *truly* original." Swedien recommended Chuck Wild, from the revolutionary new-wave group Missing Persons. Jackson decided to bring him on board. "I'll never forget the first conversation Michael and I had in 1994," recalls Wild. "He said, 'Chuck, I want you to manufacture sounds the ear has never heard. I want them to be fiery and aggressive, unusual and unique.' Off and on over the next three years, working with about 25 synths, three samplers, and a couple of Macintosh computers, I created a library of sounds and soundscapes."

Jackson also brought in famed Minneapolis duo Jimmy Jam and Terry Lewis, who had produced all of his sister Janet's albums, including the groundbreaking *Rhythm Nation*. Jam and Lewis were thrilled to finally work with Michael. Before meeting him in New York, they tested out a handful of tracks with Janet. "Over a couple of days, we came up with about eight different track ideas," recalls Jimmy Jam. "Interestingly enough, Janet knew that he'd love the demo that ended up being

'Scream.' I said, 'How do you know?' [She said] 'I know my brother." Janet, of course, was right. When Jam and Lewis arrived at the Hit Factory, Michael and Janet listened to the demos together. "He put on our tracks, which we'd pared from eight down to six," recalls Jimmy Jam. "'Scream' was the fifth. He'd listen to each track for a couple of minutes. 'I like this.... This is real good,' he'd say. Then at the end, he told us: 'All of these really work, you did a great job. Can we go back to track five?' He played 'Scream' again. 'I think this one here, I think I hear something for this track,' he said. 'Let's go with this one.' Janet looked at me and started laughing. 'I told you that's the one he was going to pick.'"

Jackson on the set of his music video for ***Earth Song*****, his most ambitious anthem at that time.**

The next day they met again in Jackson's suite at Trump Towers, and Jackson came up with the melody and lyrics for the song. "It was amazing," recalls Jam. "The writing process was like that on all the songs we did together.... He was very fast, very intense. Everything was written in a whirlwind. It just came to him. It was exhilarating." In total, three Jackson/Jam-and-Lewis collaborations—"Scream," "Tabloid Junkie," and "History"—would make the album.

For a handful of other tracks, Jackson enlisted up-and-coming R&B producer Dallas Austin (coproducer of TLC's *CrazySexyCool*), who helped out with "This Time Around" and "2Bad," and R. Kelly, who contributed "You Are Not Alone." "I grew up with the music of Michael and I've been inspired a great deal by Michael," said R. Kelly. "To actually have him call me up, call my management, saying he wants me to do a song for him was a great inspiration for me to go forward in my career.... And up to the day I met him it was like a big countdown." When the two finally went into the studio together, R. Kelly wasn't disappointed. "Michael was at another level," he said of the experience, "and it was a hell of a level to go to."

For the orchestral tracks, meanwhile, Jackson turned to renowned composer/producer David Foster (who had worked with nearly every major artist in the industry). Jackson had worked briefly with Foster before on *Off the Wall*, but they hadn't had the chance to collaborate since. "Michael asked me to bring my family along," Foster recalls. "He was big on making sure everyone was comfortable. I took three of my daughters and my two stepsons who, of course, were all very excited. Michael puts us up in this incredible five-bedroom suite at the Plaza." Foster helped produce two of the album's most emotional statements—"Childhood" and "Smile"—as well as helping finish work on "Earth Song."

As work progressed on the album, Jackson, as always, was tuned into the latest trends and innovations in popular music and was determined to stay ahead of the curve. "I think very few people realized how deeply [Michael] was involved in his records," says assistant engineer Rob Hoffman. "He had an incredible music vocabulary—from show tunes to jazz, and whatever was on the radio. He studied, and I think you can hear it in his music." Indeed, while recording *HIStory*, he listened to and enjoyed albums as diverse as Nine Inch Nails' *Downward Spiral* and the Notorious B.I.G.'s *Ready to Die*. Fortunately for Jackson, the respect he commanded from his peers meant virtually anyone he wanted to collaborate with would jump at the opportunity. For *HIStory*, Slash once again contributed his virtuosic guitar work, Boyz II Men provided background vocals, and basketball superstar Shaquille O'Neal was called in to rap. In an indication of the hip-hop world's growing respect for Michael Jackson, the Notorious B.I.G.—who was then at the height of his career—not only eagerly contributed a rap to Jackson's "This Time Around," but also shyly asked for Jackson's autograph afterward.

Wyclef Jean of the Fugees also recorded with Jackson during the *HIStory* sessions. "He's the only person in my life where, when I saw him, my whole voice-box went," he recalled of their first meeting. "I didn't know what to say. My hands were trembling." According to nearly everyone who worked with him, however, Jackson was always humble and treated his collaborators as equals. "Working with Michael is a different type of work," reflected producer/songwriter Dallas Austin. "You're pressured by time, but not by creativity or money. So you're left with mad freedom. You'd think he'd be very controlling, but if he likes you enough to work with you, he wants your expertise."

Jackson's *HIStory* teaser incited an uproar. Here, he marches at the head of a synchronized army.

Others concurred. "Michael's the most intense person I've worked with," offered Jimmy Jam. "For him, everything is about the music and how to make it better. [But] he also makes work a lot of fun. He's a kid at heart—his office is not like a normal office. He has all the kids' toys. A lot of times we'd be in session, in the middle of playing a video game, and he'd be, like 'Well, we got to do this. But go ahead and finish your game, though—I don't want to mess your game up.'"

The initial album release date was set for the winter of 1994—just before the holidays. In what had become standard Jackson form, however, the album was delayed. He wasn't yet satisfied with enough material. "I believe in perfection," he would later explain, "and I try to create that in everything I do. We never seem to totally get there, but I believe in perfect execution. And when we don't get at least 99.9 percent, I get really upset." Jackson was pleased with the way *HIStory* was evolving though. That winter, he and the rest of the creative team moved back to Los Angeles, where recording continued at Record One, Larrabee, and Westlake studios. "Sometimes we'd look up and it would easily be 3 or 4 in the morning," recalls Jimmy Jam. "There were days when Michael would leave the studio at 3 a.m. and be back in action first thing the next day."

The next several months were spent pruning and polishing, while Jackson also worked on short films, new choreography for performances, and other projects.

"The last weekend of recording on *HIStory*," recalls assistant engineer Rob Hoffman, "[Michael] came to me and Eddie Delena, and said, 'I'm sorry, but I don't think any of us are going to sleep this weekend. There's a lot to get done, and we have to go to Bernie [Grundman for mastering] on Monday morning.' He stayed at the studio the entire time, singing, and mixing. I got to spend a couple quiet moments with him during that time. We talked about John Lennon one night as he was gearing up to sing the last vocal of the record—the huge ad-libs at the end of 'Earth Song.' I told him the story of John singing 'Twist and Shout' while being sick, and though most people think he was screaming for effect, it was actually his voice giving out. He loved it, and then went in to sing his heart out."

Jackson and his team of engineers continued to work all the way to the finish line. "Later that night, while mixing," recalls Hoffman, "everyone left the room so [Michael] could turn it up. This was a common occurrence during the mixes, and I was left in the room with ear plugs, and hands over my ears, in case he needed something. This particular night, all the lights were out and we noticed some blue flashes intermittently lighting up the room during playback. After a few moments we could see that one of the speakers (custom quad Augspurger) was shooting blue flames. [Michael] liked this and proceeded to push all the faders up."

When they finally had all the songs finished (fourteen tracks out of an estimated forty to fifty that were worked on during the sessions), however, they ran into a familiar problem: there was too much material to fit on a CD. Bruce Swedien tasked assistant engineer John Van Nest with paring it down. "This was no small undertaking, as about seven minutes needed to be trimmed somewhere," recalls Van Nest. "I laid this all out in Sound Tools and came to know every bar of every song very intimately. I found places where songs could be tightened up and came up with many suggestions. On the night of mastering, I was put in a room at Bernie Grundman's with my

Sound Tools rig, and in this room, I would have to 'negotiate' with Michael about what to take out. I'll never forget this night.... Michael came in, and Bruce told MJ that we would have to remove either one whole song or edit the others to fit onto a CD. We chose the latter. I started with song one and played Michael my edits, 'Oh no, we can't take *that* out, it's my favorite part of the album!' 'Okay,' [I said.] 'Let's try another. 'Oh no, we *must* keep those four bars.' Okay, let's go to the vamp, which carries on for two minutes—how about removing these eight bars, 'Oh no, that's my favorite part of the vamp!' Well, you get the picture. Meanwhile, Jimmy Jam was in with us, telling Michael that all these edits were killer and actually make things better. And over the course of about five hours, we got it down. By this time, it was probably 3:00 a.m., and I was wiped out." The album was finally mastered by Bernie Grundman a few hours later.

***HIStory* was completed** in the spring of 1995. Before its release, Sony unleashed the beginning of a $30-million-dollar promotional campaign that once again turned Michael Jackson into a worldwide spectacle and subject of controversy. The blitz began with an elaborate four-minute teaser shot in Budapest featuring Jackson marching at the head of a perfectly synchronized army to the stirring music of Basil Poledouris's "Hymn to Red October." Directed by Rupert Wainwright, the video is a spectacular visual tour de force. As Jackson marches down a broad street resembling the Champs-Élysées, he is identified gradually through his iconic trademarks (a glove, an eye, a silhouette), masterfully establishing an aura while building suspense. When he is finally revealed in his entirety, he is adorned in shiny military regalia as fans gaze, scream, and moan in adulation. Soon after, he is unveiled again, this time literally larger than life as an enormous statue while helicopters swarm overhead. The response from the crowd is a mixture of ecstasy and reverence.

While the short video promo accomplished its purpose of generating excitement, it also elicited widespread controversy. "The clip doesn't just stop at representing previously known levels of Michael mania," wrote the *Los Angeles Times'* Chris Willman, "it goes well beyond the bounds of self-congratulation to become perhaps the most baldly vainglorious self-deification a pop singer has yet deigned to share with his public, at least with a straight face." Others argued, with its use of imagery and symbols, it was modeled after the Nazi propaganda film *Triumph of the Will*.

Jackson responded to the controversy by saying it was "art" and had "nothing to do with politics, or Communism, or Fascism." Yet as the rest of the promotional campaign unfolded—including the unveiling of several thirty-two-foot steel and fiberglass statues of the singer throughout Europe, some of which floated down prominent rivers like the Thames in London—the criticism began to build. The promo and statues played into media memes about Jackson. He was a megalomaniac, a narcissist, a child with a compulsive need for attention. However, this diagnosis was a bit too simplistic.

The *HIStory* album cover of Jackson as a statue, and its accompanying promotional efforts, certainly convey a certain audacity. Yet for Jackson, after being declared down and dead after the abuse scandal, it was also a Muhammad Ali-like declaration of defiance ("I am the greatest"). The cover image reveals him standing like a militant prizefighter; bold, fists clenched, confident. For

A thirty-two-foot statue of Jackson floats down the River Thames in London to promote *HIStory*.

a dancer in particular, the immortalizing of the body, the literal transformation of his likeness into a work of art makes sense.

It was also, of course, a publicity stunt—classic P. T. Barnum showbiz. "I wanted everybody's attention," he told Diane Sawyer. Jackson liked to surprise people, to present something they had never seen before. It was a classic demonstration of the paradox of Michael Jackson. As a person, friends say, he was shy, humble, and didn't take himself too seriously; but he knew how to perform, how to put on a show, how to hide away for years and then reappear larger than life. With the promotion for *HIStory*, that's exactly what he had done. Just a year before, he was deemed irrelevant by critics. Now, once again, he was making headlines: people were talking, people were angry, people were excited. But, everyone in the world knew his new album was coming out.

This strategy, however, had its repercussions. Jackson first concocted the idea of being "the greatest show on earth" before releasing *Bad*. The plan had indeed turned him into a spectacle of never-ending intrigue and fascination; yet it also dehumanized him for many people. This was particularly the case after the allegations. Many critics were lined up and ready to fire.

Still, as the countdown shortened until the release of the album, the excitement level was high—within the music industry as well as for fans around the world. The lead single, "Scream," was so highly anticipated, in fact, it was illegally leaked to a Los Angeles radio station two weeks early (this was before the days of illegal downloading when such leaks became commonplace). Not only was the track a showcase of two of the most prominent entertainers in the world (who happened to be siblings), it was also Jackson's first single since the allegations of child abuse—and it directly addressed his state of mind. The futuristic video (a groundbreaking, $7 million production) premiered on ABC's *Primetime Live* during Jackson and Presley's interview with Diane Sawyer to an estimated U.S. audience of more than 64 million viewers.

When "Scream" was officially released on May 31, 1995, along with the accompanying music video, it didn't disappoint, soaring to #5 on the *Billboard* charts. It replaced the Beatles' "Let It Be" as the highest debut in the thirty-seven-year history of the *Billboard* Hot 100. It was quite a comeback indeed for an artist many critics claimed was professionally finished. The album itself followed suit, becoming Jackson's fourth album in a row to hit #1 in the United States with 391,000 first-week sales (782,000 discs). "It's now common for albums to enter at #1 based on first week sales," notes John Branca. "But back when *HIStory* was released, you really did have to have a very big album to get to #1." When the album dropped out of the Top Ten a few weeks later, however, critics were already labeling it a flop. Part of the lower sales numbers likely had to do with it being a two-disc album and, therefore, more expensive. Yet interest in Jackson did also seem to be waning in America. While debuting high, "Scream" failed to hit #1 on the *Billboard* chart, marking the first time in Jackson's solo career the lead single didn't top the charts (beside "The Girl Is Mine," which reached #2). Yet *HIStory* was far from a flop. While his performance in the United States was solid if not overwhelming, Jackson retained enormous popularity throughout Europe, Asia, Australia, and Africa, all continents that saw the album hit number one and go multi-platinum. Indeed, after just six weeks, *HIStory* had sold nearly eight million copies worldwide (sixteen million discs).

In spite of its commercial successes, however (and more importantly, its artistic quality), *HIStory* was largely dismissed by critics who, predictably, could only interpret it through the lens of Michael Jackson, the media caricature. *All Music*'s Stephen Thomas Erlewine called it "a monumental achievement of ego." The *Daily News*' Jim Farber labeled it "whiny Jackson jive about his perceived mistreatment." In his reductive, condescending review, he writes: "Let's see a show of hands. How many of you out there were forced to cancel your last world tour and suffered the loss of a multi-million-dollar endorsement deal from Pepsi because every media outlet in creation trumpeted accusations that you molested a young boy? If this describes the last

Jackson poses on the set of the music video for *Scream*. The award-winning video proved that Jackson remained at the cutting edge of the medium.

"They Don't Care About Us," and "Stranger in Moscow" is as good a trio as one will find on any Jackson record. By turns intense, gritty, and haunting, these tracks reveal a progression even from the openers on *Dangerous* ("Jam," "Why You Wanna Trip On Me," and "In the Closet"). The lyrics are sharper and more sophisticated, and the sounds more distinct. "The crisp, staccato clip and compressed harmonies of 'They Don't Care About Us,'" observes Loudon Wainwright, "or the layered, meticulously arranged textures of the fluid 'Stranger in Moscow,' could come from no one else but Jackson."

Sonically, *HIStory* presented a new standard for how albums are made and recorded. "Whatever one makes of the hoopla surrounding the album," writes Daniel Sweeney, "one can scarcely ignore its amazing production values and the skill with which truly vast musical resources have been brought to bear upon the project. Where most popular music makes do with the sparse instrumentation of a working band fleshed out with a bit of synth, *HIStory* brings together such renowned studio musicians and production talents as Slash, Steve Porcaro, Jimmy Jam, Nile Rodgers, plus a full sixty piece symphony orchestra, several choirs including the Andraé Crouch Singers Choir, star vocalists such as sister Janet Jackson and Boyz II Men, and the arrangements of Quincy Jones and Jeremy Lubbock. Indeed, the sheer richness of the instrumental and vocal scoring is probably unprecedented in the entire realm of popular recording."

Jackson on the set of his music video for *They Don't Care About Us*, in Rio de Janeiro, Brazil.

Jackson basks in a moment of serenity on tour.

Sweeney continues: "But the richness extends beyond the mere density of the mix to the overall spatial perspective of the recording. Just as Phil Spector's classic popular recordings of thirty years ago featured a signature 'wall of sound' suggesting a large, perhaps overly reverberant recording space, so the recent recordings of Michael Jackson convey a no less distinctive though different sense of deep space—what for want of other words one might deem a 'hall of sound.'"

Such results, of course, were the product of an immensely talented creative team. Jackson, however, was the driving force. "I don't know that many people would ever have the patience or work ethic to create the records that [Michael] did," says assistant engineer Rob Hoffman. "We'll never have the budgets again, that's for sure. . . . There was this constant pursuit for 'sounds the ear has never heard.'"

In terms of style, where *Dangerous* mixed new jack swing, rock, and gospel, *HIStory* was more hip-hop and hard funk on the rhythm tracks and cinematic, orchestral pop on the ballads. This unusual juxtaposition was one of the criticisms of the album. Could songs as diverse as "Scream," "Childhood," and "2Bad" really work together as a cohesive listening experience? The answer partially depends on the listener. Yet throughout his career, Jackson consistently presented these sonic and thematic contrasts to achieve specific effects. It wasn't just from song to song either. On many of the rhythm tracks, a dense, aggressive bottom is overlaid with an airy, melodic top (see "Tabloid Junkie") to create contrast and tension.

Another criticism was the album's overload of "angry" songs. This concern, however, held more currency in 1995, when every song was interpreted through the lens of his personal life, than it does today. Like John Lennon's later works, *HIStory* is intended to capture the emotional turbulence of life. Everything comes out in a torrent of intense and varied emotions: sometimes angry, sometimes vulnerable, sometimes pained, sometimes joyous and triumphant, sometimes brash and blunt.

HIStory is certainly less accessible than many of Jackson's other albums; but it can also be more rewarding. The album's high points are probably as high as in any album since *Thriller*. In addition to the brilliant opening trio, "Earth Song," "Little Susie," and "Smile" stand as some of Jackson's finest musical achievements. None of these are conventional pop songs, yet they each offer something unique, powerful and timeless.

HIStory is also, without question, Jackson's most political album. It explores everything from discrimination ("They Don't Care About Us") to media manipulation ("Tabloid Junkie," "Scream") to rampant materialism and institutional corruption ("Money," "D.S.") to environmental concerns ("Earth Song"). While *Off the Wall* offered blissful escapism and liberation via music and dance, *HIStory* is a more mature effort, forcing listeners to confront unsettling realities about the world we live in.

HIStory's unique mixture of sounds, styles, and themes makes it difficult to draw comparisons, particularly within its own decade. Its sonic innovation at times recalls Nine Inch Nails' *The Downward Spiral*, while its vulnerable melancholy contains strains of R.E.M.'s *Automatic for the People*. Yet perhaps *HIStory*'s most apt parallel in the nineties is Radiohead's 1997 masterpiece, *OK Computer*, which similarly addresses themes of alienation, despair, greed, apathy, and social outrage. Radiohead and Jackson are obviously working from different life experiences and aesthetic styles (rock/punk versus R&B/hip-hop); but both also experiment liberally with different genres (classical, jazz, industrial, techno, etc.), sounds, and arrangements to create unusual, visceral, atmospheric soundscapes. Entering each album is like looking through a mirror, darkly. The open and attentive listener comes through the experience disturbed, enlightened, and changed.

With more than twenty million units (forty million discs) now sold, *HIStory* is the best-selling multiple-disc album of all time. However, it also remains one of Jackson's most unknown and underappreciated in comparison to its artistic achievement (particularly in the United States). Along with *Dangerous*, it will no doubt experience a major reappraisal (and rediscovery) in the years to come.

THE SONGS

1. SCREAM

(Written and composed by Michael Jackson, Janet Jackson, James Harris III, and Terry Lewis. Produced by James Harris III, Terry Lewis, Michael Jackson, and Janet Jackson. Lead and background vocals: Michael Jackson and Janet Jackson. Keyboards and synthesizers: Jimmy Jam and Terry Lewis)

"Scream" is a statement song. After the intense scrutiny and demoralization of the previous few years, Jackson was ready to fight back with the most powerful weapon he possessed: his music. Perhaps no other song in Jackson's career has the kind of roundhouse punch of "Scream," a furious expression of indignation. In previous tracks such as "Wanna Be Startin' Somethin'," "Leave Me Alone," and "Why You Wanna Trip On Me," of course, he had expressed some of these "pressures," denouncing media lies and societal hypocrisies. Never before, though, had the singer been this direct, personal, and viscerally angry. "Superstars don't make records like this," wrote one critic in 1995. "They make safe, nice records. You know, easy on the ear, simple, friendly.... This is Michael fighting back. And he's delivered what could be a knockout blow."

The track begins with Jackson screaming as if trapped in a glass box. It is a brilliant aural effect that captures the entrapment and suffocation he feels as a dehumanized media subject. The guttural scream contains a sense of desperation, anguish, and rage, and as he lets it out, the imprisoning glass shatters. Instead of being a spectacle or victim, he is empowered. His music, once again, provides a sense of liberation. "Tired of injustice," he begins. "Tired of the schemes." It is an appropriate opening line for *HIStory*—the most political album of Jackson's career—and he bites into the lyrics with an intensity that assaults the listener's ears. Indeed, sonically, "Scream" was far ahead of the curve, blending Nine Inch Nails industrial metal with TV on the Radio electro-funk, the mechanical angularity of *Rhythm Nation* with the techno-alienation of *OK Computer*. With its hair-raising fuzz bass and glass-shattering backbeat, it is a song that demands good speakers or headphones for full effect.

"Scream" also made a statement with its language. A once famously devout Jehovah's Witness with a Peter Pan image, Jackson shocked many listeners when his opening single replaced the refrain in the chorus, "Stop pressurin' me" in one line with the brash, "Stop fucking with me!" (Jackson would also not-so-discreetly flip the bird in the music video.) According to assistant engineer Russ Ragsdale, Jackson was reluctant to swear on the track. "I was in the room when Jimmy Jam asked him to sing the chorus of 'Scream,'" he recalls, "and he would not say the F-word. He kind of made it very percussive instead of singing the full word. Janet carried the majority of that background vocal. It was not in his nature to use words like that at all. I never heard him swear. So it was a surprise that he used other words like that on the record. We all kind of smiled when we heard it." The language incited disapproval and condemnation among some parents and critics. For Jackson, however, it was a means of expressing his fierce outrage at deceitful and hypocritical media.

Ironically—given the "family values" controversy about the language—the song was actually a symbolic demonstration of family solidarity in the face of adversity. "Scream" was Jackson's first and only duet with his sister Janet. (She would later powerfully perform the song at the 2009 MTV Music Video Awards soon after her brother's death.) Hearing the superstar siblings sing together for the first time—and in such circumstances—gave the song even more power and drama. Janet was at her peak of popularity in the early to mid-nineties; her loyal support mattered deeply to Michael. Her contribution wasn't tepid either. In the second verse she comes with just as much indignation as her brother. "You're sellin' out souls," she sings, "but I care about mine/I've got to get stronger/And I won't give up the fight." The chorus has the two perfectly harmonized as they demand their dignity and respect.

The music video for "Scream," directed by the talented Mark Romanek, was equally ambitious. With a $7 million budget, it was the most expensive music video ever made. It also became one of Jackson's most critically acclaimed. Featuring Michael and Janet as anime androgynes trapped in an insulated spacecraft, the siblings alternately observe art, play games, dance, meditate, and go crazy in their isolated pop "pleasure-dome." Its inspiration was part David Bowie, part *2001: A Space Odyssey*, but perhaps most significantly, from Jackson's complicated life as information age celebrity. "Michael and Janet's isolation comes from the need to connect and is troubled by the need to escape," observes film critic Armond White. "Romanek literalizes today's high-tech lynching by linking it to the far edge of electronic communication and complicating it with references to Warhol, the internet and modern art."

Throughout the video, the Jackson's talent is on full display, as they sing and dance with explosive energy while addressing their critics. Described as "innovative," "exciting," "electric," and "cutting-edge," the video would continue Jackson's success in representing his music visually, winning numerous awards, including an unprecedented eleven nominations at the MTV Music Video Awards and a Grammy Award for Best Video.

While both the song and video were clearly personal, however, it would be reductive to view "Scream" as mere autobiography. As with most songs on the album, Jackson attaches his personal struggles to larger social concerns. The injustice he has experienced is only a small part of a larger system of deceit and corruption. In the bridge of the song, in fact, as sirens blare, we hear a faint report: "A man has been brutally beaten to death by police after being wrongly identified as a robbery suspect. The man was an eighteen-year-old black male . . ." This subtle allusion to another victim of the system—in this case, of racial profiling, police brutality, and media exploitation—is a testament to Jackson's sharp cultural awareness. On *Dangerous*, his method of defiance was to "jam"; four years later, the pressure had increased to such a degree he could only scream.

2. THEY DON'T CARE ABOUT US

(Written and composed by Michael Jackson. Produced by Michael Jackson. Strings arranged by Michael Jackson. Vocals: Michael Jackson. Keyboards and programming: Brad Buxer, Chuck Wild, Jeff Bova, and Jason Miles. Guitar: Trevor Rabin and Rob Hoffman. Los Angeles children's choir conducted by Annette Sanders)

"They Don't Care About Us" is one of the most powerful protest songs to come out of the 1990s. In the midst of the intense racial and political turmoil of the time (Rodney King, race riots, O. J. Simpson, James Byrd Jr.), it delivers a targeted blow against an abusive, corrupt, and oppressive apparatus of power. Interestingly, while the song became a Top Ten hit in countries around the world, it failed to make it past #30 in the United States. In spite of being dismissed (and stigmatized) in the United States, however, "They Don't Care About Us" stands as one of the strongest tracks in Jackson's entire catalog.

It also became his most controversial. Before *HIStory* was even released the *New York Times*' Bernard Weinraub described the entire album as "profane, obscure, angry, and filled with rage." In particular, he singled out "They Don't Care About Us," calling it "pointedly critical of Jews." Weinraub was referring to the lines—"Jew me, sue me/Everybody do me/ Kick me, kike me/ Don't you black or white me"—which he claimed were clearly anti-Semitic. In the context of the song, of course, Jackson was intending the exact opposite. "The idea that these lyrics could be deemed objectionable is extremely hurtful to me, and misleading," he said in a statement. "The song in fact is about the pain of prejudice and hate and is a way to draw attention to social and political problems. I am the voice of the accused and the attacked. I am the voice of everyone. I am the skinhead, I am the Jew, I am the black man, I am the white man. I am not the one who was attacking. It is about the injustices to young people and how the system can wrongfully accuse them. I am angry and outraged that I could be so misinterpreted."

This statement didn't keep critics from piling on and labeling Jackson, who had numerous close Jewish friends, an anti-Semite. In his review of *HIStory*, the *New York Times'* Jon Pareles went so far as to claim "[Jackson] gives the lie to his entire catalogue of brotherhood anthems with a burst of anti-Semitism." The narrative quickly caught on and spread like wildfire. Others, however, particularly in the African American community, defended Jackson, claiming his use of language was no different than rappers using the term "nigger" as a rhetorical device or "reverse discourse." It was intended to take charged epithets and deploy them to opposite ends.

Under continued pressure, however, Jackson eventually recorded an alternate version of the song that smeared over the "offensive" lyrics; in addition, Sony included a disclaimer and apology on all subsequent albums.

Overlooked in the manufactured controversy was the song itself: a brilliant, politically potent, street-inspired rap-pop hybrid. It became a song that not only resonated for the disenfranchised in America, but also for those around the world. Sonically and lyrically it hits like a sledgehammer, with Jackson hurling rhymes over a crackling militant beat, ominous strings, and a haunting choir. It is an anthem of the oppressed, a rap of resistance. "The song's percussive rhythm could be the handclaps of a schoolyard game or the forceful face-slaps of a lunch-counter sit-in," observes Armond White.

Indeed, the track begins in what sounds like a city school yard with a woman leading children in a call-and-response chant of indignation—"All I wanna say is that they don't really care about us.... Enough is enough of this garbage." For those who assume that every Michael Jackson song must be about Michael Jackson, it is significant to note that he begins this track with someone else's voice. When he comes in, he is simply inhabiting and witnessing for these previously unheard or unacknowledged voices. It is, in this way, an act of identification and empowerment.

The lyrics throughout the song are some of Jackson's most compelling and provocative. "Tell me what has become of my rights," he sings. "Am I invisible because you ignore me? Your proclamation promised me free liberty." He later speaks of those who are victims of hate, shame, and police brutality. "You're raping me of my pride," he sings from the perspective of the oppressed. "I can't believe this is the land from which I came."

In the bridge, a jagged guitar solo lets loose over swirling synth effects and layers of tight percussion, clapping, and a sampled police scanner. "The bridge section consisted of over 300 tracks," recalls assistant engineer Rob Hoffman. "[In the early stages the song] it was basically a click track ... with Michael and Brad adding new percussion elements every day, and Andrew and I building sample libraries for it every night. Sticks, claps, snares, hits. [The] basic groove was started on the MPC, the rest of the percussion was EIII and EIIIxp; Brad [Buxer]'s 909 is the main kick. Some of the crazy fx sweeps and sounds were added at the very end by Chuck Wild. The bridge of that song is crazy. We had tons of programmers and guitar players come in and everyone filled up their own 24 track tape with overdubs.... Eddie [De Lena] and Michael edited and comped it down to a manageable number of tracks for Bruce [Swedien] to mix."

Jackson worked with renowned filmmaker Spike Lee for the song's two excellent music videos. The first was set in an impoverished *favela* in Rio de Janeiro, Brazil. Initially, local government officials attempted to block the video from being shot, fearing it would draw attention to the city's poverty. "I don't see why we should have to facilitate films that will contribute nothing to all our efforts to rehabilitate Rio's image," said State Secretary for Industry, Commerce and Tourism Ronaldo Cezar Coelho. Yet many residents felt differently. "Everybody's suddenly paying attention to Santa Marta, talking about the social, sanitary and other conditions here," Mr. de Souza, a local resident, told the *New York Times*. "It's a poor world surrounded by a rich world, an island of misery surrounded by wealth." Courts eventually ruled in favor of allowing Jackson and Spike Lee to film the video, which featured the singer in casual jeans and local shirts, dancing and engaging with the people in various locations throughout the city. In a crowded cobbled street, he dances alongside the two hundred-member Afro-Brazilian percussion group Olodum, who bring a raw energy and immediacy to the track. While the video didn't receive much attention in the United States, it had an international appeal and made a political statement that used Rio de Janeiro as a microcosm for poverty around the globe. Yet it also showed the vitality and energy of the people. The chemistry between Jackson and the people is remarkably natural and spontaneous. Through music and dance, the video suggests, comes a joyful solidarity that might potentially combat oppressive barriers.

The second video was shot in a New York prison and was immediately banned by networks due to its montage of disturbing images, including police beatings, war, genocide, and starvation. Because of the ban (ironically), most people have never seen the prison version, which is one of the boldest videos of Jackson's career. The prison setting carries profound implications not merely about the plight of literal prisoners, but also about the condition of ordinary people in a society disciplined by constant surveillance and a more internalized form of power. Jackson delivers his message dressed as a prisoner himself. Along with his fellow inmates, he brashly defies the status quo, jumping on tables, raising his fist, and leading an uprising of table-pounding prisoners to demand justice and humanity. "Some things in life they just don't want to see," he sings. Yet in the video, Jackson makes sure some of these disturbing realities are revealed. It wasn't as fun or easy to watch as "Beat It," but it certainly reinforced the song's powerful expression of outrage at injustice.

3. STRANGER IN MOSCOW

(Written and composed by Michael Jackson. Produced by Michael Jackson. Lead and background vocals by Michael Jackson. Arrangement by Michael Jackson and Brad Buxer. Keyboards, synthesizers, and bass: Brad Buxer, David Paitch, and Steve Porcaro. Beatbox percussion: Michael Jackson. Percussion: Brad Buxer. Strings: Brad Buxer. Background guitar: Steve Lukather and Brad Buxer. Synclavier: Andrew Scheps)

Although it never made any of his greatest-hits collections, "Stranger in Moscow" is one of Michael Jackson's most impressive artistic achievements and, over time, will no doubt be recognized as such.

Poetic and evocative, "Stranger in Moscow" reveals what is underneath the rage of the previous two songs. It is Jackson's version of the Beatles' seminal "A Day in the Life": a haunting expression of isolation, disillusionment, and alienation. Music critic Tom Molley describes it as an "ethereal and stirring description of a man wounded by a 'swift and sudden fall from grace' walking in the shadow of the Kremlin." Long-time engineer Bruce Swedien felt it was one of the best songs the singer ever created. Armond White concurred, calling it Jackson's "finest track since 'Billie Jean.'" Its tale of out-of-step but soul-deep anguish is eloquent enough to mythify alienation in pop terms and elicit a reconsideration of post-cold war, post-civil rights angst."

Jackson wrote the song while touring in Moscow in 1993 during a particularly difficult and lonely time in his life. "It fell into my lap," he recalled, "because that's how I was feeling at the time. Just alone in my hotel and it was raining and I just started writing it." Indeed, the morning the inspiration for the song came, Jackson called up his music director and keyboardist Brad Buxer, who was also staying in the hotel. It was 10:30 in the morning and at Jackson's request Buxer came right over. "I knocked on the door and said, 'Okay, Michael, I think you called me 'cause you want to hear the Sega stuff [Jackson had agreed to create a tune for the video game, *Sonic the Hedgehog 3*].' And he goes, 'No, no, I want to just work.' And so there was a piano there and I started playing stuff, and he said, just play, just play." Buxer, who was classically trained and played numerous instruments, had worked closely with Jackson for the past four years. "Stranger in Moscow," however, was their most significant collaboration to date. In the hotel session, Jackson would sometimes direct and sometimes simply listen until he heard something he liked. "I played him a verse and he loved it," recalls Buxer. "Then he said, 'Play something else,' and I just went to these chords. It's a simple progression, but there's this weird modulation. Thirds and sevenths are everything in music.... If you take the root and fifth of a triad—such as A flat and E flat of an A flat triad and then use those very same notes as the major 3rd and the major 7th of a new chord (in this case E major 7)—you can bend the air a little bit and make some psychological things happen. You get a powerful, but almost invisible modulation that affects the psyche simply by altering one note. And so I did that. And there's a new section that's E major 7 to A and D major 7 to G, which is just a whole step down, same progression. Those were the two progressions and that was 'Stranger in Moscow.'" Once they had the basic progression, Jackson developed the melody, which floats on the top note of the chords. In just an hour and a half, Jackson and Buxer had essentially created the entire song. (Jackson would later finish the remarkable lyrics and add other embellishments.)

It wasn't long after writing and recording the song that Jackson decided to create an entire album of new material instead of just a few new tracks to tack onto a greatest-hits collection. Both Jackson and Buxer knew they had created something special. While a seemingly simple minor-key ballad, "Stranger in Moscow's" sparse arrangement perfectly captures the detached, empty feeling of a man estranged from the world around him. The track begins with the sound of rain, then a slow, mechanical beat (built on Jackson beatboxing), and a soft-strumming guitar.

In the verses, Jackson sings in exquisite call and response lines; the echoing effect perfectly captures his feeling of isolation. "I was wanderin' in the rain," he sings. "Mask of life, feelin' insane." It begins what are likely the most impressive lyrics in Jackson's career, recalling the poetry of T. S. Eliot or Rainer Maria Rilke. The fragmented narrative he presents is about cognitive dissonance: Either the world is insane or he is. Or perhaps it is both. In the chorus, he asks repeatedly, "How does it feel?/How does it feel?/When you're alone and you're cold inside." The question, however, is left hanging, unanswered throughout the song.

Later, Jackson sings of being "abandoned in his fame." He feels a sense of betrayal, loneliness and despair that, as *Rolling Stone* put it, would "rival any Seattle rocker's pain." He is a tragic, Jay Gatsby-like character ("it is what preyed on [him], what foul dust floated in the wake of his dreams"). Jackson describes his state of mind as "Armageddon of the brain."

"The word pictures he paints with the verses are so vivid," observes music critic Jonathan Conda, "—narrating a life of pain against mental images and feelings of Cold War Russia." Toward the end of the song, Jackson samples a KGB interrogator, asking: "Why have you come from the West? Confess! To steal the great achievements of the people, the accomplishments of the workers."

For Michael Jackson, icon of the Western world (and capitalism), the song presents a fascinating paradox: once a black child from the run-down streets of Gary, Indiana, he became the most famous pop star in the world; he was a veritable symbol of the American dream. At the height of *Thriller*, the then-Soviet Union wouldn't allow his music to be heard; it had to be bootlegged. Now, ten years later, Jackson was performing to hundreds of thousands of fans in places such as Prague and Moscow, while essentially being banished from America. In the song, therefore, he is a "nowhere man," a vagabond. He has been used up and spit out by his own country and system (a "swift and sudden fall from grace"). But he is also a "stranger" in Russia—trapped in a hotel where "Stalin's tomb won't let [him] be." He is an outcast, an invisible man, feeling dejected, homeless and alone.

A certain redemption, however, comes through in the music video (which like the song itself is vastly overlooked). Music critic Owen Hatherly calls it an "impressionistic, semi-noir, sub-Le Carre tale of surveillance . . . beggars and imposing edifices . . . set in a cityscape that is one part Tim Burton, one part Andrei Tarkovsky." Directed by Nicholas Brandt, it passes on the showbiz theatrics and choreographed dancing of many of Jackson's short films in favor of something more understated and bleak: a visual narrative in which the lives of six isolated strangers play out as the world moves around them in slow motion. Jackson is identified with these "regular people": he too is alone, and wanders the streets in a black trench coat like a ghost, unacknowledged. About midway through the video, however, he and the other characters step out into the pouring rain. As they are individually baptized by the water, something changes: it is as if the aching alienation they each feel is temporarily washed away; they are cleansed and connected by a common experience: their suffering. The paradox of the video, then, is that only in expressing or opening to each other's common loneliness and pain can they find some degree of connection.

4. THIS TIME AROUND

(Song and lyrics written by Michael Jackson. Music composed by Dallas Austin, Bruce Swedien, and Rene Moore. Produced by Michael Jackson and Dallas Austin. Coproduced by Bruce Swedien and Rene Moore. Additional programming: Simon Franglen. Keyboards and synthesizer: Dallas Austin. Rap by the Notorious B.I.G.)

Following the somber "Stranger in Moscow" comes the slinky hip-hop-funk of "This Time Around." The effect of such a vastly different song—both thematically and sonically—can be a bit jarring for the listener. (A song like "In the Back" might have worked as a better bridge between the two masterpieces.) Yet Jackson wanted sharp contrasts on the album, and this certainly provided it.

Composed by Jackson and Atlanta producer Dallas Austin (coproducer of TLC's *CrazySexyCool*), the track follows up on the outrage of "Scream," as Jackson makes clear he won't be a victim. "This time around," he bluntly promises his accusers and critics, "I'm takin' no shit!" Once again, Jackson shows no inclination toward self-filtering. "This Time Around" is a tough, gritty throw down, in which Jackson's growing outrage is on full display. "Even in my home I ain't safe as I should be," raps Biggie Smalls, "Things always missin'/Maybe it could be my friends/They ain't friends if they robbin' me." With its thumping beat and funky guitar riffs, it was praised by *Rolling Stone* as a "dynamite jam . . . ripe for remixes."

The song is also notable for its rap bridge by the Notorious B.I.G., then at the height of his popularity, and along with Tupac Shakur, probably the biggest rapper in the world. "He was quite an imposing figure when he walked in," recalls John Van Nest of the studio session. "I had no idea what to expect from him in terms of attitude, but he seemed nice when he walked in. . . . But almost immediately, he blurted out, 'Yo, Dallas, can I meet Mike?' To which, Dallas replied that he thought so. Biggie went on to talk about how much this opportunity meant to him, as Michael was his hero." Biggie recorded his rap in just two takes, before waiting for Michael to come listen. "[When] Michael came in, Biggie nearly broke out in tears," recalls Van Nest. "I could tell how much this meant to him. Michael could have this effect on anyone, even the most hardcore rappers! Biggie was tripping up on his words, bowing down and telling Michael how much his music had meant to him in his life. Michael was, as always, very humble and kept smiling while Biggie just went on and on how much he loved Michael."

After the unlikely pair had talked for a while, Jackson asked to hear his rap. "We popped it up on the big speakers and let her go," recalls Van Nest. "Michael loved it. 'Oh, let's hear it again,' [he said], and we listened again. Michael just loved it and thanked Biggie for coming all the way from Philadelphia. Biggie asked rather sheepishly whether he could get a photo, and Michael agreed. A shot was taken, we listened again, and Michael thanked Biggie. Michael said good-bye and stepped out, leaving Biggie standing there looking completely stunned."

5. EARTH SONG

(Written and composed by Michael Jackson. Coproduced by Michael Jackson, David Foster, and Bill Bottrell. Background vocals: Andraé and Sandra Crouch and the Andraé Crouch Singers Choir. Piano: David Paich. Guitar: Michael Thompson. Orchestration: Bill Ross)

"Earth Song" stands with "Stranger in Moscow" as one of Jackson's greatest artistic achievements (though it reaches this status in a very different way). Where "Stranger in Moscow" is subtle and understated, "Earth Song" is epic and theatrical. Incorporating elements of gospel, blues, opera, and pop-rock, Jackson delivers a dramatic plea for the planet that has been called "the most popular green-themed tune ever." Indeed, it is not an overstatement to say it is one of the most powerful anthems of the past century.

A monumental hit just about everywhere outside the United States (where, strangely, it wasn't released as a single), "Earth Song" continues in the vein of previous socially conscious message-anthems such as "Heal the World" and "We Are the World." Yet "Earth Song," in many ways, reveals a more mature Michael Jackson. In the declining wasteland it evokes, there are no illusions about where things stand. "Earth Song" is primarily a lamentation. It paints a devastating panoramic picture of the present. "What have we done to the world?" he cries. "Look what we've done." Later, he speaks of the profound disillusionment and confusion that has resulted:

I used to dream
I used to glance beyond the stars
Now I don't know where we are
Although I know we've drifted far

The bass that comes in after the final line is so powerful it literally shakes the listener as Jackson lets out his wordless cry for the state of the Earth.

It was a theme Jackson cared about deeply. "I was feeling so much pain and so much suffering at the plight of the planet earth," said Jackson at the time (the song was actually written during the *Dangerous* sessions but not fully completed until 1995). "And for me, this is 'Earth Song,' because I think nature is trying so hard to compensate for man's mismanagement of the Earth.... I think earth feels the pain, and she has wounds ... and that's what inspired it."

Upon its release, many critics panned the anthem as cloying or over the top. *Rolling Stone* dismissed it as a "showpiece—something with which to knock 'em dead in Monte Carlo." Years later, however, with some of the then-knee-jerk cynicism against Jackson's music dissipated, "Earth Song" has gained admirers for its prescience and raw power. It's difficult to think of another pop/rock anthem that paints such a devastatingly apocalyptic picture of the world, before asking bluntly, "Do we give a damn?" What Top 40 hit of the past twenty years so brilliantly fuses gospel and opera, blues and pop (not to mention Jackson's urgent, pain-filled, passionate delivery)?

Listener reviews describe it as "majestic," "powerful," and "healing." "The song has no words in the chorus," observes one reviewer, "words can't express the pain and suffering humans have caused in this world ... the chorus is simply a cry, Michael's expression of the world's pain. The climax of the song is truly phenomenal, and all you can do is sit back, crank up the speakers and let the emotions pour through you."

Indeed, as the song builds to a crescendo, Jackson's voice soars with the music. "What about the bleeding earth?" he pleads in a dramatic call-and-response with the Andraé Crouch Singers Choir. "Can't we feel its wounds? ... What about the holy land?/Torn apart by creed ... What about the common man?/ Can't we set him free ... What about children dying?/ Can't you hear them cry?/Where did we go wrong?/ Someone tell me why ..."

Its accompanying video, directed by Nicholas Brandt (who also directed "Stranger in Moscow"), is a tour de force in its own right (it went on to win a *Le Film Fantastique* Video Award and a Grammy nomination). Shot on four different continents, the seven-minute short film depicts the various ways in which man, technology, and greed are destroying the world: rain forests are cut down by loggers; beautiful animals, killed by poachers; a North American forest, burned to stumps; the devastation of war in Croatia. About halfway through the video, Jackson, in unison with other men and women of different countries and cultures, drops to his knees and sinks his hands into the earth. As they all dig into the soil in desperation, pleading, a great wind sweeps across the globe, forcing people to cling to tree stumps, the ground, and each other. Then they watch in amazement as the destruction is reversed and life is restored: elephants and zebras, once dead, rise again; the devastation of war is undone; starving children are fed; dolphins swim free; pollution is swallowed back into pipes; trees reach to the sky, and Earth is restored to its natural state. It is redeemed. "Jackson's distinctive impulse [in the video] ignores apocalypse in favor of change: transubstantiation, rebirth, resurrection," observes film critic Armond White. "These great images are complicated by the way Michael's looking for hope is constantly interrupted by disaster (reaching out to touch a tree trunk, he jumps back at an intrusive buzz saw). His reflex makes anger indivisible from action—a typical, revolutionary paradox.... These scenes actualize struggle, while the soaring music and the secular use of the gospel choir realize triumph: The sight of a ripped tree trunk healed is unforgettable."

As with the song itself, the video's critics felt it was too idealistic and naïve. They also criticized Jackson for the messianic nature of both the video and his performances of the song. At the 1996 BRIT Awards, Pulp frontman Jarvis Cocker famously stormed the stage for what he perceived to be Jackson's "offensive" performance as a Christ-figure. Yet as cultural critic Marcello Carlin points out: "What was the more egocentric—[Jackson's] 1996 BRIT Awards performance of 'Earth Song' or Jarvis Cocker's interruption of it? 'Earth Song' plaintively, and then with increasing ferocity, asks questions of the 1967 which spawned it; why haven't we got this golden paradise now? Why, in fact, are we killing everything off, including ourselves? ... It's a complex and passionate protest song. Cocker's bum, in contrast, was reductionist [and] petty."

In spite of the controversy, "Earth Song" became one of Jackson's most successful singles ever, reaching the Top 5 in countries all over the world. It was his best-selling single in Great Britain since "Billie Jean," topping the charts for more than six weeks and selling an astounding one million copies. Jackson had prepared a new presentation of the song for his *This Is It* O2 concert series, which was partly re-created in tribute at the 2010 Grammy Awards. Jackson rightfully felt it was one of his most significant compositions.

6. D.S.

(Written and composed by Michael Jackson. Produced by Michael Jackson. Lead and background vocals by Michael Jackson. Additional programming: Chuck Wild. Keyboards and programming: Brad Buxer. Guitar: Slash)

Jackson is back on the attack in "D.S."—a thinly veiled reference to Tom Sneddon, the infamously overzealous Santa Barbara County District Attorney who would lead two investigations of child abuse against Jackson (in 1993 and 2005). Against a driving guitar riff (provided courtesy of Slash) and funky beat, Jackson lashes out against his arch-nemesis: "They wanna get my ass dead or alive," he sings, "You know he really tried to take me down by surprise." By turns mocking and vengeful, Jackson links Sneddon to institutional corruption and discrimination. Because Jackson felt Sneddon unjustly dragged his name and reputation through the mud, he returns the favor, accusing the conservative DA of being antisocial, a friend of the KKK, and stopping at nothing to "get his political say."

Sneddon is, in essence, the anti-artist: a cold, clinical authority figure bent on ridding the world of "freaks" (those who don't fit his definition of "normal").

When asked if he had heard the song, Sneddon smugly replied: "I have not, shall we say, done him the honor of listening to it, but I've been told that it ends with the sound of a gunshot." Indeed, it does, though what the ending symbolizes can be interpreted in different ways. The track once again shows Jackson's refusal to be a victim. It also provided a soundtrack for fans attending his trial in 2005 (which was prosecuted unsuccessfully by Tom Sneddon).

7. MONEY

(Written and composed by Michael Jackson. Produced by Michael Jackson. Arrangement: Michael Jackson. Lead and background vocals: Michael Jackson. Keyboards and programming: Brad Buxer)

In 1995, it was easy to view the next track, "Money," as a continuation of Jackson's personal grievances. Fortunately, years later it can simply be appreciated for what it is: an intricate sonic gem with an all-too-relevant message denouncing greed and materialism. Like Pink Floyd's single by the same title, the track explores how the love of money—and the system of self-interest it symbolizes—can (and often does) consume people whole. "Are you infected with the same disease of lust, gluttony, and greed?" Jackson asks his listeners. In the verses, he near-whispers his ominous indictments: "So you go to church/Read the holy word/In the scheme of life/It's all absurd." Religion, he is suggesting, is often nothing but a façade, when one's real object of worship is money. "Want your pot of gold," he sings in another verse, "Need the Midas touch/Bet you sell your soul/Cuz your God is such." These are incisive words directed at a culture of televangelists, get-rich-quick schemes, corporate corruption, and a socially driven obsession with wealth and status.

Composed and produced entirely by Jackson, the song is built on three brilliantly juxtaposed bass lines and a spoken rap. "Michael is a master craftsman," says Brad Buxer, who worked with Jackson on the track. "He came up with this groove. We were using Emulator 3 samplers, and he said, 'I like this sound in the middle of the loop.' So we took elements of the loop, isolated certain transients, and relayered them. Basically, I just followed Michael's instructions." As the song progresses, it builds into a fantastically layered array of rhythms and harmonies that hearkens back to his best work on *Off the Wall*.

8. COME TOGETHER

(Written and composed by John Lennon and Paul McCartney. Produced by Michael Jackson and Bill Bottrell. Synth programming: Bill Bottrell. Lead and background vocals: Michael Jackson. Guitar: Bill Bottrell. Percussion: Bill Bottrell)

Recorded several years earlier with producer Bill Bottrell (it first appeared on the 1989 film *Moonwalker*), "Come Together" was originally intended for the *Days of Thunder* soundtrack starring Tom Cruise. The high-energy Beatles cover would have likely been a big hit had it been released with the movie. As it turned out, however, it stayed in the vault for nearly six more years before its 1995 inclusion on *HIStory*. The song was never released as a single.

Jackson had long admired the Beatles' music, having famously purchased the Beatles/ATV Catalog in 1985. Since the acquisition, Jackson and attorney John Branca had discussed recording some of the songs that he now owned (he also recorded a cover of Sly and the Family Stone's classic, "Hot Fun in the Summertime"). In the late eighties, Bill Bottrell recalls driving around Los Angeles listening to Beatles tunes with Jackson, trying to determine a good song to cover. They eventually settled on "Come Together" (the runner-up was McCartney's more obscure, "You Know My Name").

John Lennon, Jackson felt, was in many ways a kindred soul: someone who didn't quite fit into conventional society, yet whose genius rested in that very unorthodoxy. It is only fitting then that Jackson picked "Come Together," a song that famously defies all conventions and openly embraces freedom from the strictures of language, institutional authority, and ideology. "It pitches a stream of self-confessed 'gobbledygook' at the violent antagonisms of an unenlightened world," writes Beatles critic Ian MacDonald, "implying that the language deployed in such confrontations is a trap and a potential prison."

Like Lennon, Jackson loved playing with words; he liked to form them in unusual, surprising sequences (see "Wanna Be Startin' Somethin'") and he especially liked to twist and contort them vocally. Of course, since *Off the Wall*, one of the major themes of his music was its ability to liberate and unify. "Come Together's" famous line—"One thing I can tell you is you got to be free"—is what both Lennon and Jackson believed at their cores. It is, as Ian MacDonald astutely observes, "a call to unchain the imagination and, by setting language free, loosen the rigidities of political and emotional entrenchment."

Sonically, where the Beatles chose to adopt a "laid-back" or "spaced-out" style to capture the feeling of being high, Jackson opts for a high-octane reinterpretation that synthesizes the famed guitar riff, highlights the song's inherent funk, and infuses the wild lyrics with loads of energy and excitement. That visceral energy is on full display in the live version at the end of *Moonwalker* in which Jackson struts and stomps with abandon as the music takes him (and his audience) into a state of ecstasy.

"I think his cover is the best cover of a Beatles song that I've heard," says recording engineer Matt Forger. "Because of that energy. He has that energy that you feel when you first heard the Beatles' recording. Michael tapped into that emotional place. And you can feel it." While it was delayed for years, "Come Together" is certainly one of the more noteworthy Beatles covers as well as a symbolic linking between two eccentric but brilliant music icons.

9. YOU ARE NOT ALONE

(Written and composed by R. Kelly. Produced by Michael Jackson and R. Kelly. Programming: Peter Mokrin and Andrew Scheps. Solo and background vocals: Michael Jackson. Choir: Andraé Crouch Singers Choir. Keyboards: R. Kelly and Steve Porcaro)

"You Are Not Alone" was the first single in the thirty-seven-year history of the *Billboard* Hot 100 chart to debut at #1. The song was written by R. Kelly, one of the hottest R&B songwriters of the nineties. Jackson quickly fell in love with the melody and decided to coproduce and include the song on *HIStory*. A gorgeous expression of isolation and longing, it ranks, according to many critics, among his best ballads. Music critic Nelson George describes it as "lovely and supple" while Stephen Thomas Erlewine praises it as "well-crafted" and "seductive." "On listening to 'You Are Not Alone'," writes biographer J. Randy Taraborrelli, "one wonders how many times Michael tried to tell himself, during his most desperate and anguished times, that he did have support in his life, from a higher power, or even friends and family, whether he actually believed it or not." Music critic Ann Powers describes the song as "beautiful, if you can take the pain. . . . The song . . . uncovers the depths of loss, and lostness, behind Jackson's attempts to be tender." With the elevated buildup of the Andraé Crouch Singers Choir, it also seems to be a summoning of strength, à la "Will You Be There."

The video featured the singer with his new wife, Lisa Marie Presley, in the semi-nude, which caused a minor uproar for some squeamish watchers and critics. Yet for Jackson, it was "art": art that wasn't ashamed of the human body, art that was naked and vulnerable (as love is), and art that pushed the envelope of expectations. Filmed partly in Jackson's private theater and partly against a majestic backdrop inspired by Maxfield Parrish's classic painting, *Daybreak*, the visual is indeed stunning. Recalled video director Wayne Isham, "The warmth displayed in the 'You Are

Not Alone' video is for real. The shots in the last scene were done without Michael and Lisa Marie knowing it, literally off-camera. Michael never at any point indicated that this was a marketing thing. It was more personal than that. The nude scenes were Michael's idea. I thought it was ballsy and honest; you can't get any more open than that. They're saying, 'Here we are, you want to see us?' I didn't look at it as a marketing thing. I thought it was a statement."

"You Are Not Alone" was Jackson's final #1 hit in the United States during his lifetime.

10. CHILDHOOD

(Written and composed by Michael Jackson. Produced by Michael Jackson and David Foster. Vocals: Michael Jackson. New York Children's Choir: Tracy Spindler, Natalia Harris, Jonathon Ungar, Brandi Stewart, Reeve Carney, Caryn Jones, and Brian Jones. Orchestration: Jeremy Lubbock. Piano: Brad Buxer, David Foster. Strings: Brad Buxer)

"Childhood" meant a lot to Michael Jackson. Of all the songs he composed, he considered it his most personal. "If you really want to know about me," he would say in a 2004 interview, "there's a song I wrote, which is the most honest song I've ever written.... It's called 'Childhood.' [People] should listen to it [if they want to understand me]. That's the one they should really listen to." Indeed, while there are many layers to the enigma that is Michael Jackson, the trauma of his "lost" childhood is where it all begins. The rest of his life, in a way, was an ongoing attempt at recovery.

The public and even many of his friends, advisors, and peers, endlessly scrutinized that personal recovery. People were quick to scoff, mock, or offer advice. Yet very few could imagine what his life was actually like: the loneliness, abuse, exploitation, and constant expectations in the early years; working all day in the studio, while other kids played in the park across the street; not being able to leave the house without being mauled from the time he was ten years old; hiding in a dark closet because of the shame and fear of fans seeing him with acne and rejecting him; the looming presence of an abusive father who might yell at or hit him for any perceived imperfection. "Our personal history begins in childhood," said Jackson in interview, "and the song 'Childhood' is a reflection of my life . . . it's about the pain, some of the joys, some of the dreaming, some of the mental adventures that I took because of the different life I had, in being a child performer. I was born on stage and 'Childhood,' it's my mirror—it's my story."

Indeed, this is the sentiment Jackson tries to convey in "Childhood," a Broadway-esque confession with the accompaniment of a full orchestra. He understands he's not "normal" to the world. People say he's "not okay." "They view it as such strange eccentricities." But have they seen his childhood? The question recurs throughout the song and works in different ways. On the one hand, it is literally asking the listener to consider the challenges of his early life. Yet it is also presented as an irrecoverable abstraction; his "ideal" childhood doesn't exist. "I'm searching for the world that I come from," he sings, but the tragic irony is it always eludes him. As in "Stranger in Moscow," he is homeless, between worlds, an alien. Childhood, like Neverland, is a constructed reality, a fantasy. Because of this, he realizes, "it's been my fate to compensate/For the childhood I've never known." Because he was forced to be an adult as a child, in other words, he wants to at least access some of the joy, wonder, and magic of childhood as an adult. However, he can never really be a child again—a reality made all too cruel and real when allegations were brought against him. It is that threatening presence that perpetually looms on the edges of so many of his songs, including "Childhood's" sequel, "The Lost Children." He can compensate, or escape into a world of "adventurous dreams" for a time, but before long reality will intrude. He wakes up in the adult world.

Recognizing this bleak truth, he simply asks his listeners: "Before you judge me/ Try hard to love me/ The painful youth I've had . . ." The pathos in these final lines is palpable. Sure, it can be (and has been) written off by cynics as maudlin and indulgent. Yet there is genuine emotion in the vocals and tragedy in the song's simple dreams. Like much of the work of Wordsworth or Barrie, it is both an ode and elegy to innocence. While it can easily be written off as sentimental, "Childhood" is also a revealing confession, a desperate plea for compassion, a song, finally, about the vulnerabilities and tragedies of being human.

11. TABLOID JUNKIE

(Written and composed by Michael Jackson, Jimmy Jam, and Terry Lewis. Produced by Michael Jackson, Jimmy Jam, and Terry Lewis. Lead and background vocals: Michael Jackson. Keyboard and synthesizers: Jimmy Jam and Terry Lewis)

Following the pleading vulnerability of "Childhood" is the provocative "Tabloid Junkie," a full-fledged indictment of the news media and its increasing penchant for sensationalism, exploitation, and misinformation. Critics have typically reviewed such songs as examples of Jackson's persecution complex and self-pity, but such a dismissal misses a more important fact: unlike most pop music, content to dwell in shallow sentimentality and recycled clichés, Jackson, in this rather ambitious track, is singing truth to power on an issue with relevance far beyond his personal life.

The song begins with the authoritative voice of a newscaster mindlessly repeating tabloid fodder as fact. It is a sort of postmodern, Orwellian moment in which the mainstream media becomes the controller and manipulator of its audience's social reality. Truth is irrelevant. What matters is entertainment, ratings, and a drug-like addiction to endless spectacle. Facts are whatever is printed or broadcast on TV to a passive, noncritical audience. In the song, as the newscaster speaks, keyboards begin typing frantically, illustrating how quickly stories (whether true or false, important or unimportant) are consumed, copied, and spread.

In this case, many of the stories involve the "strange and weird" Michael Jackson, who, to both the reporters and audience, is no longer a human but a consumable object (à la "Wanna Be Startin' Somethin'). Jackson allows the breathless reporting to build until it turns into an all-out feeding frenzy with the sounds of wild animals representing so-called journalists (the song was almost titled "Tabloid Jungle").

"Speculate to break the one you hate," Jackson sings in a gritty opening rap, "Circulate the lie you confiscate/Assassinate and mutilate/As the hounding media in hysteria." Interestingly, in this track and others, Jackson chooses to use the vehicle of hip-hop to deliver a political message. In this case, the verses are conveyed in short, biting rhymes, before the melody comes in the chorus, repeating the mantra: "Just because you read it in a magazine/See it on the TV screen/Don't make it factual, actual." Jackson, in essence is providing counterprogramming to the "news." Between verses the newscaster continues to recite stories before Jackson pleads with his audience not to believe them. "It's slander," he proclaims later in the song. "You say it's not a sword/But with your pen you torture men/You'd crucify the Lord." He later refers to the media as "parasites in black and white." These are some powerful lyrics from an artist one reviewer claimed had "a woefully narrow awareness of life."

"Tabloid Junkie" is a deftly constructed, sonically layered (the percussion is once again built on Jackson's beatboxing), four-and-a-half-minute polemic that demands truth and accountability. *Rolling Stone* described the track as a "mammoth funk-rock construction" with "lush vocal harmonies" and "quick-voiced warnings about the failings of media truth." Indeed, in an age when the mainstream media and tabloid coverage are conflated more than ever, when celebrity obsession consistently trumps far more important news, and undiscerning viewers are frequently distracted from or deceived about the truth, Jackson's song remains a relevant rebuttal and warning.

12. 2BAD

(Written and composed by Michael Jackson, Bruce Swedien, and Rene Moore. Produced by Michael Jackson, Bruce Swedien, and Rene Moore. Horn arrangement by Jerry Hey and Michael Jackson. Rap solo: Shaquille O'Neal. Keyboards and programming: Rene Moore. Additional programming: Jimmy Jam, Rob Hoffman, Michael Jackson)

"2Bad" may or may not have been intended as a sequel to "Bad," but it certainly follows in the same tradition. Brash and street-savvy, it is both a provocation (in the vein of much hip-hop) and a declaration of resiliency ("I'm standin' though you're kickin' me"). The song begins with a sample of Run DMC's famous "King of Rock," a track that challenged the white establishment's control over the music industry. It is a deft gesture that simultaneously shows respect for fellow musical pioneers and makes a statement about the song's political intentions. Once again, Jackson is not simply attacking individuals but rather institutions and ideologies. He feels targeted because of both his race and status, but he's not about to back down. Instead he calls out his various enemies: "You're aiming just for me," he sings, "You are disgustin' me/You got blood lust for me." In past albums, Jackson often used femme fatale women ("Dirty Diana," "Dangerous," etc.) as symbols of his fears and distrust, but on *HIStory* this changes. The various threats he feels—racism, media lies, government corruption, corporate power, and greed—are connected and omnipresent. "What do you want from me?" he demands of this invisible enemy. "What do you want from me?/Tired of you haunting me."

The song contains elements of funk, rock, rap and even a hint of gospel. Jackson was listening to Sly and the Family Stone (a long-time favorite) and wanted to incorporate some of their sound into the song. One can hear a bit of "Thank You (Falettinme Be Mice Elf Agin)" in the groove. Jackson's vocals, meanwhile, are delivered with verve over intricately layered drums (much of the percussion is built on Jackson's beatboxing). Jackson also helped arrange the horns. "If you listen to the bridge," says assistant engineer Rob Hoffman, "the entire horn thing was Michael's idea. He had Jerry Hey come in, and sang him all the parts." Following the horn bridge, basketball star Shaquille O'Neal comes in for a brisk rap solo. (In an excellent reggae-style remix of the song on *Blood on the Dance Floor* by members of the Fugees, John Forte performed the honors.)

13. HISTORY

(Written and composed by Michael Jackson, Jimmy Jam, and Terry Lewis. Produced by Michael Jackson. Vocals: Michael Jackson. Background vocals: Boyz II Men, Andraé and Sandra Crouch, and the Andraé Crouch Singers Choir. Orchestration from Pictures at an Exhibition, *composed by Modeste Mussorgsky, and arranged by Maurice Ravel. Performed by The Philadelphia Orchestra, conducted by Eugene Ormandy. Child solo: Leah Frazier)*

Following "2Bad," the listener is immediately struck by the triumphant, grandiose strains of Mussorgsky's epic "Great Gate of Kiev" from *Pictures at an Exhibition*. From a biographical standpoint, it seems to symbolize Jackson's victory over his trials and adversaries. It is the appropriate musical companion to the album cover, in which Jackson is shown defiant and immortalized in the form of a statue ("He dares to be recognized/The fire's deep in his eyes"). The obstacles he has endured, he seems to be saying, have only made him stronger and more powerful. His response, however, isn't for recrimination, hate, or violence, but "harmony all around the world." It is classic utopian Michael Jackson, in which all the injustices and tragedies of life are redeemed and healed by the power of music.

"HIStory," however, is perhaps Jackson's most unusual anthem. While earlier pieces such as "Heal the World" were completely melody-driven, "HIStory" is more experimental, juxtaposing short, rhyming call-and-response verses (which recall the rhythmic tempo of African American work songs) with a more traditional melodic chorus. "Don't let no one get you down/Keep movin' on higher ground," Jackson implores. "No force of nature can break/Your will to self-motivate." These are the words of a leader trying to offer hope and strength in the face of adversity. There is a grinding, uphill climb to the verses; when the chorus arrives, it feels like standing on top of a mountain. The breezy melody, with backing vocals by Boyz II Men, soars with invigorating force.

In spite of its impressive structure, however, the lyrics can at times seem rather simplistic ("Every soldier dies in his glory," "Every hero dreams of chivalry," etc.). Are such lines sincere, naïve, ironic? Sitting beside lyrics that decry "victims . . . slaughtered in vain across the land" and a mother mourning her dead child, one would have to assume Jackson is intentionally complicating such clichés à la Wilfred Owen's "Dulce et Decorum est." Where traditional national anthems celebrate "conquest" and inherent superiority, Jackson offers an alternative vision of creative achievement and borderless "harmony." The aural collage interspersed throughout the track includes everything from a speech by Martin Luther King Jr. to the opening of Disneyland. (To give some idea of the ambition of the song, it took over 192 tracks sprawled over four Sony 3348 48-track digital tapes to contain all of the song's different elements.)

At its climax, Jackson ad-libs passionately over the swelling choir and an exuberant, Fats Waller-esque piano workout. It is an incredibly ambitious song—essentially bridging the divide between Western and African-rooted music—that doesn't completely hit its mark, but manages a great deal in trying. At its core, it is about suffering, perseverance, and triumph. It is a civil rights speech set to music.

"HIStory" is also noteworthy for being the song Jackson chose to play on his website immediately following his acquittal and vindication in 2005.

14. LITTLE SUSIE

(Written and composed by Michael Jackson. Produced by Michael Jackson. Programming: Brad Buxer, Steve Porcaro, and Andrew Scheps. Engineered and mixed by Bruce Swedien. Vocals: Michael Jackson. Orchestration: Brad Buxer and Geoff Grace. Child solo: Markita Prescott)

"Little Susie" is yet another testament to Jackson's range and depth as an artist. The song also demonstrates his commitment to his creative vision regardless of whom it might alienate. Many critics were simply baffled that a "mini-opera" about such a dark and grotesque subject could land on a mainstream pop record. "What it's doing on an album with Dallas Austin and Jam and Lewis is anyone's guess," wrote *Rolling Stone*.

For Jackson, however, the reasoning for "Little Susie" (and other nontraditional inclusions) was quite simple: He believed it was a great piece. Commercial viability or audience expectations didn't matter. What mattered was the personal connection, the story, the melody. Jackson had actually written and recorded a version of the song more than fifteen years earlier in 1979. He tinkered with it a few times over the years, but it wasn't until working on the piece with Brad Buxer in 1994 that it finally began to unfold itself for Jackson.

While "Little Susie" remains mostly unknown, it is one of the most poignant and unique songs in his entire catalog. "If he ever decides to stop being a pop singer," wrote Anthony Wynn, "this song [is] proof he could compose music for movies and seriously win Oscars for it. It's sad, haunting, beautiful." Indeed, "Little Susie" reaffirms his substantial abilities as a songwriter. A tragic, piercing account of loneliness and loss, the song also boldly veers from traditional pop/rock instruments and expectations, featuring Broadway-style orchestration and strings borrowed from *Fiddler on the Roof*'s "Sunrise, Sunset." The song begins with the "Pie Jesu" segment of Maurice Duruflé's majestic masterpiece, Requiem Op. 9. Following this interlude, a little girl's voice (sung by Markita Prescott) hums a simple melody to the sound of a music box. The effect is both enchanting and disturbing.

Then comes the devastating story, narrated in what has to be considered one of Jackson's most moving vocal performances. In vivid (often gruesome) detail, we learn of an orphaned girl who dies of neglect (and likely abuse). "She was there screaming/Beating her voice in her doom," Michael sings, "But nobody came to her soon."

For years, she sings a beautiful tune but goes unheard. "Father left home/Poor mother died/Leaving Susie alone." The ongoing loneliness she feels eventually causes utter despair. "To be damned to know hoping is dead/And you're doomed/Then to scream out/And nobody's there." The pathos in these lines is profound. They convey the terrifying feeling of being completely alone, invisible, unloved, of feeling as if there is absolutely nothing to live for. "She knew no one cared."

"Neglection [sic] can kill," Jackson warns, "like a knife in your soul."

When Susie is finally "discovered," she is dead. "So blind stare the eyes in her head." Has she killed herself? Fallen down the stairs? Been murdered? In Jackson's narrative, it remains a "mystery so sullen in air." The more important truth is how she was ignored and mistreated in life. "Her face bears such agony, such strain." Only one man really knew her, but he couldn't prevent her tragic fate. Instead, as he sees her limp body on the floor, he reaches down to close her eyes. "She lie there so tenderly," Jackson sings, "Fashioned so slenderly/Lift her with care/Oh, the blood in her hair."

It is possibly the most gut-wrenching song Michael Jackson ever sang. And its resonance only strikes deeper given some of the parallels to the singer's own life and tragic death.

15. SMILE

(Words written by John Turner and Geoffrey Parsons. Music composed by Charlie Chaplin. Produced by David Foster and Michael Jackson. Vocals: Michael Jackson. Orchestration: Jeremy Lubbock)

"Smile" is Jackson's heartfelt homage to his longtime hero, Charlie Chaplin. The song originally appeared on the soundtrack of Chaplin's 1936 movie, *Modern Times*. (Jackson's rendition is taken from the stage version.)

From a very early age Jackson was fascinated with Charlie Chaplin, the enigmatic actor and filmmaker who conveyed so much humor, joy, sadness, and magic through his silent expressions. "How could you not admire his genius," Jackson said in an interview. "He was the king of pathos.... He knew how to make you laugh and cry at the same time.... I relate to him. I sometimes feel like I am him." Indeed, at several stages in his life, beginning in the 1970s, Jackson dressed up like his idol, top hat, mustache and all. He also devoured books about him, watched all his films, and incorporated some of his styles and movements into his own performances.

The two icons, of course, shared much in common: both became the biggest entertainers of a generation; both were deeply misunderstood and attacked throughout their lives; both were plagued by incessant controversy and scandal; and both were eccentric, childlike, and in many ways, tragic figures. Jackson's identification with the legendary comic, therefore, made sense. "Smile"—with its lyrical embrace of smiling (i.e., laughter and humor) to conceal, and sometimes heal, pain—was one of his all-time favorite songs.

Jackson recorded "Smile" at the Hit Factory in New York in 1994. The song was recorded live in the studio with a complete orchestra. "They rehearsed a bit without vocals in, then during the first take Michael sang, [he] just about knocked them out of their chairs," recalled assistant engineer Rob Hoffman. "The take we did that day was amazing and perfect," remembers Bruce Swedien, Jackson's longtime sound engineer. "But Michael is such a perfectionist that he insisted on recording his vocals again the next day." Ultimately, they ended up keeping the first version.

"I think I've worked with everyone, seriously," said acclaimed British orchestra conductor and producer Jeremy Lubbock. "But my most memorable recording session remains Michael Jackson's 'Smile' from the

HIStory album. Great song, great artist, painless!" Indeed, after recording the song, Jackson went in to thank the orchestra and received a standing ovation. "During the recording," recalls Swedien, "[they] had been listening to Michael sing through their individual headphones. When Michael walked out in the studio . . . every member of the fifty-piece orchestra stood up and tapped their music stands with their bows, as loud as they could. Jeremy [Lubbock] stood on the conductor's podium and also applauded as loud as he could. I was applauding by myself in the control room as loud as I could!"

"Smile" has subsequently become a classic in Michael Jackson's catalog. Biographer J. Randy Taraborrelli described the track as a "stand out" on *HIStory*: "What a vocal performance and delivery he gives to this song! Never has he sounded more sincere, more gorgeous." The *New York Times* called it "a dramatic tour de force. Over quivering strings and a nonchalant piano, Jackson sounds like he's barely holding back tears. His voice trembles, breaks, pulls together and heads for another emotional brink. It ends with an indrawn breath, a sob on the verge of a crying jag."

In the outro, Jackson hums, laughs, and whistles his way to the end. It completes a turbulent, emotionally exhausting journey, from the rage and fury of "Scream" to the temporary solace of "Smile." Even in this seemingly joyful conclusion, however, like the best Chaplin performances, a residue of sadness remains. *HIStory* is ultimately a tragedy—and like the best tragedies, its protagonist beats on, against the current, in perpetual resistance to fate.

OTHER NOTABLE HIS*TORY*-ERA SONGS

IN THE BACK (recorded 1997, released on *Michael Jackson: The Ultimate Collection*, 2004)
"In the Back" is a direct descendant of earlier atmospheric masterpieces "Billie Jean" and "Who Is It." While it is not one of Jackson's more well-known tracks, it is one of his most impressive. An intricate, ethereal jazz-blues piece, the track is an astounding demonstration of Jackson's musical prowess. Listen to the mournful trumpet, the lush strings, the entrancing harp, the pounding bass line. The song is about betrayal and despair, and Jackson conveys its deep, conflicting emotions to perfection. Experiencing its strange, hypnotic beauty is like traveling from hell to heaven and back again.

Jackson worked on the track primarily with Brad Buxer, who describes it as "unbelievable and it proves once again how Michael was a genius. I play almost every instrument on this song, but all [the] ideas are Michael." Jackson revisited the song numerous times over the years, including in Switzerland while on tour. Multiple versions exist, some of which include legendary keyboardist Billy Preston. In *The Ultimate Collection* version, Jackson scats through parts that didn't have lyrics yet. Like some of the best jazz pieces, however, the ambience, subtlety, and texture of the music communicate far more than words.

MUCH TOO SOON (recorded 1994, released on *MICHAEL*)
(See Appendix)

ON THE LINE (recorded 1995, released on *Michael Jackson: The Ultimate Collection*, 2004)
A beautiful track about opening oneself to life, with echoes of "Keep the Faith." The song was written by Jackson and Babyface and intended for Spike Lee's *Get On the Bus*. The song has become a fan favorite.

WHY (recorded 1995, released on 3T's *Brotherhood* in 1996)
A lush mid-tempo R&B track written by Babyface and intended for Jackson's *HIStory* album. When Jackson's nephews heard it, however, they loved it so much Jackson decided to give it to them for their debut album, *Brotherhood*. Jackson's vocals were kept on for the chorus.

If you wanna see/Eccentric oddities/I'll be grotesque before your eyes.

MICHAEL JACKSON, "IS IT SCARY," 1997

CHAPTER 6 BLOOD ON THE DANCE FLOOR:

*HIS*TORY IN THE MIX

Just two years after the release of *HIStory* came an unexpected postscript: a hybrid collection of five new songs and eight remixes titled *Blood on the Dance Floor: HIStory in the Mix*.

The album was in many ways an anomaly for the King of Pop. Its release in the United States went practically unnoticed. There was no elaborate unveiling, no promotion, no big music videos or hit singles (it did do much better abroad, particularly in Europe, where it received far better advertising and airplay). Because all of the songs were written during the *Dangerous* and *HIStory* sessions, *Blood on the Dance Floor* didn't receive the drawn out, excruciating attention and time Jackson usually gave his projects. The artistry was still as high as ever, but the album felt more raw, more experimental, and without all the hype and expectations that typically accompanied a Michael Jackson album.

Ironically, the low-key release—and the singer's "disappearance," as he traveled overseas on tour—allowed some critics to actually pay attention to the considerable merit of the music. *Rolling Stone* called it arguably his most "revealing record." Others saw it as a creative breakthrough. "His singing on the first five tracks of new material has never been so tormented, or audacious," observed Armond White. "*Blood on the Dance Floor* has the vitality of an intelligence that refuses to be placated.... [It] is a throwdown, a dare to the concept of innocuous Black pop."

White's characterization is apt. At this stage in his life and career, Jackson had little interest in creating mindless, formulaic radio fodder (1997 saw songs such as the Spice Girls' "Wanna Be" and Hansen's

---

RELEASED: *May 20, 1997*

PRODUCER: *Michael Jackson*

NOTABLE CONTRIBUTORS: Teddy Riley *(producer/songwriting)*, Jimmy Jam and Terry Lewis *(producing/songwriting)*, Brad Buxer *(synthesizers/keyboards)*, Bryan Loren *(songwriting/keyboards)*, Andraé Crouch Singers Choir *(vocals)*, Slash *(guitar)*, Mick Guzauski *(engineer/mixing)*

SINGLES: *"Blood on the Dance Floor," "Ghosts," "Is It Scary"*

ESTIMATED COPIES SOLD: *6 million*

Jackson disguised as the mayor of "Normal Valley" in his 1997 film, *Ghosts*.

"MmmBop" top the charts). In contrast, *Blood on the Dance Floor* explores complex psychological and social issues, including addiction, sexual obsession, abnormality, and fear.

Indeed, picking up where *HIStory's* most intense tracks left off, the album is often shocking in its bluntness, awareness, and sonic innovation. "There is real pain and pathos in these new songs," writes the *New York Times'* Neil Strauss. "In keeping with Jackson's darker mood the music has grown more angry and indignant. With beats crashing like metal sheets and synthesizer sounds hissing like pressurized gas, this is industrial funk.... Creatively, Jackson has entered a new realm."

In many ways, *Blood on the Dance Floor* can be viewed as a mini-concept album. While sonically eclectic—it incorporates elements of house, industrial, techno, funk, Gothic, and operatic pop—it is essentially an exploration of social decay. From the fear and betrayal of the title track, to the desperation of "Morphine," to the lamentation of "Superfly Sister," to the metaphorical horror capsules of "Ghosts" and "Is It Scary," Jackson is assessing a world of fear, corruption, and confusion. It is without a doubt his darkest album, even more so than *HIStory*, as he struggles for his sanity amid enclosing pressures and anxieties. The only real sliver of hope is that in holding up a mirror to its "grotesqueness," society might actually see itself for what it is and change. That is part of the point of the album's capstone, "Is It Scary." However, on *Blood on the Dance Floor*, there is no feel-good anthem explicitly calling for such change. *Blood* is a dark vision, but it is also some of the most compelling work in Jackson's career.

In spite of its relatively low profile, *Blood on the Dance Floor* became the best-selling "remix album" of all time, with an estimated eleven million records sold. The eight remixes, all derived from *HIStory*, are primarily club mixes carried out by producers such as Jam and Lewis, Frankie Knuckles, and Wyclef Jean. Of these, the standouts are Wyclef's reggae-infused reworking of "2Bad" and Jam and Lewis's funky variation of "Scream" (entitled "Scream Louder").

In terms of its critical reassessment, the focus will undoubtedly be on the five original songs, which form a sort of concept EP, as well as on the accompanying short film, *Ghosts*, Jackson's more socially pointed sequel to *Thriller*.

Jackson in his Gothic-themed film, *Ghosts*. *Blood on the Dance Floor* was Jackson's darkest effort to date.

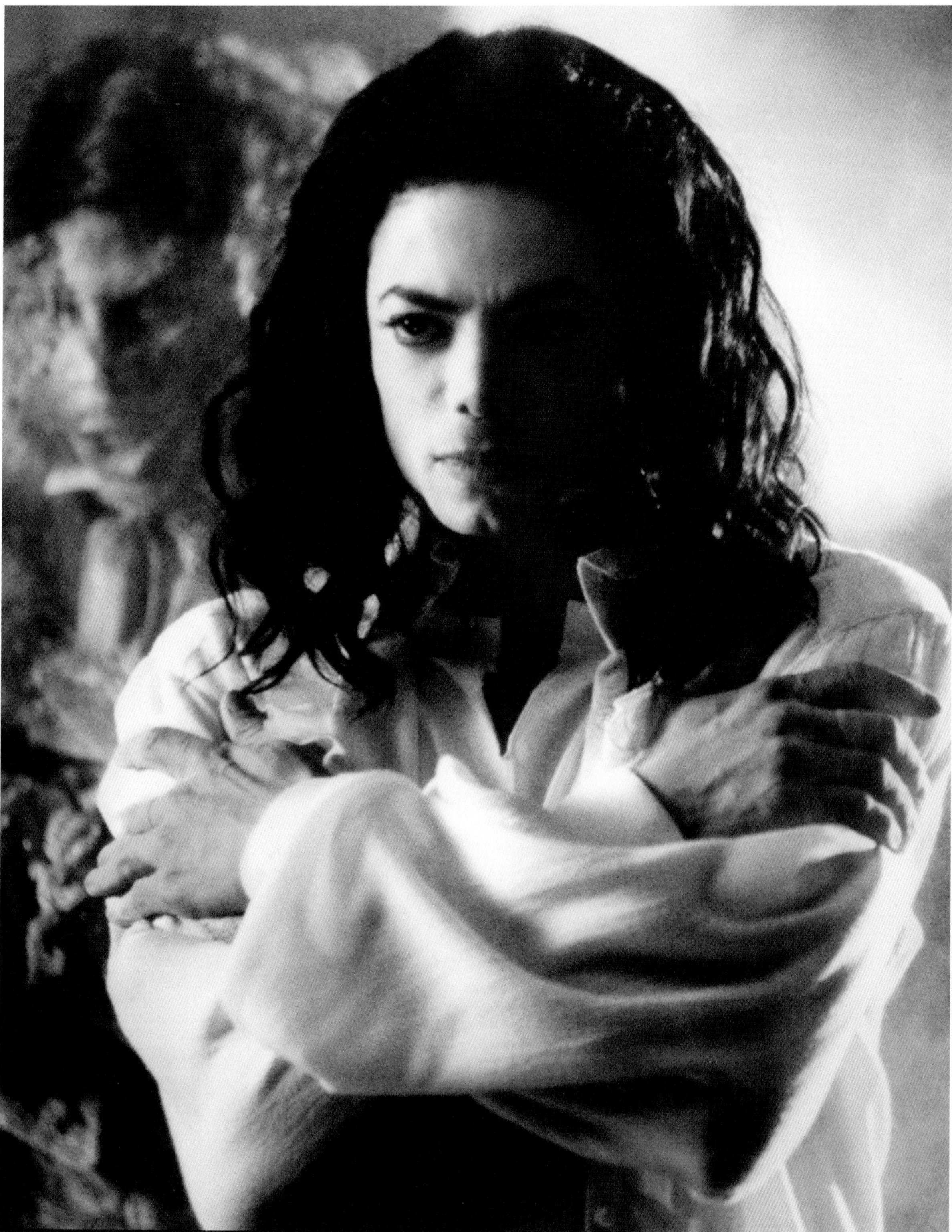

THE SONGS

1. BLOOD ON THE DANCE FLOOR

(Written and composed by Michael Jackson and Teddy Riley. Produced by Michael Jackson and Teddy Riley. Engineered by Teddy Riley, Dave Way, and Mick Guzauski. Drum programming: Teddy Riley and Brad Buxer. Mixed by Mick Guzauski. Digital systems programming: Matt Carpenter. Additional engineering: Eddie De Lena and Andrew Scheps. Solo and background vocals: Michael Jackson. Vocal arrangement: Michael Jackson. Keyboards and synthesizers: Teddy Riley and Brad Buxer)

The title track is classic Michael Jackson: a high-energy, thumping rhythm piece with the mystery and intrigue of "Billie Jean" and the film-noir drama of "Smooth Criminal." The song was originally written and recorded during the *Dangerous* sessions with producers Teddy Riley and Bill Bottrell (who came up with the title). "I thought I'd be a clever salesman," Bottrell recalled, "and I teased Michael about this great song I had called '*Blood on the Dance Floor*.' He was out of town and I was trying to tweak the song and this went on for weeks. He was really intrigued, so much so that before he ever heard what I did, he wrote his *own* '*Blood on the Dance Floor*.'" Jackson continued to tinker with it during the *HIStory* sessions and finished it in Montreux, Switzerland, while on his *HIStory* World Tour. "We took Teddy's DAT [Digital Audio Tape] and worked it over in Montreux with a four-man crew," recalls Brad Buxer. The result was one of his most invigorating dance tracks of the decade.

Like the album as a whole, the song was initially overlooked in the United States; yet it has subsequently become one of Jackson's better-known nineties singles due to consistent play in clubs and dance routines. It was also a major hit worldwide, reaching the Top Ten in more than fifteen countries and #1 in the United Kingdom, Spain, and New Zealand. *Billboard*'s Robert Miles describes the song as a "jeep-styled groove that provides a firm foundation for a lip-smacking vocal and a harmony-laden hook that is downright unshakeable."

The song's subject is familiar territory for Jackson. The "Susie" in the track, like "Dirty Diana" and "Billie Jean," represents something seductive but deceptive. (The *New York Times*' Neil Straus suggested she might be a metaphor for AIDS.) "Susie got your number/And Susie ain't your friend," Jackson sings in the chorus. "Look who took you under/With seven inches in." While it is clear some kind of violence has taken place, Jackson wisely leaves the interpretation of the song's mystery up to the listener. However, the track does reveal one of the more interesting twists in Jackson's catalog as the song essentially deconstructs itself.

"To escape the world," Jackson sings, "I've got to enjoy that simple dance/And it seemed that everything was on my side." As the song reveals, the sense that "everything is on his side" is an illusion. "Blood is on the dance floor," a space he once thought was safe, free, and joyous. Now, he recognizes, even his "escapes" aren't really insulated from outside threats. In essence, Jackson casts doubt on numerous forms of escapism—whether sex, dance, drugs, or perhaps, even the innocence he once so fully embraced. All of these things, like "Susie," are seductive but can also leave one targeted and vulnerable. In this way, it is one of Jackson's more disturbing tracks, a profound expression of disillusionment and uncertainty: "Susie" lures with promises and pleasure but will ultimately stab you when you least suspect it.

2. MORPHINE

(Written and composed by Michael Jackson. Produced by Michael Jackson. Engineered by Keith Cohen, Eddie De Lena, Mick Guzauski, and Tim Boyle. Mixed by Keith Cohen. Arrangement: Michael Jackson. Classical arrangement: Michael Jackson and Brad Buxer. Orchestral arrangement: Jorge Del Barrio. Rhythm arrangement: Michael Jackson. Vocal arrangement: Michael Jackson. Lead vocals: Michael Jackson. Background vocals: Michael Jackson, Brad Buxer, Bill Bottrell, and Jon Mooney. Keyboards: Brad Buxer and Keith Cohen. Synthesizers: Brad Buxer. Grand piano: Brad Buxer. Percussion: Michael Jackson, Brad Buxer, and Bryan Loren. Drums: Michael Jackson. Guitar: Michael Jackson and Slash. Choir: Andraé Crouch Singers Choir. Sample from "The Elephant Man")

In the gritty, haunting masterpiece, "Morphine," Jackson tackles a subject he never had before: drug addiction. It is a deeply personal expression, not only written and composed by the singer but also produced and arranged by him (Jackson also assists on percussion, drums, and guitar). "Michael knew exactly what he wanted to hear [from] each instrument," recalls Brad Buxer. "He sang all the parts . . . the piano in the middle of the song [and] those sheets of synth on the chorus." Particularly given the cause of his untimely death in 2009, "Morphine" is as revelatory as it is tragic.

The song begins with what sounds like an electric injection. To a relentless, industrial funk beat, the singer lashes out in visceral bursts of anger, aggression, and pain. "Is truth a game daddy," he screams at one point. "To win the fame baby/It's all the same baby/You're so reliable." The rage and disappointment, combined with its ear-assaulting sound (music critic Tom Sinclair described it as "alternating Trent Reznor-style sturm-und-clang with Bacharachian orchestral pomp"), make for a jarring listening experience, particularly for those accustomed to the more melodic pop of *Off the Wall* and *Thriller*. But "Morphine" is best understood as an experiment—both sonically and lyrically—in representing the experience of physical and psychological suffering and its temporary release (most literally in the form of narcotic pain relievers such as Demerol and morphine, both of which Jackson had been addicted to, on and off, since the early nineties).

This experience is also brilliantly conveyed in the song's form: About midway through the track, the grating beat subsides, symbolically representing the pacifying effect of the drug. "Relax, this won't hurt you," Jackson sings soothingly from the perspective of the drug/doctor.

Before I put it in
Close your eyes and count to ten
Don't cry
I won't convert you
There's no need to dismay
Close your eyes and drift away

Demerol, Demerol
Oh God he's taking Demerol
Demerol, Demerol
Oh God he's taking Demerol

He's tried
Hard to convince her
To be over what he had
Today he wants it twice as bad
Don't cry
I won't resent you
Yesterday you had his trust
Today he's taking twice as much

Demerol, Demerol
Oh God he's taking Demerol
Demerol, Demerol
Oh God he's taking Demerol

These verses are some of the most devastatingly poignant Jackson ever sang. Beyond the literalness of the drug is Jackson's persistent yearning to escape from pain, loneliness, confusion, and relentless pressure. In this brief interlude, he beautifully conveys the soothing, seductive, but temporary, release from reality. There is a sense of pleading, of desperation, before the high abruptly ends, and the listener is slammed back into the harsh world of accusations and anguish.

Sputnikmusic's Adam Gilham described this musical sequence as a "moment of absolute genius." The song as a whole contains a primal power and anguish that compare to the most viscerally raw work of John Lennon, Trent Reznor and Kurt Cobain. Music critic Thor Christensen calls "Morphine" "easily one of the most ambitious songs he's ever recorded." It is a confession, an intervention, a witness, and a warning.

3. SUPERFLY SISTER

(Written by Michael Jackson. Composed by Michael Jackson and Bryan Loren. Produced by Michael Jackson. Vocal arrangement: Michael Jackson. Drum programming: Bryan Loren. Arranged by Michael Jackson and Bryan Loren. Recorded by Richard Cottrell and Dave Way. Mixed by Dave Way. Lead and background vocals: Michael Jackson. Lead and rhythm guitars: Bryan Loren. Keyboards and synthesizer: Bryan Loren)

After the industrial assault of "Morphine," comes the more vintage-sounding eighties funk of "Superfly Sister," which some have compared to the classic grooves of Prince and Rick James. "When we began working [together]," recalled the song's co-composer, Bryan Loren, "it was my hope to return to a form of feeling that you got from the *Off The Wall* or even the *Thriller* LP where there was a very organic feeling about the content." Clocking in at nearly six-and-a-half minutes, "Superfly Sister" largely accomplishes that aim, mixing a solid groove with smooth harmonies and bright, playful production. Sonically, it provides a stark contrast to the industrial austerity of the previous track. Yet as funky and buoyant as its sound may be, the song continues *Blood on the Dance Floor*'s trenchant social commentary.

Indeed, in a genre and musical climate characterized by hypersexuality, "Superfly Sister" brashly subverts such expectations, exposing the risks and illusions of the world's favorite obsession. "Love ain't what it used to be," he sings repeatedly in the chorus, "That is what they're tellin' me/Push it in stick it out/That ain't what it's all about." Not a typical pop refrain by any stretch.

Yet the lyrics are anything but Jehovah's Witness-prudishness. In Jackson's sometimes playful, sometimes sarcastic, and, frequently, blunt lyrics, the target of his critique isn't sex itself, but the recklessness and hypocrisy that surrounds it. It is about deceit and infidelity—behaviors Jackson had witnessed his entire life. The repeated philandering of his father, in particular, and the deep pain it caused his mother infuriated him. He saw the same destructive pattern in many of his brothers' relationships. "Mother's preachin' Abraham," Jackson sings, "Brothers they don't give a damn." It also indicts the abuse and control his sisters suffered with domineering, exploitative husbands. "Sister's married to a hood/Sayin' that she got it good/ Holy Mary Mercy me/I can't believe the things I see." The song reveals Jackson's increasing disillusionment about marriage and love.

Of course, beyond this biographical reading, the song can also be interpreted more broadly as addressing other ramifications of reckless sex, including AIDS, abortion, and teen pregnancy. It certainly isn't a popular thing to preach in a culture that thrives on a glorified (and commodified) sexuality without consequences. Jackson's funky lamentation for the dissolution of real love and commitment is as bold as it is unique.

4. GHOSTS

(Written and composed by Michael Jackson and Teddy Riley. Produced by Michael Jackson and Teddy Riley. Engineered by Teddy Riley and Eddie DeLena. Mixed by Dave Way. Vocal arrangement: Michael Jackson. Drum programming: Matt Carpenter, Doug Grigsby, Andrew Schepps, Rob Hoffman, and Alex Breuer. Solo and background vocals: Michael Jackson. Keyboards and synthesizers: Teddy Riley, Brad Buxer, and Doug Grigsby)

Jackson jerks the listener in yet another direction with "Ghosts," the first of two new songs on *Blood on the Dance Floor* to descend into the dark corridors of the Gothic. It is a remarkable update to one of Jackson's most persistent fascinations (going back to songs such as "Heartbreak Hotel," and, of course, "Thriller")—an exploration of what Edgar Allen Poe once called "the terrors of the soul." Indeed, Jackson's well-known interest in subjects such as fear, horror, paranoia, transformation, the supernatural, and the grotesque have led critics to call him the "world's first Gothic megastar."

Part of Jackson's genius was his ability not only to understand the history of the Gothic tradition (of which he was an avid student), but also to reappropriate it in new and interesting ways. With songs and music videos such as *Thriller* and *Ghosts*, he essentially invented a new genre for popular music—what might be called Gothic Pop. This subversive aesthetic—now utilized most prominently by Lady Gaga—allowed Jackson to challenge the society that labeled him a monster or a freak. A host of academic studies have explored ways in which his life and work "embodied the Gothic." From his cryptic Neverland "castle" to his amorphous identity, to his music's persistent paranoia and horror motifs, he became a generation's most prominent Gothic hero-villain.

In this transgressive aesthetic, "Ghosts" is one of his best efforts. To a harsh, metal-clanging bass line and a haunting choir, he narrates the surrounding threats:

There's a ghost down in the hall
There's a ghoul up on the bed
There's something in the walls
There's blood up on the stairs
And it's floating through the room
And there's nothing I can see
And I know that that's the truth
Because now it's onto me.

The ghouls and ghosts, of course, are largely psychological ("There's nothing I can see"). Yet, the visceral terror and paranoia he conveys are real. The ghosts function as metaphors for all the real-world intrusions that haunt him, including those emanating from within. "Who gave you the right to shake my family tree?" he demands indignantly. "And who gave you the right to scare my baby, she needs me?" In these verses, Jackson feels under siege and lashes out at invisible enemies ("There's a ghostly smell around/ But nobody to be found"). He asks repeatedly if the ghosts and ghouls are jealous, hoping to at least ascertain their motives, but there is no response, no "peace of mind." The song ends in uncertainty.

"Ghosts" became the theme song for the 1997 film *Michael Jackson's Ghosts*, a thirty-nine-minute extended music video in the tradition of *Thriller* (*Ghosts* also featured the songs "2Bad" and "Is It Scary"). Unlike *Thriller*, however, whose unveiling was a cultural event in the United States, *Ghosts* was only shown at a handful of theaters in America and never released on video (though internationally it did quite well, premiering at the prestigious Cannes Film Festival in France and later released in Europe as a deluxe box set).

In retrospect, this fate seems ironically appropriate for a dark, socially pointed film about mainstream America's tendency to marginalize and fear what is different. The script for *Ghosts*, which drew from a range of inspirations, including Poe, Bram Stoker, *Frankenstein*, and *Phantom of the Opera*, was cowritten by Jackson and horror novelist Stephen King. Jackson told King he wanted to create something "terrifying," something that would "shock the world." The unlikely collaboration took place mostly over the phone. "The core story he described to me that day," recalls King, "was about a mob of angry townspeople—buttoned-down suburbanites, not torch-carrying peasants—who want the 'weirdo' who lives in the nearby castle to leave town. Because, they say, he's a bad influence on their children. I associated that with the view parents held toward rock & roll when I was growing up."

Work on the film commenced in 1993. "Nobody knows this, but it was originally going to be a video to promote *Addams Family Values*," said then-director Mick Garris. "I worked with him throughout preproduction and two weeks of production. It shut down for three years before resuming under Stan Winston, who was doing the effects work when I was directing. I recommended him to finish shooting when it resumed, as I was about to shoot *The Shining*."

Stan Winston, who had previously worked on such groundbreaking movies as *The Terminator*, *Edward Scissorhands*, and *Jurassic Park*, turned out to be a natural fit for the project. In addition to working with Jackson previously on *The Wiz*, his forte was special effects and makeup, talents that were used to full effect on *Ghosts*. As they worked together, Winston was thoroughly impressed by Jackson's still-dynamic imagination and ability. "It started out being 12 to 15 minutes long," he recalled of the project, "but as we were shooting it grew in power and length."

The finished product, however, contained mixed results. On the one hand, it is a stunning fusion of music, dance, and visual effects. Jackson's transformation into the conservative, overweight, middle-aged Mayor is well executed and humorous, and his incarnation (and dancing) as a skeleton presented cutting-edge CGI effects. Some of the dance sequences, particularly on "2Bad," are brilliant. Stephen King called it "some of the best, most inspired dancing of Jackson's career."

While the overall concept is strong, however, it doesn't fully develop, sacrificing what might have been interesting nuances, emotions, and details for some predictability and a stagnant plot. In addition, the acting is a bit corny (particularly by the parents and children), and the ending rather heavy-handed. In spite of these weaknesses, however, *Ghosts* is a classic Gothic subcultural expression, offering—as the *Black or White* video did—a surprisingly self-aware and challenging indictment of the rigidities and hypocrisies of suburban America.

The film begins in black and white. Where *Thriller* was part homage, and part parody of campy '70s-era horror films, *Ghosts* was inspired by the more traditionally Gothic Universal films of the 1930s and '40s such as *Dr. Jekyll and Mr. Hyde*, *Frankenstein*, *Dracula*, and *Freaks*. Like those movies, *Ghosts* deals primarily with themes of identity, particularly in how society responds to those it deems freaks.

In *Ghosts*, this freak comes in the form of a strange, reclusive "Maestro" living in a castle at the edge of town who is perceived as a bad influence on the community. In an effort to eliminate this influence, the zealous Mayor of "Normal Valley"—inspired, no doubt, in part by Santa Barbara District Attorney Tom Sneddon—leads a group of fearful citizens to demand that the Maestro leave immediately. "We want you out of town," he says. "We have a nice normal town. Normal people. Normal kids. We don't need freaks like you telling them ghost stories."

For the Mayor (and some in the community), the Maestro represents a threat to the status quo. He doesn't look the same, dress the same, or act the same as "normal" people. He also seems to possess some strange form of dark magic and tells "ghost stories." To quell his influence, the Mayor labels and marginalizes him. "Freaky Boy! Freak! Circus freak," he taunts at one point, while the townspeople passively look on. The words *freak* and *weirdo* are used repeatedly as slurs to "otherize" Jackson's character, to humiliate and dehumanize him. Interestingly, though, rather than try to assimilate to the town's expectations, to prove his normalness, Jackson's character openly defies them. He "becomes grotesque before [their] eyes," contorting his face, transforming into various monstrosities, and demonstrating demonic power. "Did I scare you?" he repeatedly asks the Mayor and townspeople.

The children in the film, who are much quicker to look past surfaces and labels, represent the relatively unsocialized. While the adults are prone to judge and fear what is different or new, the children are more open and willing to give the benefit of the doubt.

The remainder of the film is essentially a duel between the Maestro and the Mayor. "The most interesting aspect of this film," writes cultural critic Chad Helder, "is the double relationship between the eccentric Vincent Price-like Maestro and the conservative, bigoted Mayor. This doubling is reinforced by the fact that Michael Jackson plays both characters.... At one point, the Maestro takes over the Mayor's body and the Mayor, complete with pudgy prosthetics, dances for everyone, followed by a pivotal scene where a hand with a mirror comes out of the Mayor's stomach and shows the Mayor his own monstrousness. This doubling of the characters, emphasized by Jackson playing both parts, enhances the complexity of the film. Neither side can be as black/white as the mentality of a traditional horror film." The film once again demonstrates Jackson's substantial ability as a conceptualist in all forms. In *Ghosts*, he not only acted multiple parts and sang, he also co-wrote the screenplay, composed the music, and helped choreograph the dances and direct. *Ghosts* isn't perfect, but its intelligence, humor, cinematography, and dancing make it a fascinating sequel to *Thriller*.

5. IS IT SCARY

(Written and composed by Michael Jackson, Jimmy Jam, and Terry Lewis. Produced by Michael Jackson, Jimmy Jam, and Terry Lewis. Keyboard programming: Andrew Scheps. Drum programming: Jeff Taylor. Additional programming: Rob Hoffman. Vocal arrangement: Michael Jackson. Arranged by Michael Jackson, Jimmy Jam, and Terry Lewis. Recorded by Steve Hodge. Mixed by Steve Hodge. Solo and background vocals: Michael Jackson. All instruments performed by Jimmy Jam and Terry Lewis)

"Is It Scary" is the climax of Jackson's forays into the Gothic. It is also perhaps his best response to the public perception of him as some combination of spectacle, villain, and freak. If "Childhood" is, as Jackson once claimed, his most personal song, "Is it Scary" is the necessary counterpoint. Chilling, evocative, and revealing, it is an appropriate finish to the dark five-song conceptual masterpiece that is *Blood on the Dance Floor*.

Jackson co-wrote an early version of the track with Jimmy Jam and Terry Lewis in the early nineties. Jackson, however, wasn't satisfied with the cut, and continued to mold it and "let it speak to him" in the following years. Comparing the early Downtempo Groove Mix with the album edition provides an insightful glimpse into Jackson's process of developing a song until it is just right. The finished version not only adds some of the song's most important lyrics but also gives it the necessary atmosphere, drama, and passion to allow the "real pain and pathos" of the lyrics to resonate.

The song begins with nearly identical descriptions as "Ghosts," images of enclosing apparitions and ghouls, creaky stairs and confining walls; sonically, a door shuts, the air is compressed, and a heart begins to beat rapidly, evoking a sense of claustrophobia, fear, and panic. It is a symbolic descent into a prison-like chamber. It is here, significantly, that Michael Jackson holds up a mirror to his audience.

"I'm gonna be/Exactly what you wanna see," he sings. In this enclosed space, in other words, he is prepared to perform, to entertain. What one wants to see in him or through him, however, will reveal as much about the observer as the subject. "It's you who's taunting me," he continues, directly addressing his critics, "Because you're wanting me/To be the stranger in the night." The *taunting* here serves to marginalize, to turn his difference into something freakish and unrecognizable. He becomes a sort of modern-day minstrel; the audience gasps, claps, mocks, and laughs but fundamentally misunderstands the true nature of the performer and performance. Cultural critic Judith Coyle argues that Jackson "assimilated the personae of a range of minstrels, including Long Tail Blue, Dandy Blue Jim, Zip Coon, Master Juba, and even Jim Crow at different points in his career and life."

A minstrel, of course, is supposed to entertain according to expectations, not on his own terms. Jackson's refusal to do this subverts his consigned role. "The history of American entertainment (and Jackson's own place in that history) is never far from Jackson's mind," observes cultural critic David Yuan. "He has made it clear that he believes African American music should not be relegated to 'sideshow' status in American cultural history.... It is important to recognize how the oft-told history of Michael Jackson's rise to stardom resembles the institutional history of African American entertainment—and the institutional history of the freak show."

His inability or unwillingness to fulfill societal expectations, to become "normal," then, simultaneously angers, bewilders, and fascinates people. "Michael Jackson," Yuan continues, "is the definitive celebrity freak of our times.... [And] for a perplexed public, ... he is viewed as the agent of his own 'enfreakment.'" In other words, his "choice" to be a freak compounds the backlash even further.

A perceptive Jackson realizes this conundrum and confronts his listeners with a series of questions: "Am I amusing you/Or just confusing you/Am I the beast you visualized." He is essentially asking if he is perceived as less than human. In Margo Jefferson's *On Michael Jackson*, she writes of the historical context for such a query. "When the Civil War began, [P. T.] Barnum had just put an English circus performer in black makeup and a furry tunic, given him a jungle backdrop and asked the public: 'What is it?' In 1875, he put an African American in the part: '... Is it a Lower Order of MAN? Or is it a higher order of MONKEY? None can tell! Perhaps it is a combination of both. It is beyond dispute THE MOST MARVELOUS CREATURE LIVING ...'" "Michael Jackson," continues Jefferson, "contains trace elements of all this history.... His race, gender, sexuality, age are all utterly ambiguous, difficult to classify. So he becomes, for many, a 'What is it?'"

This context allows lines such as "And if you wanna see/Eccentric oddities/I'll be grotesque before your eyes" to hit on a deeper level. He'll be grotesque because that is what a prejudiced culture sees and wants to see. It is what they have made him. He is a product of American culture in every sense of the word. If I am scary to you, he is saying, I should be; I want to be.

Later, however, he reminds us that behind the "masquerade" hides "a hurting soul." "If you came to see," he sings, "The truth, the purity/ It's here inside/ A lonely heart." The paradox, however, is that he can only reveal himself by performing, perpetuating the ambiguous line between entertainer and human, persona and personhood. Resigned to this complicated fate, Jackson declares what could be the motto for his life: "So let the performance start!"

The climax showcases Jackson powerfully channeling his rage over a choir of ghosts, pouring out his pain in what feels like an exorcism. This is what the *New York Times*' Neil Strauss was referring to when he spoke of Jackson, "like the elephant man, screaming that he is a human being." It concludes one of the most pain-filled, but powerful, artistic expressions in Jackson's career.

Jackson poses with ghosts and ghouls in this rare photo from the set of *Ghosts*. *Blood on the Dance Floor* was the closest Jackson came to a concept album.

"*Invincible is just as good or better than* Thriller, *in my true, humble opinion. It has more to offer. Music is what lives and lasts.* Invincible *has been a great success. When the* Nutcracker Suite *was first introduced to the world it totally bombed. What's important is how the story ends.*"

MICHAEL JACKSON, *USA TODAY*, 2001

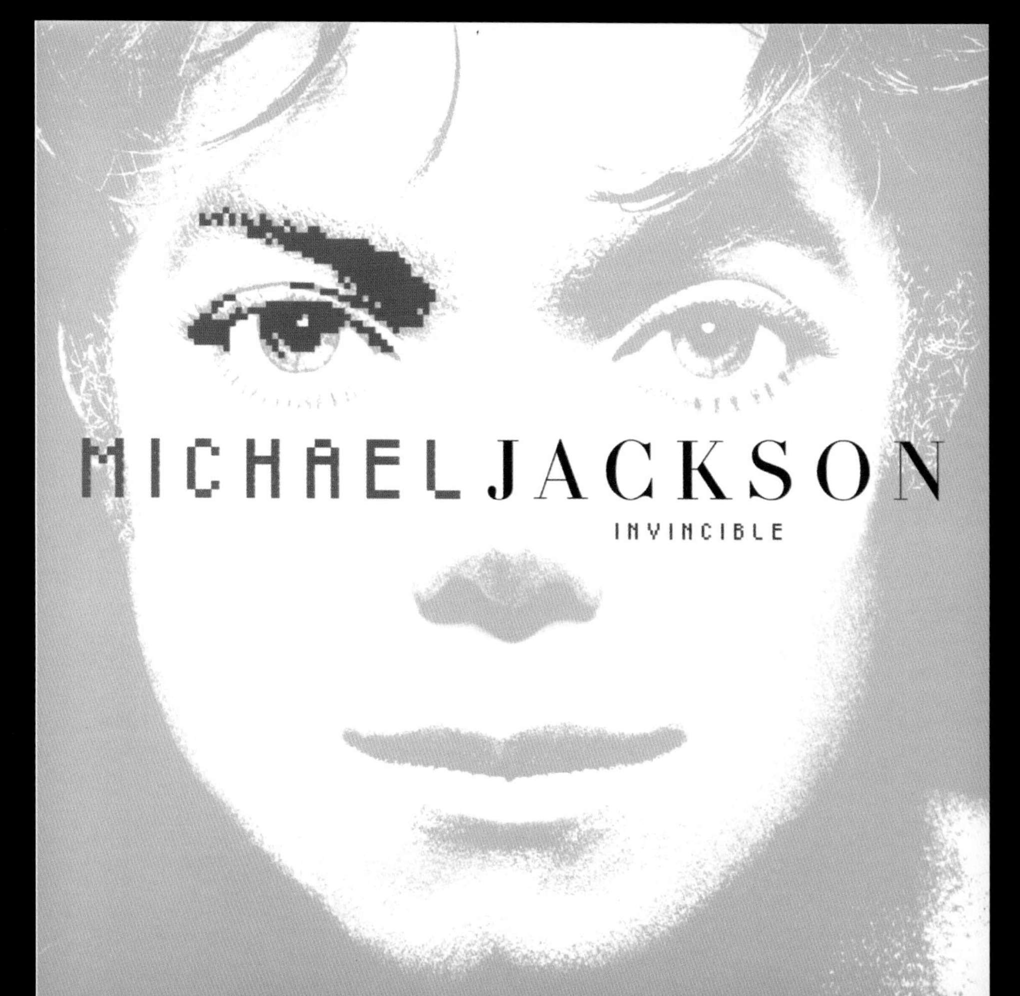

CHAPTER 7 INVINCIBLE

Released in 2001, *Invincible* was Michael Jackson's final studio album. It was also his least commercially successful (though it did manage to become his fifth consecutive album to top the charts, and ended up selling more than ten million copies worldwide). Buried by Sony's lack of promotion—due to a complicated and emotionally charged contract dispute—only one single was officially released instead of the planned six. There were also no music videos beyond *You Rock My World* and no tour. Critics generally panned the album for being too long (it ran seventy-seven minutes and contained sixteen tracks) and uneven. After several years of anticipation over Michael Jackson's "big comeback album," *Invincible* was widely viewed as a disappointment.

Ironically, though, given its relatively obscure status, *Invincible* was probably Jackson's most accessible album since the 1980s. From the retro jazz of "Butterflies," to the Latin pulse of "Whatever Happens," to the R&B heartache of "Heaven Can Wait," it was, in some ways, a return to basics. In still-brilliant vocal performances, Jackson showcases his adroit versatility, producing music that feels both classic and contemporary. *All Music*'s Stephen Thomas Erlewine described it as a "sparkly, post-hip-hop update of *Off the Wall*." *Invincible* doesn't contain the same ecstatic abandon and joy of the former album; however, its mood is unquestionably lighter than his previous three albums. It is Jackson's *Imagine*: a gentler, less anguished, more conventionally intimate expression (inspired, no doubt in part, by the births of two of his children).

The final product tended to polarize fans and critics alike. Some saw it as his most enjoyable album since *Bad*. Others, however, saw it as a bit of a regression from the challenging work he had been engaged

---

RELEASED: *October 30, 2001*

EXECUTIVE PRODUCER: *Michael Jackson*

NOTABLE CONTRIBUTORS: Rodney Jerkins *(producer/songwriting)*, Teddy Riley *(producer/songwriting)*, Brad Buxer *(arrangement/ keyboard/ programming/mixing)*, R. Kelly *(songwriting)*, Babyface *(songwriting)*, John McClain *(songwriting)*, Carol Bayer Sager *(songwriting)*, Dr. Freeze *(songwriting)*, Andre Harris and Floetry *(songwriting)*, Tyrese Gibson *(songwriting)*, The Andraé Crouch Singers Choir *(vocals)*, Santana *(guitar)*, The Notorious B.I.G. *(rap)*, Fats *(rap)*, Stuart Brawley *(engineer/mixing)*, Bruce Swedien *(engineer/mixing)*, Humberto Gattica *(engineer/mixing)*

SINGLES: *"You Rock My World," "Cry," "Butterflies"*

ESTIMATED COPIES SOLD: *11 million*

in over the past decade, an album that repeated some formulas and didn't consistently attempt the risks and depth of *Dangerous*, *HIStory*, and *Blood on the Dance Floor*. Yet regardless of how it stacks up against his other albums, there is no question *Invincible* contains very high-quality music. From "Unbreakable" to "Threatened," one can still see the innovation, range, and ability that put Jackson head and shoulders above his pretenders, even at this stage in his career.

***Invincible* was released** just weeks after the terrorist attacks of September 11, 2001. It was a time of shock and sadness in America. In the weeks and months that followed, there was an atmosphere of both paranoia and patriotism. The psyche of the entire country was shaken as the horrific images were played and replayed endlessly on TV. People feared more attacks were underway. However, from New York to California there was also a surge in national unity and resolve. Indeed, much of the world responded with compassion, holding vigils and sending support.

Michael Jackson happened to be in New York City on the day of the attack, just blocks from the World Trade Center. The night before, he and hundreds of the biggest stars in the entertainment industry were gathered for his 30th Anniversary Celebration at Madison Square Garden, which would turn out to be the final concert performances of his life. The next morning, Jackson recalled, "I got a call from friends in Saudi Arabia that America was being attacked. I turned on the news and saw the Twin Towers coming down, and I said, 'Oh my God'... It was unbelievable—I was scared to death."

Instead of fleeing for the safety of Neverland, however, Michael Jackson went to work. "I'm not one to sit back," he explained to *Rolling Stone*. "I want to do something, to help those who lost their parents, who lost their mothers and their fathers. Those are our people. Those are our children. Those are our parents." Just five days after the attacks, on September 16, Jackson announced a project that he hoped would raise $50 million for the survivors and the families of the victims of September 11.

In addition, he quickly rewrote and rerecorded a song, "What More Can I Give," that would be used as an anthem for the project. "I believe in my heart that the music community will come together as one and rally to the aid of thousands of innocent victims," said Jackson in a statement. "There is a tremendous need for relief dollars right now and through this effort each one of us can play an immediate role in helping comfort so many people. We have demonstrated time and again that music can touch souls. It is time we used that power to help us begin the process of healing immediately."

In contrast to Jackson's call for love and healing, however, the United States was soon gearing up for war: first in Afghanistan, and then, more controversially, in Iraq. Global opposition was fierce but ultimately futile, as the Bush administration carried out its "shock and awe" campaign with a handful of allies. The war, which stretched through the rest of the decade, became a symbol of the polarization, fear, and uncertainty that would permeate the years ahead.

Fear also seeped into the music industry as companies and artists scrambled to adapt to new cultural and technological changes, including Internet file-sharing services like Napster. Napster's rise was as rapid as it was revolutionary.

Almost overnight, high school and college students across the country were downloading thousands of songs online. In less than a year, Napster generated twenty-five million users, becoming the fastest-growing website in history. By 2001, in spite of legal challenges, its popularity peaked at a staggering thirty-eight million users. Eventually, in July 2001, Napster was forced to shut down. By then, though, the file-sharing genie was out of the bottle. Many music fans described it as a revolution in which the music was being liberated from an obsolete corporate system.

Industry executives, however, weren't as jubilant. Music sales were already on the decline in the late nineties. Now, even though enthusiasm for popular music seemed to be as strong as ever, the bottom line continued to drop. CD sales went from 730 million in 2000 to 593 million in 2005. In the United States, total revenue for music sales and licensing fell almost sixty percent in the 2000s, from $14.6 billion to $6.3 billion. Meanwhile, music stores became nearly extinct.

What to do about all this became the defining issue of the decade for a disoriented music industry. "The Internet," wrote *Rolling Stone*, "appears to be the most consequential technological shift for the business of selling music since the 1920s, when phonograph records replaced sheet music as the industry's profit center." Potential solutions to this dramatic change divided executives, artists, and listeners alike. Some prominent musicians, including Metallica and Dr. Dre, were quick to denounce file sharing, calling it destructive and dishonest (both filed lawsuits against Napster). Others, including Radiohead and Chuck D, felt it generated enthusiasm for music, particularly for new or lesser-known artists.

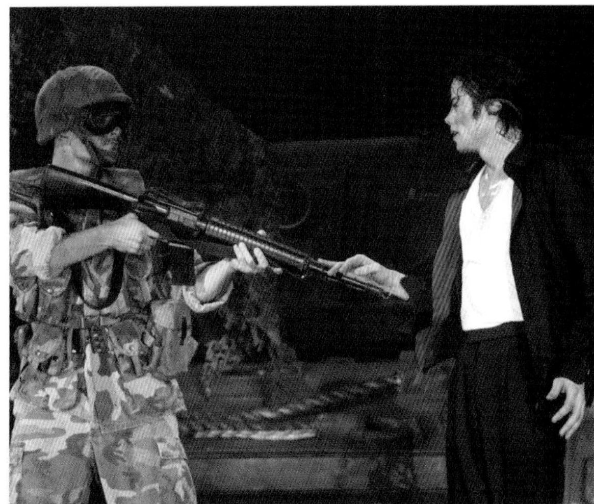

Jackson delivers an anti-violence plea on his *HIStory* World Tour.

Regardless of one's opinion about file sharing and digital music, the transformation was undeniable and unstoppable. By the end of the decade, music distribution, organization, consumption, and listening had been fundamentally altered. iPods became ubiquitous and iconic, replacing not only Walkmans and Discmans, but also the need to carry physical tapes or CDs at all. Music was now stored primarily on computers instead of on shelves and cases; it was also easily sorted and organized into individualized playlists. Listeners continued free downloads of music; however, with increasing fears of legality, sound quality, and viruses, more and more people turned to online music stores such as iTunes and Amazon.com, where songs could be purchased cheaply and reliably. By 2009, more music was purchased digitally than physically.

It was at the cusp of this transformation that Michael Jackson released *Invincible*. The music industry and technology, however, weren't the only things that had changed. Popular music was radically different than when Jackson released *HIStory* in 1995. The late nineties saw an enormous resurgence of pop in the form of boy bands, girl bands, and teen idols. In 1997, it was the Spice Girls and the Backstreet Boys; in 1998, it was Hansen, Usher, Destiny's Child, Monica, Leann Rimes, and Shania Twain; in 1999, Britney Spears and Christina Aguilera as well as the Latin Explosion led by Ricky Martin, Marc Anthony, and Enrique Iglesias; 2000 saw the emergence of *N Sync and Jessica Simpson; and in 2001, Jennifer Lopez and Mary J. Blige arrived on the scene.

The *New York Times*' Jon Pareles described it as "a general return—post-grunge, post-gangsta—to peppy, happy-faced pop songs: a reaction to too much self-importantly gloomy music." The period from 1997 to 2002 was utterly saturated with teen pop. Britney Spears became perhaps the biggest pop icon since Michael Jackson. Songs such as "... Baby One More Time" and "Oops ... I Did It Again" dominated the radio and charts, while her debut album sold more than thirteen million copies. The Backstreet Boys had became the most successful boy band since the Jackson 5, producing fourteen Top 40 hits and selling more than 130 million albums, including an estimated forty million copies of their 1999 album, *Millennium*. *N Sync picked up right where the Backstreet Boys left off: *No Strings Attached* was the second best-selling album of the 2000s (behind the Beatles' greatest-hits collection) in the United States with more than eleven million copies sold. To add to this trend, 2002 saw the beginning of the enormously popular reality television series, *American Idol*.

While teen pop was the dominant force, however, rock still had a presence in the mainstream via the revived Irish trio U2 and Brit-pop crossover

Jackson proved he hadn't lost the magic in a spectacular performance of "Billie Jean" at his 30th Anniversary Special in 2001. The two Madison Square Garden concerts would end up being the final public performances of his life.

Coldplay. The alternative was led by groups such as Radiohead, The Flaming Lips, and The Strokes. By the late nineties, hip-hop had also become successfully mainstreamed, transforming from gangsta rap to an eclectic mix of pop flash (Puff Daddy, Will Smith), sexual bluntness (Nelly, Sisqo), and innovation (Jay-Z, Kanye West). The most commercially successful rapper of this period, however, was Eminem, whose 2000-released *The Marshall Mathers LP* became the fastest-selling album of all time (with 1.79 million copies sold in its first week). The record would go on to sell nineteen million copies, while Eminem became the best-selling artist of the decade.

Michael Jackson's reentry into this eclectic, new musical scene was difficult to predict. On the one hand, the entire pop revival was something of an homage to earlier versions of him. One could see his influence everywhere in the dance steps, the styles, the tension between innocence and adult sexuality. By the beginning of the new millennium, there was a sense that America (and the world) might be ready for the return of the King of Pop himself. As successful as his protégés had become, after all, none came anywhere close to Jackson's creativity, originality, and cross-cultural impact.

Jackson wasn't young anymore though. In 1999, he turned forty. The nineties had been a challenging decade for him personally and professionally. In January 1996, he and Lisa Marie Presley divorced after just twenty months of marriage. For many people, it was confirmation that the marriage was a "sham" all along. For both Jackson and Presley it was a very difficult decision and time in their lives.

Throughout 1997, Lisa Marie and Michael spent time together during his *HIStory* World Tour. As much as they still cared for each other, however, neither was convinced it would ever work again. For years after their divorce, Jackson kept a framed picture of Presley on his nightstand. By the early 2000s, however, both had finally begun to move on.

To the public, Jackson's remarriage to his longtime nurse Debbie Rowe less than a year after his divorce to Presley was confusing at best. Jackson first met Debbie Rowe in the late eighties while making regular visits to his dermatologist, Arnold Klein. She and Michael quickly became friends. Before Jackson and Presley even began dating, Debbie Rowe, knowing how desperately Jackson wanted children, offered to make him a father via surrogacy. It wasn't until his marriage with Presley was ending that he started to seriously consider Rowe's offer. Jackson's relationship with Debbie Rowe, according to most sources, was platonic. Rowe wanted to give Jackson a child as a friend. In interviews, she would describe it as a "gift."

Debbie Rowe originally intended to be a surrogate mother. She wanted Jackson to be a father, but marriage never entered into the discussions. Eventually, of course, that changed, though the reasons aren't exactly clear. Regardless, Jackson and Rowe were married in November 1996 in a private, low-key ceremony in Australia. The unlikely couple would never live together. Their "arrangement" was simple: Michael would raise the child, and Debbie would occasionally visit. It was what she offered before the tabloid scrutiny and hasty wedding, and it was the plan the couple stuck to.

Rowe wanted to give Jackson a child as a friend. In interviews, she would describe it as a "gift."

Less than four months later, on February 13, 1997, Jackson's first son, Prince Michael, was born. Jackson described it as the best day of his life. "Words can't describe how I feel," he said in a written statement. "I have been blessed beyond comprehension and I will work tirelessly at being the best father that I can possibly be. I appreciate that my fans are elated, but I hope that everyone respects the privacy that Debbie and I want and need for our son. I grew up in a fish bowl and will not allow that to happen to my child. Please respect our wishes and give my son his privacy."

The statement, predictably, fell on deaf ears. To appease the ensuing tabloid frenzy to get the first picture of his newborn son—which had escalated to the point of helicopters flying over the hospital and reporters attempting to sneak into the gates of Neverland—Jackson finally decided to take matters into his own hands. He hired a professional photographer and sold pictures of him and his son to *OK Magazine* (a British tabloid). The money was donated to charity.

In the years that followed, however, he would go to enormous lengths to ensure his children's privacy. For someone as relentlessly stalked by paparazzi as Michael Jackson, it is remarkable how few photos were ever taken of his children. He was, of course, criticized for the elaborate masks and costumes they wore in public. For Jackson, however, it was an attempt to protect them.

More than anything, he wanted to give his children the "normal" childhood he never had. "I want him to have some space," he told Barbara Walters of Prince Michael in a 1997 interview, "where he can go to school. I don't want him to be called 'Wacko Jacko'—that's not nice. They call [me] that.... Did they ever think I would have a child one day ... that I have a heart? It's hurting my heart. Why pass it on to him?"

The following November, he and Debbie Rowe announced that they were expecting another child, this time a girl to be named Paris Michael Katherine. The 7-pound, 7-ounce baby girl was born a few months later on April 3, 1998. Jackson was elated.

Later that year, Jackson and Rowe mutually decided to divorce. Even though she never lived with Jackson, Rowe had been hounded by paparazzi since the day news broke of their first child. She wanted her old life back, and Jackson wanted to give it to her.

Jackson's final child, Prince Michael II (nicknamed Blanket), was born shortly after the release of *Invincible* in 2002 to an unknown surrogate mother. "I don't want anybody to know [the mother]," Jackson told Martin Bashir in 2003. "She doesn't want to be in papers and tabloids ... she doesn't want it, and I don't blame her." Jackson also explained the meaning behind the child's nickname: "It's an expression I use with my family and my employees. I say 'you should blanket me' or 'you should blanket her,' meaning like a blanket is a blessing. It's a way of showing love and caring.... So the third one is Blanket, and Blanket is really sweet."

While the setup of his new family wasn't traditional, it was still a family—something Jackson desperately wanted. With Prince, Paris, and Blanket, he finally had something, besides his music, that he could love unconditionally.

In many ways this was a happy time in Jackson's life; however, he still struggled with pain and addiction. Since the allegations in 1993, he continued to periodically suffer from a dependence on painkillers such as Demerol, OxyContin, and morphine, especially while on tour. To deal with persistent insomnia after concerts, he also reportedly began using propofol, a sedative agent generally used for the induction of anesthesia. "Physically, touring takes a lot out of you," Jackson acknowledged in 2001. "When I'm on stage, it's like a two-hour marathon. I weigh myself before and after each show, and I lose a

A despondent Jackson sits in a Santa Maria court, facing yet another lawsuit. In part because of numerous distractions, *Invincible* was Jackson's most difficult album to complete.

good 10 pounds. Sweat is all over the stage. Then you get to your hotel and your adrenaline is at its zenith and you can't fall asleep. And you've got a show the next day. It's tough." Jackson reportedly traveled with an anesthesiologist (who would sedate the singer at night) during much of the *HIStory* World Tour.

Many family members and close friends who became aware of Jackson's addiction tried to help him. "He was surrounded by enablers," said longtime friend Deepak Chopra, "including a shameful plethora of MDs in Los Angeles and elsewhere who supplied him with prescription drugs. As many times as he would candidly confess that he had a problem, the conversation always ended with a deflection and denial."

More obvious to the public at the time was Jackson's continued addiction to plastic surgery. The exact number of procedures he underwent is unknown; but it is clear Jackson continued to struggle with his appearance, which changed repeatedly and dramatically from 1995 to 2001. "I wish I could never be photographed and I wish I could never be seen," he confessed to Rabbi Shmuely Boteach in 2000.

Perhaps most debilitating to Jackson's career at the time, however, were the endless lawsuits and financial entanglements he was forced to confront. His representation had become a revolving door. Increasingly, he didn't know who to trust. Part of the reason for the repeated delays of his album, then, had to do with these behind-the-scenes struggles. Needless to say, his life had become far more complicated than it was when he was working at Westlake Studios with Quincy Jones and the A-Team.

As he prepared for his big "comeback," many wondered whether he still had the time, energy, and desire to make it happen. In an interview at the end of the millennium, Jackson seemed exhausted but still optimistic. Asked who his audience was in the new millennium, he answered: "I don't know. I just try to write wonderful music, and if they love it, they love it. I don't think about any demographic. The record company tries to get me to think that way, but I just do what I would enjoy hearing." Asked if he thought people would finally be able to forget the sensationalism and focus on his music, Jackson was realistic: "I don't think so 'cause the press has made me out to be this monster, this crazy person who's bizarre and weird. I'm nothing like that."

"Is there anything you can do to change that impression?" Jackson was asked.

"Well, all I can do is be myself," he responded, "and create from my soul. But they take that and manipulate it."

"I'm putting my heart and soul into [the album]," he said in an interview that year, "because I'm not sure if I'm gonna do another one after this. . . ."

Still, Jackson was excited about the future. "I think the best work is coming," he said, "but I would like to go into other areas, not keep doing album after pop album." Among his many plans was a lead role in the film, *The Nightmares of Edgar Allen Poe*. Jackson had long desired to become more involved with film, both in directing and in acting. He was also interested in doing a classical album and a children's book. "I think it's going to be totally different than what I did before," he predicted. "The idea is to take it a step forward and to innovate or else why am I doing it? I don't wanna be just another can in the assembly line."

***Invincible* was initially** scheduled for release on November 9, 1999. To the frustration of fans, however, the album was postponed repeatedly and wouldn't be released for another two years. "I'm putting my heart and soul into [the album]," he said in an interview that year, "because I'm not sure if I'm gonna do another one after this.... This will be my last proper album, I think."

Gone were the simpler days of recording in one location. Beginning in 1997, Jackson worked in studios around the world, from Montreux, Switzerland, to Norfolk, Virginia (where Teddy Riley was located). He also recorded in Los Angeles, New York, and The Hit Factory in Miami (where most of his work with Rodney Jerkins was completed).

Jackson's list of collaborators for *Invincible*, meanwhile, seemed to never end. At various stages he worked with Teddy Riley, Dr. Freeze, Babyface, R. Kelly, Will Smith, Puff Daddy, Boyz II Men, K-Ci & JoJo, Carole Bayer Sager, David Foster, Tom Bahler, Walter Afanasieff, Lenny Kravitz, Wyclef Jean, Floetry, Brandy, Sisqo, and Santana among numerous others. He also retained the services of longtime partners Brad Buxer and Bruce Swedien to work alongside newcomers such as Stuart Brawley, George Mayers, and Harvey Mason Jr. Perhaps the biggest contributor, however, ended up being a young producer named Rodney "Darkchild" Jerkins. The son of a minister from New Jersey, Jerkins got his break from none other than the King of New Jack Swing, Teddy Riley. He subsequently produced songs for some of the hottest artists in the late nineties, including Destiny's Child, Brandy, Monica, and Jennifer Lopez.

Jerkins was thrilled at the opportunity of working with Michael Jackson. "[Michael] is the best," he said in a 2000 interview. "There's no other artist at his level—and I've worked with many. He is great to work with because he knows exactly what he wants.... He is so innovative—he doesn't want the usual stuff that they play on the radio all the time, and he is very hands on. Everything has to be as he wants it."

Indeed, while Jerkins was heavily involved as producer and cowriter on several tracks, Jackson continued to act—as he did on *Dangerous* and *HIStory*—as executive producer for the album.

"He was super vocal," recalls Jerkins. "He was so hands on. I'm talking about from the high hat to everything. The sound quality was so important to him. He looked at everything under a microscope, like, 'The middle frequency is too much'—he was very technical. He use to always say, 'Melody is king' so he really focused in on melody."

Throughout 1999 and 2000, Jackson and Jerkins wrote and recorded songs together. Jerkins' role was very similar to Teddy Riley's on *Dangerous*: he was there to help Jackson develop a new "sound" for the rhythm tracks. Jackson actually paid Jerkins enough money to ensure he worked with no one else for three years (although Jerkins did end up producing an album by Brandy toward the end). Over this time, they developed a close working relationship and by early 2000, they had already created close to thirty tracks together.

The first batch of songs, according to Jerkins, was more vintage-sounding Jackson, including "You Rock My World." Jerkins, like other keen producers of R&B and hip-hop of the time, was beginning to return to late-seventies disco, soul, and funk for inspiration. In fact, around this time, Jackson's management was also offered several retro-sounding grooves by talented producer-duo the Neptunes. They, however, apparently didn't feel they were up to snuff. The Neptunes ended up recording the songs—which included Top Ten hits "Señorita" and "Rock Your Body"—with Justin Timberlake for his debut album, *Justified*. (According to Neptunes member Pharrell, Jackson had a great sense of humor about his management passing over the songs.)

The incident, however, symbolized an internal debate from the beginning: should the album be forward looking or backward looking (or both)? Jackson enjoyed *Off the Wall* and knew many people would be thrilled if he recycled it, but he hated the idea of doing something he had already done. Jackson told Jerkins he wanted *some* classic, vintage tunes, but he wanted the album as a whole to be more "futuristic." At one point, after they had been working for more than a year, Jackson actually suggested they throw out everything and start from scratch. Jerkins was shocked.

Jackson's concerns with his new sound extended to how it was recorded and engineered. While many producers were switching to digital recording, Jackson wanted to retain the warmth of analog. "He was a little scared of Pro Tools," said Rodney Jerkins. "We tried to get him to use it, but he didn't want to go that route yet and I understand: He came from the school of analog." The new team of engineers did use Pro Tools to manage tracks for *Invincible*, some of which had at least thirty different versions. Part of the challenge to Jackson was trying to balance his desire to innovate (technologically and sonically), with the wealth of experience and knowledge he had learned about recording from people such as Quincy Jones and Bruce Swedien.

It wasn't an easy task. There were huge expectations from all sides—from the record company, from collaborators, from fans, but most significantly, from himself. "Of all my albums I would say this one was the toughest [to make]," Jackson acknowledged in 2001. "I was hardest on myself. I wrote so many songs ... just to get to the 16 that I think are acceptable. And, um, it's the album where ... I didn't have children before other albums, so I caught a lot of colds; I was sick a lot ... So we had to stop and start again and stop and start."

Some days he and Jerkins reportedly worked "16 to 18 hours a day" at the studio, recording material over and over again. "I pushed Rodney," acknowledged Jackson. "And pushed and pushed and pushed and pushed him to create, to innovate more. To pioneer more. He's a real musician and he's very dedicated and he's real loyal. He has perseverance. I don't think I've seen perseverance like his in anyone. Because you can push him and push him and he doesn't get angry." Indeed, the challenge for Jerkins, while frustrating at times, was also invigorating. Working with Jackson took patience, but he was ecstatic with the results. "All I can tell you," Jerkins said at the time, "is that it's a sound you have never heard before in your life. Definitively different from everything else.... Definitively something no one has heard before. It's gonna be the best album that he's ever made."

Everyone who worked with Jackson on *Invincible* returned with similarly glowing reviews. "We think we've got the next *Thriller*," said former Jodeci member DeVante, who worked on several potential tracks (none of which made it onto the album). R. Kelly, who penned and coproduced Jackson's #1 hit, "You Are Not Alone," wrote five potential songs for *Invincible*. "If he just picks two, I'll be so happy," he said. (Jackson ultimately chose "Cry" for the final cut.)

While *Invincible*'s final track list contained an abundant sixteen songs, some outstanding material was left off, including work with DeVante, Dr. Freeze, Lenny Kravitz, Brad Buxer, and Jerkins (including "Can't Get Your Weight Off of Me," "Escape," and "We've Had Enough"). With such a deep well of material, Jackson could have gone numerous directions with the record. He was experimenting in a range of styles. One song with Kravitz—"Another Day"—was a cosmic neo-funk rock tune that was unlike anything Jackson had done before. Several songs with Brad Buxer—including "Beautiful Girl," "The Way You Love Me," and "Hollywood Tonight"—could have easily been chosen. The same might be said for two outstanding Dr. Freeze collaborations: "Blue Gangsta" and "A Place With No Name." Another gorgeous outtake was "Fall Again," a unique, haunting ballad written by Walter Afanasieff and Robin Thicke, but never fully finished.

One of the earliest tracks to be mentioned for the album was an anthem called "I Have This Dream," a collaboration with Carole Bayer Sager and David Foster. Sager described the track as "a song to take us into the year 2000 with hope." The song, however, ultimately failed to make it on to *Invincible*. Also missing was Jackson's 1998-penned charity anthem, "What More Can I Give." Needless to say, Jackson easily had enough great material to make *Invincible* a double album.

Jackson's perfectionism not only prevented many great songs from being included, but continued to delay the album's release. As the summer of 2001 approached, Jackson's fans (not to mention executives at Sony) were growing restless for the long-promised new album. He had been recording, on and off, for almost four years now and spent an estimated $30 million but still felt unsatisfied. That summer, however, under extreme pressure, he finally picked the final lineup of songs and let it go.

Late that summer, the release date for *Invincible* was finally set in stone (October 20, 2001), and the excitement began to build. "I'm recording across the hall from him at the Hit Factory," said singer Luther Vandross, "and you should hear the buzz.

The assistant engineers, that's a real good monitor, a real good gauge for whether or not it's hot in there. They come back and they say, 'Oh it's so hot in there, it's great, the music is really sounding good, everybody's gonna really love this.'"

Epic and Sony executives were thrilled with the finished product. "Michael is singing better than ever," Epic president David Glew confided. "The ballads! The ballads are beautiful, and they're all there. The dance songs are full of melodies. We're going to get a single out by mid-July, at least 8 weeks before the album hits stores. Michael's done his work, now we have to do ours. It's all about how it's marketed." Sony president Tommy Mottola called it "some of the best music Michael's ever made."

As the day grew closer for *Invincible*'s release, predictions varied as to how it would be received. Some felt the musical climate made it ripe for success; others felt it couldn't compete with the teen pop and contemporary R&B that appealed to young listeners. "The problem he faces right now is having to reach out to an audience that doesn't know who he is," said *Rolling Stone* music editor Joe Levy. "It's the first time he's had to try and connect with an audience that did not grow up with him.... It's similar to what Elvis faced at the time of his 1968 comeback special. Jackson's in a position where the [record-buyers] either don't know or care who he is or consider him a punch line to a joke. But Elvis proved 'em wrong. When he wanted them to care about the music, he could do a good job. It seems possible to me that Michael Jackson could do the exact same thing."

Michael Jackson certainly proved just that when he hit the stage at Madison Square Garden in New York that September. The New York concerts, which sold out within hours, commemorated Jackson's thirty years as a solo recording artist. It was his first time performing on the mainland in more than eleven years. Nearly the entire entertainment industry came out to witness the "big comeback" and pay homage. The list of guests and performers included music legends Quincy Jones, Diana Ross, Ray Charles, Gladys Knight, and Whitney Houston; screen icons Elizabeth Taylor, Marlon Brando, and Liza Minelli; and a new generation of recording artists including Beyoncé, Justin Timberlake, Usher, Alicia Keys,

Jackson poses with friend and actor Chris Tucker, who would appear in his video for "You Rock My World."

Jackson performing his classic, "The Way You Make Me Feel," with pop star Britney Spears for his 30th Anniversary Special at Madison Square Garden.

Missy Elliot, Ricky Martin, Britney Spears, Puff Daddy, and Jay-Z, among hundreds of others.

In the days leading up to the concerts, the excitement in the city—and the music industry—was palpable. "I think that it just shows how hungry everybody is for Michael. They want to see him, so people are trying to [imitate him], because they want to see him so bad," said Destiny's Child member Kelly Rowland. "The nearest we have [in America] to royalty is Michael Jackson," said hip-hop star Sisqo.

Jackson didn't disappoint. After a rather tedious couple of hours of tributes, he took the stage with his brothers for the first time since the 1984 Victory Tour. The atmosphere in the arena was electric as they went through a medley of classic Jackson 5 tunes. When Jackson appeared in silhouette for his solo performances, the roof nearly came off the building. At forty-three years of age, it was clear to everyone that Michael Jackson still had it.

Condensed and broadcast on CBS a couple of months later, the concerts were watched by more than twenty-five-million viewers, the largest music special on any network in more than six years. It was a promising start to Jackson's long-awaited comeback. Sadly, the next morning saw the chaos and destruction of 9/11. Suddenly pop music, among many other things, seemed superfluous and took a backseat as people tried to reorient themselves and recover from the trauma.

Just over a month later, *Invincible* was finally released worldwide. Featuring a half-digital, half-human face of Jackson on the cover, the album certainly had the look of something relevant to the information age. Released in five different colors, *Invincible* sold quickly the first week, debuting at #1 in America, the United Kingdom, France, Australia, Japan, Germany, Italy, and throughout most of the rest of the world.

In spite of receiving lukewarm reviews from critics, *Invincible* sold a healthy 366,300 copies in its first week in the United States alone (where many predicted it would fail). Within five days, it had reportedly sold three million copies globally.

The public, however, seemed to respond somewhat tepidly to Jackson's first single, "You Rock My World." While it reached #10 on the *Billboard* Hot 100, it was also criticized for not being particularly original or new, especially given how much the album had been hyped. "You Rock My World" was Jackson's only lead single as a solo artist not to crack the Top Five in the United States. (The single did do much better internationally, reaching #2 in the United Kingdom and #1 in France). The video for the song only reinforced the perception that Jackson's visionary days were behind him. Directed by Paul Hunter (who had worked with Mariah Carey, Will Smith, and Michael's sister Janet), it felt like a cheap knockoff of "Smooth Criminal," this time set in Cuba. Despite cameos by comedian Chris Tucker and screen legend Marlon Brando, the video never really took off. Of course, it wasn't just problems with the video itself. By this time, music videos in general no longer had nearly the same impact they did in the eighties and early nineties. MTV and VH1 were shifting more toward reality television, while YouTube didn't yet exist.

According to those close to Jackson, he wasn't happy with the short film either. He also wasn't happy with Sony's sequencing of the singles (he favored releasing "Unbreakable" first). Behind the scenes, much more serious problems were brewing. A major feud had developed between Jackson and then-Sony head, Tommy Mottola. The stakes had escalated to the point that Jackson threatened to leave Sony while Tommy Mottola informed the singer he was trapped by clauses in his contract.

Within months, despite its promising start, *Invincible* began falling down the charts, and Sony abruptly ended all promotions. "Butterflies," which was scheduled for a single release, soared to #2 on the R&B charts on air play alone, but Sony delayed and then canceled its release. Also canceled was the video for "Unbreakable" and a planned Grammy performance of "Whatever Happens."

Fans were bewildered and angry. *Invincible* had reportedly sold five million copies worldwide in its first few months. So what was happening? Was Sony giving up on the album already? Was Michael tired of working on it?

Jackson's previous two studio albums, *Dangerous* and *HIStory*, were promoted for nearly two years. *Invincible* was dropped after less than two months (even though Mottola, just months earlier, said that it was Jackson's best work since *Thriller*). Jackson was justifiably irate. He felt Mottola had used and betrayed him. According to one source, Mottola threatened to "ruin" Jackson. "Not physical threats," the source told *Fox News*, "but certainly the threat that Michael would be destroyed and his career would be over if he didn't agree to Tommy's terms."

Producer Rodney Jerkins felt bad that all the hard work he and Jackson put into the album was now being abandoned because of a power struggle. "I think it's at a stalemate," he said, "because there is no promotion, there is no video. If there's nothing to promote or see, how can you sell records?" Sony even refused to distribute Jackson's charity single, "What More Can I Give," which was supposed to raise money for the survivors of 9/11. "I would like to see Sony at least have the decency to let a neutral third-party record company release the songs," said executive producer Marc Shaffel. "Everyone who has heard the two songs feel they are both number-one hits, and they will raise a lot of money for good causes."

While Tommy Mottola's motives for canceling promotions for *Invincible* have been the subject of immense speculation, the truth remains somewhat clouded. Some felt the primary motive was payback for the enormous sum of money Jackson had spent making *Invincible*; others claimed Mottola was after the famed Beatles catalog. What is known for certain is that the dispute hit a sensitive nerve for Michael Jackson. It wasn't just business to him; it was personal betrayal. Since his days at Motown, he had worked tirelessly at his craft and put his heart and soul into his career. In the process, he had made billions of dollars for record companies, including CBS/Epic and Sony, who had steadfastly supported him. Now, he felt, that support was gone. In many ways, the mistreatment was a repeat of the trauma he felt with his father: He felt like a puppet, a product, exploited endlessly for what he could offer but not given the basic dignity of a respected artist. The pain was made worse when many former friends and colleagues sided with Mottola. As in 1993, Jackson felt abandoned when he needed the support the most.

The issue of race further exacerbated the situation. Michael Jackson was well aware of the history of black artists in the music industry. From Chuck Berry to Little Richard, Bo Diddley to Jackie Wilson, Jackson saw revolutionary African American artists not only slighted in proportion to their accomplishments, but also exploited by white record companies. He watched his hero, James Brown, tour into his old age to make money because white executives owned the rights and royalties to the songs that made him a legend (this, in fact, was one reason Jackson—with the help of attorney John Branca—not only made sure he owned all of his own material, but also actively acquired music-publishing rights from other artists).

Michael Jackson felt so strongly that his case was part of a larger trend of racism and exploitation in the music industry that he began to plead his case publicly. It was a rare overt political act for the singer. At a press conference in Harlem for the National Action Network, supported by Johnnie Cochran and Al Sharpton, Jackson laid out his case:

> It's very sad to see that these artists really are penniless because they created so much joy for the world. And the system, beginning with the record companies, totally took advantage of them.... And I just need you to know that this is very important, what we're fighting for because I'm tired—I'm really, really tired of the manipulation.... I'm here to speak for all injustice. You gotta remember something, the minute I started breaking the all-time record in record sales—I broke Elvis's records, I broke the Beatles' records—the minute [they] became the all-time best-selling albums in the history of the

Jackson on the set of *MTV's Total Request Live* with Carson Daly. After an initial marketing blitz, all promotions, singles, and videos were canceled for *Invincible* due to a feud between Jackson and then-Sony head Tommy Mottola.

> [*Guinness World Records*], overnight they called me a freak, they called me a homosexual, they called me a child molester, they said I tried to bleach my skin. They did everything to try to turn the public against me.

"I tired—I'm really, really tired of the manipulation."

While there may have been some hyperbole in Jackson's claims, there was also a significant amount of truth to the larger point he was making. Regardless of the pigment of his skin, Jackson clearly still identified with the struggles of African American artists and musicians. Most in the media, however, simply dismissed his grievances as sour grapes because his album hadn't performed as well as expected.

Regardless of the controversy and disappointment surrounding *Invincible*, as Jackson put it, "The music is what lives and lasts." And much of *Invincible*, in retrospect, still sounds quite fresh and impressive.

The standard for Michael Jackson, of course, has always been himself. An album could have several very good songs (as *Invincible* did), but if it didn't sell fifty-million copies and produce a string of #1 hits, it was labeled a failure. "The fact that [Michael Jackson] is a great musician is now often forgotten," observed music critic Robert Christgau in 2001. "I use the present tense because a) his skills seem undiminished and b) as only Frank Kogan has listened dispassionately enough to remark, he's doing new stuff with them—his funk is steelier and his ballads are airier, both to disquieting effect."

Such reviews, however, proved to be the minority. As usual, very few critics were able to focus on the music without injecting their opinions about Michael Jackson's eccentricities, physical appearance, and personal controversies. However, if one was able to get past the distractions and extraneous comparisons, *Invincible* contained its rewards. "Of every album I have listened to," said rapper Eminem in 2002, "the best of the year by far has been *Invincible*. Michael Jackson deserves a lot more credit than he is getting."

Indeed, from the "fleet, durable R&B minimalism" of its up-tempo tracks to the rich soulfulness of its mid-tempo grooves, to the pathos and vocal purity of its ballads, *Invincible* continued to showcase Jackson's unique and diverse talents. The front end was loaded with sharp, edgy rhythm tracks intended to appeal to a new generation of

listeners. "Unbreakable" and "Heartbreaker," both cowritten with Rodney Jerkins, are sonically explosive songs that represent a new millennium techno-funk. The tempo is balanced with smooth retro jams such as "Heaven Can Wait" and "Butterflies" and sublime ballads like "Speechless." Mark Anthony Neal described it as "a return of sorts to the kind of solid infectious R&B that marked the best of Jackson's recordings with his brothers and his 'adult' debut with *Off the Wall*." Thematically, the album has a similar arc to that of *Dangerous*, beginning with the resolve and defiance of "Unbreakable," peaking with the personal transcendence of "Speechless" and "You Are My Life," shifting to the social awareness of "Cry" and "The Lost Children," and ending with the provocative twist of "Threatened."

One of the major debates about *Invincible*, however, had to do with its array of producers and collaborators. Some felt its "unevenness" was due to "too many cooks in the kitchen" and believed that Jackson would have been better served just sticking with one or two producers. "'Butterflies,'" argued Mark Anthony Neal, "is the best example of why Jackson's investment in Jerkins was such a misstep as [Andre] Harris and other splinters of the 'Touch of Jazz' camp could have legitimately done the whole project themselves." Others felt Teddy Riley, Jackson's partner for one of his most creative efforts (*Dangerous*), collaborated on the album's most compelling tracks. "Teddy Riley proves with just two songs that he's a hundred times the composer the young hipsters flooding most of this album are," writes Nikki Transter. "While the jivin' beats of the tracks by Jerkins, et al., are funky and fun, it's the Riley-influenced efforts such as 'Whatever Happens' and 'Don't Walk Away' that are most intriguing and that allow Jackson greater room to experiment lyrically, vocally, and instrumentally."

In the end, however, it seemed one's argument for best producer or best album vision had more to do with aesthetic preferences. In reality, all of Jackson's main collaborators—Rodney Jerkins, Teddy Riley, R. Kelly, Floetry, and Babyface—were enormously talented; but together, their work felt cluttered to some listeners. Jackson himself later acknowledged he might have overworked the album and left off some early material that should have gone on.

Invincible's legacy, then, is still somewhat unsettled. Its cultural impact was relatively minimal upon its initial release. The average music listener would probably recognize one or two of its songs. In addition, unlike previous albums, there were no visual interpretations to attach to it via music videos or performances. It was an album plagued by controversy, unfulfilled expectations, and disappointment.

However, the album has sold more than ten-million copies and was recently voted the "best album of the decade" by readers of Billboard.com. Many of the songs, meanwhile, never heard the first time around, are being rediscovered by new generations without the baggage and distractions that previously accompanied them. For Jackson's fans, meanwhile, the *Invincible* album and its outtakes are a veritable treasure trove of underrated material that represents Jackson's last fully realized work.

Jackson on the set of his only music video for *Invincible, You Rock My World*.

THE SONGS

1. UNBREAKABLE

(Written and composed by Michael Jackson, Rodney Jerkins, Fred Jerkins III, LaShawn Daniels, Nora Payne, and Robert Smith. Produced by Michael Jackson and Rodney Jerkins. Recorded by Stuart Brawley. Digital editing by Stuart Brawley and Paul Foley. Mixed by Bruce Swedien, Rodney Jerkins, and Stuart Brawley. Lead vocal: Michael Jackson. Background vocals: Michael Jackson. Additional background vocals: Brandy. Rap performed by The Notorious B.I.G. All musical instruments performed by Michael Jackson and Rodney Jerkins)

"Unbreakable" introduces the sound of the new-millennium Michael Jackson. As with his previous techno-industrial sonic forays ("Dangerous," "Scream"), the track begins with a prelude of machine sounds, almost as if the music is discovering how to create itself. Thematically, it perfectly correlates with the hybrid identity conveyed on the album cover: the creative act is consummated by a combination of the biological and technological, organic and digital, human and machine.

Jackson allows this opening tension to build with what sounds like an engine idling, an animal growl, and an approaching stomp, before the song explodes into a relentless piano-driven hook. The effect is outstanding. For an artist who had been on the sidelines for six years, it was a strong opening statement. "The song is without doubt the album's standout," wrote music critic Nikki Tranter in a 2001 review. Jackson considered the track one of his favorites on the record and pushed for it to be the first single and short film. ("You Rock My World" was ultimately deemed more radio-friendly by Sony.)

The decision to pass on the track as the opening single was perhaps also due to its bluntness. While the majority of *Invincible* deals with "love and relationships," "Unbreakable" is a bold declaration of defiance. "When you bury me underneath all your pain," Jackson taunts in one line. "I'm steady laughin', while surfacing."

In some ways, the song is also a message to himself, a summoning of confidence and strength in the face of adversity. As he explained to Anthony DeCurtis in a simulchat interview: "I've been through hell and back. I have, to be honest, and still I'm able to do what I do and nothing can stop me. No one can stop me, no matter what. I stop when I'm ready to stop. You know, and uh, I'm just saying [in 'Unbreakable'], you know, I will continue to move forward no matter what."

The recurring piano-bass hook conveys that determination and perseverance well. Clocking in at more than six minutes, "Unbreakable's" pulsing, persistent beat nearly pushes through the speakers as Jackson's staccato vocals bite into the lyrics. "'Unbreakable' is so striking," wrote Robert Hilburn, "that savvy stereo retailers could use it to demonstrate the wonders of their latest sound systems."

At about the 3:50 mark, The Notorious B.I.G. makes a posthumous appearance, offering a smooth rap solo, before Jackson closes the song in classic improvisational form. The song sent a clear message: Michael Jackson was back. As one review put it: "He's not going to leave his pop crown behind without a fight."

2. HEARTBREAKER

(Written and composed by Michael Jackson, Rodney Jerkins, Fred Jerkins III, LaShawn Daniels, Mischke, and Norman Gregg. Produced by Michael Jackson and Rodney Jerkins. Music programmed by Michael Jackson and Rodney Jerkins. Recorded by Bruce Swedien and Stuart Brawley. Digital editing by Alex Greggs, Stuart Brawley, and Fabian Marasciullo. Rap recorded by Bob Brown. Mixed by Bruce Swedien, Rodney Jerkins, and Stuart Brawley. Lead vocal: Michael Jackson. Rap performed by Fats. Background vocals: Michael Jackson, Mischke, LaShawn Daniels, and Nora Payne)

With its wildly ricocheting beats and sounds, "Heartbreaker" feels like the work of a mad scientist in the studio. The *Los Angeles Times'* Robert Hilburn describes it as a "sonic marvel" that moves the artist into "daring new territory." Even the *New York Times'* Jon Pareles, notoriously critical of Jackson, acknowledged his "percussive genius" on rhythm tracks like "Heartbreaker": "[He] breaks up his singing with grunts and breaths and yelps ... against a rhythm track of electronic noises that ratchet and sputter like a truckload of joy buzzers on a rough road."

As with previous albums, this sonic novelty was actively pushed for by Jackson. "A lot of sounds on the album aren't sounds from keyboards," he explained, "[they] are, you know, pretty much programmed into the machines. We go out and make our own sounds. We hit on things, we beat on things, so nobody can duplicate what we do. We make them with our own hands, we find things and we create things. And that's the most important thing, to be a pioneer. To be an innovator."

"Heartbreaker" is a clear example of this innovation, mixing techno, pop, hip-hop and funk (it also features Jackson's renowned beatboxing) to achieve something the "ear hasn't heard." *NME* described it as a "busy, percussive groove with a compulsive repetitive chorus but a classic soaring [Jackson] middle eight."

Lyrically, "Heartbreaker" continues a well-established trope for Jackson. It is a song of seduction and spurned love. "She speaks the lines that can control my mind," he sings. It is a thematic obsession that began with "Heartbreak Hotel" and continued in tracks such as "Billie Jean," "Dirty Diana," and "Dangerous." For Jackson, there is a perpetual distrust, even fear, of a certain type of woman (or at least what she represents). There is also, of course, the persistent temptation and fascination.

Jackson succeeds better on building tension and painting a story in earlier seduction tracks. "Heartbreaker's" achievement lies primarily in its sonic inventiveness. "I find extraordinary beauty in [such] fast songs," writes the *Village Voice*'s Frank Cogan, "He and Rodney Jerkins ... pull in fuzzes and buzzes and whirs—the edginess of techno—truncated clangs, little frog-croaking bass notes.... I don't know if it's a beauty I'll ever care about. The beauty in previous Michael Jackson albums found *me*. But sometimes this took a while: I was several months into *Bad* before I suddenly felt it when he sang, 'He came into her apartment/He left the bloodstains on the carpet'—but once I did, much of the album seemed deft, sharp, and sad."

3. INVINCIBLE

(Written and composed by Michael Jackson, Rodney Jerkins, Fred Jerkins III, LaShawn Daniels, and Norman Gregg. Produced by Michael Jackson and Rodney Jerkins. Recorded by Bruce Swedien and Stuart Brawley. Digital editing by Stuart Brawley. Rap recorded by Bob Brown. Mixed by Bruce Swedien, Rodney Jerkins, and Stuart Brawley. Music programmed by Michael Jackson and Rodney Jerkins. Lead vocal: Michael Jackson. Background vocals: Michael Jackson. Rap performed by Fats)

By the time the title track rolls around (the third Jackson–Jerkins collaboration), some listeners might feel a bit overwhelmed by the sonic assault. Previous Jackson records typically used this space to ease into a ballad or mid-tempo joint ("Stranger in Moscow," "Baby Be Mine"). However, Jackson offers one more heavy-hitting rhythm track, before delving into variations of R&B/soul on the next four songs.

"Invincible" is a clear example of Jackson's attempt to be current and relevant in the new-millennium R&B scene. There are elements of Timbaland, Usher, Jay-Z, and R. Kelly (all of whom, of course, drew inspiration from Jackson for their own sound). A steely hip-hop/soul hybrid, the track moves to a slow, rugged, metal-clanging beat as Jackson pleads for the love of a girl. In its 2001 review, *Rolling Stone* described it as "fleet, durable R&B minimalism."

The rapper Fats—who was also featured on "Heartbreaker"—makes a return appearance, free-styling over the song's heavy backbeat. Jackson, meanwhile, simultaneously laments a breakup and seduces with promises. "His singing is sassy, defiant, and forceful," wrote Robert Hilburn. Yet there is also a semi-detached pathos to the song as he longs for a love he seems to know will always elude him.

"Invincible" concludes the opening chamber of the album, a showcase of pristine, cutting edge, sonically experimental R&B rhythm tracks that earned the praise and respect of critics and peers alike.

4. BREAK OF DAWN

(Written and composed by Dr. Freeze and Michael Jackson. Produced by Michael Jackson and Dr. Freeze. Lead vocal: Michael Jackson. Background vocals: Michael Jackson and Dr. Freeze. All musical instruments: Michael Jackson, Dr. Freeze, Rodney Jerkins, and Teddy Riley. Recorded by Mike Ging, Brad Gilderman, Humberto Gatica, Dexter Simmons, and George Mayers. Drum programming: Michael Jackson and Brad Buxer. Digital editing: Harvey Mason Jr. and Stuart Brawley. Mixed by Humberto Gatica, Teddy Riley, and George Mayers)

After the up-tempo grind of the first three tracks, "Break of Dawn" is a smooth and sensual release. "Rarely since *Thriller* has the performer exuded so much warmth," wrote music critic Sal Cinquemani. "The subtle harmonies and simple arrangements . . . not only recall the time period but wisely update it." Actually, perhaps the track it most closely resembles is "Liberian Girl" from *Bad*. Its sonic ambience, lush production, and romantic lyrics are intended to capture the way love and imagination can transport us. Where Jackson in the past often associated sex with secrecy ("In the Closet") or guilt ("Dirty Diana"), here he embraces sexual intimacy with no reservations or fears. It is as natural and beautiful as the birdsong that unobtrusively appears throughout the track.

Indeed, the entire song is a Keats-like celebration of the senses. The couple is literally in a world of their own making. It's physical ("Hold my hand/Feel the sweat"), but it is also metaphysical. He asks her to use her imagination to experience things she's "never known." There are numerous travel metaphors and escape metaphors. The idea is that they are moving away from social constraints into something more natural, connected, pure and beautiful.

Jackson cowrote and coproduced the song with Dr. Freeze (who also worked with Michael on excellent non-album cuts such as "A Place With No Name" and "Blue Gangsta"). Its fluid rhythm, exotic atmosphere, and passionate vocals make "Break of Dawn" a favorite on the album for many fans.

5. HEAVEN CAN WAIT

(Written and composed by Michael Jackson, Teddy Riley, Andreao Heard, Nate Smith, Teron Beal, E. Laues, and K. Quiller. Produced by Michael Jackson and Teddy Riley. Coproduced by Andreao Heard and Nate Smith. Recorded by Teddy Riley, Bruce Swedien, and George Mayers. Digital editing: Teddy Riley and George Mayers. Mixed by Teddy Riley, Bruce Swedien, and George Mayers. Orchestra arranged and conducted by Jeremy Lubbock. Lead vocal: Michael Jackson. Background vocals: Michael Jackson. Additional background vocals: Dr. Freeze and "Que")

The first of four *Invincible* collaborations with *Dangerous* producer Teddy Riley, "Heaven Can Wait" is every bit as smooth as "Break of Dawn," but explores a different emotion. With its tight, textured harmonies and classic R&B feel, it feels like an updated variation of the Bee Gees. Many critics praised the song as one of the album's best offerings. While *Invincible*'s rhythm tracks convey a mechanical minimalism, the feel here is warm and rich. Jackson's passionate pleadings ride a stuttering beat in the verses before dissolving like air into the chorus. Mark Anthony Neal described it as "one of Jackson's best vocal performances since *Thriller*'s 'Lady in My Life.'" It is a song that undoubtedly had the potential to be a big R&B hit, had Sony released it as a single.

Jackson was introduced to an early demo of the track by producer Teddy Riley. "When I did that song with him," Riley recalls, "he held his heart and he said 'Teddy, is this mine?' I said, 'It's yours if you want it,

Michael.' He's like: 'I want it, let's go get it!' He was so excited. . . . He said, 'I want that song. I need that song in my life.' Jackson subsequently tweaked the structure, sound and lyrics.

The song is about the desire to elude death. The singer has finally found love and joy, but now dreads it will be taken from him. "Tell the angels no," he sings, "I don't want to leave my baby alone." This fear is in some ways perfectly consistent with Jackson's earlier work. Yet when previous tracks conveyed isolation ("leave me alone," "Billy Jean is not my lover"), Jackson now speaks for a collective "us." "Just leave us alone," he pleads at the end. "Please leave us alone" (interestingly, however, in the final gasps he returns back to "leave me alone").The painful emotion conveyed in these final lines is genuine. The fear isn't so much death itself as it is separation and a return to loneliness. The track is a supplication for time, to love and be loved without interference or intrusion.

6. YOU ROCK MY WORLD

(Written and composed by Michael Jackson, Rodney Jerkins, Fred Jerkins III, LaShawn Daniels, and Nora Payne. Produced by Michael Jackson and Rodney Jerkins. Recorded by Brad Gilderman, Rodney Jerkins, Jean-Marie Horvat, Dexter Simmons, and Stuart Brawley. Digital editing by Harvey Mason Jr. and Stuart Brawley. Mixed by Bruce Swedien and Rodney Jerkins. Lead vocal: Michael Jackson. Background vocals: Michael Jackson. Intro: Michael Jackson and Chris Tucker. All musical instruments performed by Michael Jackson and Rodney Jerkins)

"You Rock My World" was Jackson's last *Billboard* Top Ten hit, peaking at #10 in the United States (the song did better abroad, where it reached #1 in France and #2 in the United Kingdom). The initial reaction to the song was mixed. Some critics and fans felt Jackson was simply repeating formulas and described it as "safe" and "unoriginal." Others, however, saw it as a return to form. "[It is his] least forced, most seamless single [in ages]," wrote *Entertainment Weekly*'s David Browne. "A simple, taut mesh of unwavering dance beat and strings."

The album cut begins with a slightly humorous (and slightly awkward) exchange with comedian Chris Tucker that once again seems like an attempt to be current (for some reason it was difficult to imagine Michael Jackson really saying, "She's bangin'" about a girl). Once the bass line sets in, however, he slides into the song as naturally as into a sequined glove. From there, it's vintage Michael Jackson: a pulsing beat, exuberant strings, and a vocal performance that, as *Rolling Stone* observed, "recall[s] the singer's work with Quincy Jones by way of finely sculpted and exquisitely voiced rhythm tracks and vibrating vocal harmonies."

This indeed was what cowriter and coproducer Rodney Jerkins was going for on the song. "It's like Michael back to the melodies," he explained. "It makes you want to dance. It's a feel-good song."

Indeed, the high-energy, infectious tune holds up well with other similar Jackson dance classics ("The Way You Make Me Feel," "Remember the Time," "P.Y.T."). "Jackson sings with more funk finesse than he has in ages," writes Jon Dolan, "gelling perfectly with disco strings, lush harmonies and a sumptuous groove."

7. BUTTERFLIES

(Written and composed by Andre Harris and Marsha Ambrosius. Produced by Michael Jackson and Andre Harris. Recorded by Andre Harris and Bruce Swedien. Assistant engineering by Vidal Davis. Mixed by Bruce Swedien. Lead vocal: Michael Jackson. Background vocals: Michael Jackson and Marsha Ambrosius. Horns: Norman Jeff Bradshaw and Matt Cappy. All music instruments by Andre Harris)

For many fans and critics, the soulful "Butterflies" is one of the hidden gems of Michael Jackson's late career. Like "Heaven Can Wait," it reminds people of what made Jackson's voice such a revelation in the first place, yet benefits from added maturity and sophistication. Though Sony never officially released "Butterflies" as a single, it quickly became an underground hit, particularly in urban areas like New York City. Given the enthusiastic response, many people simply couldn't understand why it wasn't promoted as the new sound of Michael Jackson. "It would have opened people's minds," music critic Steven Ivory told NPR. "Butterflies" still managed to reach #13 on the *Billboard* Hot 100 and #2 on the Hot R&B/Hip-Hop Singles chart on the strength of air play alone.

The song was introduced to Jackson by longtime friend and record executive, John McClain. Jackson liked what he heard in the track by Floetry, a young neo-jazz/soul duo from England. Marsha Ambrosius recalls receiving a message from the King of Pop in 2000: "This really light voice comes out of the answering machine: 'I'm really interested in that stuff coming out of *A Touch of Jazz*. That Floetry stuff is really cool.' It was Michael Jackson!"

After receiving several potential demos, Jackson chose "Butterflies." A few months later Ambrosius and Natalie Stewart were in the studio working with him on the song. "It was incredible," recalled Ambrosius of the experience, "because he continually asked, 'Marsh, what's the next harmony? Girls, does this sound right? What do you think? Is this what you were looking for?' He was so open."

"It is not too overstated to suggest that 'Butterflies' is one of Jackson's most significant R&B recordings in some time," argued music critic Mark Anthony Neal. "Jackson opens the song with a growl-like murmur of a tenor, but the song takes off in the second verse when he pushes his range to a breathy lilting falsetto that powerfully captures the vulnerability that the song's lyrics attempt to convey."

"Butterflies" has become one of Jackson's most highly regarded late works, and continues to be "discovered" by music lovers who missed it the first go-round.

8. SPEECHLESS

(Written and composed by Michael Jackson. Produced by Michael Jackson. Digital editing by Brad Buxer and Stuart Brawley. Recorded by Bruce Swedien, Brad Buxer, and Stuart Brawley. Mixed by Bruce Swedien. Arranged by Michael Jackson. Lead vocal: Michael Jackson. Orchestra arranged and conducted by Michael Jackson and Jeremy Lubbock. Choir by Andraé Crouch and the Andraé Crouch Singers Choir. Keyboards: Brad Buxer. Viola/ Contractor: Novi Novoq. Viola: Thomas Tally. Violins: Peter Kent, Gina Kronstadt, Robin Lentz, Kirstin Fife, and John Wittenberg)

The ballads on *Invincible* were generally considered hit or miss by critics. As sentimental as it may be, "Speechless" is a hit. Written, composed, and arranged by Jackson, the song is a gorgeous Broadway-esque ballad that puts Jackson's signature vocal ability on full display. *NME* described it as the "first really soaring tune on the album." It is certainly one of his purest expressions of joy. Like his gospel songs, the climax reaches a sort of spiritual transcendence that is uncommon to most pop music.

The track begins a cappella, conveying a vulnerability and intimacy that recalls "She's Out of My Life," before gradually building to a sublime crescendo. The soaring orchestra—co-arranged by Jackson, Brad Buxer, and Jeremy Lubbock—is simple, but breathtaking at its climax. "He wanted it to be this kind of ecstasy," said Buxer. "He said, 'I want you to play these arpeggios.' I thought it would be too busy, too sweet. When the modulations start coming, you hear all this arpeggiating going on on the keyboard. It's not sequenced; it's all playing. That's what he wanted."

Jackson wrote the song while staying in Germany. He recalls playing with children when the inspiration for the song came. "There are these two sweet little kids, a girl and a boy, and they're so innocent," he said in a 2001 interview. "They're the quintessential form of innocence, and just being in their presence I felt completely speechless, 'cause I felt I was looking in the face of God whenever I saw them. They inspired me to write 'Speechless.'" Once Jackson had the song in his head, he immediately called Brad Buxer. "I got a call at 4:30 in the morning," recalls Buxer. "He sang all the parts over the phone. At 6:30 a.m. it was done."

The result was a love song about a pure, unconditional, safe kind of love he had never really sung about before (perhaps because he had never fully experienced it until he had children). "When I'm with you," he sings, "I'm in the light/Where I cannot be found/It's as though I am standing in/The place called Hallowed Ground."

9. 2000 WATTS

(Written and composed by Michael Jackson, Teddy Riley, Tyrese Gibson, and J. Henson. Produced by Michael Jackson and Teddy Riley. Recorded by Teddy Riley and George Mayers. Digital editing: Teddy Riley and George Mayers. Additional keyboard programming: Michael Jackson and Brad Buxer. Mixed by Bruce Swedien, Teddy Riley, and George Mayers. Lead vocal: Michael Jackson. Background vocals: Michael Jackson. Additional background vocals: Teddy Riley)

Many listeners hardly recognized Jackson on "2000 Watts," an ode to sound (and sound technology) that features the singer in an uncharacteristically deep baritone voice. There has been some debate, in fact, about whether it is Jackson's "natural voice" or whether it has been digitally altered in some way. According to Teddy Riley and engineer Stuart Brawley, however, it is indeed his real voice. Following the high tenor/falsetto bliss of "Speechless," it provides a sharp contrast, showcasing Jackson's range and versatility (vocally and stylistically).

"2000 Watts" was cowritten by Riley and R&B singer Tyrese Gibson for the latter's album by the same title; Jackson, however, fell in love with a demo of the song, and Gibson gladly handed it over. True to its title, "2000 Watts" tests the strength of speaker systems. "Hard, hammering and chant-like," observed *New Music Express*, "this is a definite highlight. With minimal industrial production, it's a rough equivalent to 'They Don't Care About Us' on *HIStory*. The tribal feel underlines that this album is really good at rhythm."

Indeed, many pointed to the song as one of the album's most instantly accessible and energetic dance tracks. "Jackson connects marvelously with '2000 Watts,'" wrote music critic Robert Hilburn, calling it a "celebration of dance music's therapeutic powers that should be a club anthem." A cursory glance at the lyrics also reveals its sexual undertones. For "2000 Watts," eroticizing the sound and machinery of the medium shows how exhilarating music-making can be.

10. YOU ARE MY LIFE

(Written and composed by Michael Jackson, Babyface, Carol Bayer Sager, and John McClain. Produced by Michael Jackson and Babyface. Engineered by Paul Boutin. Mixed by John Gass. Strings arranged by Meyers. Engineered by Tommy Vicari. Lead vocal: Michael Jackson. Background vocals: Michael Jackson and Babyface. Acoustic guitar: Babyface. Keyboards: Babyface. Drum programming: Babyface. Bass guitar: Babyface. Choir: Jason Edmonds, Nathon Walton, Tabia Ivery, and Lynne Fiddmont-Lindsey)

"You Are My Life" was a last-minute inclusion on *Invincible*, replacing the up-tempo "Shout" just five weeks before the album was released. "The writers first played it for Michael on a Thursday," wrote biographer J. Randy Taraborrelli. "He loved it—changed the lyrics from 'You Are My World' to 'You Are My Life,' and then recorded it the next evening."

The song no doubt had personal significance for Jackson, whose two young children had brought new meaning to his life. Indeed, in many ways, it is the most honest musical expression of what his children meant to him.

"Once, all alone," he sings,

I was lost in a world of strangers
No one to trust
On my own, I was lonely
You . . . suddenly appeared
It was cloudy before, but now it's all clear
You took away the fear
And you brought me back to the light

Later in the song, he further describes the transformation/salvation they inspired:

Now I wake up every day
With this smile upon my face
No more tears, no more pain
'Cause you love me
You help me understand
That love is the answer to all that I am
And I'm a better man
Since you taught me by sharing your life

"You Are My Life" was the collaborative effort of some gifted songwriters—Babyface, Carole Bayer Sager, John McClain, and Jackson. Many critics, however, felt it was the weakest of the ballads, citing its lethargic pacing and cliché-ridden chorus. *Rolling Stone* called it a smooth L.A. production with a "terribly off Babyface."

Yet "You Are My Life" is a song that has been reevaluated a bit more compassionately since Jackson's death. J. Randy Taraborrelli called it a "sparkling . . . standout" ballad. What starts as a slow, guitar-strumming lamentation, gradually builds momentum and grows into a sublime celebration of life. Jackson wrings the song for all its worth in the last half. "You gave me hope when all hope is lost," he cries. "You opened my eyes when I couldn't see/Love was always here waiting for me."

11. PRIVACY

(Written and composed by Michael Jackson, Rodney Jerkins, Fred Jerkins III, LaShawn Daniels, and Bernard Bell. Produced by Michael Jackson and Rodney Jerkins. Recorded by Rodney Jerkins, Jean-Marie Horvat, and Brad Gilderman. Digital editing: Harvey Mason Jr. and Paul Cruz. Mixed by Jean-Marie Horvat and Rodney Jerkins. String arrangement: David Campbell. Lead vocal: Michael Jackson. Background vocals: Michael Jackson and LaShawn Daniels. Guitars: Michael Thompson. Bass: Nathan East. Drums: Gerald Hayword and Emanuel Baker)

"Privacy" has Jackson on the attack, as he growls about the increasingly unethical tactics of the media over a grinding beat and the sound of flashing cameras. The song hits as hard as anything on the album, its aggressive tone supplemented by symphonic strings and Slash's ripping guitar fills. The content is, of course, a Michael Jackson staple. Indeed, it is fair to say that no popular musician of the 20th century was as consistently fierce a media critic as Michael Jackson. As a mass-communicator himself, he understood the enormous power the media held over the public's perception of reality. Songs like "Privacy" were intended to both alert people to its deception ("You've got the people confused . . .") and assert his humanity in the face of dehumanizing tactics ("You try to get me to lose the man I really am").

As on previous media-aimed tracks, Jackson is shrewd enough to make the song about more than himself. In the second verse, he recounts the senseless death of Lady Diana, who was, notoriously, being chased by tabloid reporters when her car fatally crashed in 1996. "My friend was chased and confused, like many others I knew/But on that cold winter night, my pride was snatched away."

Jackson's identification with another "celebrity" hounded by the paparazzi may not elicit much sympathy from the average listener. Yet Jackson clearly feels there is a larger "message" at stake in such a tragedy. His "pride is snatched away" because of a realization that his value as a human being is reduced to how much profit he can generate for a preying media. He is addressing, in other words, a system of enslavement and exploitation. Desperate to avoid this fate, he shakes his fist at the enclosing paparazzi, warning, "Get away from me!"

12. DON'T WALK AWAY

(Written and composed by Michael Jackson, Teddy Riley, Richard Carlton Stites, and Reed Vertelney. Produced by Michael Jackson and Teddy Riley. Coproduced by Richard Stites. Recorded by Teddy Riley and George Mayers. Digital editing by Teddy Riley and George Mayers. Mixed by Bruce Swedien, Teddy Riley, and George Mayers. Lead and background vocals: Michael Jackson. Additional background vocals: Richard Stites)

"Don't Walk Away" isn't a song that drew much attention, yet it could be Jackson's most understated, authentic expression of heartbreak since "She's Out of My Life." Cowritten by Jackson, Teddy Riley and Richard Stites, the track is different than the typically lavish Jackson ballad. Indeed, it is probably as close to country as Jackson got in his entire solo career. With a stripped-down, blues-tinged soul, Jackson articulates its emotions with nuance and conviction. Music critic Mike Heyliger described the track as a "stunningly heartbreaking ballad that the Backstreet Boys would still salivate in their sleep for."

In its most literal interpretation, the song could be about Jackson's relationship with Lisa Marie Presley. More generally, it is simply about the pain and despair of lost love. "Don't walk away," he pleads. "See I just can't find the right thing to say/I try but all my pain gets in the way." Later in the song, he laments all his dreams being broken but feels helpless to do anything about it. Jackson brilliantly captures the emptiness and anguish of the lyrics in his vocal. As Motown legend Marvin Gaye once put it: "Michael will never lose the quality that separates the merely sentimental from the truly heartfelt. It's rooted in the blues, and no matter what genre Michael is singing, that boy's got the blues."

13. CRY

(Written and composted by R. Kelly. Produced by Michael Jackson and R. Kelly. Recorded by Mike Ging, Brad Gilderman, and Humberto Gatica. Mixed by Michael Jackson and Mick Guzauski. Choir arrangement: R. Kelly. Drum programming: Michael Jackson and Brad Buxer. Keyboard programming: Michael Jackson and Brad Buxer. Lead vocal: Michael Jackson. Choir: Andraé Crouch and the Andraé Crouch Singers Choir. Percussion: Paulinho Da Costa. Drums: John Robinson. Guitars: Michael Landau)

Following the heartache of "Don't Walk Away" comes a more universal lamentation. "Cry" revisits a sentiment Jackson had been delivering his entire solo career. Its roots go back as far as the Old Testament as poet-prophets like Job and Jeremiah assessed a world of suffering, injustice, and despair and tried to find hope in the darkness. They also tried to provoke awareness and action. Similarly, Jackson "cries" because he sees tragedy all around him and internalizes it. He sings of people barely holding on, not knowing when the pain will end; he sings of "stories buried and untold," of people "hiding the truth"; he sings of illusions and masks ("faces filled with madness"; "people laugh when they're feeling sad"). Then, in the chorus, he makes a plea (with his listeners and himself) to somehow overcome. What connects us isn't pretending the tragedy doesn't exist, but seeing it for what it is and confronting it as a collective.

The idea of being connected to one another through our suffering and grief was certainly relevant to its historical context. Released shortly after the tragedy of September 11, 2001, "Cry" was exactly the kind of song that was needed in such a devastating moment. Some critics claimed it was too simplistic and messianic; parts of the chorus can indeed come across that way. But the core of the song is much deeper, looking inward and outward at the same time, and offering no easy answers. As a lamentation, it conveys the "sound of trauma." Listen to the desolate wind blow in the beginning and the slow, aching drumbeat. It conveys an alienation that recalls the intro to "Stranger in Moscow." Jackson's vocals are not celebratory, but melancholy and restrained. As with previous anthems, it takes the help of the choir (symbolizing community) for him to find hope and resolve. The majestic call and response he engages in at the climax is classic Michael Jackson, demonstrating the purposeful communication that must take place if we are ever to "change the world."

14. THE LOST CHILDREN

(Written and composed by Michael Jackson. Produced by Michael Jackson. Arranged by Michael Jackson. Keyboard programming: Michael Jackson and Brad Buxer. Narrative: Baby Rubba and Prince Jackson. Youth choir: Tom Bahler. Digital editing: Brad Buxer and Stuart Brawley. Recorded by Bruce Swedien, Brad Buxer, and Stuart Brawley. Mixed by Bruce Swedien. Audio snippets from The Twilight Zone *courtesy of CBS Broadcasting Inc.)*

"The Lost Children" was an easy target for critics, one of whom called it a "creepy, airheaded companion piece to the pictures of missing kids on milk cartons." Music executives undoubtedly discouraged its inclusion on *Invincible*. While it is a finely crafted pop waltz with a beautiful melody, it didn't fit the image, style or sound of a traditional pop/R&B star (it also, of course, reminded people of Jackson's long-speculated-about relationship with children). In terms of album coherence, it seemed strange on the surface next to songs such as "2000 Watts" and "You Rock My World." It says something then about Jackson's guts and creative independence that the song made it onto his high-stakes "comeback album." He knew the majority of critics would scoff; but he also knew for whom and for what the song was written—and that mattered more to him.

Jackson was never as actively engaged on behalf of children's rights as he was in the years leading up to *Invincible*. He worked with a range of people, including Nelson Mandela and Rabbi Shmuley Boteach, to raise funds and political will; he worked on a book about the importance of parenting with unconditional love; he gave a well-received speech at Oxford University calling for a renewed focus on reversing disturbing trends of neglect, abuse, and hyper-socialization. Along with his artistic ambitions, he saw his work on behalf of children as his life's purpose. "The Lost Children," then, was Jackson's attempt to fuse his music with a cause that mattered deeply to him. If "Cry" was a lamentation for the world, "The Lost Children" was a prayer for those most vulnerable.

In his Oxford speech, he explained:

> Here is a typical day in America—six youths under the age of 20 will commit suicide, 12 children under the age of 20 will die from firearms—remember this is a *day*, not a year—399 kids will be arrested for drug abuse, 1,352 babies will be born to teen mothers. This is happening in one of the richest, most developed countries in the history of the world.... It is self-evident that children are thundering against the neglect, quaking against the indifference and crying out just to be noticed. The various child protection agencies in the US say that millions of children are victims of maltreatment in the form of neglect, in the average year. Yes, neglect. In rich homes, privileged homes, wired to the hilt with every electronic gadget. Homes where parents come home, but they're not really home, because their heads are still at the office. And their kids? Well, their kids just make do with whatever emotional crumbs they get. And you don't get much from endless TV, computer games and videos. These hard, cold numbers which for me,

wrench the soul and shake the spirit, should indicate to you why I have devoted so much of my time and resources into making our new Heal the Kids initiative.

A simple plea on behalf of the neglected and abandoned, "The Lost Children" may not fit the typical mold for a pop album, but for Jackson it didn't matter. He wrote and recorded the song for children like him—those forced to endure too much too soon. He felt it was crucial, regardless of the backlash, to give them a voice through his music.

15. WHATEVER HAPPENS

(Written and composed by Michael Jackson, Teddy Riley, Gil Cang, J. Quay, and Geoffrey Williams. Produced by Michael Jackson and Teddy Riley. Recorded by Teddy Riley, George Mayers, and Bruce Swedien. Digital editing: Teddy Riley and George Mayers. Mixed by Bruce Swedien, Teddy Riley, and George Mayers. Lead and background vocals: Michael Jackson. Additional background vocals: Mario Vasquez and Mary Brown. Orchestra arranged and conducted by Jeremy Lubbock. Guitar: Carlos Santana and Rick Williams. Whistling: Carlos Santana and Stuart Brawley)

"Whatever Happens" is arguably the best song on the album. A haunting Latin-infused dance groove featuring guitar legend Carlos Santana, it was intended to be one of the album's major singles and music videos before Sony decided to cancel all promotions. Still, critics nearly unanimously praised the track. *Rolling Stone* described it as an "exceptional song" while *Pop Matters* called it "brilliant." "It would've made for an inspired choice for a single," wrote music critic Mike Heyliger, "and could've made for an awesome video. It's got a slow motion, cinematic feel, Michael's voice is top-notch, and Carlos Santana comes on board to add a blistering guitar solo. Classic stuff here."

Indeed, with its eerie whistling and passionate vocals, "Whatever Happens" evokes something intoxicating. "The music is Latin-based," wrote *Rolling Stone*'s James Hunter, "a deep brew of Jeremy Lubbock's strings and Carlos Santana's guitar. Jackson and producer Teddy Riley make something really handsome and smart: They allow you to concentrate on the track's momentous rhythms, Santana's passionate interjections and Lubbock's wonderfully arranged symphonic sweeps" as Jackson narrates with "a jagged intensity."

Lyrically, it is one of Jackson's more subtle and mature efforts. Cowritten with Teddy Riley, "Whatever Happens" narrates the story of two people who still love each other deeply, but fear their relationship is in peril. "He gives another smile," Jackson sings,

Tries to understand her side
To show that he cares
She can't stay in the room
She's consumed
With everything that's been goin' on

Jackson smartly allows these lines to hint without fully revealing why they are at odds, with what she is "consumed," or what's been "going on." The ambiguity allows the listener to fill in the gaps. In a later verse, Jackson describes a couple desperately trying, but failing, to communicate.

He's working day and night, thinks he'll make her happy
Forgetting all the dreams that he had
He doesn't realize it's not the end of the world
It doesn't have to be that bad
She tries to explain, "It's you that makes me happy,"

Whatever, whatever, whatever

The final line of seeming indifference ("whatever, whatever, whatever") paradoxically leads into the chorus ("Whatever happens, don't let go of my hand"), casting an uncertainty about the promises they make each other. In the outro, Jackson continues to plead desperately, but finds no resolution.

The song returns the listener to the intimate pain and isolation of "Don't Walk Away." With the tension still lingering in the air, it sets the stage perfectly for the album's final statement.

16. THREATENED

(Written and composed by Michael Jackson, Rodney Jerkins, Fred Jerkins III, and LaShawn Daniels. Produced by Michael Jackson and Rodney Jerkins. Recorded by Stuart Brawley. Digital editing: Stuart Brawley. Mixed by Bruce Swedien, Rodney Jerkins, and Stuart Brawley. Lead and background vocals: Michael Jackson. All musical instruments played by Michael Jackson and Rodney Jerkins. Audio snippets of Rod Serling courtesy of CBS Broadcasting Inc.)

While it is relatively unknown (buried at the end of Jackson's least-known album), "Threatened" is a worthy capstone to its horror-themed predecessors ("Thriller," "Ghosts," "Is It Scary"). It is also an appropriate official finale to Michael Jackson's catalog, exploring so many of the themes—monstrosity, metamorphosis, fear, deception, and the interrogation of normative values and expectations that preoccupied him throughout his career. People often forget that Jackson remained just as fascinated by the dark terror of Poe as he did the innocent whimsy of J. M. Barrie. "Threatened" represents this dark, cryptic, Gothic dimension of Jackson. Featuring creepily patched-together narration from a resurrected Rod Serling (creator of *The Twilight Zone*), the bone-crunching track ends *Invincible* with a wickedly subversive twist.

Jackson planned to create a horror-themed short film for the song, complete with cutting-edge special effects, but when Sony canceled promotions for the album, it meant no budget for videos. Sonically and lyrically, however, "Threatened" leaves plenty of stimuli for the imagination: enclosing walls, distant screams, dark halls, ominous warnings. Against a "compulsive upward chord sequence" and tomb-sliding backbeat, Jackson sings from the perspective of the monster: "I'm the living dead, the dark thoughts in your head."

By "becoming" a monster, Jackson is able to speak through an imagined voice or character. "You're fearing me, 'cause you know I'm a beast," he says. It is a role he clearly relishes (going back to "Thriller" and even before). In the chorus, he warns: "You should be watching me, you should feel threatened/While you sleep, while you creep, you should be threatened." Music critic Sal Cinquemani described the track as a "stand-out . . . new millennium 'Thriller.'" While the comparison to "Thriller" is natural, however, "Threatened" must also be understood as a continuation of Jackson's Gothic expressions on *Blood on the Dance Floor*, in which he really began to explore the psychological and social implications of the genre. One of the implications of a song like "Threatened" is that monstrosity is a social construction that makes its way into people's minds. Michael Jackson is a monster because of what he represents to some people, because he disrupts society's sense of what is normal and natural. Like "Is It Scary," however, "Threatened" turns the tables, forcing us to question how we delineate normality and monstrosity. Often those most "normal" on the outside are most "monstrous" inside. In Gothic art, this logic is often reversed: the grotesque is often presented on the exterior (in exaggerated form), but it often symbolizes something deeper, something more deeply buried.

"The major ingredient of any recipe for fear is the unknown," says Rod Serling in the song's introduction. "Threatened," then, forces us to consider the ingredients that make a monster a monster. Why do we fear it? Why is it threatening? How do we deal with this fear and perceived threat?

"Threatened" also returns the album to the technological questions it raises on the first track (and the cover). It is, in essence, a digital "Frankenstein"—a patchwork of disparate parts reassembled into something strange and new. The lines from Rod Serling were pieced together from a variety of different *Twilight Zone* episodes. The sound effects—ravens cawing, bells tolling, etc.—were also pulled from a technological time machine and reappropriated for the song. Nothing about the song is analog—the drums, keyboards, everything is technologically produced. The only thing that is natural is Jackson's voice—though toward the end of the song, he distorts that as well through a sort of intentional glitch-effect, brilliantly conveying his singularity with the machines that mediate what we hear. There are a variety of potential interpretations for this, one being (to paraphrase Marshall McLuhan), that the medium is the monster. Perhaps it is only perceived as such because it is "unknown" and, therefore, threatening. As Dennis Yeo Kah Sin notes: "These transhuman manifestations . . . interrogate fundamental assumptions of our humanity and existence as the horror of the artificial human . . . re-emerges in an up-to-date form with the possibility of new kinds of simulated life . . . The terror of the Gothic monster lies precisely in its indeterminate constitution."

The song ends with Serling's provocative conclusion: "What you just witnessed could be the end of a particularly terrifying nightmare. It isn't; it's the beginning."

A fascinating techno-Gothic expression at the cusp of the Information Age, "Threatened" is a fitting conclusion to Jackson's last fully realized album.

OTHER NOTABLE *INVINCIBLE*-ERA SONGS:

A PLACE WITH NO NAME (recorded 1998, unreleased)
A very nice revision of America's classic hit, "A Horse With No Name." Jackson recorded the track in 1998 with R&B producer Dr. Freeze. A portion of it was leaked shortly after Jackson's death in 2009.

ANOTHER DAY (recorded 1999, unreleased)
(See Appendix)

BEAUTIFUL GIRL (recorded 1998, released on *Michael Jackson: The Ultimate Collection*, 2004)
A lush ballad Jackson wrote and worked on with Brad Buxer. The song contains sublime production and gorgeous harmonies. It also features Jackson singing in a deeper register than usual to wonderful effect.

BLUE GANGSTA (recorded 1999, unreleased)
The long-lost sequel to "Smooth Criminal," "Blue Gangsta" is an outstanding yet-to-be-released gem that draws inspiration from sources as disparate as Old Hollywood-era gangster films, Westerns (note the standoff whistling), cabaret, funk, and jazz. It makes for an adventurous and exciting listening experience. From the big cinematic brass, to the Italian-style accordion, to the wonderful harmonies, this is undoubtedly a landmark track for Jackson that would have made for a great short film. An unofficial hip-hop remix of the song was leaked by rapper Tempamental in 2006. The original song was recorded with Dr. Freeze in 1999.

CAN'T GET YOUR WEIGHT OFF OF ME (recorded 2000, unreleased)
A hip Jackson–Jerkins rhythm track with a similar sound to "Invincible."

ESCAPE (recorded 2000, unreleased)
A funky, sonically inventive rhythm track that juxtaposes a taut, mechanical beat with smooth, airy harmonies. The song, which begins with a jail break, is a sort of cross between "Speed Demon" and "Scream" as Jackson expresses his desire to "get away from a system" that stifles and entraps him. He worked on the song with Rodney Jerkins. A version leaked in 2002. It has since become a fan-favorite, but has yet to be officially released.

FALL AGAIN (recorded 1999, released on *Michael Jackson: The Ultimate Collection*, 2004)
A gorgeous, haunting ballad Jackson worked on with Walter Afanasieff and Robin Thicke. Jackson never fully completed the song, but an excellent demo was released on *The Ultimate Collection*. It is one of many non-album hidden gems and a fan favorite.

I HAVE THIS DREAM (recorded 1999, unreleased)
A new-millennium anthem Jackson worked on with David Foster and Carole Bayer Sager. It was talked about quite a bit before *Invincible* was released but ultimately failed to make the album.

ONE MORE CHANCE (recorded 2001, released on *Number Ones*, 2003)
A nice mid-tempo ballad that almost feels like *Thriller*-era Jackson. It was written by R. Kelly along with "Cry," but ultimately passed up for *Invincible*. The song was later released as the only new track on the greatest hits collection, *Number Ones*.

SHOUT (recorded 2000, unreleased)
A rock/hip-hop adaptation of the Isley Brothers' 1959 hit by the same name. Rather than celebrating like the original, Jackson raps some intense lyrics over a jagged beat and screaming guitar. "Living encaged like animals and cannibals," he says in one verse, "Eating each other alive just to survive the nine to five." It was scheduled to appear on *Invincible* until the final month when Jackson decided to replace it with "You Are My Life."

SLAVE TO THE RHYTHM (recorded 2003, unreleased)
A great electro-pop club banger Jackson originally worked on with Jimmy Jam and Terry Lewis. Jackson reportedly revisited it many times over the years, most recently with Tricky Stewart.

THE WAY YOU LOVE ME (recorded 2000, *Michael Jackson: The Ultimate Collection*, 2004)
(See Appendix)

WE'VE HAD ENOUGH (recorded 2000, released on *Michael Jackson: The Ultimate Collection*, 2004)
A powerful antiwar track written and produced by Jackson along with Carole Bayer Sager and Rodney Jerkins. One of many tracks strong enough to be on *Invincible*, but instead was released on *The Ultimate Collection* in 2004.

WHAT MORE CAN I GIVE (recorded 1998 and 2001, released in 2001 as digital download)
This Jackson-penned anthem was first used for Nelson Mandela charity concerts—"Michael and Friends and What More Can I Give"—and later to benefit families of the victims of 9/11. One version features just Jackson on vocals while the other features Beyoncé, Céline Dion, and Mariah Carey, among others.

Jackson promotes *Invincible* in Times Square.

CHAPTER 8 THE FINAL YEARS

Michael Jackson's final interview took place in the fall of 2007. He was in Brooklyn with his children where he had agreed to a rare one-on-one exchange and photo shoot with *Ebony* magazine to celebrate the twenty-fifth anniversary of *Thriller*. It was nearly a year before he would commit to the fifty-date *This Is It* O2 Arena concert series in London. It was the first time he had spoken at length since his 2005 trial and acquittal.

Following the trial—an exhausting and arduous six months of humiliation and scrutiny—Jackson had seemingly disappeared. The one-time face of popular music had become a sort of vagabond, an artist in exile. Tabloids occasionally speculated on his whereabouts (Bahrain, Ireland, Las Vegas) or caught glimpses of him with his children in a bookstore or an amusement park. For the most part, though, he had slipped from the public's consciousness. Most assumed his career was over.

Behind the scenes, however, a still compulsively creative and restless Jackson told *Ebony* he was as busy as ever. Indeed, in the years after his 2005 trial, he wrote and recorded dozens of new songs. Some of these were made with longtime creative partners Brad Buxer and Michael Prince; some were with friends such as Eddie Cascio; and some were with contemporary artists and producers such as Will.i.am, Neff-U, Ne-Yo, RedOne and Akon. The new studio album was rumored to be as strong as ever; it was his proof that he hadn't lost the creative magic. In his final years, he would also begin work on a classical album with composer David Michael Frank, and start preparations for his remarkable concert spectacle, *This Is It*, a fifty-show run in London's O2 Arena that may have been the biggest comeback in popular music history.

"I always want to do music that inspires or influences another generation.... I give my all to my work. I want it to just live."

MICHAEL JACKSON, *EBONY*, 2007

Jackson was overwhelmed with the response to his *This Is It* concert series in London.

The public, of course, knew very little of this. In his final years, Jackson was more reclusive than ever, and his management and finances were in disarray. However, those who worked with him or interviewed him during these years could sense a renewed passion and determination. "Sitting on the sofa next to him," observed *Ebony*'s Bryan Monroe in 2007, "you quickly look past the enigmatic icon's light, almost translucent skin and realize that this African American legend is more than just skin deep. More than an entertainer, more than a singer or dancer, this grown-up father of three reveals a confident, controlled and mature man who has a lot of creativity left inside him."

In his final months, Jackson would tell his fellow collaborators that he was so "supercharged" he couldn't sleep at night; his mind wouldn't shut down. "I'm channeling," he told Kenny Ortega. "I'm writing music, and ideas are coming to me and I can't turn it off." Ortega asked him if it was possible that he might put these ideas "on the shelf until after July 13 [when his concert series began]." Jackson replied half-jokingly, "You don't understand—if I'm not there to receive these ideas, God might give them to Prince."

In the period between Michael Jackson's final studio album, *Invincible*, and his death, he continued to work on new material and return to songs that hadn't been released. Jackson had described his most recent work as a potpourri of styles and sounds, ranging from electro to synth-pop to classical. "I like to take sounds and put them under the microscope and just talk about how we want to manipulate the character of it," he explained in a 2007 interview.

Of course, numerous other songs were left off previous albums (many of which have been described in this book). "Michael had a tendency to over-record," said co-executor John Branca said. "He would record 20, 30, 40 songs for one album." Some of these songs were just as good, if not better, than songs that made the final cut. The reasons for not including them were various: sometimes Jackson was saving them or hoping to improve them; sometimes he felt they just didn't fit with the rest of the material. There are an estimated forty to fifty fully finished or close-to-finished songs in the vault that were written and recorded for *Off the Wall* to *Invincible* and were left off his studio albums. Numerous other demos are in various states of completion.

In March 2010, the Michael Jackson estate and Sony announced a seven-year distribution deal that included up to ten new Michael Jackson projects, some of which would include older, unreleased material and some newer. The deal, worth an estimated $250 million, was by far the largest recording contract in history. "We and Sony feel that the future for Michael Jackson is unlimited," said John Branca. "If you look at Elvis and the Beatles, and how their brands are thriving, they only hint at what the future holds for Michael."

Jackson's newer material was recorded with a variety of collaborators in studios all over the world. In the summer of 2002 he recorded some songs with longtime friend, Barry Gibb, including a gorgeous string-laden anthem, "Pray for Peace" (later worked on with Brad Buxer), and a soaring duet entitled "All in Your Name," protesting war in the name of religion. Even during his trial in 2005, he continued to work on new material. His spokeswoman at the time, Raymone Bain, remembers him saying that writing new songs was therapeutic, and he was working on new ideas whenever he could. One of these songs, "From the Bottom of My Heart" (a variation of "I Have This Dream"), was a charity recording intended to benefit the victims of Hurricane Katrina. Another, "You Are So Beautiful," was a tribute to his loyal fans.

Following his 2005 trial, Jackson and his children moved to the Kingdom of Bahrain, a small Middle Eastern island close to Saudi Arabia. There, they lived with a member of the Bahraini royal family, Abdulla Hamad Al-Khalifa, for several months. (The arrangement was set up by Jackson's older brother Jermaine, who was close friends with Sheik Abdulla.) "[Michael] looked beaten," recalls Ahmed Al Kahn. "And so people here, Abdulla, myself, all the people around him really helped Michael recover really quickly. They gave him his space. They let him recoup. They gave him rest. They gave him his privacy." In 2006, a short-lived recording deal was announced between Jackson and Sheik Abdulla's new label, Two Seas Records. Just months later, Jackson and Abdulla parted ways, forming Jackson's own label (the Michael Jackson Company) instead. Jackson worked sporadically in the palace studio during this time, including on songs entitled "Light the Way" and "He Who Makes the Sky Grey." Producer Bill Bottrell, who had worked with Jackson on several tracks in the late eighties and early nineties (including "Black or White"), was called out to work with the singer in Bahrain. However, by the time he arrived, Jackson was gone. Bottrell decided to lay down some grooves at the palace studio anyway in case he and Jackson got together in the future. Unfortunately, they never reunited, and the tracks were never realized. Around this time, Jackson also reached out to old friends such as Rod Temperton and Teddy Riley as well as young contemporary talents such as 50 Cent (who later performed on "Monster") and Kanye West (who later remixed "Billie Jean" for *Thriller 25*).

Later that year, Jackson relocated to Ireland, where he stayed at several beautiful, secluded countryside estates over the next several months. Patrick Nordstrom, who rented his Blackmore Castle in Cork to Jackson for a couple of weeks, described him as a "restless soul," but said Jackson found some peace, refuge, and rejuvenation in his stay. He could play with his children without the constant presence of the paparazzi; he could read and write and plan his future. (One summer night in Cork, Jackson reportedly took his children to a Bob Dylan concert.)

Jackson also spent some time at the estate of friend and fellow dancer Michael Flatley in Castlebridge. "I felt that he was inspired here," said Flatley. "He could be himself completely somehow here, away from the world's eyes." The majority of Jackson's time in Ireland, however, was spent in Westmeath at Grouse Lodge and its nearby Coolatore House, owned by Paddy Dunning. Dunning remembers Jackson being interested in everything about Ireland. He would read the local paper every morning and was fascinated with the country's history, mythology, and music.

Grouse Lodge also had a state-of-the-art studio, which Jackson utilized frequently during his stay. "Michael actually spent most of his time recording in Studio Two," recalls Dunning. "He really seemed to like the sound of that room. What was amazing for me was discovering just how incredible Michael was at playing any instrument. He'd sit at the piano and play all the Beatles songs for us to all sing along to, or get on the drums, or play guitar. Michael was working with people like [Neff-U], Rodney Jerkins, Will.i.am and other musicians, but the tracks he recorded were never finished."

In a rare 2006 interview with *Access Hollywood*, Jackson, shown in the studio with Black Eyed Peas front man Will.i.am, was asked if it felt good to be writing music again. "I never stopped," he said.

Over the next couple of years, Jackson and Will.i.am became close creative partners, recording at least a half-dozen songs together. "I think he's doing wonderful, innovative, positive, great music," Jackson said of Will.i.am. For his part, Will.i.am was thrilled to work with his idol. "Something needs to put a jolt back in the music industry," he said, "and the only thing that can do that is the jolt itself, the energy that sparked the imagination of kids [like me in the first place]."

In Ireland (and later in Las Vegas and Los Angeles), Jackson and Will.i.am worked on a range of grooves, with elements of electro, hip-hop, and disco. "It was going to be out of this world," Will.i.am told the *Daily Mirror*, describing it as primarily a dance album. "Of course they were melodic and as he would say juicy. 'It's so juicy it sounds like something you would just want to eat,' [he said]. The way he described music was just awesome." One song titled "The Future" addressed environmental issues, but with a killer Latin beat. "It was very demanding," Will.i.am told the BBC. "It ordered and demanded people to the dance floor." Another mid-tempo track, called "I'm Gonna Miss You," was inspired by James Brown's death in 2006. Other songs included "I'm Dreamin'") and "The King," which was intended to include Jackson protégés Usher and Ne-Yo. "Man, he still sings like a bird," Will.i.am said in 2006. "He could go anywhere. I think we have a real opportunity to do something here." Once they finished a track, Jackson was careful to ensure it didn't leak. "He was very protective and kept it under lock and key," explained Will.i.am. "After we made it I had to hand back every demo. He was a perfectionist and didn't want anyone to hear it until it was ready." Three Jackson–Will.i.am collaborations were reportedly completed (or nearly completed), with a fourth about seventy-five percent done, and the rest left in the early stages. Some of Jackson and Will.i.am's work was later poised to appear on his first posthumous album, *Michael*; however, Will.i.am later changed his mind, reasoning that since Jackson was such a perfectionist and wasn't able to see the tracks to completion, it would be "disrespectful" to release them.

"He was a great father. People don't realize much of the time he didn't even have a nanny."

After a six-month stay in Ireland, Jackson finally returned to the United States in the winter of 2006, where he rented a home in Las Vegas for several months. Here, Jackson reached out to several former collaborators, including longtime friend Brad Buxer. Jackson, Buxer, and recording engineer Michael Prince worked together, on and off, frequently over the next couple of years. Most of their work took place in Jackson's home, where a makeshift studio was set up in a large second story space that included a dance floor and an office. It allowed Jackson to work in a comfortable environment with people he trusted. Some days he would simply wake up and work in his pajamas; other days, they would drive over to the Palms Hotel and use the studio there.

Jackson was happy to be working with old friends again. "Some days we would work two hours, some days eight hours, depending on his kids' schedule," recalls Michael Prince. "He was a great father. People don't realize much of the time he didn't even have a nanny. He was a single father. He'd make them breakfast, talk to them, take them out to see shows, let them watch him work. Then he'd call a tutor over and they would study while we recorded."

Jackson also recorded with producer Ron "Neff-U" Feemster (who had previously worked with Beyoncé and Ne-Yo) and Senegalese-American recording artist Akon in 2007. "He's incredible," said Akon, after recording with Jackson in Las Vegas. "He's a genius. Just to be in the same room, I felt everything I wanted to accomplish in life has been achieved. That aura... that's how incredible that aura is.... The way he thinks... some artists think regional, some think national, I was thinking international. He thinks planets. It's on another level."

Jackson and Akon worked on a few songs together, but only one was completed and it leaked just a couple of months later, in January of 2008. The good news was the fans—and even some skeptics—liked what they heard. With its lush harmonies and infectious melody, "Hold My Hand" revealed Jackson was still in good shape vocally. It wasn't a groundbreaking track, but it showed promise for his future work. As the buzz gradually started building around a new "comeback album," a "longtime Jackson associate" told a *Chicago Suns-Times* reporter: "This is something Michael is carefully planning. I think the album is going to be amazing."

In the spring of 2007, a financially strapped Jackson temporarily moved to Northern Virginia, before showing up at the doorstep of longtime friends, the Cascio family, in Franklin Lakes, New Jersey later that summer. Jackson had become friends with Frank and Eddie Cascio in the mid-1980s and had remained close ever since. That fall, while staying in their home for nearly four months, Jackson, Eddie Cascio, and singer/producer James Porte (who had worked as an assistant engineer on *Invincible*) worked on several new songs in a makeshift recording studio in the basement.

In the beginning, Jackson simply assisted them with their work, but before long, he was also collaborating, writing, and singing. While occasionally stressed about money and other aspects of his life, Jackson mostly seemed energized and happy during his stay in New Jersey. According to the Cascios, Jackson recorded about a dozen demos that fall, including three tracks ("Breaking News," "Keep Your Head Up," and "Monster") that appeared on his first posthumous album, *Michael*, and several others ("Burn Tonight," "Water," "Carry On," "All I Need") that may appear on subsequent releases. Jackson also recorded vocals for *Thriller 25* during his stay.

"Jackson was still plotting his comeback, waiting for the right opportunity. He continued to keep his finger on the pulse of the music industry."

After a four-month residence in New Jersey, Jackson returned to Las Vegas, where he resumed work with Brad Buxer and Michael Prince and reached out to several other new collaborators, including renowned Swiss producer RedOne (who also produced Lady Gaga's debut album, *The Fame*, that year). "All I can say is, he is the best," said RedOne of the experience. "He is very inspirational and very open. It seems like there is no limit in what he knows about music, about productions and about emotions." RedOne worked with Jackson on several songs in 2008 and 2009. "The music we were doing was good, really good… very energetic, uplifting. It's sad that we never finished [it]." RedOne does say, however, that a few tracks are complete enough to be released and he plans to do so in the coming years, as long as the money goes to charity.

That February, Sony released *Thriller 25*, a reissue of Jackson's seminal classic, which included five new remixes by popular contemporary artists such as Kanye West, Will.i.am, and Akon, and a re-recorded outtake from the *Thriller* sessions called "For All Time." Considering Jackson's virtual disappearance since his 2005 trial, many were surprised at how well the album sold. It hit #1 in eight countries. Even in the United States, where Jackson was thought to be commercially dead, it reached #2 on the *Billboard* Albums Chart, selling more than 106,000 copies. By Halloween, it had sold close to 700,000 copies in the United States (making it the top-selling catalog album of 2008) and an estimated three million worldwide.

While the album reissue succeeded both commercially and critically—reminding people why it became the biggest-selling record of all time in the first place—the artist himself was nowhere to be found. No interviews (beside with *Ebony* the previous summer), no appearances, no announcements. Jackson was reportedly scheduled to perform at the Grammy Awards show in February. However, as the date grew closer, conversations between show producer Ken Ehrlich and Jackson's team broke down and, in spite of being hyped in commercials, Jackson was a mysterious no-show. Some said he was too nervous to take the stage again or that his expectations for himself were too high.

Jackson was still plotting his comeback, waiting for the right opportunity. He continued to keep his finger on the pulse of the music industry.

He was intrigued by Lady Gaga and planned to collaborate with her in the near future. He was also interested in the work of Ne-Yo, an artist whose soulful pop and smooth melodies hearkened back to Jackson's early work. In 2008, he called Ne-Yo about collaborating for his new album. "My hands were shaking like never before," recalled Ne-Yo. "But the great thing is that I get to work with my idol and he is really cool." Asked what Jackson was looking for from him, Ne-Yo responded, "His music is all about the melody, and that's the only sort of real direction he gave me: 'Just make sure the song is as melodic as possible. I want to get back to that.'" Ne-Yo quickly learned, however, of Jackson's high expectations. "He wants killer melodies. He'll call me back and say 'I really like song number three, song number four the hook could be stronger. Song number one, change the first verse.... Okay, bye.' Click. And then I redo them and he's like, 'Okay, they're perfect. Send me more.' So I don't know what he's keeping, what he's getting rid of, what he's recording."

Indeed, very few people did. What is now known is that Jackson was busy at work during these years, continuing to develop new songs or song ideas. "Wanna come back tomorrow," he would often say to Brad Buxer and Michael Prince after a successful recording session. "He was incredibly focused, completely coherent, always in a good mood," recalls Michael Prince. "[In 2008] you could tell he was getting ready for his comeback. He was looking good, looking stronger, plotting his next move."

Later that year, Buxer had to inform Jackson that he couldn't remain full-time in Vegas, though Jackson tried his hardest to convince him to stay. "When things slowed down [after *Invincible*]," Buxer explained, "I wanted to finish my flying training, so I did that. I was flying for a major airline and when I wasn't flying I was commuting to work with him in Las Vegas. It worked for a while, but he didn't like the idea that I wouldn't quit the airlines." Buxer told Jackson if there was a major tour or album, he would join on, but otherwise he couldn't afford to quit the airline; he had to keep his job. One night Jackson pleaded with Buxer. "I don't want to work with anyone else. You're flying an airplane every night; with me, you're making history." Reluctantly, however, Buxer had to pass up the opportunity. Before parting in 2008, however, they worked on numerous songs, including "Days in Gloucestershire," "Changes," "Hollywood Tonight," and "Best of Joy." (Ron Feemster coproduced the latter two tracks for the *Michael* album, as well as a new version of Jackson and Buxer's 2000 track, "The Way You Love Me.")

Soon after, Jackson informed Michael Prince, Neff-U, and others he was heading to Los Angeles. At first, his collaborators didn't even realize the move was permanent. Over the next several months Jackson lived in the Bel-Air Hotel. All the gear and hard drives were brought over from Las Vegas as he continued to work on the new album and business plans. It was here that Jackson recorded the vocals for several nearly finished songs, including "Best of Joy" and "I Was the Loser." Several months later, after finalizing a deal with AEG for his O2 concert series, Jackson moved into a rented home in Holmby Hills. By this time, Jackson had dozens of song titles written on 3×5-inch index cards. He was getting closer to determining what would make it onto the final track list. He also had a unique plan in store for the new music's release. According to recording engineer Michael Prince, his vision was to finish many of the tracks while his concerts were going in London and release them one-by-one as singles, not as a full album. It was a brilliant idea. Jackson, as always, was keenly attuned to the music industry and felt this was the ideal way to disseminate his music in the age of digital downloading. He also realized that with the publicity generated by his ongoing stay at the biggest venue in the world, the anticipation for each new song would be huge. Rather than give critics a chance to immediately dismiss his new album as a flop, he would outsmart them by having hit single after hit single, and finally, once he reached ten to twelve songs, release it as a full album.

Jackson continued to record even in his final months, while most of his time was consumed preparing for his upcoming tour. Two days before he died, he called his longtime friend Deepak Chopra about a new environmental song he had been working on called "Breed." "I've got some really good news to share with you," he said in a voice-mail about the song. Chopra said he sounded "upbeat" and "excited." The demo he sent was a majestic reminder of our connection to the planet, not unlike his 1995 hit, "Earth Song." Chopra, however, wasn't able to reach Jackson to talk to him about it. "The music demo he sent me lies on my bedside table as a poignant symbol of an unfinished life."

While Jackson's vision for the album will, sadly, never be fully realized, however, he did leave dozens of songs and fragments of songs that will be heard in the coming years. The estate of Michael Jackson now possesses the majority of the work he was engaged in during this time and plans to release at least two to three albums containing much of this material. The first of these, *Michael*, was released in December 2010.

Another project Michael Jackson was engaged in during his final months might surprise many people who didn't know him well. Jackson always had a deep affinity for classical music, and it had long been a dream of his to compose a classical album. To this end, in the spring of 2009, he arranged a meeting with prolific, award-winning composer David Michael Frank.

When Frank arrived at Jackson's Holmby Hills home, he wasn't sure what to expect. "I drove up to the front door, and was met by an assistant who told me to go inside," he recalled. "I was reluctant to shake his hand because I had heard that he was concerned about germs, but he immediately stuck his hand out and gave me a very firm handshake. He was very skinny, but not the least bit frail. He was wearing a suit and a hat. He was going to rehearsal later for the tour. He said, 'You look familiar.' I told him a long time ago I worked on a TV tribute to Sammy Davis Jr. at Shrine Auditorium [that he had participated in]. I told him I had met him briefly there. He said, 'I never forget a face.'"

Jackson proceeded to tell Frank of the three major projects in which he was engaged: his *This Is It* concert show, a pop album, and a classical album. "He said he listened to . . . classical music all the time; it was his absolute favorite. I was impressed with the pieces he mentioned: Aaron Copland's *Rodeo*, *Fanfare for the Common Man*, and *Lincoln Portrait*; Leonard Bernstein's *West Side Story*. I mentioned Bernstein's *On the Waterfront*. Then Michael mentioned that he loved Elmer Bernstein's film music, too, and he specifically mentioned *To*

Kill a Mockingbird. I realized that almost all the classical pieces he mentioned are childlike, very simple and pretty, like Prokofiev's *Peter and the Wolf* and Tchaikovsky's *Nutcracker Suite*. He also mentioned Debussy several times, specifically *Arabesque* [No. 1] and *Clair de Lune*. He was very soft-spoken when we were talking about music, but when he got animated about something, he was very changed. When he mentioned how he loved Elmer Bernstein, and I said I liked *The Magnificent Seven* score, Michael started singing the theme very loudly, almost screaming it."

Jackson had his oldest son, Prince, retrieve a demo he had recorded, and together, he and Frank listened to it. "It's very pretty music," Frank recalls. "One piece had an Irish quality about it. I suggested that we could use a Celtic harp. The pieces sound like pretty film score music, with very traditional harmony, and definitely very strong melodies. One of them was a little John Barry-ish, like in *Out of Africa*—that kind of John Barry score. I could hear [in my head] sweeping strings and French horns in unison."

Jackson and Frank went to the piano to flesh out parts that were still incomplete. "I sat at the piano," recalls Frank, "and Michael hummed the missing part of one of the pieces. I had taken a little digital recorder with me and asked if I could record him. He was in perfect pitch. I tried to figure out chords to go with it as he hummed. He said, 'Your instincts are totally right about the chords.'" Jackson later told friends how amazed he was that Frank could immediately play any piece he mentioned.

Jackson, Frank remembers, was anxious to get the pieces orchestrated. After the first meeting, they continued to talk on the phone. "He asked me how the project was going and I said I was waiting to hear from someone so we could set the deal. I suggested we could record the music in London while he was doing the show there. He liked the idea. He again brought up [Debussy's] *Arabesque*. I laid the music all out on my computer and started on the orchestrations. Finally, a week before Michael died, his manager, Frank DiLeo, called and asked me for an e-mail with the budget and an electronic mock-up of the music, the costs of orchestration." Unfortunately, as with his pop album, Jackson wasn't able to see his vision realized. Frank, however, says Jackson "had the tunes pretty much worked out." Each piece was about seven to ten minutes long and most of the missing parts had been filled. Jackson also told Frank about other instrumental music he had worked on, including a jazz piece.

"I hope one day his family will decide to record this music as a tribute," Frank concluded, "and show the world the depth of his artistry.... I told Michael I was going to use one of Leonard Bernstein's batons I had bought at auction when we did the recording. I knew he would have gotten a big kick out of that." As of late 2011, the estate of Michael Jackson had yet to announce any plans to release Jackson and Frank's classical album.

Of all his final projects, however, the *This Is It* concert series at the O2 Arena in London was poised to make the biggest splash. Indeed, in some ways the statement was already made before Jackson even began rehearsing for the show. When he announced the concerts in London to a crowd of hysterical fans, networks around the world, including the BBC and CNN, gave it more than an hour of live coverage. It was impossible to think of another artist in the world who could command that kind of attention by simply announcing concert dates. By the next day, more than 1.6 million people had signed up on Jackson's website to buy tickets. Then came what AEG executive Randy Phillips described as "the most astonishing [thing] I have seen in my career in the entertainment business." After years out of the public spotlight and nearly a decade since being on a stage, Jackson sold out ten, then thirty, then fifty dates at the O2 Arena. Demand was so high, the website froze and crashed repeatedly. "Tickets sold at a rate of 11 per second, 657 per minute and nearly 40,000 an hour," said concert organizers, who called it the fastest-selling show in history. "We often talk about unprecedented demand, but this week we have witnessed a live entertainment phenomenon," said Ticketmaster's managing director. "This was undoubtedly the busiest demand for tickets for an event which we have ever experienced."

It was an astonishing turn of events. The media, which had wondered days before "who, beyond the most devoted fans, would pay £50 [$80] and upwards for a ticket," were shocked. Jackson had just pulled off the biggest one-city gig ever at the hottest new arena in the world. Experts predicted he could generate close to £1 billion for the London economy. His album sales were up more than two hundred percent. "Michael Jackson has floored his critics," wrote the *Times*' Veronica Schmidt. Indeed, at fifty years old, he was set to make history again. Even his peers were amazed and excited to see the shows. "To sell out like that is a testament to talent," said Coldplay's Chris Martin. "It is just amazing to sell out 50 shows in one city in a big arena. It's the biggest comeback since Lazarus."

Jackson first met with AEG executive Randy Phillips about the possibility of the shows in late 2007. At that point, Jackson was still skeptical about doing an extended show or tour. By the next year, however, he had changed his mind. In the fall of 2008, he flew to Los Angeles to meet with Randy Phillips again. This time Phillips could see Jackson was serious and focused. He was "ready to stop living like a vagabond." He wanted to clear up his financial mess; he wanted a new permanent home for his family; and, most importantly, he wanted his children to see him perform on stage for the first time. "My kids are old enough now to appreciate what I do," he told Phillips, "and I'm still young enough to do it."

Within months, preparations were underway. Renowned director Kenny Ortega was tapped as director, Travis Payne as choreographer, and Michael Bearden as music director. Rehearsals started at Center Staging (a small venue where the earliest foundation was laid), then moved to the Forum, and finally, to the Staples Center. By this time (March 2009), Jackson had moved to his Holmby Hills chateau and was struggling with insomnia and anxiety. He wanted to do the shows, but there was an enormous amount of pressure and stress. Many on the outside (and even some on the inside) were skeptical about whether Jackson could actually pull off fifty concerts. He was not young any more and had a recent history of unreliability. The dates were spread out to give Jackson recuperation time, but there were still justifiable concerns about his health. Most who worked closest with him, however, said that he seemed to be in good condition, mentally and physically. He had begun training with Lou Ferrigno (of *The Incredible Hulk*), he was strengthening his voice, he was dancing and building stamina. When Grammy producer Ken Ehrlich saw his rehearsals, he was blown away by how good Jackson looked. "He wasn't giving it full out," recalls Ehrlich. "But vocally he had started to really project. I thought he was in great form."

There is no question that behind the scenes Jackson still struggled with many personal demons concerning his sleep, medication, physical appearance, finances, and other pressures. Yet what was plain to nearly everyone around Jackson in his final months was his passion and commitment to create "the greatest show on earth." "In his final days," wrote *Rolling Stone*'s Claire Hoffman, "he not only dreamed of a comeback, he worked as hard as he could to pull it off, maybe as hard as he ever had in his life." Indeed, Jackson was engaged in every aspect of the show, from selecting the dancers, to creating the visual effects, to designing the costumes, to developing the choreography. It would have been very easy for him to simply do a show like most "oldies" acts—to go through the motions and allow people some nostalgia about the good old days. As Jackson's former wife, Lisa Marie Presley, put it: "Mediocrity was not a concept that would even for a second enter Michael Jackson's being or actions."

Michael Jackson wanted to shock the world with his concerts. "The show we create here has to have people leaving and not being able to turn it off," Jackson told Kenny Ortega. "They shouldn't be able to go to sleep. They have to see the sun come up and still be talking about it." He wanted it to be unlike anything people had seen at a concert before. "I don't even care if they're applauding," he told Ortega. "I want their jaws on the ground."

Jackson and *This Is It* director Kenny Ortega working on a short film for his O2 concert series.

When the world finally saw a glimpse of what Jackson was preparing behind the scenes in his final months—via the posthumously released *This Is It* documentary—there was something akin to this response. Film critic Roger Ebert said it was "nothing at all like what I was expecting to see. Here is not a sick and drugged man forcing himself through grueling rehearsals, but a spirit embodied by music.... He corrects timing, refines cues, talks about details of music and dance. Seeing him always from a distance, I thought of him as the instrument of his producing operation. Here we see that he was the auteur of his shows." Indeed, it was a fascinating glimpse into how Jackson operated creatively—and how serious and passionate he was about his craft. "His directions are almost poetic," observed the *Hollywood Reporter*'s Kirk Honeycutt. "About the tempo of one number, he instructs, 'It's like you're dragging yourself out of bed.' Another time, he says, 'It has to simmer.'... At one point, Ortega asks his star how he will see a certain cue onstage. Jackson pauses and then says, 'I'll feel that.' And you know he would have." There are also some glimpses into his humanity. He humorously complains about an earpiece ("It feels like a fist in my ear") in one scene; in another, he prods his musical director to play a song the way he wrote it before laughing about a "booty" joke. "We see Jackson as a perfectionist, a generous boss, a tough taskmaster and a playful child," writes film critic Alex Fletcher. "Off guard and probably unaware that it would ever be seen by the public, we find Jackson pushing his band and production team to the limit.... It's heartening to finally view the late singer as a rounded human with regular failings and imperfections. Similarly, a scene featuring Jackson screaming 'weeeee!' with childish glee as he moves around the stage on a giant cherry picker, will surely bring a smile to even the most cynical viewer."

Jackson's vision for *This Is It* was a full-immersion concert spectacle. There were twenty-two different sets, elaborate backdrops, 3-D films, aerial dancers, huge chandeliers, fireworks, and flying ghosts. "Make sure those ghosts come through the screen," Jackson instructed Ortega. He wanted everything to be as visceral, intense, and dramatic as possible. The show was to begin with static interference permeating the arena, a cacophony of lighting, and chrome spheres multiplying on the stage. Then Jackson would be unveiled out of a giant robot that emanated historical images. Holding one of the chrome spheres, he would reflect on an image of himself. Jackson described it as a *Hamlet* moment. From there, he and his audience would be off together on a "great adventure."

Jackson didn't just want mindless spectacle and escapism. He wanted something deeper, something that changed people's consciousness. This undercurrent is present through many of his song choices, from "They Don't Care About Us" to "Black or White." However, it came through most powerfully on one of the later numbers, "Earth Song," an apocalyptic blues-operatic piece that paints a devastating picture of the destruction we are doing to the world. In the 3-D film created for the performance, a little girl falls asleep in a forest; when she wakes up everything around her is burned to the ground. Jackson liked the metaphor of people "sleeping" until the problems had escalated beyond control ("It's like a runaway train," he said). People who spoke to him personally said he was genuinely terrified about the future his children (and all children) would inhabit if we didn't begin to make changes. After the song's huge climax, Jackson wanted the girl and the tractor from the film to actually come out onto the stage and approach the audience. The tractor door was to open and a human would step out. "It's not the machines that are destroying the world," Jackson wanted to reveal. "It's the people that are destroying the world." Interestingly, it is on this bleak, but poignant, note he intended to end. "Not a happy ending," he insisted to Kenny Ortega. "I want it burning. I want it there, lasting and burning, and I want us standing there with our arms reached out, asking people 'please'!... before it becomes a travesty."

In rehearsal footage from the final day, Jackson is shown, at one moment, pointing out at his imagined audience: "You, you, you, us, we."

APPENDIX

MICHAEL

RELEASED: December 14, 2010
NOTABLE CONTRIBUTORS:
Akon *(songwriting/producing/vocals),* Stuart Brawley *(engineer),* Brad Buxer *(songwriting/producing),* C. "Tricky" Stewart *(producing),* Eddie Cascio *(songwriting/producing),* Theron "Neff-U" Feemster *(producing),* 50 Cent *(rap),* Lenny Kravitz *(songwriting/producing/vocals),* John McClain *(producing),* Jon Nettlesbey, Orianthi *(guitar),* Michael Prince *(engineer),* James Porte *(songwriting/producing/vocals),* Teddy Riley *(producing)*

Michael Jackson's first posthumous album, a ten-song collection entitled *MICHAEL*, was released in December 2010. It was accompanied by controversy before the first single was even released. Fans, family members, and even some of Jackson's former collaborators contested everything from the creative license taken to complete Jackson's unfinished work, to the tracklist, to the authenticity of certain vocals.

Posthumous works, of course, are notoriously tricky. There are essentially two philosophical approaches: (1) present the material basically as it was found; or (2) try to complete the artist's vision based on instructions and/or intuition.

For the 2009 documentary, *This Is It*, Jackson's Estate opted for the first approach, a risky move (this was footage, after all, that was never intended to be seen) that resulted in the best-selling documentary of all time. Fans and non-fans alike responded to its raw authenticity. There was something undeniably riveting and enlightening about peaking "behind the curtain" and witnessing the artist in his element. It was tragic, of course, that his full vision was never realized. But for many viewers it humanized the singer, even as it showcased his extraordinary talent.

With *MICHAEL*, however, the latter approach was taken. All of the songs were completed after his death by people who had worked with Jackson in the past, ranging from producers Teddy Riley, Tricky Stewart, and Neff-U, to estate co-executor John McClain. They wanted to make the tracks as complete as possible, believing that this is what Jackson would have wanted. The resulting album is a mixed affair, combining older songs with newer songs, songs that were mostly finished with songs that needed work, songs that were well-documented with songs that were more mysterious. Most controversial were the so-called "Cascio tracks," which were reportedly recorded in the basement of Jackson's longtime friends, the Cascios, in New Jersey. In spite of forensic examinations and reassurances from both the Cascios and Sony, questions have persisted about the origins and production of the tracks. Other songs—including "Another Day" and "Behind the Mask"—had been anticipated for years, but provoked fierce debate with their 2010 reincarnations. In addition, the album contained no tracks with Will.i.am, RedOne, or Ne-Yo (all of whom Jackson was working with in his final years).

MICHAEL, then, is inevitably different than the album Jackson would have created were he alive. Yet in spite of its limitations, *MICHAEL* still contains some fantastic new music, including a handful of gems. Songs like the sublime vocal masterwork, "(I Like) The Way You Love Me," the long-anticipated *Thriller* outtake, "Behind the Mask," the tender ballad, "Best of Joy," the funky cautionary tale, "Hollywood Tonight," and the poignant song-poem, "Much Too Soon," all make excellent additions to an already legendary catalog.

THE SONGS

1. HOLD MY HAND

(Written by Aliaune Thiam, Giorgio Tuinfort, Claude Kelly. Produced by Akon and Michael Jackson. Lead and background vocals: Michael Jackson and Akon)

Akon first presented "Hold My Hand" to Michael in late 2007. Jackson loved its simple elegance and melody. He and Akon laid down the vocals soon after in a recording session at the Palms Studio in Las Vegas. Unfortunately, just weeks after it was recorded, the song leaked onto the Internet. Jackson was very upset and disappointed. The song was close to being finished, but not yet ready to be heard.

Almost three years later, in 2010, Akon returned to "finish" the song for inclusion on *MICHAEL*. In his updated production, Akon was clearly aiming bigger than the song he and Jackson originally recorded. The strings are more prominent and lavish, and the song turns into a tribute of sorts to Jackson, complete with a soaring gospel-infused finale. Where the original conveys a more restrained, subtle emotion, the new version is dramatic and anthemic, while also splicing in more of Jackson's vocals.

Jackson's estate made the song his first posthumous single after finding a note that read: "Akon song—first single." A few weeks later, it climbed up the charts around the world, reaching the Top Ten in over fifteen countries.

"Hold My Hand" is certainly a deserving addition to Jackson's catalog, embodying much of what fans loved about the singer. With its call to connect, it is a "love song" that ties the personal to something more profound and universal (à la "You Are Not Alone"). The chord progression is a variation of Pachelbel's Canon in D Major, which is deftly blended with a Caribbean-tinged rhythm and highlighted by Jackson and Akon's lush harmonies. There is a purity to Jackson's vocal that somehow manages to communicate joy, yearning, and sadness all at once. The opening lyric ("This life don't last forever...") is a poignant reminder of the transience of life. But ultimately, this is a catharsis song as Jackson calls out to those "miserable alone," allowing the music to facilitate reunion.

2. HOLLYWOOD TONIGHT

(Written by Michael Jackson, Brad Buxer. Produced by Teddy Riley and Michael Jackson. Coproduced by Theron "Neff-U" Feemster. Lead and background vocals: Michael Jackson. Spoken bridge written by Teddy Riley)

From the Gregorian chant intro (Jackson's idea) to the slick bass line to the funky guitar riff, "Hollywood Tonight" sounds, perhaps more than any other track, like the direction Jackson may have been heading for his new album. Instantly danceable, with a chorus that sticks in the head, this is classic Michael Jackson. It is one of his best bass lines since "Who Is It."

Jackson first put down a sketch of the lyrics in 1999 while staying at the Beverly Hills Hotel. Soon after, he began working out the music with longtime friend and collaborator, Brad Buxer (who co-wrote the song). The song traveled with them from Los Angeles to New York, Miami to Neverland, during the early *Invincible* sessions. Jackson loved parts of "Hollywood"—the wordplay in the lyrics, the "westbound, greyhound" harmonies, the whistling in the outro—but stopped working on it once producer Rodney Jerkins came on board for *Invincible*.

Over the next ten years, however, he returned to the track numerous times. For the bass line, he was searching for something similar to "Billie Jean," but distinct. "Do smooth muted bass on 'Hollywood,'" he indicated in one note. His early demos feature two layered bass lines (Michael Prince added the "Billie Jean"-esque kick and snare in the last mix MJ requested). Jackson and Brad Buxer continued tinkering with it in Las Vegas in 2007.

In October, 2008, Jackson, now living in Los Angeles, asked recording engineer Michael Prince to put the latest mix of "Hollywood" on CD so he could listen to it and see what might be improved. Sadly, he never got around to working on it again.

Following Jackson's death, Theron Feemster (aka Neff-U) and Teddy Riley worked on the song, adding new production and a new bridge (written by Riley and performed by Jackson's nephew, Taryll Jackson). The track paints a narrative of a young, naïve girl seduced by the bright lights of Hollywood. Once she arrives, however, she is used and abused by men who prey on her innocence. In his notes, Jackson called it a "true story." Certainly, it was a tale he could relate to, having come to Hollywood himself at the age of nine.

3. KEEP YOUR HEAD UP

(Written by Michael Jackson, Eddie Cascio, and James Porte. Produced by C. "Tricky" Stewart and Michael Jackson. Lead vocal: Michael Jackson. Background vocals: Michael Jackson and James Porte. Additional backing vocals: Duawne Starling)

One of three songs on the album originally recorded at the Cascio residence in New Jersey, "Keep Your Head Up" is a motivational working-class anthem about an ordinary woman "looking for the hope in the empty promises." The posthumous production was carried out by Tricky Stewart, who gives the second half of the song a Jackson-esque lift with the help of a fervent gospel choir.

4. (I LIKE) THE WAY YOU LOVE ME

(Written by Michael Jackson. Produced by Theron "Neff-U" Feemster and Michael Jackson. Lead and background vocals: Michael Jackson)

"(I Like) The Way You Love Me" was one of Michael Jackson's favorite songs in his final years. After his death, it also turned out to be the one music legend Stevie Wonder singled out as his favorite. "I love that song! I just love it," he said. "It makes me feel that he's here. That's the spirit of how I like to remember his voice."

"(I Like) The Way You Love Me" originally appeared on the 2004 box set, *Michael Jackson: The Ultimate Collection*. Jackson had worked on the track with Brad Buxer during the *Invincible* sessions, recording it at the Hit Factory in 2000. In his final years, however, Jackson wanted to revisit the tune and possibly rerelease it. "It's a song he had in his heart for many years," says producer Theron "Neff-U" Feemster. An updated version of the song was being worked on in Los Angeles before Jackson passed.

Both versions contain their own virtues. While the original is more straightforward and clean, highlighting Jackson's gorgeous vocals, the new version embellishes a bit more, adding punchy piano chords, a fluttering flute, and a metallic sheen to some of the harmonies. It gives it a fresh feel while retaining the charm of the original.

The new version begins with a nostalgic touch, as Jackson explains the composition of the track in a saved phone message. It is a nice, authentic moment that also illuminates his ability as a composer. The track itself feels like something straight out of the late '50s or early '60s, a burst of classic doo-wop soul featuring innocent sentiments of love and Beach Boys-esque harmonies. Jackson was undoubtedly surrounded by such songs on the street corners of Gary, Indiana, as a young boy. It is a testament to the quality of Jackson's work that an obscure song like this contains all the hallmarks of a classic, its blissful modulating *woo-ooo-oohs* reminding people of the simple pleasures of music.

5. MONSTER

(Written by Michael Jackson, Eddie Cascio, and James Porte. Produced by Teddy Riley, Angelikson, and Michael Jackson. Background vocals: Michael Jackson and James Porte. Rap lyrics written by Curtis Jackson)

A dark, aggressive rhythm track set to a relentless beat, "Monster" probably hits harder than anything on the album. It is without question the best and most complete of the three Cascio tracks. Teddy Riley adds some nice touches to the production, including an eerie, liquid-like ambience, visceral shrieks, and lion roars sampled from Jackson's zoo. 50 Cent's rap solo ("It's home, sweet home, the land of the forbidden/All hell, run tell the King has risen") also works surprisingly well, complementing the track's grisly, defiant tone.

The song is about the claustrophobia of being trapped in a monstrous, cannibalistic world. Everywhere the singer turns, he finds people who want to use and abuse him. The result is that he begins to feel like a monster himself.

The track was originally recorded by Eddie Cascio and James Porte in 2007. It is expected to be one of the album's singles.

6. BEST OF JOY

(Written by Michael Jackson. Produced by Theron "Neff-U" Feemster and Michael Jackson. Coproduced by Brad Buxer. Lead and background vocals: Michael Jackson. Additional background vocals: Mischke)

A breezy mid-tempo ballad, "Best of Joy" can be interpreted as an ode to music itself. Jackson often referred to music as his "first love," and in this song, like the Jackson 5 classic "Music and Me," he expresses appreciation for what it has meant to him. On another level, it could be about a relationship, perhaps directed toward his fans or his children, who stood by him "when all the walls came tumbling down." Ultimately, the song is about a sustaining, secure, deep kind of love that is unconditional and eternal.

One of Jackson's final recordings, "Best of Joy," was last recorded at the Bel-Air Hotel in Los Angeles in 2008. The melody came in a moment of inspiration. "[Michael] would say melodies are ancient," recalls Theron Feemster. "They are in the heavens above waiting to be plucked. When the expressed sound of his imagination felt right he would look at me with a calm smile and say, 'It's nice, isn't it?'" That same inspiration seems to guide the song's production, which tastefully accompanies Jackson's effortless falsetto and rich harmonies. The ending beautifully captures the song's essence, as the refrain, "We are forever, I am forever . . ." slowly dissolves with the music.

7. BREAKING NEWS

(Written by Michael Jackson, Eddie Cascio, and James Porte. Produced by Teddy Riley, Angelikson, and Michael Jackson. Lead vocals: Michael Jackson. Background vocals: James Porte. Voice talents: Stuart Brawley, Sandy Orkin, Stacey Michaels, Michael Lefevre, and Lisa Orkin. Voiceover producer: Michael Lefevre)

"Breaking News" will be forever linked to the controversy surrounding its vocals, which were fiercely contested by Jackson's family and fans. In December 2010, the track's co-writer and co-producer, Eddie Cascio, appeared with his family on the *Oprah Winfrey Show* defending the veracity of his work with Jackson, claiming it was recorded in his basement in 2007. According to Cascio, the songs were mostly written and recorded before Jackson arrived at their home in New Jersey; they subsequently convinced him to lay down vocals on the material.

For some, however, Cascio's explanations—and reassurances from Sony and the Michael Jackson estate—haven't put the matter to rest. Questions continue to swirl about the song's origins, process, and unusual sounding vocals. As for the substance of the track itself, "Breaking News" is familiar territory, offering a critique of the way people feed on "breaking news" (read: scandals) with obsessive compulsion ("No matter what/You just want to read it again"). Sonically, it contains echoes of the Teddy Riley-produced 1988 hit, "My Prerogative" (by Bobby Brown). Riley, who added new production to the track after Jackson's death, uses menacing strings, punchy horns, and a pulsing, new jack beat to try to accentuate the song's ominous message.

8. (I CAN'T MAKE IT) ANOTHER DAY

(Written by Lenny Kravitz. Produced by Lenny Kravitz. Coproduced by Michael Jackson. Lead and background vocals: Michael Jackson. Background vocals: Lenny Kravitz)

"Another Day" was originally recorded in 1999 at the legendary Marvin's Room Studio in Los Angeles. "It was the most amazing experience I've had in the studio," recalls Lenny Kravitz, who wrote and produced the song. "It was done by two people who respected each other and love music." The result was a unique and powerful track that explodes out of the speakers.

The original demo has Michael summoning a cosmic power over a rugged, industrial funk beat and a soaring chorus. "I've opened up my heart I want you to come through," he pleads in one verse. "I close my eyes I'm searching for your love." The line is held in tension, building anticipation, before Jackson releases the pent-up energy over Kravitz's driving guitar and short, clipped backing vocals. It is one of Jackson's finest rock efforts since "Give In To Me" from Dangerous, yet was ultimately left off of *Invincible*.

Kravitz returned to "finish" the song after Jackson's death. The version he completed for the album features more prominent drums and guitar and a new outro. While his intent was undoubtedly to make the song better, however, the embellishments change the mood of the song. Where the original demo highlighted Jackson's vocals, conveying the wonder and mystery of the lyrics, Kravitz's update offers more of a funky, classic rock feel. While a fragment of the original demo leaked online, it is unknown whether the full version will be officially released.

9. BEHIND THE MASK

(Written by Michael Jackson, Chris Mosdell, and Ryuichi Sakamoto. Produced by Michael Jackson, John McClain, and Jon Nettlesbey, "Behind the Mask" contains a sample of the recording "Behind the Mask" as performed by Yellow Magic Orchestra. Lead and background vocals: Michael Jackson. Additional background vocals: Shanice Wilson and Alphonso Jones)

"Behind the Mask" was first recorded in Jackson's Hayvenhurst studio in 1981. It was an adaptation of a song by innovative Japanese electro-pop group Yellow Magic Orchestra. When Jackson first heard the synth-driven piece, he was mesmerized by its futuristic sound and unusual mood. He subsequently reached out to Ryuichi Sakamoto to ask permission to rework the song, including the addition of new lyrics. With Sakamoto's approval, Jackson went to work, developing a fantastic new version. The track would have been right at home on *Thriller* and likely a huge hit. Unfortunately, it never made it to Westlake Studios for the final lineup due to a song credit dispute. Jackson's version, however, was later covered by his keyboardist, Greg Phillinganes, Eric Clapton, and, ironically, Ryuichi Sakamoto. For decades, fans have anticipated hearing Jackson on the song, but even though the songwriting credits were resolved in 1985, it was never released.

Perhaps to be consistent with the mostly newer material on the album, however, coexecutor John McClain decided to completely reproduce and rearrange the song for *MICHAEL*, including a different bass, the additions of two sax solos, crowd noise, and a female singer in the outro. Such creative liberties provoked frustration among many fans who were eager to hear the version Jackson last worked on rather than a reinterpretation. It is unclear if the long-anticipated demo, which was modeled very closely by Greg Phillinganes in his 1985 recording, will eventually be released.

Yet regardless of the mix, the song itself is superb. In vocals brimming with vitality and passion, Jackson narrates a story of deceptive surfaces and illusions. "Behind the mask, you control your world," he sings. Later, cyborg-sounding background vocals deliver dystopian maxims of alienation ("There is nothing in your eyes/But that's the way you cry"). The song also features a killer bass line, Jackson's uncanny beatboxing, and an eerie "Good Vibrations"-esque electronic keyboard serving as a counter-melody. It is arguably the crown jewel in Jackson's treasure trove of non-album, *Thriller*-era songs.

10. MUCH TOO SOON

(Written by Michael Jackson. Produced by Michael Jackson and John McClain. Lead and background vocals: Michael Jackson)

The album closer showcases Jackson's ability as a singer-songwriter to magnificent effect. That a song like this—arguably Jackson's finest ballad—didn't make it onto an album while he was alive is a tragedy unto itself. "Much Too Soon" is an exquisite expression of loss and yearning that stands shoulder-to-shoulder with some of the best folk ballads of the Carpenters and the Beatles. The lyrics almost read like a W. B. Yeats poem.

The track was first written by Jackson in 1981 and revisited multiple times over the years. The vocal on this version was recorded in 1994 at the Hit Factory during the *HIStory* sessions. It was originally engineered and mixed by Bruce Swedien (this version leaked online in the weeks preceding the album release). "Michael came in one day and said he had an idea and needed a guitar player," recalls assistant engineer Rob Hoffman. "So they called in a local session guy, Jeff Mironov. He sat with MJ in the iso-booth and Michael patiently sang every note of every chord, and the melody. He had the whole thing in his head. Once Jeff had it down, Michael came into the control room and sang live while Jeff did some takes . . . I believe we did about 5 or 6 takes, all of them amazing . . . But the song was shelved and never brought up again."

The version that appears on *MICHAEL*, featuring more prominent accordion and strings, was reproduced for the album by estate co-executor John McClain.

In the song, a forlorn Jackson, accompanied by the subtle acoustic guitar work of Tommy Emmanuel, sings about being separated from a loved one "much too soon." The pathos in the vocal comes through with such purity and honesty the listener feels every ounce of his heartache. "Take away this never-ending sorrow," he pleads in one line. "Take this lonely feeling from my soul." Given the context of Jackson's life, these words carry profound depth and resonance.

The bridge features a harmonica solo that highlights the song's folk-blues essence, before Jackson returns with a final verse about "never letting fate control [his] soul." It is a beautiful, bittersweet song that perfectly balances hope and regret, loneliness and the desire for reconciliation. For all Jackson's superstardom, "Much Too Soon" reminds everyone that behind the media construct was a human being.

Michael Jackson smiles while on tour in Tokyo in 1987.

NOTES

INTRODUCTION: A GREAT ADVENTURE

1 **"He's just freeing it":** Regina Jones, "Unbreakable," *Vibe*, March 2002.

1 **"the breathtaking verve of his predecessor":** Jim Miller, "Review of the Opening Night of the Victory Tour," *Newsweek*, July 16, 1984.

2 **"I am a slave to the rhythm":** "The Man in the Mirror," *TV Guide*, November 10, 2001.

2 **"When you're dancing":** Michael Jackson, interview by Oprah Winfrey, *The Oprah Winfrey Show*, February 10, 1993.

2 **"After studying James Brown from the wings":** Michael Jackson, *Moonwalk* (New York: Doubleday, 1988), 47.

3 **"She was art in motion":** Ibid., 68.

3 **"He would always come into the studio":** Stevie Wonder, "Remembering Michael," *Time*, July 2009.

4 **"I'll never forget his persistence":** Ibid., 77.

4 **"I love great music":** Regina Jones, "Unbreakable," *Vibe*, March 2002.

5 **"He wanted to be the best of everything":** Quincy Jones, *Q: The Autobiography of Quincy Jones* (New York: Doubleday, 2001), 230.

5 **"like a hawk, observing every decision":** Jackson, *Moonwalk*, 123.

5 **"I have all kinds of tapes and albums":** Michael Jackson and Catherine Dineen, *Michael Jackson: In His Own Words* (London: Omnibus, 1993), 38.

5 **"anybody he thought would make":** Greg Tate, "Michael Jackson: The Man in Our Mirror," *The Village Voice*, July 1, 2009.

6 **"If you take an album like *Nutcracker Suite*":** Bryan Monroe, "Michael Jackson: In His Own Words," *Ebony*, December 2007, 98.

6 **"In film, you live the moment":** Michael Jackson, interview by Jesse Jackson, *Keep Hope Alive*, March 25, 2005.

9 **"the oft-repeated conventional wisdom":** Hampton Stevens, "Michael Jackson's Unparalleled Influence," *The Atlantic*, June 24, 2010.

9 **"[Michael] has some of the same qualities":** Jones, *Q: The Autobiography of Quincy Jones*, 230.

10 **"Jackson was a dancer at heart":** Neil McCormick, "Michael Jackson, Bruce Springsteen & Bono: Great Singing Is About More Than the Notes," *The Telegraph*, June 30, 2009.

11 **"He starts with an entire sound and song":** Richard Buskin, "Classic Tracks: Michael Jackson's 'Black or White,'" *Sound on Sound*, August 2004.

11 **"One morning [Michael] came in":** "Post here if you worked on Michael Jackson's DANGEROUS album," Gearslutz.com, http://www.gearslutz.com/board/4325168-post15.html (accessed June 27, 2009).

11 **"He was a consummate professional":** Brad Sundberg, "One Year Later," *BSUN Media Newsletter* (accessed June 25, 2010).

12 **"All of Michael's recordings were done":** Bruce Swedien, personal author interview. April 15, 2010.

12 **"[He] just started asking me to take more responsibility":** Bill Bottrell, personal author interview. May 14, 2010.

12 **"When you did something [Michael] liked":** Brad Buxer, personal author interview. June 23, 2010.

13 **"I don't categorize music":** Regina Jones, "Unbreakable," *Vibe*, March 2002.

13 **"bizarre disintegration":** Brooks Barnes, "A Star Idolized and Haunted, Michael Jackson Dies at 50," *New York Times*, June 27, 2009.

13 **"Given the tumult in his personal life":** Josh Tyrangiel, "Michael Jackson Dead at 50: A Life of Talent and Tragedy," *Time*, June 25, 2009.

13 **"The underlying sweetness that had made":** Jon Pareles, "Tricky Steps From Boy to Superstar," *New York Times*, June 25, 2009.

14 **"Jackson's career arc from beloved child star":** Armond White, *Keep Moving: The Michael Jackson Chronicles* (New York: Resistance Works, 2009), 4.

14 **"What is interesting is that this":** Mikal Gilmore, "Triumph and Tragedy: The Life of Michael Jackson," *Rolling Stone*, July 2009.

16 **"Though he aimed bigger and broader":** Jody Rosen, "King Michael," Slate.com, http://www.slate.com/id/2221482 (accessed June 26, 2009).

17 **"Many of his most affecting performances":** Jeff Chang, "The Man in the Mirror: Remembering Michael Jackson," *Facing South*, June 26, 2009.

17 **"the result of the alienation people":** *Michael Jackson, Dancing the Dream: Poems and Reflections* (New York: Doubleday, 1992), 143.

18 **"Black people cherished *Thriller*'s breakthrough":** Greg Tate, "I'm White!" *The Village Voice*, September 22, 1987.

18 **"Even though rooted in Black experience":** Michael Eric Dyson, "Freedom Fighter," *Ebony*, September 2009.

18 **"From a child to older people":** Piers Morgan, "My Pain," *The Mirror*, April 13, 1999.

18 **"Michael is now, quite simply":** Michael Goldberg and Christopher Connelly, "Trouble in Paradise? Michael Jackson, An Exclusive Look Inside a Musical Empire," *Rolling Stone*, March 15, 1984.

19 **"whose achievement could not be separated":** Andrew Motion, *Keats* (New York: Farrar, Straus and Giroux, 1997), 499.

20 **"fawn in a burning forest":** Gerri Hirshey, "Michael Jackson: Life in the Magic Kingdom," *Rolling Stone*, February 17, 1983.

21 **"Unlike the Beatles, [Jackson] has a vast audience":** Jay Cocks, "Why He's a Thriller," *Time*, March 19, 1984.

21 **"first pop explosion not to be judged":** Greil Marcus, *Lipstick Traces: A Secret History of the Twentieth Century* (Cambridge, MA: Harvard University Press, 1990).

21 **"Today was a seminal moment in Internet history":** Linnie Rawlinson and Nick Hunt, "Jackson Dies, Almost Takes Internet with Him." http://articles.cnn.com/2009-06-26/tech/michael.jackson.internet_1_google-trends-search-results-michael-jackson (accessed June 26, 2009).

22 **It was bigger than Elvis Presley's:** Nick Allen, "Michael Jackson Memorial Service: The Biggest Celebrity Send-off of All Time," *Telegraph* (UK), July 7, 2009.

22 **On iTunes and other online retailers:** In the U.S., *The Essential Michael Jackson* was the #1 album, "Man in the Mirror" the #1 single, and *Thriller* the #1 video.

22 **"In life, Michael Jackson was the king of pop":** Jerry Shriver, "Jackson Is the King of Media. Sales Soar After His Death," *USA Today*, June 30, 2009.

23 **"It was a moment that summed up everything":** Rob Sheffield, "Not Like Other Guys," *Rolling Stone*, June 29, 2009.

24 **"From Compton to Harlem":** Greg Tate, "Michael Jackson: The Man in Our Mirror," *The Village Voice*, July 1, 2009.

24 **"Michael Jackson and the Jackson Five were a big part":** Yolanda, comment on "Michael Jackson Memories," CNN.com, comment posted on June 27, 2009, http://newsroom.blogs.cnn.com/2009/06/27/michael-jackson-memories (accessed: June 27, 2009).

24 **"As a single child":** Bipana, comment on "Readers Pay Tribute to Michael Jackson," Yahoo! News, comment posted on June 26, 2009, http://news.yahoo.com/s/ynews/ynews_en412 (accessed June 26, 2009).

24 **"I remember when I would drive 200 miles":** Dodie, comment on "Michael Jackson Memories," CNN.com, comment posted on June 27, 2009, http://newsroom.blogs.cnn.com/2009/06/27/michael-jackson-memories (accessed June 27, 2009).

24 **"I was 11 years old and the daughter":** rbn, comment on "Michael Jackson Dies at 50," MTV.com, comment posted on June 26, 2009. http://www.mtv.com/news/articles/1614744/20090625/jackson_michael.jhtml (accessed June 26, 2009).

25 **"I can still remember being 3 years old":** Corey, comment on "Michael Jackson Dies at 50," MTV.com, comment posted on June 26, 2009. http://www.mtv.com/news/articles/1614744/20090625/jackson_michael.jhtml (accessed June 26, 2009).

25 **"We've been deprived of so many things":** RT, "The Heartbreaker Remembered In Russia," http://ru.rt.com/usa/news/the-heartbreaker-remembered-in-russia (accessed June 27, 2009).

25 **"When I was a kid":** Blesson George, comment on "Readers Pay Tribute to Michael Jackson," Yahoo! News, comment posted on June 26, 2009, http://news.yahoo.com/s/ynews/ynews_en412 (accessed June 26, 2009).

25 **"Michael Jackson was very much loved in Africa":** Nana Koram, comment on "Michael Jackson—Africa Reacts," BBC.com, comment posted on June 26, 2009, http://newsforums.bbc.co.uk/nol/thread.jspa?forumID=6656&edition=2 (accessed June 26, 2009).

25 **"a close member of our family":** "Celebrity Reaction to Michael Jackson's Death," *Los Angeles Daily News*, July 7, 2009.

27 **"It's so sad and shocking":** "World Mourns Pop Legend Jackson." *BBC News* broadcast, June 26, 2009.

27 **"In a desperate attempt to hold onto his memory":** Hillary Crosley and Gil Kaufman, "Madonna Pays Tearful Tribute to Michael Jackson at 2009 VMAs," MTV.com, http://www.mtv.com/news/articles/1621390/20090913/jackson_michael.jhtml (accessed September 13, 2009).

28 **"Often in the past, performers have":** Jackson, *Moonwalk*, 282.

28 **"an almost calm certainty":** Lisa Marie Presley, "He Knew," MySpace.com, http://www.myspace.com/lisamariepresley/blog/497035326 (accessed June 27, 2009).

28 **"Whatever his life felt like from inside":** David Gates, "Finding Neverland," *Newsweek*, June 27, 2009.

CHAPTER 1: *OFF THE WALL*

31 **"invented modern pop as we know it":** Rob Sheffield, "Not Like Other Guys," *Rolling Stone*, June 26, 2009.

33 **"seemed entirely in tune with the times":** Anthony DeCurtis, "Michael Reinvents Pop," *Rolling Stone*, July 2009.

33 **"a strangely innocent boy-child":** Rob Sheffield, "When Michael Became Michael," *Rolling Stone*, July 2009.

33 **"People came to [Studio 54] like characters":** Steve Demorest, "Michael in Wonderland," *JET*, March 1, 1980.

33 **"Disco was diametrically opposite":** Daryl Easlea, "Disco Inferno," *The Independent*, December 11, 2004.

34 **"The attacks on disco gave respectable voice":** Craig Werner, *A Change Is Gonna Come: Music, Race & the Soul of America* (New York: Plume, 1999).

34 **"like a little kid in the Manhattan playground":** J. Randy Taraborrelli, *Michael Jackson: The Magic and the Madness* (Pan Books, 2004), 167–68.

34 **"genuine acting talent":** Lisa Campbell, *Michael Jackson: The King of Pop* (Wellesley, MA: Branden Books, 1993), 41.

35 **"Most of the people involved with the film":** Jones, *Q: The Autobiography of Quincy Jones*, 229.

35 **"Michael was the best thing that came out":** Ibid., 229, 231.

35 **"[Michael Jackson] had the wisdom":** Ibid., 230.

36 **"Quincy does jazz, he does movie scores":** Steve Demorest, "Michael in Wonderland," *JET*, March 1, 1980.

36 **"He marched back into Epic":** Jones, *Q: The Autobiography of Quincy Jones*, 232.

37 **"one of the best songwriters who ever lived":** Ibid., 233.

37 **In addition to the Big Three:** Ibid., 232.

37 **"It was the smoothest album I have ever":** Tamika Jones and John Abbey, "Michael Jackson's Peacock Music," *Blues & Soul*, August 28, 1979.

37 **"We were just taking a lot of chances":** Quincy Jones. *Off the Wall* (special edition). Sony, 2001, compact disc. Originally released in 1979.

37 **"On a couple of tunes the band":** Jones and Abbey, "Michael Jackson's Peacock Music," *Blues & Soul*, August 28, 1979.

38 **"We tried all kinds of things":** Jones, *Q: The Autobiography of Quincy Jones*, 232.

39 **"He can come to a session":** J. Randy Taraborrelli, *Michael Jackson: The Magic and the Madness*, 185.

39 **"[One day], he comes in the studio":** Bryan Monroe, "*Michael Jackson: In His Own Words*," 96.

40 **"Until now, [Jackson has] understandably":** Stephen Holden, review of *Off the Wall*, *Rolling Stone*, August 1979.

40 **"a photo taken at a graduation":** Anthony DeCurtis, "Michael Reinvents Pop," *Rolling Stone*, July 2009.

40 **"Michael's approach is very dramatic":** Michael Jackson, *Michael Jackson: The Ultimate Collection*, Sony, 2004, compact disc. Liner notes, 23.

40 **"[Quincy and I] share the same philosophy":** Jackson, *Moonwalk*, 185.

41 **"Fans and industry peers alike":** J. Randy Taraborrelli, *Michael Jackson: The Magic and the Madness*, 187.

41 **"[it] looked beyond funk to the future":** Review of *Off the Wall*, *Blender*, 2001.

42 **"[It] is a dance album released":** Anthony DeCurtis, "Michael Reinvents Pop," *Rolling Stone*, July 2009.

42 **"most intricately timed, fully textured":** Barney Hoskyns, "The Boy Who Would Fly," *NME*, September 17, 1983.

42 **"Jackson brought to *Off the Wall* vocal tricks":** Jimmy Guterman, *The Best Rock 'N' Roll Records of All Time* (New York: Carol Publishing Corp., 1992).

42 **"I remember where I was":** Jackson, *Moonwalk*, 176.

42 **"That experience lit a fire in my soul":** Ibid., 184.

42 **"If you asked me to choose between *Off the Wall*":** Mark Fisher, "And When the Groove Is Dead and Gone," in *The Resistible Demise of Michael Jackson*. Edited by Mark Fisher (Washington, D.C.: Zero Books, 2009), 13.

42 **"Rosetta Stone for all subsequent R&B":** *1,001 Albums You Must Hear Before You Die*. Edited by Robert Dimery (New York: Universe, 2006).

44 **"The introduction is ten seconds":** Gerri Hirshey, "Michael Jackson: Life in the Magical Kingdom," *Rolling Stone*, February 17, 1983.

44 **"possibly the most thrilling intro":** Paul Lester, "Michael Jackson's Twenty Greatest Hits," in *The Resistible Demise of Michael Jackson*. Edited by Mark Fisher (Washington, D.C.: Zero Books, 2009), 24.

44 **"'Don't Stop' practically leads you":** Mark Fisher, in *The Resistible Demise of Michael Jackson*, 13.

44 **"as a kind of group":** Jackson, *Moonwalk*, 161.

44 **"Michael is rarely discussed as an arranger":** Jackson. *Michael Jackson: The Ultimate Collection*, 23.

44 **"mean whatever people want it to mean":** Chris Cadman and Craig Halstead, *Michael Jackson: For the Record* (Bedfordshire: Authors OnLine, 2007).

45 **"[It] captures [him] the way":** Rob Sheffield, "A New Kind of Hollywood Musical," *Rolling Stone*, July 2009.

45 **"What's remarkable about 'Rock With You'":** J. Edward Keyes, "Michael Jackson: The Essential Playlist," *Rolling Stone*, June 26, 2009.

45 **"It was perfect for me to sing":** Jackson, *Moonwalk*, 158.

45 **"[It] manages the amazing feat":** Fisher, *The Resistible Demise of Michael Jackson*, 13.

45 **"The part where Michael sings":** Steven Hyden, "Favorite Songs," AVClub.com, http://www.avclub.com/articles/favorite-songs,25055 (accessed March 13, 2009).

46 **"Is there any record":** Fisher, *The Resistible Demise of Michael Jackson*, 13.

47 **"Jackson lets loose over a slap-bass":** David Abravanel, review of *Off the Wall* Cokemachineglow.com, http://cokemachineglow.com/record_review/4632/michaeljackson-offthewall-1979 (accessed June 26, 2009).

47 **"It was particularly satisfying":** Jackson, *Moonwalk*, 160.

47 **"Not a lot of people give 'Get On The Floor'":** Andre Grindle, review of *Off the Wall*, Amazon.com, http://www.amazon.com/Off-Wall-Spec-Michael-Jackson/product-reviews/B00005QGAT (accessed June 25, 2009).

48 **"I knew he liked Charlie Chaplin":** Cadman and Halstead, *Michael Jackson: For the Record*, 242.

48 **"At one point, you can hear":** Timothy Pernell, review of *Off the Wall*, TheMidnightMan.com, http://midnightman84.wordpress.com/2009/04/08/off-the-wall-epic-michael-jackson (accessed: July 9, 2009).

48 **"engaging melody":** Jackson, *Moonwalk*, 160.

49 **"It's a very mature emotion":** Michael Jackson, *Off the Wall* (special edition), Sony, 2001, compact disc. Originally released in 1979.

49 **"[Jackson] takes huge emotional risks":** Stephen Holden, review of *Off the Wall*, *Rolling Stone*, August 1979.

49 **"[It] became a Jackson signature":** Jackson. *Michael Jackson: The Ultimate Collection*, 23.

49 **"I had been letting so much build up inside me":** Jackson, *Moonwalk*, 163.

49 **"He cried at the end of every take":** Michael Jackson, *Off the Wall* (special edition). Sony, 2001, compact disc. Originally released in 1979.

49 **"one of the loneliest people in the world":** Jackson, *Moonwalk*, 162.

50 **"knowing that the barriers that have separated":** Ibid., 162.

50 **"I just love the bass line":** Alicia Keyes, "Our Favorite Songs," *Time*, July 2, 2009.

50 **"Floating just above a lush bed of organ":** J. Edward Keyes, "Michael Jackson: The Essential Playlist," *Rolling Stone*, June 27, 2009.

52 **"The scream was the kind":** Jackson, *Moonwalk*, 172.

52 **"This is the first example of a cinematic":** Jackson. *Michael Jackson: The Ultimate Collection*, 23.

52 **"['This Place Hotel'] was the most ambitious":** Jackson, *Moonwalk*, 172.

CHAPTER 2: *THRILLER*

55 **"In today's world of declining sales":** Alan Light, "Dancing Into Immortality," *Rolling Stone*, July 2009.

57 **"We live now in the world":** Tom Ewing, review of *Thriller: 25th Anniversary Edition*, *Pitchfork*, February 15, 2008.

57 **"By November 1982, the month *Thriller*":** Luke Crampton and Dafydd Rees, *Rock & Roll: Year By Year* (London: DK Publishing, 2003), 362.

57 **"In the late '70s, I heard":** Bruce Swedien, *In the Studio with Michael Jackson* (New York: Hal Leonard, 2009), 38.

58 **"Rock videos are firing up a musical revolution":** Jay Cocks, "Sing a Song of Seeing," *Time*, December 26, 1983.

58 **"a diverse but irresistible mix of sounds":** J. D. Reed, "New Rock on a Red-Hot Roll," *Time*, July 18, 1983.

59 **"After four years of slumping sales and stagnating sounds":** Ibid.

59 **"There is no question that *Thriller* was the driving":** Gail Mitchell and Melinda Newman, "How Michael Jackson's *Thriller* Changed the Music Business," *Billboard*, July 3, 2009.

59 **"the quality of [*Thriller*] inspired many people":** Michael Jackson, *Thriller 25th Anniversary: The Book, Celebrating the Biggest Selling Album of All Time* (Orlando: ML Publishing, 2008), 64.

59 **"In general, record companies never believe":** Jackson, *Moonwalk*, 181.

60 **"I remember being in the studio":** Ibid., 181.

60 **"pinnacle of analog tape production":** Matt Forger, personal author interview. May 20, 2010.

61 **"Quincy wants his arrangements and his recordings":** Ibid.

61 **"There was a misconception":** Ibid.

61 **"We didn't use all these tracks just to record":** Ibid.

61 **"What we did on *Thriller*":** Ibid.
61 **"It was all about the emotional content":** Ibid.
63 **"with complete bass lines, counter lines, and all":** Jones, *Q: The Autobiography of Quincy Jones*, 236.
63 **"never had a piece of paper in front of him":** Peter Lyle, "Michael Jackson's Monster Smash," *The Telegraph*, November 25, 2007.
63 **"The producer's main job is to find the right tunes":** Jackson, *Thriller 25th Anniversary: The Book, Celebrating the Biggest Selling Album of All Time*, 13.
63 **"That was a very magical night":** Lyle, "Michael Jackson's Monster Smash," *The Telegraph*, November 25, 2007.
63 **"Michael had already written fantastic songs":** Jackson, *Thriller 25th Anniversary: The Book, Celebrating the Biggest Selling Album of All Time*, 81.
64 **"He and I both agreed that the song":** Jackson, *Moonwalk*, 197.
64 **"I like my songs":** Ibid., 185.
64 **"We did the final mixes and fixes and overdubs":** Jones, *Q: The Autobiography of Quincy Jones*, 238.
64 **"It was a disaster":** Ibid., 238.
64 **"I felt devastated":** Jackson, *Moonwalk*, 199.
65 **"We'd put too much material on the record":** Jones, *Q: The Autobiography of Quincy Jones*, 238.
65 **"We put it dead in the pockets":** Ibid., 239.
65 **"When it was done—boom—it hit us hard":** Jackson, *Moonwalk*, 199–200.
65 **"From the beginning, Epic intended to live":** Mitchell and Newman, "How Michael Jackson's *Thriller* Changed the Music Business," *Billboard*, July 3, 2009.
65 **"iconic sun-god relaxing after quitting time":** Jackson, *Thriller 25th Anniversary: The Book, Celebrating the Biggest Selling Album of All Time*, 65.
66 **"*Thriller* is a wonderful pop record":** John Rockwell, "Michael Jackson's *Thriller*: Superb Job," *New York Times*, December 19, 1982.
66 **"On ballads he is hushed, reverent":** Jim Miller, "The Peter Pan of Pop," *Newsweek*, January 10,1983.
67 **"When you have two strong names":** Jackson, *Moonwalk*, 188.
67 **"So when Jackson's first solo single":** Christopher Connelly, review of *Thriller*, *Rolling Stone*, November 1982.
67 **"CBS screamed, 'You're crazy.'":** Jackson, *Moonwalk*, 207.
67 **"At some point, *Thriller* stopped selling":** Taraborrelli, *Michael Jackson: The Magic and the Madness*, 226.
68 **"The pulse of America and much of the rest":** Jay Cocks, "Why He's a *Thriller*," *Time*, March 19, 1984.
70 **"When *Thriller* came along, it really changed everything":** L. A. Reid, interview by Ann Curry, NBC, June 26, 2009.
70 **"I don't categorize music":** Regina Jones, "Unbreakable," *Vibe*, March 2002.
70 **"The sound of 'Beat It' was simply":** Light, "Dancing Into Immortality," *Rolling Stone*, July 2009.
70 **"Today we do things called mash-ups, right?":** L. A. Reid, interview by Ann Curry, NBC, June 26, 2009.
70 **"MTV was arguably the best example":** Debra Alban, "Michael Jackson Broke Down Racial Barriers," CNN.com, http://articles.cnn.com/2009-06-28/us/michael.jackson.black.community_1_mark-anthony-neal-mtv-raps-popular-culture? (accessed June 28, 2009).
70 **"But if you're saying music":** "Why It Took MTV So Long to Play Black Music Videos," *JET*, October 9, 2006.
71 **"At the time I would look at what people":** Jackson, *Moonwalk*, 200.
72 **"Certain executives from MTV will deny it now":** John Branca, personal author interview. April 13, 2010.
72 **"He was MTV's Jackie Robinson":** Touré, "MTV's Jackie Robinson," *The Daily Beast*, June 26, 2009. www.thedailybeast.com/blogs-and-stories/2009-06-26/mtvs-jackierobinson
73 **"It was amazing working with Michael at the time":** Peter Lyle, "Michael Jackson's Monster Smash," *The Telegraph*, November 25, 2007.

73 **"No, that's what I love about":** Andy Warhol and Bob Colacello, "The Very Private World of Michael Jackson," *Interview*, August 20, 1982.

75 **"I've been to the Oscars and I've been to the BAFTAs":** Jackson, *Thriller 25th Anniversary: The Book, Celebrating the Biggest Selling Album of All Time, 56.*

75 **"If you were young then, the *Thriller* video":** Mike Celizic, "'*Thriller*' Video Remains a Classic 25 Years Later," TodayShow.com, http://today.msnbc.msn.com/id/24282347/ns/today-today_entertainment/ (accessed April 26, 2008).

75 **"For the first time in the history of MTV":** "Why It Took MTV So Long to Play Black Music Videos," *JET*, October 9, 2006.

76 **"the first making of documentary of its kind":** Stan Sinberg, "Shaman at the Negotiating Table," *Southern California Super Lawyers*, February 2006.

76 **"destroy the tapes of the video":** Branca, personal author interview. April 13, 2010.

76 **"When they chastised me, it really hurt me":** Shmuley Boteach, *The Michael Jackson Tapes* (New York: Vanguard, 2009), 105.

76 **"[It] was the unveiling of a marvelous, mature Jackson":** Stephen Thomas Erlewine, review of *Thriller* 25, *All Music Guide*, February 2008.

77 **"It was like watching quicksilver in motion":** "Stars Remember Michael Jackson," Life.com, http://www.life.com/image/74713120/in-gallery/29292#index/21 (accessed June 2009).

77 **"He would watch tapes of gazelles":** Jones, *Q: The Autobiography of Quincy Jones*, 230.

78 **"Once the music plays, it creates me":** Sylvie Simmons, "Interview: Michael Jackson," *Creem*, 1983.

78 **"I'm pretty blasé about crowd response":** Christopher Smith, "Michael Jackson's 'Motown 25' Performance—In Person," *Los Angeles Times*, June 27, 2009.

79 **"body that forgets its fetters":** Dominic Fox, "Serious Joy: Michael Jackson Against the Spirit of Gravity," in *The Resistible Demise of Michael Jackson*. Edited by Mark Fisher (Washington, D.C.: Zero Books, 2009), 92.

79 **"You're a hell of a mover":** Jackson, *Moonwalk*, 213.

79 **"It was the greatest compliment":** Ibid.

79 **"Forget the red jacket and sparkling glove":** Jackson, *Michael Jackson: The Ultimate Collection*, 23.

79 ***"Thriller's* parts added up":** Jody Rosen, "King Michael," Slate.com, http://www.slate.com/id/2221482, June 26, 2009.

80 **"a subtle black-pride anthem":** Kelefah Sanneh, review of *Thriller* 25, *Blender*, February 12, 2008.

80 **"purest form of genius on *Thriller*":** Mark Anthony Neal, review of *Thriller* 25, NewBlackMan, February 2008.

80 **"Hot as Jackson was after the quantum leap":** "Ann Powers and Other Pop Critics Remember Michael Jackson's '*Thriller*,'" *Los Angeles Times*, June 25, 2009.

80 **"Hands clap, horns blare":** Jim Miller, "The Peter Pan of Pop," *Newsweek*, January 10, 1983.

81 **"Jackson seemingly summons the gods":** Neal, review of *Thriller* 25, NewBlackMan, February 2008.

81 **"These are the . . . moments that most casual":** Ibid.

81 **"The sweet midtempo glide of 'Baby Be Mine' would have":** "Ann Powers and Other Pop Critics Remember Michael Jackson's '*Thriller*,'" *Los Angeles Times*, June 25, 2009.

81 **"John Coltrane-style progressive jazz":** Light, "Dancing Into Immortality," *Rolling Stone*, July 2009.

82 **"positively incandescent, perhaps because it isn't as familiar":** Stephen Thomas Erlewine, review of *Thriller* 25, *All Music Guide*, February 2008.

82 **"The song I've just done with Michael Jackson":** Miller, "The Peter Pan of Pop," *Newsweek*, January 10, 1983.

82 **"The lift Jackson gives the word":** "Ann Powers and Other Pop Critics Remember Michael Jackson's '*Thriller*,'" *Los Angeles Times*, June 25, 2009.

82 **"[The Girl Is Mine] sounds very pretty":** Miller, "The Peter Pan of Pop," *Newsweek*, January 14. 1983.

83 **"If ever a video killed the radio star":** "Ann Powers and Other Pop Critics Remember Michael Jackson's '*Thriller*,'" *Los Angeles Times*, June 25, 2009.

83 **"easy to overlook the song's inherent":** J. Edward Keyes, "Michael Jackson: The Essential Playlist," *Rolling Stone*, June 26, 2009.

83 **"'*Thriller*' is about as epic as a pop song gets":** Tyler Fisher, review of *Thriller*, Sputnikmusic, September 27, 2009.

83 **"On the intro, there's a little rhythm":** Bruce Swedien, *In the Studio with Michael Jackson* (New York: Hal Leonard, 2009), 33.

84 **"such spectacular robo-funk":** Keyes, "Michael Jackson: The Essential Playlist," *Rolling Stone*, June 26, 2009.

84 **"asphalt aria":** Jay Cocks, "Why He's a Thriller," *Time*, March 19, 1984.

84 **"hip-hopped to it in clubs and break-danced":** Ibid.

84 **"I wanted to write the type of rock song":** Jackson, *Moonwalk*, 194.

84 **"We knew he'd come up with the nitroglycerin":** Jones, *Q: The Autobiography of Quincy Jones*, 237.

84 **"this-ain't-no-disco AOR track":** Christopher Connelly, review of *Thriller*, *Rolling Stone*, November 1982.

85 **"'Billie Jean' is not only one of the best singles":** Mark Fisher, "'And When the Groove Is Dead and Gone,'" in *The Resistible Demise of Michael Jackson*. Edited by Mark Fisher (Washington, D.C.: Zero Books, 2009), 14–15.

85 **"greatest dance record of all time":** "Billie Jean Voted Top Dance Song." BBC News, http://news.bbc.co.uk/2/hi/entertainment/7507218.stm (accessed July 15, 2008).

86 **"one of the most revolutionary songs in the history":** Joe Queenan, The Vinyl Word, "How Billie Jean Changed the World," *The Guardian*, July 12, 2007.

86 **"It's been said before, but it's worth repeating":** "The 500 Greatest Songs of All Time," *Rolling Stone*, December 2004.

86 **"Even while we were getting help":** Jackson, *Moonwalk*, 192.

86 **"The intro to 'Billie Jean' was so long":** Jackson, *Thriller 25th Anniversary: The Book, Celebrating the Biggest Selling Album of All Time*,13.

86 **"a very unusual instrument, the lyricon":** Swedien, *In the Studio with Michael Jackson*, 37.

86 **"ran through his part on every guitar":** "The 500 Greatest Songs Since You Were Born," *Blender*, April 1, 2009.

86 **"Michael always knew how he wanted it to sound":** Ibid.

86 **"I recorded the bass, drums, and guitars":** Swedien, *In the Studio with Michael Jackson*, 36.

87 **"Then I went back into the control room":** Jackson, *Thriller 25th Anniversary: The Book, Celebrating the Biggest Selling Album of All Time*, 32.

87 **"'Billie Jean' is hot on every level":** "The 500 Greatest Songs Since You Were Born," *Blender*, April 1, 2009.

87 **"one of the most sonically eccentric":** Ibid.

88 **"Twenty-five years later, *Thriller's* central chamber":** "Ann Powers and Other Pop Critics Remember Michael Jackson's '*Thriller*,'" *Los Angeles Times*, June 25, 2009.

88 **"a thing of unnatural beauty":** David Stubbs, "The 'King' Is Dead. Long Live Everything Else," *The Resistible Demise of Michael Jackson*. Edited by Mark Fisher (Washington, D.C.: Zero Books, 2009), 74.

88 **"probably the best musical composition on the album":** Eric Henderson, review of *Thriller*, *Slant Magazine*, October 18, 2003.

88 **"The way his voice tumbles down":** Keyes, "Michael Jackson: The Essential Playlist," *Rolling Stone*, June 26, 2009.

89 **"It's all about the chipmunk":** "Ann Powers and Other Pop Critics Remember Michael Jackson's '*Thriller*,'" *Los Angeles Times*, June 25, 2009.

89 **"The breakdown in 'P.Y.T.,' with its ecstatic":** Tom Ewing, review of *Thriller* 25, *Pitchfork*, February 15, 2008.

89 **It reached #10 on the *Billboard* Hot 100:** Rob Sheffield, review of *Thriller 25*, *Rolling Stone*, February 2008.

89 **"'Lady' shines for its classic simplicity":** "Ann Powers and Other Pop Critics Remember Michael Jackson's '*Thriller*.'" *Los Angeles Times*, June 25, 2009.

90 **"[It] was one of the most difficult tracks to cut":** Jackson, *Moonwalk*, 197–198.

90 **"Jackson's closing minute-and-a-half ad-lib":** Mark Anthony Neal, review of *Thriller*, NewBlackMan, February 2008.

CHAPTER 3: *BAD*

93 **"Jackson's free-form language keeps us aware":** Davitt Sigerson, review of *Bad*, *Rolling Stone*, October 22, 1987.

93 **"a combination of digital drum sounds":** Jackson. *Michael Jackson: The Ultimate Collection*, 24.

94 **"Was there ever a more surreal meeting":** Lester, "Michael Jackson's Twenty Greatest Hits," in *The Resistible Demise of Michael Jackson*, 24.

97 **"Prince was it when Purple Rain came out":** Ed Kiersh, "Beating the Rap," *Rolling Stone*, December 4, 1986.

97 **"He's the best man in the world":** Ibid.

98 **"As Michael planned it":** Taraborrelli, *Michael Jackson: The Magic and the Madness*, 355.

98 **"It was a strange summit":** Quincy Troupe, "The Pressure to Beat It," *Spin*, June 1987.

98 **"I was there for a couple of the meetings":** Swedien, *In the Studio with Michael Jackson*, 42.

99 **"Many observers find in the ascendancy":** Jay Cocks, "Why He's a Thriller," *Time*, March 19, 1984.

100 **"He's not afraid to look into the worst suffering":** Taraborrelli, *Michael Jackson: The Magic and the Madness*, 382.

100 **"Michael would kneel down at the stretchers":** Ibid.

100 **"My dear brothers, we have forty-six stars":** Jones, *Q: The Autobiography of Quincy Jones*, 253.

100 **"Around this time, I used to ask":** Jackson, *Moonwalk*, 261.

100 **"I love working quickly":** Campbell, *Michael Jackson: King of Pop*, 110.

100 **"I have never before or since experienced the joy":** Jones, *Q: The Autobiography of Quincy Jones*, 258.

101 **"more than an unprecedented communal":** Stephen Holden, "The Pop Life. Artists Join in Effort for Famine Relief," *New York Times*, February 27, 1985.

101 **"Anybody who wants to throw stones":** Jones, *Q: The Autobiography of Quincy Jones*, 258.

103 **"Pioneering new ideas is exciting to me":** Jackson, *Moonwalk*, 260.

104 **"It was great, exciting stuff":** Matt Forger, personal author interview. May 20, 2010.

104 **"[*Captain EO* is] about transformation":** Jackson, *Moonwalk*, 259.

104 **"the most powerful backlash in the history":** Quincy Troupe, "The Pressure to Beat It," *Spin*, June 1987.

104 **"In record time, he went from being":** Ibid.

104 **"The year 1985 has been a black hole for Michael":** Gerri Hirshey, "The Sound of One Glove Clapping," *Rolling Stone*, December 1985.

105 **"I visited John Merrick's remains":** Robert E. Johnson, "Michael Jackson Comes Back," *Ebony*, September 1987.

105 **The parallels between Jackson and John Merrick:** David Yuan "The Celebrity Freak: Michael Jackson's 'Grotesque Glory,'" *Freakery: Cultural Spectacles of the Extraordinary Body*. Edited by Rosemarie Thomson (New York: New York University, 1998), 368–384.

105 **"Freaks are called freaks and are treated":** James Baldwin, "Freaks and the American Ideal of Manhood," *Playboy*, January 1985.

106 **"Once I saw Michael sitting on the bathroom":** Russ Ragsdale, personal author interview. April 11, 2010.

106 **"Like the old Indian proverb says":** Cutler Durkee, "Unlike Anyone, Even Himself," *People*, September 14, 1987.

106 **"It's a great paradox about Michael":** Taraborrelli, *Michael Jackson: The Magic and the Madness*, 350.
106 **"whole career to be the greatest":** Ibid, 357.
106 **"This is going to be my bible":** Ibid, 357.
106 **"As generally understood, 'humbug' consists":** *The Colossal P .T. Barnum Reader*. Edited by James Cook (Champaign, IL: University of Illinois, 2005), 95.
107 **"It's like I can tell the press":** Taraborrelli, *Michael Jackson: The Magic and the Madness*, 360.
107 **"It's rhythm and timing":** Boteach, *The Michael Jackson Tapes*,144–146.
107 **"It's too late, anyway":** Michael Goldberg and David Handelman, "Michael Jackson in Fantasyland," *Rolling Stone*, September 24, 1987.
107 **"Michael was growing and wanted to experiment":** Bill Bottrell, personal author interview. May 15, 2010.
108 **"He was able to take some finished demos,":** Ibid.
109 **"[Quincy and I] disagreed on some things":** Jackson, *Moonwalk*, 263.
109 **"There was so much stress":** Jon Dolan, "King of Pain," *Rolling Stone*, July 2009.
109 **"Bruce Swedien recalls a tradition":** Swedien, personal author interview. April 25, 2010.
109 **"On a few occasions, Michael would want":** Ragsdale, personal author interview. April 11, 2010.
109 **"sending long streams of cigar smoke":** Troupe, "The Pressure to Beat It," *Spin*, June 1987.
109 **"spread of fried chicken, potato salad":** Ibid.
109 **"We tried our best to just treat Michael":** Ragsdale, personal author interview. April 11, 2010.
109 **"Alone in the semidarkness, illuminated softly":** Troupe, "The Pressure To Beat It," *SPIN*, June 1987.
110 **"Jackson has 62 songs":** "Michael Jackson in Fantasyland," *Rolling Stone*, September 24, 1987.
110 **"Fifty percent of the battle is trying":** Taraborrelli, *Michael Jackson: The Magic and the Madness*, 352.
110 **"Michael's vision [is] to start making a record":** Ragsdale, personal author interview. April 11, 2010.
110 **"A lot of people are so used to just seeing":** Robert E. Johnson, "Michael Jackson Comes Back," *Ebony*, September 1987.
110 **"You need a dramatic deadline":** Goldberg and Handelman, "Michael Jackson in Fantasyland," *Rolling Stone*, September 24, 1987.
111 **"It's a jubilation, is what it is":** Johnson, "Michael Jackson Comes Back," *Ebony*, September 1987.
111 **"I can't answer whether or not I like":** Jackson, *Moonwalk*, 270.
112 **"Jackson the singer can get bushwhacked":** Jay Cocks, "The Badder They Come," *Time*, September 14, 1987.
112 **"The backlash has more to do with the singer's":** Guy D. Garcia and David E. Thigpen, "People," *Time*, February 29, 1988.
113 **"[Michael Jackson] couldn't imagine recording an album":** Taraborrelli, *Michael Jackson: The Magic and the Madness*,, 374.
113 **"The albums that *Thriller* displaced":** Jon Pareles, "How Good is Jackson's '*Bad*'?" *New York Times*, September 3, 1987.
114 **"Many of the attacks [on Jackson's artistry]":** Quincy Troupe, "The Pressure to Beat It," *Spin*, June 1987.
114 **"Anybody who charges studio hackery":** Robert Christgau, review of *Bad*, *Consumer Guide Reviews*, October 1987.
114 **"a state-of-the-art dance record":** Cocks, "The Badder They Come," *Time*, September 14, 1987.
114 **"*Bad* is not only a product but also a cohesive anthology":** Davitt Sigerson, review of *Bad*, *Rolling Stone*, October 22, 1987.
115 **"widest variety of soundfields":** Swedien, personal author interview. April 25, 2010.
115 **"*Bad* . . . cranks up the music's intensity":** Jon Dolan, "King of Pain," *Rolling Stone*, July 2009.
115 **"It's interesting to me to reflect on the album *Bad*":** Swedien, *In the Studio with Michael Jackson*, 43.

115 **"some of the sharpest black pop ever recorded":** "Michael Jackson." Rock and Roll Hall of Fame. http://rockhall.com/inductees/michael-jackson/bio (accessed July 2009).

116 **"'*Bad*' needs no defense":** Sigerson, review of *Bad*, *Rolling Stone*, September 22, 1987.

116 **"When Jackson declares that the 'whole world":** Ibid.

116 **"Michael's concept of what really is bad":** Taraborrelli, *Michael Jackson: The Magic and the Madness*, 372.

117 **"Scorsese's best post-'70s film":** Armond White, "In MJ's Shadow," *New York Press*, June 30, 2009.

117 **"This is going to sound strange":** Eric Ditzian, "'*Book of Eli*' Director Allen Hughes Calls Michael Jackson Incredible Actor Who Got 'Too Weird and Freaky,'" MTV.com, http://moviesblog.mtv.com/2010/01/11/book-of-eli-director-allen-hughes-calls-michael-jackson-incredible-actor-who-got-too-weird-and-freaky (accessed January 11, 2010).

117 **"When we worked together on '*Bad*'":** Jocelyn Vena, "Michael Jackson Honored By Justin Timberlake, Will.I.Am, Diddy," MTV.com, http://www.mtv.com/news/articles/1614756/20090625/jackson_michael.jhtml (accessed June 25, 2009).

117 **"four and a half minutes of unadulterated bliss":** Keyes, "Michael Jackson: The Essential Playlist," *Rolling Stone*, June 26, 2009.

117 **Two weeks later, he had written and demoed:** Katherine Jackson with Richard Wiseman, *My Family, The Jacksons* (New York: St. Martin's Press, 1990), 161–162.

117 **"It's a really intense shuffle":** Jon Dolan, "Bigger, Tougher, Riskier," *Rolling Stone*, July 2009.

118 **"I would hate to record Michael with what I would":** Swedien, *In the Studio with Michael Jackson*, 45.

118 **"Amid the modern electronics, there's a taste of older":** Pareles, "How Good is Jackson's '*Bad*'?" *New York Times*, September 3, 1987.

118 **"Every piece of this song is in perfect place":** Keyes, "Michael Jackson: The Essential Playlist," *Rolling Stone*, June 26, 2009.

119 **"In a year in which Whitney Houston's":** Andy Roberts, "21 Years of *Bad*," *The Vine*, December 28, 2008.

119 **"There is a great singer at work here":** Cocks, "The Badder They Come," *Time,* September 14, 1987.

120 **"All of his stuff is so different":** Michael Jackson. *Bad* (special edition). Sony, 2001, compact disc. Originally released in 1987.

120 **"one of my absolute favorites of all the music":** Swedien, *In the Studio with Michael Jackson*, 45.

121 **"During the vocal session, we had apparently":** Russ Ragsdale, personal author interview. April 11, 2010.

121 **"the most ripping synth solo":** Ibid.

122 **"heavy R&B riffer . . . [with] a timely salute":** Ibid.

122 **"one of [his] most powerful vocals":** Josh Tyrangiel, "Top Ten Michael Jackson Songs of All Time," *Time,* June 26, 2009.

122 **"This, more than any other":** Paul Lester, "Michael Jackson's Twenty Greatest Hits," in *The Resistible Demise of Michael Jackson*, 33.

122 **"Siedah and I wrote it for him directly":** Paul Zollo, "Behind 'Man in the Mirror' With Glen Ballard," *Rolling Stone*, July 24, 2009.

122 **"The song was this really magical moment":** Ibid.

122 **"Here the fantasies found elsewhere":** Thom Duffy, "Jackson Re-emerges, Still Thrills With '*Bad*,'" *Orlando Sentinel*, September 1, 1987.

123 **"Affirmations are easy fodder":** White, *Keep Moving: The Michael Jackson Chronicle*, 92.

123 **"No one since Dylan has written an anthem of community":** Sigerson, review of *Bad*, *Rolling Stone*, August 1987.

123 **"It is a remarkable dramatic performance":** Cocks, "The Badder They Come," *Time,* September 14, 1987.

123 **"amazing performances . . . Jackson took the song":** Rob Sheffield, "Michael Jackson: The Essential Moments," *Rolling Stone*, July 2009.

124 **"Churls may bemoan . . . Jackson's duet":** Sigerson, review of *Bad*, *Rolling Stone*, August 1987.

125 **"What really makes 'Smooth Criminal' stand out":** Christopher Sunami, "Reviews: Smooth Criminal," Kitoba.com, http://kitoba.com/pedia/Smooth%20Criminal.html (accessed November 5, 2008).

125 **"None of the signature moves that appear in the video":** Ibid.

126 **"some of [Jackson's] most slashingly":** Owen Gleiberman, "Michael Jackson: Why the Weirdness WAS the Greatness," *Entertainment Weekly*, July 21, 2009.

126 **"awesome for its dancing, cinematography":** Jay Ziegler, "Ridiculously Awesome Music Videos: 'Smooth Criminal,'" *Consequence of Sound*, June 15, 2008.

126 **"It's a song that remains, after more than twenty years":** Gleiberman, "Michael Jackson: Why the Weirdness WAS the Greatness," *Entertainment Weekly*, July 21, 2009.

126 **"I worked hard on the song":** Jackson, *Moonwalk*, 270.

126 **"a batch of thick chords for Jackson to vamp over":** Dolan, "King of Pain," *Rolling Stone*, July 2009.

126 **"the album's best song":** Stephen Thomas Erlewine, review of *Bad*, *All Music Guide*, August 1987.

127 **"While poking fun at the wildest tabloid rumors":** Jim Farber, "Ghosts of Pop," *Connoisseur*, May 1989.

CHAPTER 4: *DANGEROUS*

134 **"galvanized pop music":** Robert Doerschuk, "Interview with Teddy Riley," *Keyboard*, February 1992.

134 **"Classic rap assaults your guts with its maxed-out":** Ibid.

134 **"Three words in one capsule":** Ibid.

135 **"Michael was not angry with Quincy":** "Brad Buxer Interview," *Black & White Magazine*, November/December 2009.

135 **"With Michael, he never stopped creating":** Matt Forger, personal author interview. May 20, 2010.

135 **"It was pretty unbelievable really":** Buxer, personal author interview. June 18, 2010.

135 **"He was always open to my suggestions and ideas":** Ibid.

136 **"I was an engineer when he first hired me":** Bill Bottrell, personal author interview. May 15, 2010.

136 **"It was Michael who actually drew":** Richard Buskin, "Classic Tracks: Michael Jackson's 'Black or White,'" *Sound on Sound*, August 2004.

136 **"Michael was always prepared to listen":** Ibid.

136 **"He's a fucking brilliant entertainer":** Omoronke Idowu, Shani Saxon, et al, "Michael and Me," *Vibe*, June/July 1995.

137 **"We recorded some twenty-plus tracks together":** Bryan Loren, "Michael and Me." Myspace.com, http://www.myspace.com/bloren2/blog (accessed July 11, 2009).

137 **"Michael loved finding new sounds":** "Brad Buxer Interview," *Black & White Magazine*, November/December 2009.

138 **"There was more pressure":** "Michael Jackson: Recording *Dangerous* with Teddy Riley," MusicRadar.com, http://www.musicradar.com/news/tech/michael-jackson-studio-secrets-from-teddy-riley-211776 (accessed July 3, 2009).

138 **"He started scatting and beatboxing different parts":** *The Official Michael Jackson Opus*. Edited by Jordan Sommers and Justyn Barnes (Guernsey: Opus Media Group, 2009), 142.

138 **"I didn't check out until a year":** Ibid, 142.

138 **"the biggest experience in my life":** Ibid, 142.

138 **"Listen, you're going to really produce":** "When Heaven Can Wait: Teddy Riley Remembers Michael Jackson," *Hip Hop Wired*, July 2009.

138 **"Teddy was very professional":** Michael Goldberg, "Michael Jackson's '*Dangerous*' Mind: The Making of the King of Pop," *Rolling Stone*, January 9, 1992.

138 **"I was using a lot of vintage stuff":** "Michael Jackson: Recording *Dangerous* with Teddy Riley," MusicRadar.com, http://www.musicradar.com/news/tech/michael-jackson-studio-secrets-from-teddy-riley-211776 (accessed July 3, 2009).

138 **"'You know what I'd like to have overlaid":** Ibid.

138 **"We used a variety of drum machines":** Doerschuk, "Interview with Teddy Riley," *Keyboard*, February 1992.

138 **"Michael likes to listen [to music] even louder":** Goldberg, "Michael Jackson's '*Dangerous*' Mind: The Making of the King of Pop," *Rolling Stone*, January 9, 1992.

139 **"He always pushed me to be different":** "Michael Jackson: Recording *Dangerous* with Teddy Riley." MusicRadar.com, http://www.musicradar.com/news/tech/michael-jackson-studio-secrets-from-teddy-riley-211776 (accessed July 3, 2009).

139 **"I felt confident 'Remember the Time' would make":** Sommers and Barnes, *The Official Michael Jackson Opus*, 142.

139 **"We're not going home until you've sung":** Ibid., 142.

140 **"I sat with him for hours":** Deepak Chopra, "A Tribute to My Friend, Michael Jackson," *Huffington Post*, June 26, 2009.

141 **"When I did certain things in the past that I didn't realize":** Shmuley Boteach, *The Michael Jackson Tapes*, 105.

141 **"It's strange that God doesn't mind expressing":** Michael Jackson, *Dancing the Dream: Poems and Reflections* (New York: Doubleday, 1992), 69.

142 **"Do you care, have you a part":** Ibid., 4.

142 **"Through endless rumors to get him tired":** Ibid., 7.

142 **"When a whale plunges out of the sea":** Ibid., 50.

142 **"What delight nature must feel when she makes":** Ibid., 50.

142 **"All of life is in me":** Ibid., 146.

143 **"You and I were never separate":** Ibid., 136.

143 **"This world we live in is the dance of the creator":** Ibid., 1.

143 **"I really believe that God chooses people":** Robert E. Johnson, "Michael Jackson: Crowned in Africa, Pop King Tells Real Story of Controversial Trip," *Ebony*, May 1, 1992.

143 **"I'm never satisfied with anything":** Michael Jackson, interview by Oprah Winfrey, *The Oprah Winfrey Show*, February 10, 1993.

144 **"We'd drive to the studio and work":** Goldberg, "Michael Jackson's '*Dangerous*' Mind: The Making of the King of Pop," *Rolling Stone*, January 9, 1992.

144 **"'*THRILLER*'—CAN MICHAEL JACKSON BEAT IT?":** Richard W. Stevenson, "'*Thriller*'—Can Michael Jackson Beat It?" *New York Times*, November 10, 1991.

144 **"This is the challenge Jackson":** Goldberg, "Michael Jackson's '*Dangerous*' Mind: The Making of the King of Pop," *Rolling Stone*, January 9, 1992.

145 **"video nightmare":** David Browne, "Michael Jackson's Black or White Blues," *Entertainment Weekly*, November 29, 1991.

145 **"It's like using bathroom talk to get attention":** Ibid.

145 **"sleeve so symbol-laden it could":** Mat Snow, "Michael Jackson, Dangerous Hip-hop and Gospel, Slash and God, Sublime and Ridiculous," *Q* magazine, January 1992.

148 **"loping, melodic electro-groove patented by [Teddy] Riley":** Mark Coleman, "Dangerous Liaisons," *US*, January 1992.

148 **"triumph . . . that doesn't hide from the fears":** Alan Light, review of *Dangerous*, *Rolling Stone*, November 1991.

148 **"a much sharper, harder, riskier album than *Bad*":** Stephen Thomas Erlewine, review of *Dangerous*, *All Music Guide*, November 1991.

148 **"On *Dangerous*, humanity lets Michael Jackson":** David Browne, review of *Dangerous*, *Entertainment Weekly*, November 29, 1991.

148 **"Of all the bizarre apparitions in current popular music":** Jon Pareles, "Michael Jackson in the Electronic Wilderness," *New York Times*, November 24, 1991.

149 **"least confident album since he became a solo superstar":** Ibid.

149 **"I have been cleansing myself":** Michael Jackson, Grammy Award acceptance speech, Shrine Auditorium, Los Angeles, California, February 24, 1993.

150 **"Jackson's dread, depression and wounded-child sense":** Dolan, "King of Pain," *Rolling Stone*, July 2009.

150 **"In all the swooning at *Thriller's* album sales":** Ben Beaumont-Thomas, "*Dangerous* Was Michael Jackson's True Career High," *The Guardian*, July 6, 2009.

152 **"reminiscent of Jackson's solo album":** Light, review of *Dangerous*, *Rolling Stone*, November 1991.

152 **"a dense, swirling [Teddy] Riley track":** Ibid.

152 **"We had been experimenting with the 'looping'":** Swedien, *In the Studio with Michael Jackson*, 49.

153 **"clipped, breathy up tempo voice":** Alan Light, review of *Dangerous*, *Rolling Stone*, November 1991.

153 **"By keeping the beat straight-ahead":** Doerschuk, interview with Teddy Riley. *Keyboard*, February, 1992.

153 **"Only Jackson would use that title":** Pareles, "Michael Jackson in the Electronic Wilderness," *New York Times*, November 24, 1991.

153 **"It's the kind of song that made Jackson a megastar":** Ibid.

154 **"We used a variety of drum machines":** "Michael Jackson: Recording *Dangerous* with Teddy Riley," MusicRadar.com, http://www.musicradar.com/news/tech/michael-jackson-studio-secrets-from-teddy-riley-211776 (accessed July 3, 2009).

154 **"Even the bass is a car horn":** "Michael Jackson: Recording *Dangerous* with Teddy Riley." MusicRadar.com, http://www.musicradar.com/news/tech/michael-jackson-studio-secrets-from-teddy-riley-211776 (accessed July 3, 2009).

154 **"If there's nothing new happening on this record":** Chuck Eddy, "Sound of Breaking Glass," *The Village Voice*, December 17, 1991.

155 **"smooth tenor [that] flutter[s] over":** Timothy Pernell, review of *Dangerous*, *The Midnight Man*, July 11, 2009.

155 **"One of the biggest things Michael really surprised":** "Michael Jackson: Recording *Dangerous* with Teddy Riley," MusicRadar.com, http://www.musicradar.com/news/tech/michael-jackson-studio-secrets-from-teddy-riley-211776 (accessed July 3, 2009).

155 **"Michael asked if he could sing the hook":** "Michael Jackson Recording in the Studio," Gearslutz.com, http://www.gearslutz.com/board/so-much-gear-so-little-time/160901-michael-jackson-recording-studio.html (accessed December 13, 2007).

155 **"'Remember the Time' adopts an African heritage":** White, *Keep Moving: The Michael Jackson Chronicles*, 34–35.

156 **"Their kiss characterizes the hyphen":** Ibid., 33.

156 **"fiendishly intricate, loaded with scratching":** Ben Beaumont-Thomas, "*Dangerous* Was Michael Jackson's True Career High," *The Guardian*, July 6, 2009.

156 **"Michael's ecstatic gasps and whoops are still":** Eddy, "Sound of Breaking Glass," *The Village Voice*, December 17, 1991.

157 **"I must have recorded over a hundred kids":** Forger, personal author interview. May 20, 2010.

157 **"I started editing it to take out some":** Ibid.

157 **"When an audience lights candles and sways":** Deepak Chopra, "Michael Jackson and the God Feeling," *Washington Post*, June 29, 2009.

158 **"one of the best music videos ever made":** Armond White, *Keep Moving: The Michael Jackson Chronicles*, 30.

158 **"As soon as we got to Westlake [Studio]":** Richard Buskin, "Classic Tracks: Michael Jackson's 'Black or White,'" *Sound on Sound*, August 2004.

158 **"put down this big, slamming":** Ibid.

158 **"He just accepted it when he first heard it":** Ibid.

158 **"That's the sort of thing he does":** Ibid.

158 **"The guy's an absolute natural":** Ibid.

159 **"For my part, I didn't think much of white rap":** Ibid.

159 **"effervescent pop hit":** Rob Sheffield, "Michael Jackson: The Essential Moments," *Rolling Stone*, July 2009.
159 **"Just before this saccharine image can pall":** White, *Keep Moving: The Michael Jackson Chronicles*, 23.
160 **"White America's proverbial resistance to the music":** Ibid, 23.
160 **"It is a fiercely jarring coda":** Margo Jefferson, *On Michael Jackson*, 102.
160 **"It creates a strange tension":** Ibid. 102.
160 **"This is a film noir version of Gene Kelly's famous":** White, *Keep Moving: The Michael Jackson Chronicles*, 25–26.
161 **"I want[ed] to do a dance number where I [could] let":** Alex Colletti, "Michael Jackson's Video Legacy, In His Own Words," MTV, December 8, 1999.
161 **"I've gone on about it at length":** White, *Keep Moving: The Michael Jackson Chronicles*, 29–30.
161 **"If you solely pay attention to Michael":** Alban, "Michael Jackson Broke Down Racial Barriers," CNN.com, http://articles.cnn.com/2009-06-28/us/michael.jackson.black.community_1_mark-anthony-neal-mtv-raps-popular-culture? (accessed June 28, 2009).
162 **"criminally underrated song":** Adam Gilham, review of *Dangerous*, Sputnikmusic.com, http://www.sputnikmusic.com/review/6454/Michael-Jackson-Dangerous/ (accessed April 24, 2006).
162 **"I just remember him coming to me":** Bottrell, personal author interview. May 14, 2010.
162 **"The parts came about instantly":** Buxer, personal author interview. June 18, 2010.
162 **"The process is creating a vocal rhythm":** "Michael Jackson Simulchat," MTV, August 17, 1995.
162 **"My official all-time-favorite Michael clip":** Greg Tate, "Michael Jackson: The Man in Our Mirror," *The Village Voice*, July 1, 2009.
162 **"trance ending":** Bottrell, personal author interview. May 15, 2010.
163 **"['Give In To Me'] was like a revelation":** Bottrell, personal author interview. May 15, 2010.
163 **"We sat on two stools in Record One":** Ibid.
163 **"looser, more instinctive vocals":** Ibid.
163 **"He sent me a tape of the song that had no guitars":** Goldberg, "Michael Jackson's *'Dangerous'* Mind: The Making of the King of Pop," *Rolling Stone*, January 9, 1992.
164 **"Michael Jackson was often at his best":** Keyes, "Michael Jackson: The Essential Playlist," *Rolling Stone*, June 27, 2009.
164 **"one of the best efforts of his career":** John Kays, "Michael Jackson's *'Dangerous'* Stands As One of His Best Albums Ever!" NewsBlaze.com, http://newsblaze.com/story/20090705121607kays.nb (accessed July 5, 2009).
165 **"He was brilliant with that stuff":** Buxer, personal author interview. June 18, 2010.
165 **"It was modeled after Michael's beatbox":** Ibid.
165 **"The Music of Negro Religion still remains":** W. E. B. Du Bois, *The Souls of Black Folk* (New York: Cosimo, 2007), 116.
165 **"The lyrics are like a proper sermon":** John Kays, "Michael Jackson's *Dangerous* Stands As One of His Best Albums Ever!" NewsBlaze.com, http://newsblaze.com/story/20090705121607kays.nb (accessed July 5, 2009).
166 **"This is an experience that is best described":** Robert Darden, *People Get Ready!: A New History of Black Gospel Music* (London: Continuum International Publishing, 2004), 214.
166 **"He didn't care what race you were":** "Ryan White's Mother Remembers Michael Jackson," CBS.com, http://www.cbsnews.com/stories/2009/07/03/earlyshow/leisure/celebspot/main5131656.shtml (accessed July 3, 2009).
166 **"One can never choose to forget how much":** Jason King, "Michael Jackson: More Than Black and White," *New Black Magazine*, July 7, 2009.
167 **"I told Michael, I like Billy'":** Doerschuk, "Interview with Teddy Riley," *Keyboard*, February 1992.

167 **"I never felt competition with Teddy":** "Post Here If You Worked on Michael Jackson's DANGEROUS Album," Gearslutz.com, http://www.gearslutz.com/board/so-much-gear-so-little-time/403276-post-here-if-you-worked-michael-jacksons-dangerous-album-24.html (accessed September 16, 2009).

CHAPTER 5: *HISTORY: PAST, PRESENT AND FUTURE, BOOK I*

173 **"She was very kind, very loving, very sweet":** Michael Jackson, interview with Barbara Walters, *20/20*. September 12, 1997.

174 **"Competition among news organizations became so fierce":** Mary Fisher, "Was Michael Jackson Framed?" *GQ*, October 1994.

174 **"a frenzy of hype and unsubstantiated rumor":** Ibid.

174 **"Imagine having someone going through all of your stuff":** Taraborrelli, *Michael Jackson: The Magic and the Madness*, 501.

174 **"What became of the massive investigation":** Fisher, "Was Michael Jackson Framed?" *GQ*, October 1994.

175 **"There are other people involved that are waiting":** Ibid.

175 **"I could never harm a child":** Michael Jackson, interview with Diane Sawyer, *Primetime Live*, June 14, 1995.

175 **"I talked to my lawyers":** Ibid.

176 **"You have to have that tragedy":** Edna Gunderson, "Michael in the Mirror," *USA Today*. December 14, 2001.

176 **"In truth, I really didn't want the album":** Craig Halstead and Chris Cadman, *Michael Jackson: The Solo Years* (Bedfordshire: Authors OnLine, 2003), 132.

176 **"I was on tour and it seemed like I was in Armageddon":** Robert E. Johnson, "Where I Met Lisa Marie and How I Proposed," *Ebony*, October 1994.

176 **"The brilliant thing about us is that we were often":** Ibid.

177 **"We fell in love":** Chris Heath, "Elvis' Girl," *Rolling Stone*, April 2003.

177 **"Our relationship was not 'a sham'":** Presley, "He Knew," MySpace.com, http://www.myspace.com/lisamariepresley/blog/497035326 (accessed June 26, 2009).

177 **"They acted like two kids in love":** "Post Here If You Worked on Michael Jackson's DANGEROUS Album," Gearslutz.com, http://www.gearslutz.com/board/so-much-gear-so-little-time/403276-post-here-if-you-worked-michael-jacksons-dangerous-album-24.html (accessed June 27, 2009).

178 **"When Michael walks into the recording area":** Uri Geller, "My Friend, Michael Jackson," http://site.uri-geller.com/my_friend_michael_jackson, May 2001.

178 **"could think of anyone who was truly":** Bruce Swedien, *In the Studio with Michael Jackson*, 55.

178 **"I'll never forget the first conversation Michael and I":** Ibid., 63.

178 **"Over a couple of days, we came up":** *The Official Michael Jackson Opus*. Edited by Sommers and Barnes, 132.

179 **"He put on our tracks, which we'd pared":** Ibid, 132.

179 **"It was amazing. The writing process was like that":** Ibid, 132.

179 **"I grew up with the music of Michael":** Omoronke Idowu, Shani Saxton, et al, "Michael and Me," *Vibe*, June/July 1995.

180 **"Michael asked me to bring my family along":** *The Official Michael Jackson Opus*. Edited by Sommers and Barnes, 124.

180 **"I think very few people realized how deeply":** "Post Here If You Worked on Michael Jackson's DANGEROUS Album," Gearslutz.com, http://www.gearslutz.com/board/so-much-gear-so-little-time/403276-post-here-if-you-worked-michael-jacksons-dangerous-album-24.html (accessed June 18, 2009).

180 **"Working with Michael is a different type of work":** "Michael & Me," *Vibe*, June/July 1995.

180 **"Michael's the most intense person I've worked with":** Ibid.

181 **"I believe in perfection":** "*HIStory*: The Michael Jackson Interview," VH1, November 10, 1996.

181 **"Sometimes we'd look up and it would easily":** "Michael & Me," *Vibe*, June/July 1995.

181 **"The last weekend of recording on *HIStory*":** "Post Here If You Worked on Michael Jackson's DANGEROUS Album," Gearslutz.com, http://www.gearslutz.com/board/so-much-gear-so-little-time/403276-post-here-if-you-worked-michael-jacksons-dangerous-album-24.html (accessed June 27, 2009).

181 **"Later that night, while mixing":** Ibid.

181 **"This was no small undertaking":** Ibid.

182 **"The clip doesn't just stop at representing previously":** Chris Willman, "Michael's Back, and He's Big . . . Really Big," *Los Angeles Times*, June 5, 1995.

182 **"nothing to do with politics":** Michael Jackson, interview with Diane Sawyer, *Primetime Live*, June 14, 1995.

184 **"It's now common for albums to enter at #1":** John Branca, personal author interview. January 5, 2010.

184 **"a monumental achievement of ego":** Stephen Thomas Erlewine, review of *HIStory: Past, Present and Future, Book I*, *All Music Guide*, June 1995.

184 **"whiny Jackson jive about his perceived mistreatment":** Jim Farber, "Michael's 'HIS'-sy Fit," *New York Daily News*, June 19, 1995.

184 **"Let's see a show of hands":** Ibid.

184 **"He's not pretending to be normal any more":** Jon Pareles, "Michael Jackson Is Angry, Understand?" *New York Times*, June 18, 1995.

186 **"remains one of the most gifted musicians alive":** Ibid.

186 **"*HIStory*'s ultimate goal is to position":** James Hunter, review of *HIStory: Past, Present and Future, Book I*, *Rolling Stone*, June 1995.

186 **"Some of the new songs":** Ibid.

186 **"[On HIStory] Jackson expresses hard experience":** Arnold White, *Keep Moving: The Michael Jackson Chronicles*, 64.

187 **"The crisp, staccato clip and compressed harmonies":** Loudon Wainwright III, review of *HIStory: Past, Present and Future, Book I*, *Entertainment Weekly*, June 23, 1995.

187 **"Whatever one makes of the hoopla":** Daniel Sweeney, "An Incredible New Sound for Engineers," *ASC*, June 1995.

188 **"But the richness extends beyond the mere density":** Ibid.

188 **"I don't know that many people":** "Post Here If You Worked on Michael Jackson's DANGEROUS Album," Gearslutz.com, http://www.gearslutz.com/board/so-much-gear-so-little-time/403276-post-here-if-you-worked-michael-jacksons-dangerous-album-24.html (accessed June 27, 2009).

190 **"Superstars don't make records like this":** "The History Years." *The Michael Jackson Archives*, http://www.the-michael-jackson-archives.com/history1.html, May 1995.

190 **"I was in the room when Jimmy Jam asked him":** Ragsdale, personal author interview. January 16, 2010.

191 **"Michael and Janet's isolation comes from the need":** White, *Keep Moving: The Michael Jackson Chronicles*, 58–59.

191 **"profane, obscure, angry, and filled with rage":** Bernard Weinraub, "In New Lyrics, Jackson Uses Slurs," *New York Times*, June 15, 1995.

191 **"pointedly critical of Jews":** Ibid.

191 **"The idea that these lyrics could be deemed objectionable":** White, *Keep Moving: The Michael Jackson Chronicles*, 55.

192 **"[Jackson] gives the lie to his entire catalogue":** Pareles, "Michael Jackson Is Angry, Understand?" *New York Times*, June 18, 1995.

192 **"The song's percussive rhythm could be the handclaps":** Armond White, *Keep Moving: The Michael Jackson Chronicles* (New York: Resistance Works, 2009).

192 **"The bridge section consisted of over 300 tracks":** Rob Hoffman, personal author interview. January 16, 2010. Also, "Post Here If You Worked on Michael Jackson's DANGEROUS Album," Gearslutz.com, http://www.gearslutz.com/board/so-much-gear-so-little-time/403276-post-here-if-you-worked-michael-jacksons-dangerous-album-8.html (accessed June 28, 2009).

192 **"I don't see why we should have to facilitate":** Diana Jean Schemo, "Rio Frets as Michael Jackson Plans to Film Slum," *New York Times*, February 11, 1996.

193 **"It's a poor world surrounded by a rich world":** Ibid.

193 **"ethereal and stirring description of a man":** Tom Molley, "Michael Jackson Seemingly Gives His Side of Story on Decade-old Album," *Associated Press*, May 22, 2005.

193 **"Its tale of out-of-step but soul-deep anguish":** White, *Keep Moving: The Michael Jackson Chronicles*, 61.

193 **"It fell into my lap because that's how":** Cadman and Halstead, *Michael Jackson: For the Record*, 234–235.

194 **"I knocked on the door and said":** Buxer, personal author interview. June 20, 2010.

194 **"I played him a verse and he loved it":** Ibid.

194 **"Jackson would later write the remarkable lyrics":** Ibid.

195 **"rival any Seattle rocker's pain":** Jon Dolan, "The Thrill Is Gone," *Rolling Stone*, July 2009.

195 **"The word pictures he paints with the verses":** "A Stranger in Moscow." *The Couch Sessions*, June 30, 2009. www.thecouchsessions.com/2069/06/a-stranger-in-moscow

195 **"impressionistic, semi-noir, sub-Le Carre tale":** Owen Hatherley, "'Stalin's Tomb Won't Let Me Be': Michael Jackson as Despot," *The Resistible Demise of Michael Jackson*, 199.

195 **"Biggie went on to talk about how:** "Post Here If You Worked on Michael Jackson's DANGEROUS Album," Gearslutz.com, http://www.gearslutz.com/board/so-much-gear-so-little-time/403276-post-here-if-you-worked-michael-jacksons-dangerous-album-8.html (accessed June 28, 2009).

195 **"[When] Michael came in, Biggie nearly broke out in tears":** Ibid.

195 **"We popped it up on the big speakers":** Ibid.

196 **"I was feeling so much pain and so much suffering":** Alex Pasternack, "Was Michael Jackson the World's Biggest Environmentalist?" Treehugger.com, http://www.treehugger.com/files/2009/06/michael-jackson-earth-song-biggest-uk-single-not-released-in-us-video.php (accessed June 26, 2009).

196 **"The song has no words in the chorus":** M. Giles, review of *HIStory: Past, Present and Future, Book I*," Amazon.com, http://www.amazon.com/review/R323CSF4BV5URO (accessed March 21, 2006).

197 **"Jackson's distinctive impulse [in the video]":** White, *Keep Moving: The Michael Jackson Chronicles*, 60.

197 **"What was the more egocentric":** Fisher, *The Resistible Demise of Michael Jackson*, 67.

198 **"I have not, shall we say, done him the honor":** National District Attorneys Association, "Prosecutor Profile: Thomas W. (Tom) Sneddon Jr," 2008.

198 **"Michael is a master craftsman":** Brad Buxer, personal author interview. June 30, 2010.

198 **They eventually settled on "Come Together":** Bottrell, personal author interview. May 14, 2010.

199 **"It pitches a stream of self-confessed":** Ian MacDonald, *Revolution in the Head: The Beatles' Records and the Sixties* (Chicago: Chicago Review Press, 2005), 358–359.

199 **"a call to unchain the imagination":** Ibid., 359.

199 **"I think his cover is the best cover of a Beatles song":** Forger, personal author interview. May 20, 2010.

199 **well-crafted and seductive:** Stephen Thomas Erlewine, review of *HIStory: Past, Present and Future, Book I*, *All Music Guide*, June 1995.

199 **"On listening to 'You Are Not Alone'":** Taraborrelli, *Michael Jackson: The Magic and the Madness*, 609.

199 **"beautiful, if you can take the pain":** Ann Powers, "Being a Michael Jackson Fan Wasn't Easy, But the Music Was Worth It," *Los Angeles Times*, June 26, 2009.

199 **"The warmth displayed in the 'You Are Not Alone' video":** Omoronke Idowu, Shani Saxon, et al, "Michael & Me," *Vibe*, June/July 1995.

200 **"If you really want to know about me":** Michael Jackson, interview with Ed Bradley, *60 Minutes*, December 28, 2003.

200 **"Our personal history begins in childhood":** Cadman and Halstead, *Michael Jackson: For the Record*, 54.

201 **"mammoth funk-rock construction":** James Hunter, review of *HIStory: Past, Present and Future, Book I*, *Rolling Stone*, June 1995.

202 **"If you listen to the bridge":** "Post Here If You Worked on Michael Jackson's DANGEROUS Album," Gearslutz.com, http://www.gearslutz.com/board/so-much-gear-so-little-time/403276-post-here-if-you-worked-michael-jacksons-dangerous-album.html (accessed June 28, 2009).

203 **"What it's doing on an album with Dallas Austin":** Hunter, review of *HIStory: Past, Present and Future, Book I*, *Rolling Stone*, June 1995.

203 **"If he ever decides to stop being a pop singer":** Anthony Wynn, review of *HIStory: Past, Present and Future, Book I*, Amazon.com, http://www.amazon.com/review/R2GPNDLAJ8RBKN (accessed October 13, 2002).

204 **"He was the king of pathos.... He knew how to make":** *Michael Jackson's Private Home Movies*," Fox, April 24, 2003.

204 **"They rehearsed a bit without vocals in":** Rob Hoffman, personal author interview. January 16, 2010.

204 **"The take we did that day was amazing":** "Interview with Bruce Swedien," *Black & White*, October 1999.

204 **"I think I've worked with everyone, seriously":** Ibid.

205 **"During the recording, they had been":** Swedien, *In the Studio with Michael Jackson*, 58.

205 **"What a vocal performance and delivery":** Taraborrelli, *Michael Jackson: The Magic and the Madness*, 610.

205 **"a dramatic tour de force":** Pareles, "Michael Jackson Is Angry, Understand?" *New York Times*, June 18, 1995.

205 **"unbelievable and it proves once again how Michael":** "Interview with Brad Buxer," *Black & White*, November/December 2009.

CHAPTER 6: *BLOOD ON THE DANCE FLOOR: HISTORY IN THE MIX*

207 **"revealing record":** Jon Dolan, Review of *Blood on the Dance Floor: HIStory in the Mix*, *Rolling Stone*, April 1997.

207 **"His singing on the first five tracks of new material":** Armond White, *Keep Moving: The Michael Jackson Chronicles*, 84–86.

208 **"There is real pain and pathos":** Neil Strauss, review of *Blood on the Dance Floor: HIStory in the Mix*, *New York Times*, May 20, 1997.

210 **"We took Teddy's DAT and worked it over":** Brad Buxer, personal author interview. June 18, 2010.

210 **"jeep-styled groove that provides":** Robert Miles, review of *Blood on the Dance Floor: HIStory in the Mix*, *Billboard*, April 12, 1997.

211 **"Michael knew exactly what he wanted":** "Interview with Brad Buxer," *Black & White*, November/December 2009.

212 **"moment of absolute genius":** Adam Gilham, review of *Blood on the Dance Floor: HIStory in the Mix*, *Sputnikmusic*, November 28, 2006.

212 **"easily one of the most ambitious songs he's ever recorded":** Thor Christensen, review of *Blood on the Dance Floor: HIStory in the Mix*, *Dallas Morning News*, May 20, 1997.

213 **"When we began working [together]":** Bryon Loren, "Michael and Me," MySpace.com, http://www.myspace.com/bloren2/blog (accessed July 11, 2009).

213 **"world's first Gothic megastar":** Sam Davies, "Glove, Socks, Zombies, Puppets: The Unheimlich Maneuvers and Undead Metonyms of Michael Jackson," in *The Resistible Demise of Michael Jackson*. Edited by Mark Fisher (Washington, D.C.: Zero Books, 2009), 227.

213 **"embodied the Gothic":** Dennis Yeo Kah Sin, "'Did I Scare You?' The Curious Case of Michael Jackson as Gothic Narrative," in *Studies in Gothic Fiction*. Ed. Franz J. Potter. Nanyang Technological University, Singapore. http://www.zittaw.com/starticlesin.htm. November 2009.

213 **"terrifying . . . shock the world":** Stephen King, "Memories of Michael Jackson," *Entertainment Weekly*, July 3, 2009.

214 **"The core story he described to me that day":** Ibid.

214 **"Nobody knows this, but it was originally going":** Michael Adams, "The Cold Case: Director Mick Garris on Michael Jackson's Forgotten Ghosts," MovieLine.com, http://www.movieline.com/2009/07/the-cold-case-director-mick-garris-on-michael-jacksons-forgotten-ghosts.php (accessed July 14, 2009).

214 **"It started out being 12 to 15 minutes long":** Christopher Pickard, "Cannes 1997," FilmFestivals.com, http://www.filmfestivals.com/cannes97/cfilm4.htm (accessed February 30, 2010).

214 **"some of the best, most inspired dancing":** Stephen King, "Memories of Michael Jackson," *Entertainment Weekly*, July 3, 2009.

215 **"The children in the film, who are much quicker":** Yet another example of Jackson's Romantic impulses (see Rousseau, Blake, Wordsworth, etc.).

215 **"The most interesting aspect of this film":** Chad Helder, "Michael Jackson's Ghosts," *Scary Fairy Tale*, December 10, 2006.

216 **"assimilated the personae of a range of minstrels":** See Coyle's insightful blog: "Is It Scary: Minstrelsy, Metamorphosis and Michael Jackson," http://amiscaryforyou-michaeljackson.blogspot.com (accessed February 26, 2010).

216 **"The history of American entertainment":** David Yuan, "The Celebrity Freak: Michael Jackson's Grotesque Glory." *Freakery: Cultural Spectacles of the Extraordinary Body*, 372.

216 **"Michael Jackson is the definitive celebrity freak":** Ibid, 372.

216 **"When the Civil War began, [P. T.] Barnum":** Margo Jefferson, *On Michael Jackson* (New York: Pantheon, 2006), 12–13.

216 **"Michael Jackson contains trace elements of all this history":** Ibid, 13.

216 **"like the elephant man, screaming":** Neil Strauss, review of *Blood on the Dance Floor: HIStory in the Mix*, *New York Times*, May 20, 1997.

CHAPTER 7: *INVINCIBLE*

219 **"sparkly, post hip-hop update of *Off the Wall*":** Stephen Thomas Erlewine, review of *Invincible*, *All Music Guide*, October 2001.

220 **"I got a call from friends in Saudi Arabia":** "Michael Jackson Exclusive," *Vibe*, March 2002.

220 **"I'm not one to sit back":** Andrew and Jenny Eliscu, "Jackson Song to Aid 9/11 Victims." *Rolling Stone*, September 17, 2001.

220 **"I believe in my heart that the music community":** Gary Susman, "Shining Stars," *Entertainment Weekly*, September 19, 2001.

221 **"The Internet appears to be the most consequential":** Brian Hiatt and Evan Serpick, "The Record Industry's Decline," *Rolling Stone*, July 2007.

222 **"a general return—post-grunge, post-gangsta":** Jon Pareles, "When Pop Becomes the Toy of Teeny Boppers," *New York Times*, July 11, 1999.

224 **"Words can't describe how I feel":** "Michael Jackson and Wife Become Parents of Baby Boy," *JET*, March 3, 1997.

224 **"I want him to have some space":** Michael Jackson, interview with Barbara Walters, *20/20*, September 12, 1997.

224 **"I don't want anybody to know [the mother]":** Michael Jackson, interview with Martin Bashir, *Living with Michael Jackson*, February 6, 2003.

225 **"Physically, touring takes a lot out of you":** Edna Gundersen, "Michael in the Mirror," *USA Today*, December 14, 2001.

225 **"He was surrounded by enablers":** Chopra, "A Tribute to My Friend, Michael Jackson," *Huffington Post*, June 26, 2009.

225 **Jackson seemed exhausted but still optimistic:** Lisa Bernhard, "The Once and Future King," *TV Guide*, December 1999.

226 **"I don't think so 'cause the press has":** Ibid.

226 **"Well, all I can do is be myself":** Ibid.

226 **"I think the best work is coming":** Ibid.

226 **"I'm putting my heart and soul into [the album]":** "Michael Jackson: My Pain," *The Daily Mirror*, April 12, 1999.

226 **"[Michael] is the best":** The Michael Jackson café, http://www.mjcafe.net/the%20legend%20speeches%20&%20faq/quotes.htm, March 1999 (accessed February 16, 2009).

227 **"He was super vocal":** Linda Hobbs, "Rodney Jerkins Talks MJ's Last Studio Album, *Invincible*," *Vibe*, September 5, 2009.

227 **"He was a little scared of Pro Tools":** Elianne Halbersberg, "Rodney Jerkins: A Rare Interview With the Hit-Making Producer," Mix.com, http://mixonline.com/mag/audio_rodney_jerkins/ (accessed December 1, 2004).

227 **"Of all my albums I would say this one":** Online audio chat with Anthony DeCurtis. GetMusic.com,. http://getmusic.mp3.com/calendar/audiochats/michaeljackson/index.html (accessed October 26, 2001).

228 **"I pushed Rodney, and pushed":** Ibid.

228 **"All I can tell you is that it's a sound":** Ibid.

228 **"We think we've got the next *Thriller*":** "The Quest for Perfection," Sonicnet.com http://www.sonicnet.com/pop/features, March 30, 2000 (accessed June 1, 2008).

228 **"If he just picks two":** "The Quest for Perfection," Sonicnet.com http://www.sonicnet.com/pop/features, March 30, 2000 (accessed June 1, 2008).

229 **"I'm recording across the hall from him":** Ibid.

229 **"Michael is singing better than ever":** Roger Friedman, "Michael Jackson Presents the '*Invincible*' Album, Record Execs Go Crazy," *Fox News 411*, June 15, 2001.

229 **"some of the best music Michael's ever made":** "Grammy Maestro Mottola Sees a Jax Comeback," Michael Jackson Fan Club, News Archive, http://www.mjfanclub.net/home/index.php?option=com_content&view=article&catid=162%3A1999&id=117%3A1999-february&Itemid=75, February 26, 1999.

229 **"The problem he faces right now is having":** Ibid.

230 **"I think that it just shows how hungry everybody":** Ibid.

232 **"Not physical threats, but certainly the threat":** Roger Friedman, "Jacko May Claim Threats By Motolla," *Fox News 411*, July 12, 2002.

232 **"I think it's at a stalemate":** Nekesa Mumbi Moody. "Michael Jackson, Sony Feud Over Sales." *Associated Press*, June 13, 2002.

232 **"It's very sad to see that these artists really are penniless":** Michael Jackson, National Action Network speech, Harlem, New York, July 9, 2002.

233 **"The fact that [Michael Jackson] is a great musician":** Robert Christgau, review of *Invincible*, *Consumer Guide Reviews*, October 2001.

233 **"Of every album I have listened to":** Michael Jackson, Wikiquote, http://en.wikiquote.org/wiki/Michael_Jackson (accessed May 2, 2007).

233 **"fleet, durable R&B minimalism":** James Hunter, review of *Invincible*, *Rolling Stone*, December 6, 2001.

235 **"a return of sorts to the kind of solid infectious":** Mark Anthony Neal, "The Return of the Scarecrow," Seeingblack.com, http://www.seeingblack.com/x122101/michaeljackson.shtml (accessed December 21, 2001).

235 **"'Butterflies' is the best example of why":** Neal, "The Return of the Scarecrow," Seeingblack.com, http://www.seeingblack.com/x122101/michaeljackson.shtml (accessed December 21, 2001).

235 **"Teddy Riley proves with just two songs":** Nikki Tranter, review of *Invincible*, popmatters.com, http://www.popmatters.com/music/reviews/j/jacksonmichael-invincible2.shtml (accessed October 30, 2001).

236 **"The song is without doubt the album's":** Ibid.

236 **"I've been through hell and back":** Online audio chat with Anthony DeCurtis. GetMusic.com, http://getmusic.mp3.com/calendar/audiochats/michaeljackson/index.html (accessed October 26, 2001).

236 **"'Unbreakable' is so striking":** Robert Hilburn, "Michael Jackson's *Invincible*," *Los Angeles Times*, October 28, 2001.

236 **"He's not going to leave his pop crown":** Adam Gilham, review of *Invincible*, sputnikmusic.com, http://www.sputnikmusic.com/review/6695/Michael-Jackson-*Invincible* (accessed May 4, 2006).

237 **"daring new territory":** Hilburn, "Michael Jackson's *Invincible*," *Los Angeles Times*, October 28, 2001.

237 **"[He] breaks up his singing with grunts":** Jon Pareles, "To Regain Glory, the New Michael Imitates the Old," *New York Times*, October 28, 2001.

237 **"A lot of sounds on the album aren't sound":** Online audio chat with Anthony DeCurtis, GetMusic.com, http://getmusic.mp3.com/calendar/audiochats/michaeljackson/index.html (accessed October 26, 2001).

237 **"busy, percussive groove with a compulsive":** Mark Beaumont, review of *Invincible*, *NME*, October 17, 2001.

237 **"I find extraordinary beauty in [such] fast songs":** Frank Cogan, "The Man in the Distance," *The Village Voice*, November 27, 2001.

237 **"fleet, durable R&B minimalism":** Hunter, review of *Invincible*, *Rolling Stone*, December 6, 2001.

238 **"His singing is sassy, defiant, and forceful":** Hilburn, "Michael Jackson's *Invincible*," *Los Angeles Times*, October 28, 2001.

238 **"The subtle harmonies and simple arrangements":** Sal Cinquemani, review of *Invincible*, *Slant Magazine*, October 29, 2001.

238 **"one of Jackson's best vocal performances":** Neal, "The Return of the Scarecrow," Seeingblack.com, http://www.seeingblack.com/x122101/michaeljackson.shtml (accessed December 29, 2001).

239 **"When I did that song with him":** Dasun Allah, "When 'Heaven Can Wait': Teddy Riley Remembers Michael Jackson," Hiphopwired.com, http://hiphopwired.com/2009/07/08/when-heaven-can-wait-teddy-riley-remembers-michael-jackson (accessed July 8, 2009).

239 **"[It is his] least forced, most seamless":** David Browne, "You Rock My World," *Entertainment Weekly*, September 7, 2001.

239 **"recall[s] the singer's work with Quincy Jones":** Hunter, review of *Invincible*, *Rolling Stone*, December 6, 2001.

239 **"Jackson sings with more funk finesse":** Jon Dolan, "Back in the Groove," *Rolling Stone*, July 2009.

240 **"It would have opened people's minds":** Steven Ivory, "Michael Jackson Leaves Behind Hits Both Large and Small," NPR, July 1, 2009.

240 **"This really light voice comes out of the answering machine":** "Floetry Biography," Universal Music Publishing Group Spotlight, http://www.umusicpub.com/spotlight.aspx?id=526, 2009.

240 **"It was incredible, because he continually asked":** Billy Johnson Jr., "Songwriter Gets the Butterflies," Yahoo.com, http://new.music.yahoo.com/michael-jackson/news/artist-name-michael-jackson-id-1013025-songwriter-gets-the-butterflies--12063973 (accessed November 15, 2001).

240 **"This song wouldn't sound out of place on *Off the Wall*":** Mike Heyliger, review of *Invincible*, Pop Dose, June 28, 2009.

240 **"It is not too overstated to suggest that 'Butterflies'":** Neal, "The Return of the Scarecrow," Seeingblack.com, http://www.seeingblack.com/x122101/michaeljackson.shtml (accessed December 17, 2001).

241 **"first really soaring tune on the album":** Mark Beaumont, review of *Invincible*, *NME*, October 17, 2001.

241 **"He wanted it to be this kind of ecstasy":** Buxer, personal author interview. June 18, 2010.

241 **"There are these two sweet little kids":** Online audio chat with Anthony DeCurtis, GetMusic.com, http://getmusic.mp3.com/calendar/audiochats/michaeljackson/index.html (accessed October 26, 2001).

241 **"I got a call at 4:30 in the morning":** Buxer, personal author interview. June 16, 2010.

241 **"2000 Watts" was cowritten by Riley and R&B singer:** Billy Johnson Jr., "Tyrese's '2000 Watts' *On Michael Jackson*'s *Invincible*," Yahoo! Music, http://new.music.yahoo.com/tyrese/news/artist-nametyrese-id1033398s-2000-watts-on-michael-jacksons-invincible--12033686, October 29, 2001.

241 **"Hard, hammering and chant-like":** Mark Beaumont, review of *Invincible*, *NME*, October 17, 2001.

241 **"Jackson connects marvelously with '2000 Watts'":** Hilburn, "Michael Jackson's *Invincible*," *Los Angeles Times*, October 28, 2001.

242 **"You Are My Life" was a last-minute inclusion:** Taraborrelli, *Michael Jackson: The Magic and the Madness*, 613.

242 **"The writers first played it for Michael on a Thursday":** Ibid., 613.

242 **"terribly off Babyface":** James Hunter, review of *Invincible*, *Rolling Stone*, December 6, 2001.

242 **"sparkling . . . standout":** Taraborrelli, *Michael Jackson: The Magic and the Madness*, 613.

243 **"stunningly heartbreaking ballad that the Backstreet Boys":** Mike Heyliger, review of *Invincible*, Pop Dose, June 28, 2009.

243 **"Michael will never lose the quality":** David Ritz, "The Bubblegum Soul Machine," *Rolling Stone*, July 2009.

244 **"creepy, airheaded companion piece to the pictures":** Justin Harung, review of *Invincible*, *Spin Cycle*, November 2001.

245 **"Here is a typical day in America—six youths under":** Michael Jackson, "Heal the Kids" speech, Oxford University, Oxford, England, March 21, 2001.

245 **A haunting Latin-infused dance groove:** There were also rumors Jackson would perform the song at the 2002 Grammy Awards.

245 **"It would've made for an inspired choice for a single":** Heyliger, review of *Invincible*, *Pop Dose*. June 28, 2009.

245 **"The music is Latin-based, a deep brew":** Hunter, review of *Invincible*, *Rolling Stone*, December 6, 2001.

247 **"stand-out . . . new millennium 'Thriller'":** Cinquemani, review of *Invincible*, *Slant Magazine*, October 29, 2001.

247 **"These transhuman manifestations . . . interrogate fundamental":** Dennis Yeo Kah Sin, "'Did I Scare You?' The Curious Case of Michael Jackson as Gothic Narrative," in *Studies in Gothic Fiction*. Ed. Franz J. Potter. Nanyang Technological University, Singapore, http://www.zittaw.com/starticlesin.htm, November 2009.

CHAPTER 8: THE FINAL YEARS

252 **"Sitting on the sofa next to him":** Bryan Monroe. "Michael: 25 Years After *Thriller*, *Ebony*, December 2007.

252 **"I'm channeling":** Craig McLean, "Kenny Ortega on Michael Jackson's Final Days," *The Times* (UK), October 24, 2009.

252 **"on the shelf until after July 13":** Claire Hoffman, "Michael Jackson's Final Days: Hope and Ruin," *Rolling Stone*, August 6, 2009.

253 **"I like to take sounds and put them under":** "An Exclusive with Michael Jackson," *Access Hollywood*, October 6, 2006.

253 **"Michael had a tendency to over-record":** Jake Coyle and Anthony McCartney. "Sony Bets MJ Fans Won't Stop 'Til They Get Enough," *Associated Press*, March 17, 2009.

253 **"We and Sony feel that the future for Michael Jackson is unlimited":** Chris Lee, "Michael Jackson Estate, Sony Music Entertainment Strike Distribution Deal," *Los Angeles Times*, March 16, 2010.

253 **"[Michael] looked beaten":** Josh Mankiewicz, "The Secret Life of Michael Jackson." Dateline/MSNBC.com, http://www.msnbc.msn.com/id/35259896/ns/dateline_nbc-newsmakers (accessed February 5, 2010).

254 **"I felt that he was inspired here":** Ibid.
254 **"I never stopped":** "An Exclusive with Michael Jackson," *Access Hollywood*, October 26, 2006.
254 **"Something needs to put a jolt back":** Ibid.
254 **"It was going to be out of this world":** Emily Wither, "Will.i.am on MJ," *BBC Music*, June 29, 2009.
254 **"It was very demanding":** Ibid.
254 **"Man, he still sings like a bird":** "will.i.am Working on Michael Jackson Comeback Album," billboard.com, http://www.billboard.com/bbcom/news/article_display.jsp?vnu_content_id=1003526647 (accessed January 4, 2007).
255 **"He was very protective and kept it under":** "will.i.am Admits Working On Michael Jackson's Dance Music Album," *The Daily Mirror*, July 1, 2009.
255 **"He's a genius. Just to be in the same room":** Ibid.
255 **"This is something Michael is carefully planning":** Bill Zwecker, "Jackson Plans His Comeback," *Chicago Sun-Times*, September 17, 2007.
256 **"All I can say is, he is the best":** Jan Blumentrath, "Interview With RedOne," *Hit Quarters*, March 23, 2009.
256 **"The music we were doing was good":** Mike Collett-White, "Star Producer RedOne Eyes Michael Jackson Release," *Reuters*, January 21, 2010.
257 **"My hands were shaking like never before":** "Michael Jackson Aiming to Outdo '*Thriller*'" With New Album," *Sawf News*, September 24, 2008.
257 **"His music is all about the melody":** Jada Yuan, "Failed Guitarist Ne-Yo on Writing Songs with Michael Jackson," *New York*, July 22, 2008.
257 **"He wants killer melodies":** Ibid.
257 **"He was incredibly focused, completely coherent":** Michael Prince, personal author interview. November 1, 2010.
257 **"When things slowed down [after *Invincible*]":** Ibid.
257 **"I don't want to work with anyone else":** Buxer, personal author interview. June 18, 2010.
258 **"The music demo he sent me lies on my bedside":** Chopra, "A Tribute to My Friend, Michael Jackson," *Huffington Post*, June 26, 2009.
258 **"I drove up to the front door, and was met":** Tim Smith, "More Details on Instrumental Album Michael Jackson Started Before His Death, and His Love of Classical Music," *Baltimore Sun*, July 10, 2009.
259 **"He said he listened to . . . classical music":** Ibid.
259 **"It's very pretty music":** Ibid.
259 **"I sat at the piano":** Ibid.
259 **"had the tunes pretty much worked out":** "Will the New Michael Jackson Music Be Released." CNN.com. http://articles.cnn.com/2009-07-16/entertainment/jackson.music.unreleased_1_jackson-and-freddie-mercury-songs-michael-jackson?_s=PM:SHOWBIZ (accessed July 16, 2009).
259 **"I hope one day his family will decide":** Smith, "More Details on Instrumental Album Michael Jackson Started Before His Death, and His Love of Classical Music," *Baltimore Sun*, July 10, 2009.
260 **"the most astonishing [thing] I have seen":** Andre Paine, "Michael Jackson's 50 Shows Sell Out In Hours." billboard.com, http://www.billboard.com/news/michael-jackson-s-50-shows-sell-out-in-hours-1003951400.story#/news/michael-jackson-s-50-shows-sell-out-in-hours-1003951400.story (accessed March 13, 2009).
260 **"Tickets sold at a rate of 11 per second":** Ibid.
260 **"We often talk about unprecedented demand":** Ibid.
260 **"who, beyond the most devoted fans, would pay £50":** Rosie Swash, "Michael Jackson Can't Fail to Sell Out the O2 Arena," *The Guardian*, March 5, 2009.
260 **"To sell out like that is a testament to talent":** Jason Gregory, "Coldplay's Chris Martin: 'Michael Jackson Comeback Bigger Than Lazarus,'" Gigwise.com, http://www.gigwise.com/news/50086/Coldplays-Chris-Martin-Michael-Jackson-Comeback-Bigger-Than-Lazarus (accessed March 24, 2009).

260 **"My kids are old enough now to appreciate":** *Michael Jackson: This Is It*, directed by Kenny Ortega (Sony Pictures, 2009), DVD.

261 **"He wasn't giving it full out":** Mike Fleeman, "Final Days: The Mystery of Michael Jackson's Death," *People*, June 26, 2009.

261 **"In his final days, he not only dreamed":** Claire Hoffman, "Michael Jackson's Final Days: Hope and Ruin," *Rolling Stone*, August 6, 2009.

261 **"Mediocrity was not a concept":** Presley, "He Knew," MySpace.com, http://www.myspace.com/lisamariepresley/blog/497035326 (accessed June 26, 2009).

261 **"The show we create here has to have people leaving":** Ben Sisario, "Revising the Image of Michael Jackson's Final Days," *New York Times*, October 21, 2009.

261 **"I want their jaws on the ground":** Hoffman, "Michael Jackson's Final Days: Hope and Ruin," *Rolling Stone*, August 6, 2009.

261 **"nothing at all like what I was expecting to see":** Roger Ebert, review of *This Is It*, *Chicago Sun-Times*, October 27, 2009.

261 **"His directions are almost poetic":** Kirk Honeycutt, review of *This Is It*, *The Hollywood Reporter*, October 27, 2009.

262 **"We see Jackson as a perfectionist:** Alex Fletcher, review of *This Is It*, *Digital Spy*, October 29, 2009.

262 **"It's not the machines that are destroying the world":** Michael Jackson's *This Is It*, directed by Kenny Ortega (Sony Pictures, 2009), DVD.

262 **"Not a happy ending":** Ibid.

One of several enourmous statues (this one located in the Netherlands) of Jackson erected during the promotional campaign for *HIStory* in 1995.

ACKNOWLEDGMENTS

This book would not be possible without the help and support of hundreds of people. I am grateful in particular to my agent, Helen Zimmermann, for believing in this project (and me) from early on. Thank you for finding this book a great home and for your assistance in overcoming countless roadblocks along the way. A big thank you also to Michael Fragnito, for catching the vision of this book and being willing to publish something that focused on Michael Jackson's music rather than sensationalism. I express my utmost appreciation to my editor, Laura Swerdloff, for overseeing such a huge project with patience, care, and enthusiasm. This book became much better as a result of your judicious eye and valuable suggestions. Thanks also to my excellent production editor Andrea Santoro and copyeditors Cathlyn Matracia and Michael Cea; also, to Chris Thompson and Margery Greenspan, for the outstanding book design.

I want to express my sincere appreciation to the Estate of Michael Jackson. To Karen Langford: You have been a pleasure to work with. Thank you for your helpful assistance with so many requests and for your kindness and support. To John Branca: Thank you for seeing the value of this project and for your kind remarks, insightful feedback and encouragement. Thanks also to John McClain, Howard Weitzman, Jim Bates, and Diana St. Amand. To Neal Preston: Your photos are works of art. Thank you for allowing them to be part of this book. Thanks also to the gifted Sam Emerson, whose beautiful work graces the cover (and many of these pages). And to Anthony DeCurtis: Thank you for a generous read and an outstanding foreword.

I also want to express my sincere appreciation to Michael Jackson's creative partners. Matt Forger, you are incredible. Thank you for our hours of conversations and so much insight ("It's about what people feel, not just what they hear."). Brad Buxer, you are brilliant. Your passion, integrity, warmth, and knowledge came through in every conversation. Bill Bottrell, your work with Michael is phenomenal. Thank you for your time and insights. Bruce Swedien: I'm not sure a recording engineer could be more universally respected than you. Thank you for your generosity and bottomless well of knowledge. To Michael Prince: Thank you for your refreshing honesty and for sharing such fascinating experiences (including the untold connection of Michael Jackson and "Legs Diamond"). To Russ Ragsdale: It was a pleasure getting to know you and learning of your amazing experiences. To Rob Hoffman: Your insights on working with Michael were always so detailed, vivid and illuminating. Also, to Quincy Jones, Rod Temperton, Greg Phillinganes, Steve Porcaro, Buz Kohan, David Foster, Teddy Riley, Andrae and Sandra Crouch, John Barnes, Jimmy Jam, Terry Lewis, Rodney Jerkins, Brad Sundberg, and Stuart Brawley: I express my profound admiration and thanks. And to so many others not mentioned: Thank you for your time and willingness to read chapters, revive memories, and offer feedback. I depended on so many of you to make this book as accurate, informative, and comprehensive as possible.

Finally, a huge thank-you to my family. Your love and encouragement means everything to me. To my wife and two beautiful children: You have sustained me and inspired me through years of difficult work, occasional triumphs, frequent uncertainty, crazy schedules, impossible juggling, and marathon writing sessions. Through it all, we always made time to share music together.

CREDITS

All song lyrics courtesy of ©Mijac Music. Used by permission.

Selections from *Moonwalk* courtesy of ©The Estate of Michael Joseph Jackson. Used by permission.

Selections from *Dancing the Dream* courtesy of ©The Estate of Michael Joseph Jackson. Used by permission.

A contemplative "portrait of the artist as a young man" captured by Neal Preston.

PHOTO CREDITS

©Corbis: 5 (Sunset Boulevard), 16 (Bob King), 19 (Gary Hershom/Reuters), 23 (Richard H. Cohen), 35 (Susan Phillips), 36 (Bettmann), 62 (Bill Nation/Sygma), 77 (Bettmann), 183 (Murray Andrew/Sygma), 222 (Beth A. Keiser/EPA), 230 (Beth A. Keiser/EPA)

©Matt Forger: 60, 107

©Getty Images: 3 (Tom Copi/Michael Ochs/Getty Images), 20 (Jorge Willian/Globo), 24 (George Dekeerle), 26, 32 (Tom Keller), 38 (Ron Gallela/Wire Image), 40 (Ron Gallela/Wire Image), 41 (Andy Freeberg), 65 (AFP), 69 (Dave Hogan), 96 (Hutton Archive), 98 (Hutton Archive), 129 (Hutton Archive), 137 (L. Cohen/Wire Image), 141 (Ian Barkley), 176 (Eric Ryan/Wire Image), 221 (Phil Dent/Redferns), 225 (Jim Ruyman), 233 (K Mazur/Wire Image), 249 (K Mazur/Wire Image), 252 (MJ Kim), 261 (John Shearer/AEG/Concerts West)

©MJJ Productions, Inc.: 30, 54, 66, 92, 130, 170, 175, 206, 218

©Optimum Productions: 7, 15, 17, 21, 39, 43, 66, 72, 74, 75, 77, 91, 102, 104, 108, 112, 115, 133, 142, 145, 172, 179, 180, 185, 187, 208, 209, 217, 229 (Jonathan Exley), 234 (Jonathan Exley), 294, 296, 298, 306

©Neal Preston: I, III, XIV, 2, 8, 10, 12, 29, 37, 71, 78, 98, 101, 111, 263, 298

©Sjors Provoost: 295 (Creative Commons)

©Triumph International, Inc.: 18, 53, 56, 59, 147, 151, 169, 186, 188, 270, 301

©White House: 94

Every effort has been made to trace copyright holders and to obtain their permission for the use of copyright material. The publisher apologizes for any errors or omissions in the above list and would be grateful if notified of any corrections that should be incorporated in future reprints or editions of this book.

LIST OF SONGS

(IN ALPHABETICAL ORDER)

2BAD (*HIStory*)
2000 WATTS (*Invincible*)
ANOTHER DAY (*MICHAEL*)
ANOTHER PART OF ME (*Bad*)
BABY BE MINE (*Thriller*)
BAD (*Bad*)
BE NOT ALWAYS (*Victory*)
BEAT IT (*Thriller*)
BEHIND THE MASK (*MICHAEL*)
BEST OF JOY (*MICHAEL*)
BILLIE JEAN (*Thriller*)
BLACK OR WHITE (*Dangerous*)
BLAME IT ON THE BOOGIE (*Destiny*)
BLOOD ON THE DANCE FLOOR (*Blood on the Dance Floor*)
BLUE GANGSTA (unreleased)
BREAK OF DAWN (*Invincible*)
BREAKING NEWS (*MICHAEL*)
BUFFALO BILL (unreleased)
BURN THIS DISCO OUT (*Off the Wall*)
BUTTERFLIES (*Invincible*)
CAN YOU FEEL IT (*Triumph*)
CAN'T GET YOUR WEIGHT OFF OF ME (unreleased)
CAN'T LET HER GET AWAY (*Dangerous*)
CAROUSEL (*Thriller-Special Ed.*)
CENTIPEDE (*Rebbie Jackson*)
CHEATER (*Michael Jackson: The Ultimate Collection*)
CHILDHOOD (*HIStory*)
COME TOGETHER (*HIStory*)
CRY (*Invincible*)
DANGEROUS (*Dangerous*)
DESTINY (*Off the Wall*)
DIRTY DIANA (*Bad*)
DO YOU KNOW WHERE YOUR CHILDREN ARE (unreleased)
DON'T STOP 'TIL YOU GET ENOUGH (*Off the Wall*)
DON'T WALK AWAY (*Invincible*)
D.S. (*HIStory*)
EARTH SONG (*HIStory*)
EASE ON DOWN THE ROAD (*The Wiz*)
EATEN ALIVE (*Diana Ross*)
ESCAPE (unreleased)
FALL AGAIN (unreleased)
FLY AWAY (*Bad–Special Edition*)
FOR ALL TIME (*Thriller 25*)
GET IT (*Characters*, by Stevie Wonder)
GET ON THE FLOOR (*Off the Wall*)
GHOSTS (*Blood on the Dance Floor*)
GIRL IS MINE, THE (*Thriller*)
GIRLFRIEND (*Off the Wall*)
GIVE IN TO ME (*Dangerous*)
GONE TOO SOON (*Dangerous*)
GOT THE HOTS (unreleased)
GROOVE OF MIDNIGHT (unreleased)
HEAL THE WORLD (*Dangerous*)
HEARTBREAK HOTEL (*see also, "This Place Hotel"*) (*Triumph*)
HEARTBREAKER (*Invincible*)
HEAVEN CAN WAIT (*Invincible*)
HISTORY (*HIStory*)
HOLD MY HAND (*MICHAEL*)
HOLLYWOOD TONIGHT (*MICHAEL*)
HOT STREET (unreleased)
HUMAN NATURE (*Thriller*)
I CAN'T HELP IT (*Off the Wall*)
I HAVE THIS DREAM (unreleased)
I JUST CAN'T STOP LOVING YOU (*Bad*)
IF YOU DON'T LOVE ME (unreleased)
IN THE BACK (*Michael Jackson: The Ultimate Collection*)
IN THE CLOSET (*Dangerous*)
INVINCIBLE (*Invincible*)
IS IT SCARY (*Blood on the Dance Floor*)
IT'S THE FALLING IN LOVE (*Off the Wall*)
JAM (*Dangerous*)
JUST GOOD FRIENDS (*Bad*)
KEEP THE FAITH (*Dangerous*)
KEEP YOUR HEAD UP (*MICHAEL*)
LADY IN MY LIFE, THE (*Thriller*)
LEAVE ME ALONE (*Bad*)
LIBERIAN GIRL (*Bad*)
LITTLE SUSIE (*HIStory*)
LOST CHILDREN, THE (*Invincible*)
LOVE NEVER FELT SO GOOD (unreleased)
LOVELY ONE (*Triumph*)
MAKE OR BREAK (unreleased)
MAN, THE (*Pipes of Peace, by Paul McCartney*)
MAN IN THE MIRROR (*Bad*)
MEN IN BLACK (unreleased)
MIND IS THE MAGIC (unreleased)
MONEY (*HIStory*)
MONKEY BUSINESS (*Michael Jackson: The Ultimate Collection*)

MONSTER (*MICHAEL*)
MORPHINE (*Blood on the Dance Floor*)
MUCH TOO SOON (*MICHAEL*)
NIGHTLINE (unreleased)
OFF THE WALL (*Off the Wall*)
ON THE LINE (*Michael Jackson: The Ultimate Collection*)
ONE MORE CHANCE (*Number Ones*)
PLACE WITH NO NAME, A (unreleased)
PRIVACY (*Invincible*)
P.Y.T. (Pretty Young Thing) (*Thriller*)
REMEMBER THE TIME (*Dangerous*)
ROCK WITH YOU (*Off the Wall*)
SAY SAY SAY (*Pipes of Peace by Paul McCartney*)
SCARED OF THE MOON (*Michael Jackson: The Ultimate Collection*)
SCREAM (*HIStory*)
SERIOUS EFFECT (unreleased)
SHAKE YOUR BODY (Down to the Ground) (*Destiny*)
SHE DRIVES ME WILD (*Dangerous*)
SHE GOT IT (unreleased)
SHE'S OUT OF MY LIFE (*Off the Wall*)
SHE'S TROUBLE (unreleased)
SHOUT (unreleased)
SLAVE TO THE RHYTHM (unreleased)
SMILE (*HIStory*)
SMOOTH CRIMINAL (*Bad*)
SOMEBODY'S WATCHING ME (*Rockwell*)
SOMEONE IN THE DARK (*Michael Jackson: The Ultimate Collection*)
SOMEONE PUT YOUR HAND OUT (*Michael Jackson: The Ultimate Collection*)
SPEECHLESS (*Invincible*)
SPEED DEMON (*Bad*)
STATE OF SHOCK (*Victory*)
STRANGER IN MOSCOW (*HIStory*)
STREETWALKER (*Bad–Special Edition*)
SUNSET DRIVER (*Michael Jackson: The Ultimate Collection*)
SUPERFLY SISTER (*Blood on the Dance Floor*)
TABLOID JUNKIE (*HIStory*)
THERE MUST BE MORE TO LIFE THAN THIS (unreleased)
THEY DON'T CARE ABOUT US (*HIStory*)
THIS IS IT (*This Is It*)
THIS PLACE HOTEL (*see also "Heartbreak Hotel"*) (*Triumph*)
THIS TIME AROUND (*HIStory*)
THREATENED (*Invincible*)
THRILLER (*Thriller*)
UNBREAKABLE (*Invincible*)
WALK RIGHT NOW (*Triumph*)
WANNA BE STARTIN' SOMETHIN' (*Thriller*)
WAY YOU LOVE ME, THE (*The Ultimate Collection/ MICHAEL*)
WAY YOU MAKE ME FEEL, THE (*Bad*)
WE ARE HERE TO CHANGE THE WORLD (*Michael Jackson: The Ultimate Collection*)
WE ARE THE WORLD (*We Are the World*)
WE'VE HAD ENOUGH (*Michael Jackson: The Ultimate Collection*)
WHAT MORE CAN I GIVE (unreleased)
WHATEVER HAPPENS (*Invincible*)
WHO IS IT (*Dangerous*)
WHY (*Brotherhood*, by 3T)
WHY YOU WANNA TRIP ON ME (*Dangerous*)
WILL YOU BE THERE (*Dangerous*)
WORK THAT BODY (Unreleased)
WORKIN' DAY AND NIGHT (*Off the Wall*)
YOU ARE MY LIFE (*Invincible*)
YOU ARE NOT ALONG (*HIStory*)
YOU CAN'T WIN (*The Wiz*)
YOU ROCK MY WORLD (*Invincible*)

Jackson in a photo shoot from the *HIStory* era.

GENERAL INDEX

INDEX OF PHOTOGRAPHS